Theodor-Heuss-Anlage 12
D-68165 Mannheim
Telefon: +49/621/86298-0
Telefax: +49/621/86298-250

Value Chain Management in the Chemical Industry

Matthias Kannegiesser

Value Chain Management in the Chemical Industry

Global Value Chain Planning of Commodities

Physica-Verlag
A Springer Company

Author
Matthias Kannegiesser
Danziger Straße 35
10435 Berlin
Germany
mkannegiesser@yahoo.com

Diss., TU Berlin, D83

ISBN 978-3-7908-2031-7   e-ISBN 978-3-7908-2032-4

DOI: 10.1007/978-3-7908-2032-4

Contributions to Management Science ISSN 1431-1941

Library of Congress Control Number: 2008930040

© 2008 Physica-Verlag Heidelberg

This work is subject to copyright. All rights are reserved, whether the whole or part of the material is concerned, specifically the rights of translation, reprinting, reuse of illustrations, recitation, broadcasting, reproduction on microfilm or in any other way, and storage in data banks. Duplication of this publication or parts thereof is permitted only under the provisions of the German Copyright Law of September 9, 1965, in its current version, and permissions for use must always be obtained from Physica-Verlag. Violations are liable for prosecution under the German Copyright Law.

The use of general descriptive names, registered names, trademarks, etc. in this publication does not imply, even in the absence of a specific statement, that such names are exempt from the relevant protective laws and regulations and therefore free for general use.

Cover design: WMXDesign GmbH, Heidelberg

Printed on acid-free paper

9 8 7 6 5 4 3 2 1

springer.com

Foreword

Over the last three decades, research and industry intensively investigated effective planning and control methods in the value chain. *Supply chain management* (SCM) and *Advanced Planning Systems* (APS) became key words at the interface between business administration, operations research and computer science. Among other industries, the process industry specifically chemicals, steel and food is a primary application area for SCM and APS due to decision complexity as well as volume and value importance of material flows. Research for these industries focused on production and supply network planning. Supply chain management started to overcome functional separation by organizational units and research disciplines in marketing, sales, logistics, production, procurement and controlling towards a process-oriented thinking. But still, there was a clear separation between demand and supply as well as volume and value focus leading to local but not global optima. While production – mostly the relatively inflexible part of the chain – was in the focus of optimization and simulation models, sales and procurement prices and volumes were mainly treated as given to be fulfilled and optimized locally. Profitability was mainly measured with ex-post or static contribution margin analysis by controlling functions.

This relatively stable system now faces increasing volatility and complexity due to volatile demand and raw material prices as well as globalization in markets and company networks. Specifically, price-volatile commodity products within the chemical industry require planning volumes together with values across sales to procurement. In this context, the work of Matthias Kannegiesser focuses on two research questions:

- How can volumes and values within the value chain be managed in an integrated way?
- Specifically, how can a global commodity value chain within the chemical industry be planned by values and volumes?

The first question targets an enhancement of *supply chain management* towards *value chain management* with integrated volumes *and* value planning. The second question is related to a specific industry type as basis to develop and evaluate a volume and value planning model in detail for a defined scope.

The study provides valuable insights for research and industrial practice. At the beginning, the author reviews different management concepts in the value chain either demand, supply or value-oriented. The author proposes an integrated framework for value chain management as an interdisciplinary structure consisting of separated concepts.

The study focuses then on value chain planning in the chemical industry and describes industry characteristics specifically for commodity products. Commodities are standard products produced in mass production of high volumes. They received less attention in supply chain management research due to a lack of complexity in production and distribution. Here, commodities are a suitable area for developing an end-to-end value chain planning model since sales and raw material price volatility needs to be jointly managed with volumes throughout the chain to ensure profitability. The study specifies planning requirements for a global commodity value chain in general. A state of the art analysis of recent literature reveals that requirements are covered only partly by developed specialized models with lack of integration.

In the main part of the study, the author develops a model fulfilling the postulated requirements and proves the applicability in a comprehensive industry case (research questions 1 and 2). The model contains new innovative solutions such as sales price and volume planning based on price-quantity functions and linear turnover approximation, planning of future inventory values, global transportation and transit inventory planning, production throughput smoothing or the handling of variable raw material consumptions rates in production. Industry case results show the importance of joined planning volumes and values in a global network: changes of prices or exchange rates require a change of volumes to ensure profitability.

As a result the study opens various new research areas investigating the joined management of volumes and values in different industries or on the strategic or operative value chain management level.

Prof. Dr. Paul van Beek
Prof. Dr. Hans-Otto Günther

Acknowledgements

Each path towards a remote goal starts with a first step. I remember the first step when discussing this project together with the first advisor Prof. Dr. Hans-Otto Günther in his Berlin office. The research approach to combine internationally-oriented, quantitative research with practice-orientation and industry application was a guiding principle for this project from the start. The research of the Department of Production Management at the Technical University of Berlin focusing on production and supply chain management as well as advanced planning systems and the process industry was a perfect competence basis for the study: many research results and practical experiences in the area of optimization, simulation and specifically supply chain management were relevant and important input. Besides, Prof. Günther provided continuous and ongoing guidance during the entire project and provided fruitful opportunities to discuss and exchange ideas with the national and international research and industry community. The second advisor Prof. Dr. Paul van Beek of the University of Wageningen (NL) is a close member of this international research community and provided very valuable specific feedback and guidance on the one hand but also broader perspectives on the research topic on the other hand. I really appreciated his personal engagement into the study as well as his detailed and constructive feedback during meetings and discussions.

Having made the first step, the up coming way in the project was sometimes stony and foggy: getting into the subject, detailing the scope and starting the model development as well as the computational implementation was a challenge specifically using specialized tools and developing new systems. Prof. Günther's team at the Department of Production Management supported me in an outstanding way during this period and along the project. His former co-worker Prof. Dr. Martin Grunow impressed me with his broad and at the same time deep expertise in very different industries and academic fields that he could challenge developed models from various perspectives and provide great guidance in moving forward. I'm also grateful being integrated into the research team of Ph.D. students at the department supported by Hanni Just with Matthias Lehmann, Ulf Neuhaus, Markus Meiler and Ihsan Onur Yilmaz. I really appreciated the intense and fruitful discussions especially on study approaches and system usages at the department, joined conferences, seminars and workshops we spent together. I would also like to send a special thanks to Christoph Habla and Derya Kurus for their master thesis contribution and ideas, which really made a difference to the model and the study results.

Half way of the journey was characterized by model evaluation and enhancement together with the industry partner. I'm very grateful to the industry partner supporting the study actively with a dedicated team and resources. I would like to thank specifically the unit leadership and the leadership team of supply chain management for establishing the basis for this study and supporting it until the end. In addition, I would like to thank the entire planning and decision support team for the joined time and many hours spent in requirements workshops, data gathering and model testing as well as evaluation. It was a joined success that the developed model was not only developed for academic research purpose but could also be used in the monthly planning process and quickly provided decision support on volumes and value decisions in order to return the invest into this research.

The total path would not have been possible without the organizational and financial support from A.T. Kearney providing the opportunity to taking a leave of absence from consulting work for this study. Specifically, I would like to thank Dietrich Neumann, Dr. Dirk Buchta, Thomas Rings, Holger Röder, Dr. Marcus Eul, Dr. Otto Schulz and Erik Thiry, who supported the project with their guidance, senior counseling and mentoring. I would also like to thank Katharina Mosters and Hans Rustemeyer supporting this process from a Human Resource perspective in a very flexible and unbureaucratic way as well as Dr. Marianne Denk-Helmold, Cornelia Colsman, Margot Jung and Ben Perry for the indispensable support in reviewing and ensuring quality from an editor perspective. Matthias Lütke Entrup inspired this project significantly with his work on *Advanced Planning in Fresh Food Industries* including many fruitful discussions around optimization in the industry: thank you not only for the insights about poultry, sausage and yogurt production!

When reaching the end of the path, I would like to share this moment with family and friends and thank them for their continuous love and support during this challenging period of life.

April 2008   M. Kannegiesser

Table of Contents

Foreword V

Acknowledgements VII

Abbreviations XIII

1 Introduction 1
   1.1 Research Field Overview 3
   1.2 Research Gaps and Questions 6
   1.3 Research Approach 7

2 Value Chain Management 11
   2.1 Value Chain 11
   2.2 Concepts to Manage the Value Chain 18
      2.2.1 Concepts to Manage Values 19
      2.2.2 Concepts to Manage Demand 22
      2.2.3 Concepts to Manage Supply 28
      2.2.4 Concepts Comparison 37
   2.3 Integrated Value Chain Management 40
      2.3.1 Value Chain Management Definition and Framework 40
      2.3.2 Value Chain Strategy, Planning and Operations 44
      2.3.3 Value Chain Management Methods 53
   2.4 Conclusions 60

3 Chemical Industry and Value Chain Characteristics 63
   3.1 Chemical Industry Characteristics 63
      3.1.1 Chemical Industry Overview 63
      3.1.2 Chemical Market and Development 69
      3.1.3 Specifics of Chemical Commodities 74
   3.2 Global Commodity Value Chain in the Chemical Industry 81
      3.2.1 Global Value Chain Network Overview 81
      3.2.2 Network Characteristics 83
      3.2.3 Sales Characteristics 86

    3.2.4 Distribution Characteristics 88
    3.2.5 Production Characteristics 89
    3.2.6 Procurement Characteristics 90
  3.3 Conclusions 91

4 Value Chain Planning Requirements and State of the Art Analysis 93
  4.1 Value Chain Planning Requirements 93
    4.1.1 Requirements Gathering Overview 93
    4.1.2 Planning Process Requirements 94
    4.1.3 Value Planning Requirements 97
    4.1.4 Sales Planning Requirements 100
    4.1.5 Distribution Planning Requirements 102
    4.1.6 Production Planning Requirements 106
    4.1.7 Procurement Planning Requirements 108
  4.2 Literature Review and State of the Art Analysis 109
    4.2.1 State of the Art Analysis Overview 110
    4.2.2 Planning-related Literature 111
    4.2.3 Global-related Literature 114
    4.2.4 Commodity-related Literature 116
    4.2.5 Chemicals-related Literature 118
  4.3 Conclusions 121

5 Global Value Chain Planning Model 123
  5.1 Model Overview and Structure 123
  5.2 Planning Basis 126
    5.2.1 Planning Framework 126
    5.2.2 Planning Objects and Basis Indices 127
  5.3 Value Planning 133
    5.3.1 Value Objective Function 133
    5.3.2 Future Inventory Value Planning 140
  5.4 Sales Planning 145
    5.4.1 Sales Index Sets, Control and Input Data 145
    5.4.2 Price Elasticity Analysis 148
    5.4.3 Turnover Approximation Preprocessing 151
    5.4.4 Sales Decision Variables and Constraints 157
    5.4.5 Sales Indicator Postprocessing 159
  5.5 Distribution Planning 161
    5.5.1 Transportation Index Sets, Control and Input Data 161
    5.5.2 Transportation Variables and Constraints 163
    5.5.3 Inventory Index Sets, Control and Input Data 169
    5.5.4 Inventory Variables and Constraints 171

5.5.5 Distribution Balance Index Sets, Variables and Constraints ... 174
5.5.6 Distribution Indicator Postprocessing..................................176
5.6 Production Planning 177
5.6.1 Production Indices, Index Sets, Control and Input Data........179
5.6.2 Production Variables, Preprocessing and Constraints 185
5.6.3 Production Indicator Postprocessing 191
5.7 Procurement Planning..192
5.7.1 Procurement Index Sets, Control and Input Data 193
5.7.2 Procurement Variables and Constraints.................................193
5.7.3 Procurement Indicator Postprocessing 194
5.8 Conclusions 194

6 Model Implementation and Case Study Evaluation 197
6.1 Model Implementation...197
6.2 Case Study Evaluation...201
6.2.1 Case Study Overview 201
6.2.2 Basis Plan Evaluation 206
6.2.3 Value Scenario Evaluation 214
6.2.4 Sales Scenario Evaluation 216
6.2.5 Distribution Scenario Evaluation...219
6.2.6 Production Scenario Evaluation 222
6.2.7 Procurement Scenario Evaluation 228
6.3 Opportunities for Model Extensions..229
6.3.1 Regional Sales Planning 230
6.3.2 Robust Planning with Price Uncertainties.............................233
6.3.3 Price Planning Using Simulation-based Optimization 240
6.4 Conclusions 244

7 Summary, Conclusions and Outlook...247

References..251

Abbreviations

3PL	3rd Party Logistics
AGVS	Automated Guided Vehicle Systems
APP	Aggregate Production Planning
APS	Advanced Planning Systems
ATP	Available-to-Promise
Bc	Base Currency
BOM	Bill of Material
C	Constraint
CEFIC	Conseil Européen de l'Industrie Chimique
CM I	Contribution Margin I
CM II	Contribution Margin II
CP	Constraint Programming
CPFR	Collaborative Planning, Forecasting and Replenishment
CRM	Customer Relationship Management
d	Day
DC	Distribution Center
e.g.	exempli gratia
EBIT	Earnings Before Interests and Tax
EBITDA	Earnings Before Interest, Tax, Depreciation and Amortization
EBT	Earnings Before Tax
ECP	European Contract Price
ECR	Efficient Consumer Response
EMEA	Europe, Middle East and Africa
EPC	Event-driven Process Chain
ERP	Enterprise Resource Planning
et al.	et alteri
EU	European Union
EUR	Euro
EVA®	Economic Value Added
EVCM	Extended Value Chain Management
fc	Foreign Currency
FIFO	First in, First out
GA	Genetic Algorithms
GATT	General Agreement on Tariffs and Trade

GDP	Gross Domestic Product
H	Hour
HPP	Hierarchical Production Planning
HR	Human Resources
IAS	International Accounting Standards
IL	Inventory Level
IR	Inventory Range
IRV	Inventory Range Valued
IT	Information Technology
JIT	Just In Time
KPI	Key Performance Indicator
LIFO	Last in, First out
LP	Linear Programming
M	Month
MILP	Mixed Integer Linear Programming
MIP	Mixed Integer Programming
MIT	Massachusetts Institute of Technology
MRP I	Material Requirement Planning
MRP II	Manufacturing Resource Planning
NAFTA	North American Free Trade Association
NOA	Net Operating Assets
NOPAT	Net Operating Profit After Taxes
NPV	Net Present Value
OEM	Original Equipment Manufacturer
OPL	Optimization Programming Language
P&L	Profit & Loss
PC	Personal Computer
PE	Polyethylene
PL	Procurement Level
POS	Point-of-Sale
PP	Polypropylene
QP	Quadratic Programming
RFP	Request for Proposal
RM	Revenue Management
ROA	Return on Assets
ROCE	Return on Capital Employed
RSM	Response Surface Methodology
S&OP	Sales & Operations Planning
SCC	Supply Chain Council
SCM	Supply Chain Management
SCOR®	Supply Chain Operations Reference
SCP	Supply Chain Planning

SD	System Dynamics
SL	Sales Level
SME	Small and Medium Enterprise
SNP	Supply Network Planning
SRM	Supplier Relationship Management
t	Ton
TP	Transfer Point
TTG	Total Relative Turnover Gap
UL	Utilization Level
US	United States
USD	United States Dollar
US-GAAP	United States Generally Accepted Accounting Principles
VA	Value-Added
VAL	Value-Added Level
VCM	Value Chain Management
VMI	Vendor Managed Inventory
WACC	Weighted Average Cost of Capital
WTO	World Trade Organization
XTG	Maximum Relative Turnover Gap

1 Introduction

In human history, global trade existed already in the ancient world, when people started to trade natural resources, animals or products with other global regions. Early examples are the imports of domesticated animals from Asia to the Sahara between 7,500 and 4,000 BC, the Silk Road from Southern Asia across the Middle East to Europe or the Amber Road. In the Middle Ages, international sea trade was fostered in Europe around cities of Venice, Genoa, Dutch and Flemish cities or by the Hanseatic League. The search for new global trade routes was a driver for discoveries like the arrival of Columbus in America looking for a new sea trade route to India (N.N. 2005a; N.N. 2005b; N.N. 2005c). Global trade in ancient world was challenged by significant transportation time, risks and costs, as well as demand and supply information asymmetry between regions and trade barriers such as tariffs or missing convertibility of currencies.

With the beginning of the 21st century, global transportation times, risks and costs decreased dramatically, communication and information technology enabled people to overcome geographical distances and to reduce information asymmetry between global regions. In addition, trade barriers and market protectionism were systematically reduced through trade agreements like the General Agreement on Tariffs and Trade (GATT) and organizations like the World Trade Organization (WTO).

On the micro-economic level, simple company value chains consisting of buying products to optionally make other products out of it, to distribute and sell these products with a margin to customers become complex networks with globally spread out locations. Globally operating companies face the task to manage volumes and values in this network in a profitable way to ensure competitiveness and business sustainability.

This work investigates the problem to jointly plan volumes and values in a global value chain network for commodity products in the chemical industry. The chemical industry is a process industry sector offering products produced in repetitive production processes carrying out specific physical and chemical reactions (Günther/van Beek 2003a, p. 2). The chemical industry is one of the key global industries with chemical product sales of € 1,776 billion globally in 2004 (CEFIC 2005, p. 3). Globalization with regional growth differences and commoditization with price pressure are important trends within the chemical industry (CEFIC 2005, p. 17 and pp. 28-30; Rammer et al. 2005, pp. 37-48). The management of global material flows poses new challenges on the chemical industry companies since considerable value can be gained from optimizing of the complex global networks (Günther/van Beek 2003a, p. 5).

Additional challenges exist specifically for chemical *commodities*. Commodities are standard products with a defined quality, where price is the key buying criterion. Commodities are often volatile in sales and purchasing prices as well as volumes: increasing crude oil prices lead to higher raw material prices in procurement while dynamic customer markets specifically in Asia lead to a sales price and volume volatility. These dynamics in volumes and values through the value chain directly impact company's profitability as shown in fig. 1.

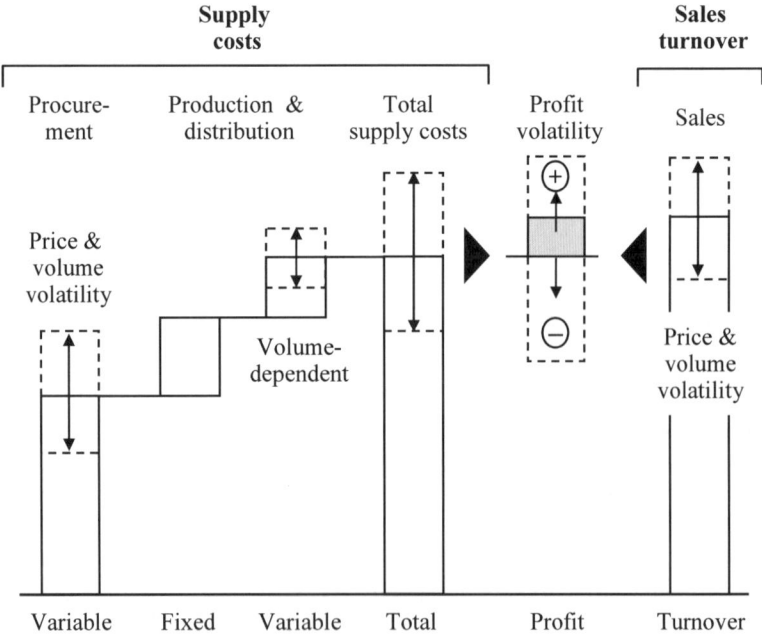

Fig. 1 Challenges to manage values and volumes in a commodity value chain

We give some explanation on fig. 1.

- Sales turnover on the right side of the figure is volatile not only by volatile sales volumes and prices
- Supply costs on the left side of the figure are volatile mainly caused by volatile procurement volumes and prices; within supply, fixed production costs are given and not decision relevant in the short/medium term;

variable production and distribution costs such as transportation and warehousing are variable dependent on volumes
- Overall commodity businesses face a high margin volatility as a consequence of the volatility in turnover and supply costs requiring to manage volumes and values in an integrated way

Cause-effect-relations of these dynamics in the value chain may still be obvious, when operating a simple value chain comprising few products, locations and production steps. Considering the global multi-stage, multi-location value chain network, price changes in raw materials cannot directly be related to intermediate or even sales products and their prices. This problem requires specific planning models and methods.

1.1 Research Field Overview

The research field related to the problem to plan values and volumes of a global chemical commodity value chain network is structured into:

- a general research field overview to define the interdisciplinary research field of value chain management as theoretic background combining specialized research fields that investigate the value chain and appropriate management concepts
- a specific research field overview of state of the art research results related to the problem of planning a global chemical commodity value chain network

General Research Field Overview

Management concepts in the value chain are the generally relevant research fields for the work. *Value chain* as a term was initially defined by Porter *"disaggregating a firm into its strategically relevant activities in order to understand the behavior of costs and the existing and potential sources of differentiation"*. Porter's value chain consists of a *"set of activities that are performed to design, produce, market, deliver and support its product"* (Porter 1985, pp. 33-40). Developed *management concept areas* for the value chain can be classified by specialization on values, demand or supply:

- *Value-oriented management concepts* focus on determination of ex-post profitability in the value chain as well as decision support value indicators based on given demand and supply volumes. Sub-fields are financial accounting, profit and cost controlling (Götze 2004; Götze/Bloech

2004) as well as recent value-based management concepts (Hostettler 2002; Revsine et al. 2004).

- *Demand-oriented management concepts* focus on sales price and sales quantity decisions to maximize turnover with a given or unrestricted supply. Demand-oriented research areas are micro-economics specifically for price mechanisms (Varian 1994), sales and marketing (Effort 1998; Kilter/Keller 2005) and recently revenue management (Cross 2001; Tallury/Van Ryzin 2005).
- *Supply-oriented management concepts* focus on procurement, production and distribution decisions to minimize supply costs for a given demand. Supply-oriented research areas are production management (Günther/Tempelmeier 2003), logistics management (Schönsleben 2004), supply chain management and advanced planning (Shapiro 2001; Chopra/Meindl 2004; Stadtler/Kilger 2005; Bartsch/Bickenbach 2002; Dickersbach 2004; Günther 2005) as well as procurement and sourcing (Dobler et al. 1977; Large 2000; Chen et al. 2002; Talluri/Narasimhan 2004; Monczka et al. 2004; Melzer-Ridinger 2004).

The specialization of management concepts lead to several problems in planning a global commodity value chain: maximizing sales volumes and production utilization only can reduce profitability due to high raw material costs; maximizing purchasing volumes only can reduce profitability due to high inventory costs and/or missing demand. The planning problem requires an integrated approach across the value chain from sales to procurement. The specialized research areas have to be combined to an integrated value chain management framework as the basis for the specific tasks for planning a global value chain for commodities in the process industry.

Problem-specific Research Field Overview

The problem to monthly plan a global value chain for commodities in the chemical industry puts specific requirements considering on the aspects of values, sales, distribution, production and procurement planning in a global network. Recent research related to value chain planning can be clustered into global-oriented, chemical industry-oriented or commodity-oriented research.

Models with a *global* scope are found mainly for strategic network design problems, where location decisions in a global company network need to be optimized (Arntzen et al. 1995; Vidal/Goetschalckx 2001; Goetschalckx et al. 2002). These models consider exchange rate, import tariffs and tax rate differences as global specifics in network design decisions. Recent papers develop also global planning models on a more tactical level

(Chakravarty 2005; Kazaz et al. 2005). Industry-specific global planning models on a monthly level considering also transportation lead times between regions or transit inventories could not be found in current literature. Supply chain management, production management and planning models in the *chemical industry* have been a field of intensive research in practice and science during the last years. Several industry studies analyze the status, requirements and areas of supply chain management also considering the chemical industry (Chakravarty 2005; Kazaz et al. 2005). Scientific research focuses on production (Günther/van Beek 2003b). Subjects to research are the production and logistics characteristics and planning requirements in the chemical industry (Loos 1997; Kallrath 2002a), detailed scheduling models especially for batch production (Blömer 1999; Neumann et al. 2000; Trautmann 2001; Neumann et al. 2002) and in some cases continuous production (Zhou et al. 2000) or hierarchical production planning (Hauth 1998) or multi-site production and supply network planning problems in complex company networks providing production synchronization planning methods (Timpe/Kallrath 2000; Berning et al. 2002; Kallrath 2003; Grunow et al. 2003a; Grunow et al. 2003b; Berning et al. 2004; Levis/Papageorgiou 2004; Yang 2005; Timpe/Kallrath 2000). Integrated production and distribution network design and planning are addressed by Grunow (2001) and Timpe/Kallrath (2000). While production and distribution are intensively investigated due to the complexity and cost-importance of capital-intensive production assets in the chemical industry, procurement and demand management in the chemical industry value chain are less investigated. An example for a procurement model is a spot and contract procurement planning model by Reiner/Jammernegg (2005). Demand-oriented models investigating demand and classical forecasting of demand quantities in the chemical industry can be found for example in practice-oriented industry cases (Franke 2004).

Commodity models are traditionally related to natural resource commodities such as agricultural products e.g. sugar, coffee, metals or crude oil. Economists investigated pricing and market mechanisms for these commodity markets especially during the 1970s and 1980s during the oil crisis from a macro-economic perspective (Meadows 1970; Labys 1973; Labys 1975; Hallwood 1979; Guvenen 1988). From a micro-economic perspective, commodities are considered in financial market research (Roche 1995, Clark et al. 2001; Geman 2005). These models focus on commodities traded on international exchanges. Regular analysis and research are conducted to analyze the development of demand, supply and prices for natural resources but also for industry commodity products (Commodity Research Bureau 2005). Planning commodities in the chemical industry has to deal with demand volatility and uncertainty in volumes and prices as with sales quantity flexibility. Several authors proposed models to handle demand uncertainty in general focusing on quantities (Cheng et al. 2003; Gupta/Maranas 2003; Cheng et al. 2004; Chen/Lee 2004). Uncertainty is reflected by demand quantity scenarios and/or probabilities. Proposed models maximize expected or robust profit. Process industry-specific models use simulation to address demand uncertainty and to determine optimal inventory levels (Jung et al. 2004).

1.2 Research Gaps and Questions

The first research field overview reveals that management research disciplines are specialized focusing on either supply, demand or values. Porter was the first to recognize the anatomy of a value chain with the interdependencies between functional units to create value. However, he did not provide a structured management framework helping companies to translate the value chain anatomy into integrated management processes. Supply chain management research made great progress towards this goal but was still limited to the integration of production and distribution decision making with focus on volumes and costs neglecting price and volume decision making in procurement and sales.

The purpose of this work is to contribute to taking supply chain management to the next level and to complete Porter's value chain mission of integrating decision making in management processes throughout the value chain overcoming separation into demand, supply and value-orientation. For that reason we believe that this work is new. The chemical industry and specifically with its price-volatile commodities is the perfect application field given the complexity in the industry value chain as well as the volatility in volumes and values. The benefits of integrated value chain management will get transparent when demonstrated in an industry case. Summarizing, the specific research gaps so far are:

- there is lack of integrated value chain management framework to integrate demand, supply and value decisions in the value chain; specifically, the integration of sales price and volume decisions with supply chain and procurement decisions is excluded in so far specialized research areas focusing either on demand, supply or values
- the specific problem to plan a monthly global commodity value chain network end-to-end is not covered so far; research is specialized on parts of the problem such as production planning and scheduling, value-based management or revenue management without providing an inte-

grated model for integrating sales prices and volumes with supply volume and value decisions

The following research questions are formulated to close the gaps:

> Research question 1: How can volumes and values within the value chain be managed in an integrated way?

The work's first objective is to combine specialized research to a value chain management framework for managing a value chain end-to-end by volumes and values.

> Research question 2: How can a global commodity value chain be optimally planned by volumes and values?

Developed frameworks are applied to the specific industry problem to monthly plan a global chemical commodity value chain by volumes and values. Sub-objectives are to elaborate characteristics and planning requirements for a global commodity value chain in the chemical industry and to develop, implement and evaluate the respective model. Research question 2 is directed to a real industry case study demonstrating the real existence of formulated requirements, showing the applicability of the developed model in reality and evaluating the model using industry data.

1.3 Research Approach

The study is structured into three parts framed by an introductory chapter and a summary, conclusions and outlook chapter at the end as shown in fig. 2.

- Chapter 2 defines the theoretical background of the work. Related research areas around the central terms *value chain* and *value chain management* are identified. Definitions, classification schemes and concepts are presented as a whole.
- Chapter 3 and 4 introduce the specific global value chain planning problem to be solved in the work. The problem is determined by the industry specifics. This part has two functions: first formalizing the problem and sharpening the work's scope; secondly, define value chain planning requirements as basis for a state of the art analysis to identify specific research gaps in the current literature.
- Thirdly, a value chain planning model is elaborated in chapter 5 and 6 to support postulated requirements and to fill identified research gaps.

Finally, the model needs to prove its applicability in reality and its performance in an industry case study. The model is evaluated with comprehensive industry case data and the relevance of the end-to-end value chain planning approach is evaluated. Opportunities for model extensions are outlined at the end.

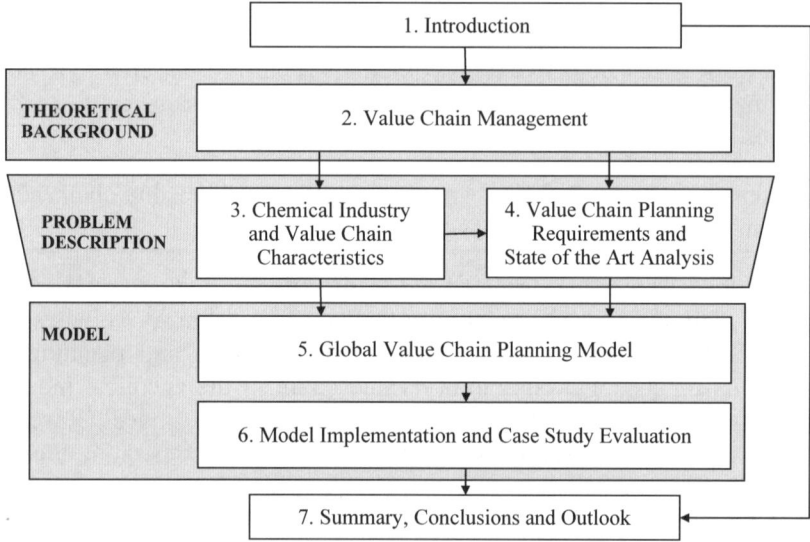

Fig. 2 Study structure and approach

The research results are summarized in chapter 7 and compared to the research questions and objectives formulated in chapter 1. A concluding outlook outlines open and potential new areas, where future research is required.

This approach combines deductive and inductive research steps (Popper 1959, pp. 27-33) and complies with the process proposed by Ulrich/Hill (1976). This process includes cases studies as one mean of deductive research. A case study serves as one basis for the definition of industry requirements existing in reality in chapter 4 as well as a test bed for the model evaluation in chapter 6. A mapping of each chapter to the research process of Ulrich and Hill (1976), p. 348 is summarized in table 1.

Table 1 Study chapters mapped to research process

Research process	Chapter	Chapter function in research process
A. Terminological-descriptive	Value Chain Management	Define the research field and basic terms
	Chemical Industry and Value Chain Characteristics	Use of descriptive studies to narrow problem area investigated within research field Definition of types and relevant dimensions in the scope
B. Empirical-inductive	Global Value Chain Planning Requirements and State of the Art Analysis	Identify planning requirements based on case studies and literature Analyze requirements coverage by state of the art research and further specify research gaps
C. Analytical-deductive	Global Value Chain Planning Model	Model development for formulated requirements
D. Empirical-deductive	Model Implementation and Case Study Evaluation	Validate applicability and requirements coverage of model in industry case

Research field and basic terms are now introduced in chapter 2.

2 Value Chain Management

The theoretical background is defined around the central term *value chain*. Chapter 2 presents research concepts *to manage the value chain* structured by their area of specialization either on supply, demand or values. Secondly, within an integrated framework, the results of the specialized disciplines are combined with the objective to manage sales and supply by values and volume. *Value chain management* is defined and positioned with respect to other authors' definitions. A *value chain management framework* is established with a strategy process on the strategic level, a planning process on the tactical level and operations processes on the operational level. These management levels are detailed and interfaces between the levels are defined. Since the considered problem is a planning problem, the framework serves for structuring planning requirements as well as the model development in the following chapters.

2.1 Value Chain

Value chain as a term was created by Porter (1985), pp. 33-40. A value chain "disaggregates a firm into its strategically relevant activities in order to understand the behavior of costs and the existing and potential sources of differentiation". Porter's value chain consists of a "set of activities that are performed to design, produce and market, deliver and support its product". Porter distinguishes between

- *primary activities*: inbound logistics, operations, outbound logistics, marketing and sales, service in the core value chain creating directly value
- *support activities*: procurement, technology development, human resource management, firm infrastructure supporting the value creation in the core value chain

Fig. 3 illustrates Porter's value chain.

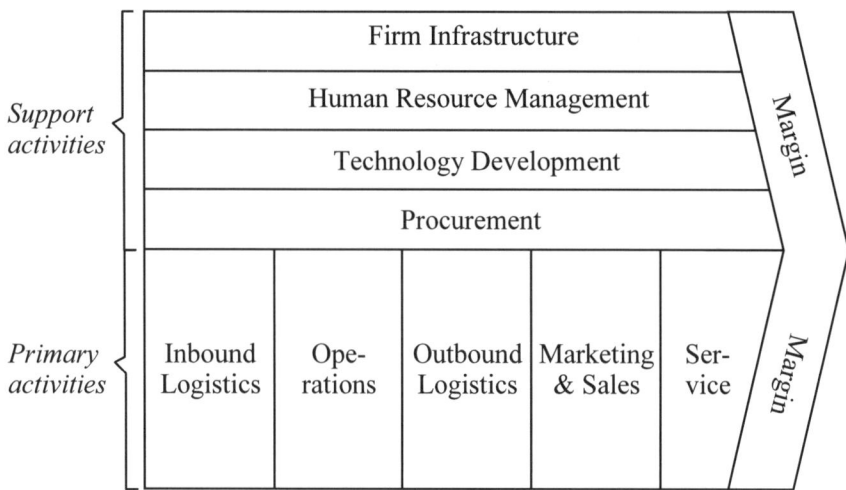

Fig. 3 Value chain by Porter

Porter formulates the general strategies for the value chain of *cost leadership* and *differentiation* to reach competitive advantage (Porter 1985, pp. 62-163). These cross-value chain strategies established a principle that competitive advantage can be reached only by managing the entire value chain as a whole including all involved functions.

Some authors argue that Porter's value chain is characterized by classical functional separation and thinking in organizational units instead of processes, since not processes but activities are listed by organizational function (Corsten 2001, p. 93). Over the years, the value chain was further enhanced towards

- cross-company-orientation defined in the term *supply chain*
- network-orientation defined by the term supply chain network

Supply Chain and Supply Chain Network

Porter's value chain is one basis for the development of the *supply chain*. The term *supply chain* was created by consultant Keith Oliver in 1982 according to Heckmann et al. (2003). Compared to the company-internal focus of Porter's value chain, the supply chain extends the scope towards intra-company material and information flows from raw materials to the end-consumer reflected in the definition of Christopher (1992): "*a supply chain is a network of organizations that are involved through upstream and downstream linkages in different processes and activities that product value in the form of products and services in the hand of the ultimate consumer*". Core ideas of the supply chain concept are:

- a better collaboration between companies in the same supply chain will help to improve delivery service, better manage utilization and save costs particular for holding inventories (Alicke 2003)
- individual businesses can no longer compete as solely autonomous entities, but rather as supply chains (Christopher 1998)

Various illustrations and definitions for the supply chain exist as shown in fig. 4.

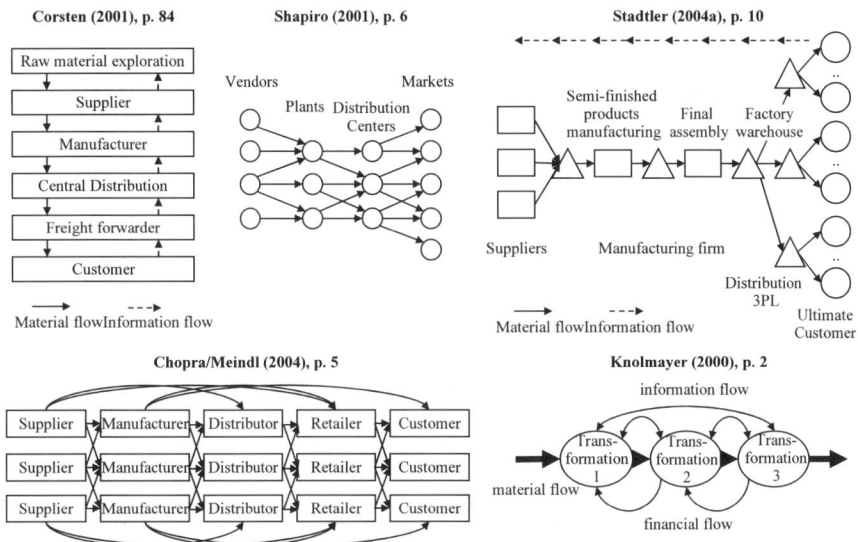

Fig. 4 Supply chain illustrations in literature

Corsten points out that a supply chain is a special type of network composed of multi-level logistic chains owned by legally separated companies. The focus in the supply chain is the coordination of flows of materials and information between these companies. Corsten's examples show the supply chain structure starting with raw materials up to the final consumer (Corsten/Gössinger 2001).

The network aspect in supply chains is illustrated by Shapiro where supply chain networks are composed by notes connected by transportation networks (Shapiro 2001, p. 6). Compared to Corsten, Shapiro extends the supply chain including many-to-many-relations between vendors, plants, distribution centers and markets.

Stadtler addresses the aspect of multi-level manufacturing of semi-finished and final assembly products as well as multi-level distribution steps. He also introduces different node types for procurement, production, distribution and sales and confirms the one-directional flow of material and the one-directional flow of information similar to Corsten. Stadtler emphasizes the difference between intra-organizational and inter-organizational supply chains (Stadtler 2004a, p. 10).

Chopra and Meindl support the aspect of many-to-many relations and a supply chain network. Additionally, they add the aspect of direct relations between partners in the supply chain across several supply chain steps. The primary purpose of the supply chain is to satisfy customer needs, in the process generating profit for itself (Chopra/Meindl 2004, p. 5).

The review of Knolmayer supports the cross-node communication to ensure collaboration across the chain. Additionally, communication is not only one-directional but bi-directional as well as supply chain does not only cover material and information but also monetary flows (Knolmayer/Mertens et al. 2000, p. 2).

While the previous illustrations are focused on the *intra-company* supply chain structures, *inter-company* structures of the supply chain are related to Porter's value chain as shown in fig. 5 (Meyr/Wagner et al. 2004, p. 113 based on Rohde/Meyr et al. 2000).

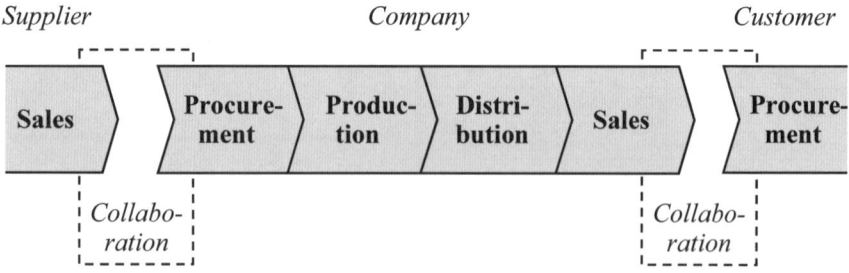

Fig. 5 Company-internal supply chain structures

Here, the focus is on the primary value-creating activities influencing directly the bottom line of the company. Different to Porter,

- *procurement* is a primary value-creating activity and core element in the supply chain and not a support function,
- market-facing activities are combined into *sales* including customer services
- inbound and outbound logistics activities are combined in *distribution*,
- operation in Porter's value chain is more specified with the term *production*.

Concluding, the supply chain and supply chain network concept extends Porter's value chain concept towards cross-company networks in order to improve efficiency and delivery service, minimize costs and inventories based on a given demand across the chain. The focus shifted from value creation within a company towards ensured supply for a given demand and cross-company material flow and information management.

This approach requires a cross-company coordination and information exchange platform in order to create transparency and accurate information about material flows in the chain as basis for decisions. In addition, full collaboration and trust rather than the competition between different companies is required. These assumptions are similar to approaches in planned economies with a central planning office trying to optimize complete industries composed by state-owned companies.

In market economies, however, companies are confronted with competition when selling to customers and they use the market competition when purchasing from suppliers. On the other hand, market constellations can change, when many customers compete for limited resources or raw materials provided by few large suppliers. In these situations, prices, values as well as ensured profitability within each company are decisive for the sustainable survival of the business. While the supply chain emphasizes the supply aspects including ensured supply and availability (Corsten 2001, p. 94), an essence of Porter's value chain underlining the value focus and the supply chain concept is required as basis for the study.

Value Chain and Value Chain NetworkUsed in the Study

The value chain in the study focuses on the company internal value creation in the primary activities consistent to the company-internal supply chain structures by Meyr et al. (2004) and Rohde et al. (2000) as illustrated in fig. 6.

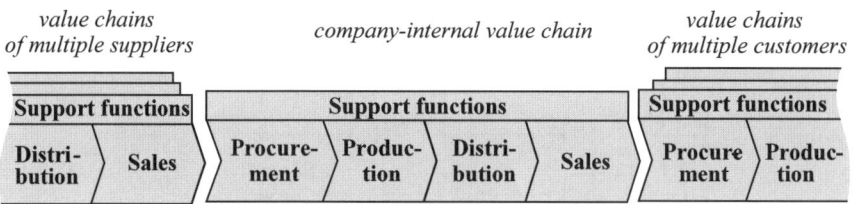

Fig. 6 Value chain considered in the study

The considered value chain is characterized by

- the primary functions of sales, distribution, production and procurement as well as the support function consistent to Porter's support functions excluding procurement

- *sales* covers besides core sales activities also marketing and sales-related service function
- *distribution* covers inbound and outbound logistics with warehousing and transportation
- *production* covers Porter's operations functions; production is not a mandatory function e.g. in case of retailers in the consumer goods industry
- *procurement* is a primary function directly impacting volumes and values
• the value chain has clear interfaces with the procurement functions of multiple customer and the sales functions of multiple supplier interfaces
• the functional structure is consistent with the value creation process and supports the definition of cross-functional management processes

The company-internal value chain is basis for end-to-end volume and value management as well as collaboration and negotiation between other value chains.

The value chain network combines illustrations of the different supply chain network (see fig. 7).

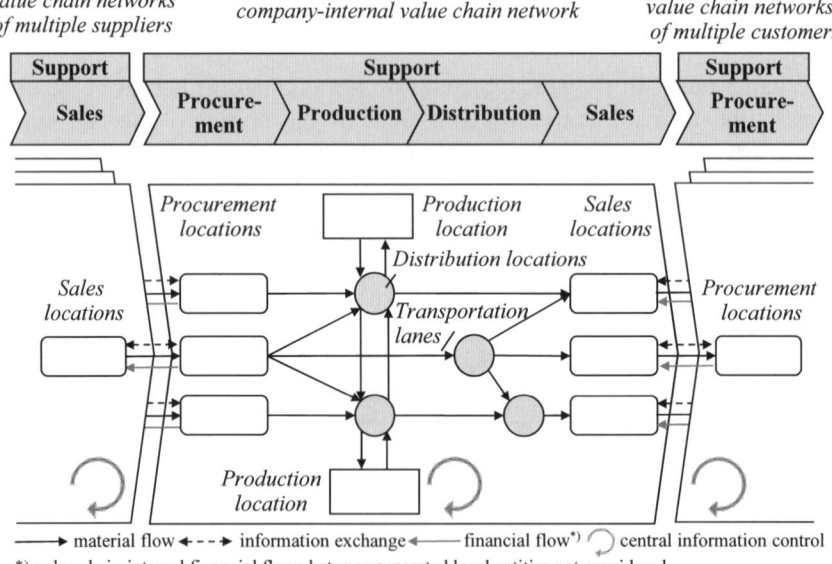

Fig. 7 Value chain network structures

The network is composed by locations and transportation lanes between these locations consistent to supply network structure definitions e.g. in

APS (Dickersbach 2004, pp. 13-15). The company-internal value chain consists of procurement, production, distribution and sales locations:

- procurement locations group one or multiple suppliers to a logical location for purchasing of raw materials and/or finished products for production or trading purpose
- production locations group one or multiple production sites to a logical location
- distribution locations group one or multiple warehousing or logical distribution centers e.g. cross-docking centers
- sales locations group one or multiple customers to a logical sales locations

The value chain network includes the aspect of aggregating multiple customers and suppliers to logical location(s), which is an important aspect in industry value chain networks operating with hundreds and thousands of customers and individual sites.

Distribution locations are included in the company-internal value chain network, if distribution volumes and values are under the control and in the books of the company independent if the warehousing and transportation is outsourced to 3PL distribution companies or not. Therefore, a company value chain network is enclosed with a central control of all volume and value information for the respective network and clear interfaces to customers and suppliers out of the network. While the internal value chain network is focused on material flows evaluated with respective internal costs, dedicated interfaces to multiple suppliers and multiple customers are characterized by material flows, financial flows and mutual instead of one-directional exchange of information as proposed for supply chains by several authors.

The value chain network structure is built on the assumption that not all but specific company-internal value chain information can be shared with customers and suppliers specifically capacity and inventory information. Capacity and inventory information are important factors in price negotiations as well as customer and supplier relationship management: excess inventory weakens the supplier position in price negotiations; shortage in capacity can lead to the fact that important customers change suppliers. Instead of *"opening the books"* between all companies, structured information exchange needs to be established at those interfaces between value chain networks with respect to the specific *demand* and *offer* information as well as *collaboration* and *negotiation processes* e.g. investigated by Dudek for supply chains (Dudek 2004).

The value chain network structure fosters an evolution towards market and pricing mechanisms at the interfaces between networks comparable to financial markets, electronic marketplaces and exchanges with multiple buyers and multiple sellers. While the supply chain concept is concentrated on the supply volume side, the value chain concept should provide the basis to integrate demand volume and overall value decision making into management concepts.

2.2 Concepts to Manage the Value Chain

Three research areas with respective sub-topics are relevant to the problem of managing a global value chain end-to-end by volume and value:

- Concepts to manage *values* in the value chain
- Concepts to manage *demand* in the value chain
- Concepts to manage *supply* in the value chain

Fig. 8 illustrates these research foci and the respective sub-fields.

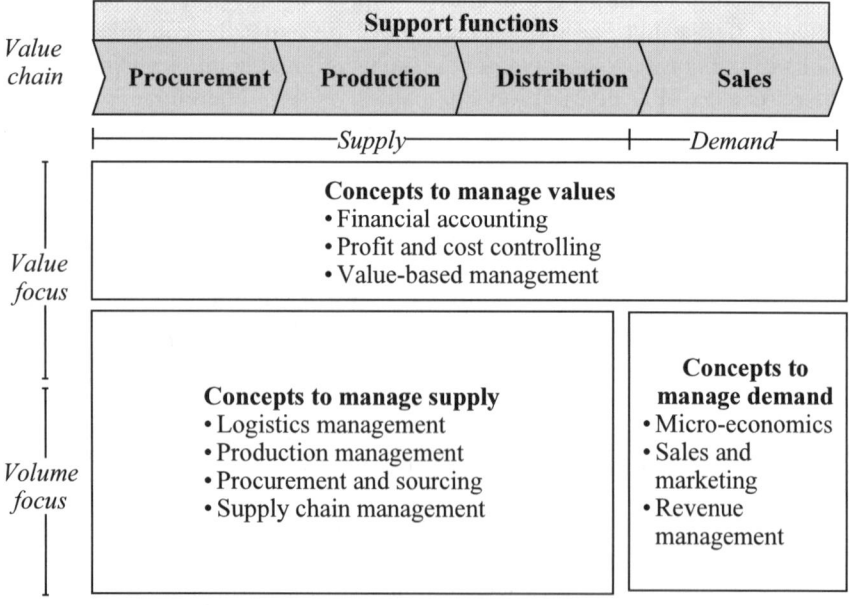

Fig. 8 Management concepts in the value chain

The management concepts focus on the primary activities in the value chain. Management concepts for support functions such as human resources, information technology or corporate finance are out-of-scope in this work. The integration of support management concepts into value chain management is an area for further research.

2.2.1 Concepts to Manage Values

Values in the industry value chain are subjects of financial accounting, profit and cost controlling as well as value-based management research. Out of the scope is the value chain support function of corporate finance concerned with getting required or investing excess financial resources in financial markets, which is not a core activity in the industry value chain and out of the scope in this work. The integration of value chain management with corporate finance is a potential area for further research.

Financial Accounting

Financial accounting is the basis for accurate measuring and evaluation of all values. External financial accounting processes for accounts receivables, e.g. payments from customers, and accounts payables, e.g. payments to suppliers, are key processes in financial accounting (Teufel/Röhricht et al. 2000, pp. 115-170). Inside the company, the accurate evaluation of values in compliance with legal accounting standards such as IAS or US-GAAP has to be ensured (Born 1999). Typical evaluation problems within the value chain are for example the accurate evaluation of assets like fixed production resource value and costs based on depreciation methods or the correct evaluation of working capital such as inventories applying inventory accounting methods e.g. Last-in-First-Out (LIFO) or First-In-First-Out (FIFO) methods (Kremin-Buch 2001; Revsine et al. 2004).

Profit and Cost Controlling

Profit and cost controlling has the objective to provide cost and profitability information as support for management decisions on business and investment using value-based indicators e.g. measuring costs and profitability of the company, customers, products and/or locations (Götze 2004; Götze/Bloech 2004). Profit and cost controlling is based on the structures of cost types, cost centers and cost objects such as products or customers (Götze 2004). Profits and costs are allocated on costs objects such as products to evaluate unit profitability. A key differentiation is fixed costs also called indirect costs and variable costs also called direct costs. Direct costs can be directly allocated to a cost object such as a product, while fixed and indirect costs require volume-oriented allocation methods to reflect potential cause-effect-relations between products and associated fixed costs. A common problem is to allocate capital-intensive production fixed costs such as shifts and depreciations on assets on produced products since the final fixed cost rate depends on the utilization of the production. Here, the calculated indicators depend on the volume situation. Calculated profitability indicators are rather static and rely on ex-post analysis as well as the chosen allocation rules.

Additionally, profit and cost controlling has to consider legal and accounting standards required and applied in formal financial reporting and company business statements.

A guiding instrument for cost and profit controlling is the company income structure as illustrated in table 2 (Revsine/Collins et al. 2004; N.N. 2006a):

Table 2 Income statement structure

Value indicators	Description
Gross revenues/gross sales	Based on gross sales quantity and gross prices
- Discounts/Provisions/Returns	Terms, conditions, provision agreement
= Net revenues/net sales (0)	Net sales turnover
- Cost of sales	Variable cost of goods sold
= Gross margin/EBITDA (1)	Earnings before interests, tax, amortization, depreciation; also contribution margin I (CM I)
- Net operating expenses	Fixed selling, administration costs incl. depreciation
= Operating Profit/EBIT (2)	Earnings before interests, tax, depreciation; also contribution margin II (CM II)
+/- Financial results	Interests payable on debts, investment income
+/- Other revenues/expenses	
= EBT (3)	Earnings/profit on ordinary activities bf. Taxation
- Tax	Based on taxes on earnings
= Net income (4)	Basis for earnings per share calculation/net operating profit after taxes

Different earning results are reported supporting different perspectives on the company's income situation:

- EBITDA has a more short-term perspective focusing on variable costs excluding fixed costs for assets
- EBIT has more a mid to long-term perspective including fixed costs
- EBT compares total earnings considering the financial structure and results of the company independent of location-specific taxes
- Net income is the effective income remaining to the company

EBIT and EBITDA are common indicators used in company-internal decision making supporting operative profitability analysis as basis for volume decisions. Recently value-based management concepts extended the set of indicators to a more shareholder and analyst-oriented perspective.

Value-based Management

Value-oriented management concepts evolved from cost and profit controlling towards value based management concepts. Transparency on profitability of invested capital for the company and its shareholders is an objective of value-based management. Profitability indicators are related to capital indicators. Common indicators are Return on Assets (ROA), Return on Capital Employed (ROCE) and Economic Value Added (EVA®) as presented in table 3 (Hostettler 2002; Revsine et al. 2004).

Table 3 Value-based management indicators

Indicator	Formula	Descriptions
ROCE	$\dfrac{EBIT}{(Total\ assets - current\ liabilities)}$	Indicator to measure pre-tax interest rate on total invested capital excluding current short-term liabilities
ROA	$\dfrac{Net\ profit}{Total\ assets}$	Indicator to compare total profit return on assets specifically in asset-intensive industries
EVA®	$NOPAT - (NOA \cdot WACC)^{1}$	Profit indicator deducting capital costs from net operating profit after taxes excluding interests; consideration of financing structure of the company

Value-based management indicators target an improved and more meaningful profitability analysis considering also required capital employed such as assets and inventories. Providing the interface to integrate value-oriented indicators into volume-oriented management concepts in the value chain would be an interesting option to link volume decisions with overall value performance of the company.

Conclusions: Value-oriented Management Concepts

Value-oriented management concepts provide the accurate basis for evaluation of volumes and profitability. Integrated management concepts in the value chain and decision support models need to be consistent with

---

[1] NOPAT is the Net Operating Profit After Taxes excluding financial results; NOA is the Net Operating Assets and WACC is the Weighted Average Costs of Capital of the company financed by equity and outside capital (N.N. 2006b; N.N. 2006k).

the value definitions from value-oriented management concepts and have to take into account effective values that are "in the books".

Value-oriented management concepts share the characteristics to determine values and profitability ex-post based on historic volumes. They currently do not support a future-oriented planning of volumes and values in global multi-level networks since future planning of volumes depends on sales and supply network planning decisions. Also, the allocation of fixed costs on products and customers based on compensation keys and metrics is problematic when operating a global, multi-stage network with hundreds of products and customers, where cause-effect relations are not direct and linear. Finally, they cannot provide information on the future value of working capital employed such as inventories derived from the monthly inventory volume plan. Hence, an integrated value chain management concept needs to provide the platform to integrate value- and volume-oriented management concepts.

2.2.2 Concepts to Manage Demand

Demand management concepts consider demand and sales as active areas of decision making with respect to pricing and sales quantity decisions. Research fields addressing these decisions are primarily micro-economics, sales & marketing research as well as recently revenue management.

Micro-economics

Micro-economics contribute to demand-oriented management with economic research on market and pricing mechanisms (Varian 1994). Relations of demand and supply from the micro-perspective of buyers and sellers as market participants are investigated. Specifically, market-constellations, price-quantity functions and pricing mechanisms are related to sales quantity and price decision making.

Market constellations depend on the number of market participants on supply and demand side differentiated in polypoly (many), oligopoly (few) and monopoly (one) as illustrated in fig. 9 (N.N. 2006c).

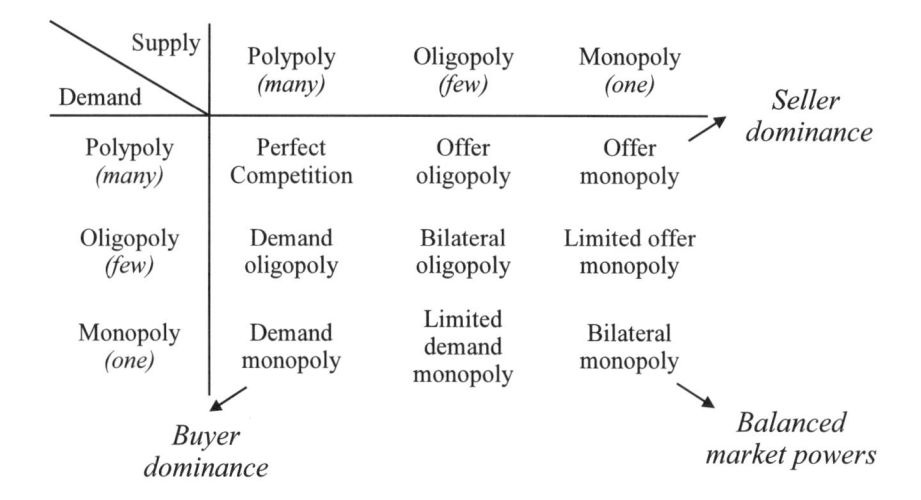

Supply / Demand	Polypoly (many)	Oligopoly (few)	Monopoly (one)
Polypoly (many)	Perfect Competition	Offer oligopoly	Offer monopoly
Oligopoly (few)	Demand oligopoly	Bilateral oligopoly	Limited offer monopoly
Monopoly (one)	Demand monopoly	Limited demand monopoly	Bilateral monopoly

Seller dominance ↗ (upper right)

Buyer dominance ↙ (lower left)

Balanced market powers ↘ (lower right)

Fig. 9 Market constellations

Depending on the market constellations, market participants can dominate sales price and quantity decisions in micro-economic theory. Relationships between and price and quantity in the market constellations are reflected by price-quantity functions as shown in fig. 10 (N.N. 2006d).

Polypoly (perfect competition): market price vs quantity, with Supply and Demand curves intersecting at $\bar{p}$, $\bar{x}$.

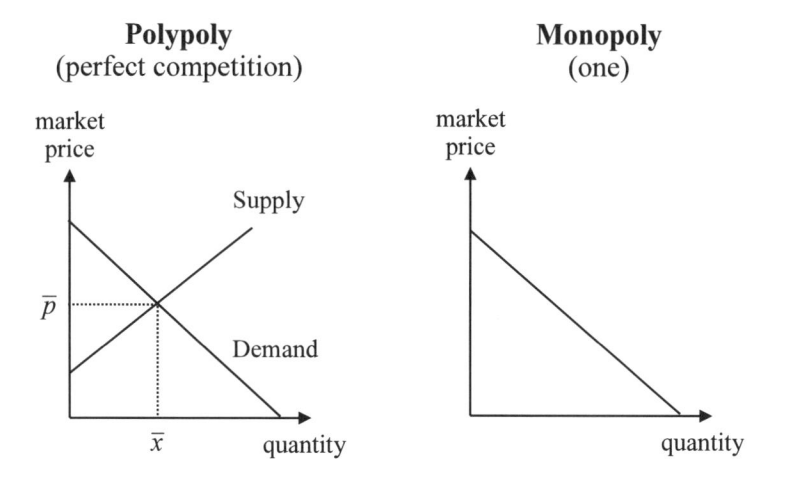

Monopoly (one): market price vs quantity, with a single downward-sloping demand curve.

Fig. 10 Price-quantity functions

Price-quantity functions reflect the negative correlation between market prices and sales quantity. In perfect competition, high market prices correlates with low demand quantities. A single supplier cannot influence the market price with his decisions, a market price and quantity is determined by demand and supply as shown in the left part of fig. 10.

In case of an offer monopoly, a single supplier can dictate the prices, while buyers can only react with their demand quantity to these prices.

The relation between prices and quantities can be expressed by the price elasticity of demand defined as relative change of quantity divided by the relative price change $E = (\Delta q / q_0) : (\Delta p / p_0)$ (N.N. 2006e). The elasticity is characterized as fully elastic (E = ∞), elastic (E > 1), unitary elastic (E = 1), inelastic (E < 1), entirely inelastic (E = 0) or negative elastic (E < 0). Market constellations, price-quantity functions and elasticity are developed from a market perspective considering market constellations, market prices and total sales quantities, not from an individual value chain perspective. However, they provide fruitful input for the integrated management of volumes and value in a value chain, since market constellations and price-quantity relations impact volume and value management in the value chain.

Finally, pricing mechanisms are an important aspect investigated in micro-economics specifically in auction theory. Three different types of pricing mechanism relations exist: bilateral negotiations, single-sided auctions and many-to-many exchanges as shown in fig. 11.

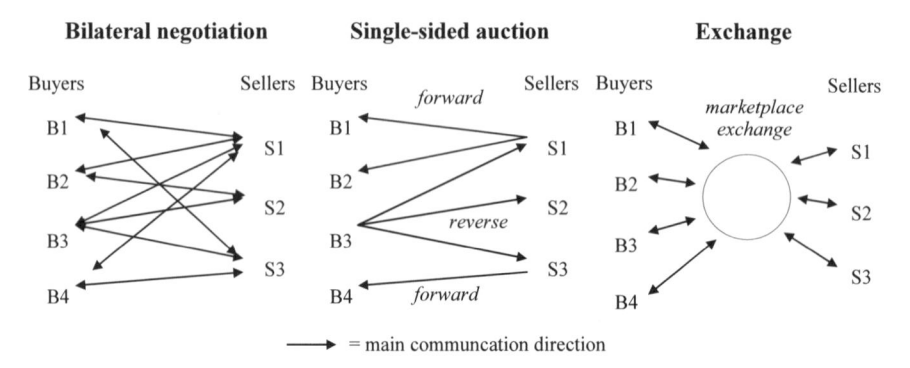

Fig. 11 Pricing mechanisms relations between buyers and sellers

A negotiation is a one-to-one pricing mechanism, where a single buyer and a single supplier negotiate price and quantities. Single-sided auctions have a structured protocol where one auctioneering participant and multiple bidders submitting bids. The winner is determined based on the bidding protocols e.g. First-price-Sealed-Bid or Vickrey auction or Dutch auction. Single-sided auctions exist for selling – called *forward auction* – and for buying – called *reverse auction* –. Finally, exchanges are many-to-many pricing mechanisms with a defined double auction protocol and multiple buyers and sellers submitting offers and bids cleared in one market price

(McAfee/McMillan 1987; Milgrom 1989). Sales price and quantity decisions in value chains needs to consider the respective pricing mechanism applied in the market and reflect it in integrated management concepts.

Sales and Marketing

The area for sales price and quantity decision within a company is a sales and marketing domain. Sales and marketing research has gained increasing importance with the change from seller to buyer markets (Wöhe 2002, pp. 463-465). In the middle of the 20th century in industrialized countries, markets changed from excess demand with insufficient supply towards excess supply and competition in saturated markets. The company focus changed from production-orientation towards sales-orientation. The sales function is an integral part of marketing (Winkelmann 2005). Marketing can be defined as *"an organizational function and a set of processes for creating, communicating and delivering value to customers and for managing customer relationships in ways that benefit the organization"* (Kotler/Keller 2005, p. 6). Marketing can be structured around the so-called marketing mix of product, price, promotion (Communication) and place (Distribution) (Kotler/Keller 2005, p.19). Marketing structures the interface to customers, defines the product portfolio and the pricing as well as the distribution strategy with respect to sales channels, e.g. via wholesalers, web-based shops, direct sales, etc. Marketing also structures the sales functions to sell the products to the customer. Sales and marketing differ in focus as shown in table 4.

Table 4 Focus areas of Marketing vs. Sales

Area	Marketing	Sales
Market	Entire market, market segments	Customers, customer groups
Product	Product lifecycle, portfolio	Customer-relevant articles
Volume	Total volumes, market shares	Sales quantities by customer
Value	Pricing strategy and gross prices Overall product profitability	Customer terms & conditions Customer contribution margins
Topics	Market strategy (segmentation, competitive analysis, positioning) Marketing Mix (product, promotion, place, price)	Customer Relationship Management and Customer Service Collaboration and negotiation, RFP processes Forecasting and sales planning Sales order management

Marketing has a more strategic orientation towards overall product portfolio and markets, while sales has a more operative orientation towards single articles and customers. Specifically, the price as well as terms and conditions are key decisions driving profitability. In industry companies, the price erosions can be observed when companies are facing competition and prices are decreased excessively, since they do not have a systematic price management in place (Homburg et al. 2005). Recent work started to investigated dynamic pricing in industry applications such as the iron and steel industry and in the US automotive industry, respectively (Spengler et al. 2007; Biller et al. 2005). Important in the context of the value chain is that both are managed mainly oriented at sales volume, value and overall profitability targets as basis for active decision making (Bestmann 1996, p. 324).

Revenue Management

Revenue management (RM) is the most recent, demand-oriented management concept in comparison (Cross 2001; Tallury/Van Ryzin 2005). Alternative terms used are yield management or dynamic pricing. Revenue management is concerned with *"demand-management decisions and the methodology and systems required making them"* (Tallury/Van Ryzin 2005, p. 2). Tallury and Van Ryzin distinguish:

- Sales decisions: decisions on where to sell and when to whom at what price
- Demand decisions: estimation of demand and its characteristics and using price and capacity control to "manage" demand

Tallury and Van Ryzin differentiate three basic categories of demand management decisions in revenue management (Tallury/Van Ryzin 2005, p. 3):

- Structural decisions with respect to pricing mechanisms (auctions, negotiations, posted prices), segmentation mechanisms, terms of trade, bundling of products
- Price decisions on how to set posted prices, individual-offer prices and reserve prices in auctions; how to price across categories; how to price over time; how to markdown (discount) over the product lifetime
- Quantity decisions: whether to accept or reject an offer to buy; how to allocate output or capacity to different segments, products or channels; when to withhold a product from the market and sell at later points in time

Revenue management is focused on *demand forecasting* – aggregated and disaggregated – *demand distribution models* or *arrival processes* to develop specific approaches such as *overbooking, seat inventory control* and *pricing approaches* (McGill/van Ryzin 1999).

Initial application fields for revenue management are rental cars (Carroll/Grimes 1995), hotel rooms, transit and highway systems (Huang 2002) or airline seats with a given, perishable capacity (Anjos et al. 2004) with the example of American Airlines to introduce first yield management to better manage profit and airline seat utilization (Smith et al. 1992). Revenue management developed since the late 1970s with the deregulation of the airline industries until web-based pricing mechanisms used in e-commerce applications starting in the 1990s (Phillips 1999, p. 2; Boyd/Bilegan 2003).

Revenue management uses computer-automated pricing mechanisms that support a differentiated pricing for the same product considering utilization and product timing, e.g. different prices for the same hotel room during the week or at the week-end. Pricing mechanisms are based on an analysis of demand patterns in order to ensure that available capacities are sold out in the most profitable way. Current studies reveal that the importance of revenue management as specific demand management concept in the German chemical industry has increased in order to utilize better excess capacities (N.N. 2005d).

Cross formulates basic principles of revenue management (Cross 2001, p. 69):

- When balancing demand and supply does not concentrate on costs but on price
- Replace cost-oriented pricing by market-oriented pricing
- Do not sell to mass markets but to segmented micro-markets
- Reserve your products for your best customers
- Make decisions not based on assumptions but based on facts
- Continuously analyze the value cycle of each product
- Continuously re-evaluate profitability opportunities

Revenue management is not a phrase-based management concept but a discipline based on quantitative methods such as statistics, simulation and optimization as well as systems including steps for data collection, estimation and forecasting, optimization and sales control (Cross 2001, pp. 17-18).

Dedicated revenue management systems are increasingly developed to be applied in airline and non-airline industries (Secomandi et al. 2002). For several recently developed revenue management systems in airlines, hotels, car rentals, telecommunication systems and cargo transportation see Gosavi et al. (2007), Bartodziej et al. (2007), Lee at al. (2007), Defregger and Kuhn (2007), Reiner and Natter (2007). These papers focus on revenue maximization based on pricing and decisions to influence the demand for services such as airline seats, rental car capacity or hotel rooms, which are in limited supply. Active sales and pricing decisions investigated in revenue management are principally relevant for the industrial planning problem considered in this work. However, in contrast to service industries this study deals with physical products and the complex decision making process in a global chemical value chain.

Concluding, revenue management is concentrated on the demand management with a given capacity and supply: *"Revenue management can be thought of as the complement of supply-chain management (SCM), which addresses the supply decisions and processes of the firm, with the objective (typically) of lowering the cost of production and delivery"* (Tallury/Van Ryzin 2005, p. 2). Examples of management practice, where pricing and supply decisions such as lead times or capacities are explicitly linked, are few (Fleischmann et al. 2004, p. 11). Dell is a first example, where PC pricing is dynamically changed based on a production push principle to allocate PCs to the best-price business (McWilliams 2001).

An integrated management concept for the entire value chain from procurement to sales would require integration of both concepts of minimizing costs for supply and maximizing turnover for demand.

Conclusions: Demand-oriented Management Concepts

Up to now, demand management concepts have shared the focus on demand, sales and price decisions to maximize turnover based on a given supply. Supply volatility by volumes – for example due to reduced production or procurement quantities – and values – for example due to volatile procurement prices – is not considered as decision variable in demand management concepts. Authors like Flint (2004) address the challenges to bring marketing and global supply chain management together for customer benefit. But since specifically commodity products require an active sales and price management, the work has to consider the status of demand management concepts and to define the interface to supply-oriented management concepts.

2.2.3 Concepts to Manage Supply

The supply side of the value chain has been subject to research since the middle of the 20th century. The research field can be structured into logistics management, production management, procurement and sourcing, as well as supply chain management.

Logistics Management

Logistics originates in the 1950s motivated by logistic problems in the military sector to coordinate and manage material and personnel in military activities. Logistics can be defined as *"the process of planning, implementing and controlling the efficient, effective flow and storage of goods, services and related information from their point of origin to point of consumption for the purpose of conforming to customer requirements"*. Logistics objective is to allocate resources, like products, services and people, where they are needed and when they are desired (N.N. 2006f). Logistics can be differentiated into inbound logistics for purchased goods, production logistics in production, distribution logistics for finished goods and disposal and reverse logistics for recycled, returned or disposed goods as summarized in fig. 12 (Corsten/Gössinger 2001, p. 81; Günther/Tempelmeier 2003, p. 9):

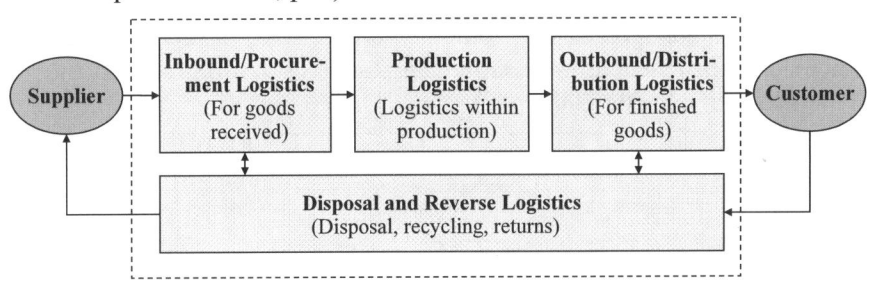

Fig. 12 Types of logistics

Characteristic is that logistics and logistic management are concentrated on the physical material flow in warehousing and transportation (Corsten/Gössinger 2001, p. 81). Logistic research investigates the management of physical material flow

- in warehousing: incl. warehouse layout planning, warehousing systems such as conveyer belts, automated guided vehicle systems (AGVS) as well as queuing, stocking systems, commissioning and packaging problems (Arnold 1995; Günther/Tempelmeier 2003, p. 9)
- in transportation: transport loading, transport routing and scheduling problems (Günther/Tempelmeier 2003, pp. 261-274)

Some authors have extended the scope of *logistics* and used the term *logistics management* comparable to the term *supply chain management* (Schönsleben 2004, p. 7): *"Logistics is defined as the organization, planning and realization of the entire flow of goods, data and information along the product lifecycle"* and *"logistics management has the objective to effectively and efficiently manage the daily intercompany and intracompany operations".*

In this book, logistics and logistics management is focused on the operative volume management in the physical distribution as part of the value chain. A clearer differentiation between logistics research targeting specialized logistic service providers for warehousing and transportation compared to supply chain management problems can be observed in recent literature (Baumgarten/Darkow et al. 2004; Günther et al. 2005).

Production Management

Production management is concentrated on management problems in industrial production. Industrial production is defined as "the creation of output goods (products) using material and immaterial input goods (production factors) based on technical processing methods" (Günther/Tempelmeier 2003, p. 6). Production is characterized by the transformation of input goods into output goods using resources such as machineries or assets as well as human resources as illustrated in fig. 13 (Günther/Tempelmeier 2003, p. 7).

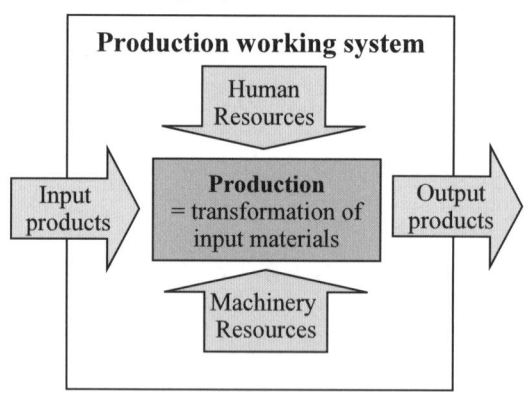

Fig. 13 Production working system structure

Production management concepts started in the 1960s and 1970s with the Material Requirement Planning (MRP I) and the Manufacturing Resource Planning (MRP II) concepts (see for example Günther/Tempelmeier 2003; Lütke Entrup 2005, pp. 5-9). The objective of MRP I was to determine the needs of orders for dependent components in production and raw materials using a bill-of-material explosion (BOM). MRP I hence supported a multi-level calculation of secondary demand for the orders, however, did not consider capacity constraints and did not include feedback loops. MRP II enhanced the concept towards integrated production planning across planning horizons from long term to short term and also between demand and production including feedback loops. Still criticism remains that the assumption of infinite capacity leads to infeasible plans. In addition, the focus of MRP II was transactional and operational for single production plans and not for the entire supply chain or value chain network. MRP I and MRP II are the basis for the evolution towards supply chain management (tools) and the so called Advanced Planning Systems (APS) as described later.

Procurement and Sourcing

Procurement and sourcing is investigated as a separate function (Large 2000; Humphreys et al. 2000; Chen et al. 2002; Talluri/Narasimhan 2004) or together with *materials (requirements) planning/management* (Dobler et al. 1977; Stadtler 2004b) or supply chain management (Melzer-Ridinger 2004; Monczka et al. 2004).

Procurement covers *„all company and/or market-oriented activities that have the purpose to make objects available to the company that are required but not produced"* (Large 2000, p. 2). Other terms found in the context of procurement are *strategic sourcing, purchasing, supply management* and/or *supplier relationship management*.

Two basic procurement functions exist: for resale or purchasing for consumption or conversion (Dobler et al. 1977, p. 4). Procurement is a core function of the business (Dobler et al. 1977, p. 5). Key objectives in procurement are to procure specified objects at a defined quality from suppliers, achieve cost savings and minimum prices for these objects and ensure continuous supply and foster joined innovations with suppliers based on contracts and a supplier relationship management.

Strategic sourcing, the centralization and strategic management of purchasing activities, is a primary cost saving lever for companies by bundling of purchasing volumes, consolidation of many to few suppliers and long contractual agreements for large volumes leading to increased economies of scale for selected supplier(s) and lower purchasing prices for the sourcing company (Talluri/Narasimhan 2004). Strategic sourcing also includes make or buy decisions, e.g. the outsourcing of non-core activities of the company to a specialized service provider (Humphreys et al. 2000). Procurement research also investigates efficient procurement processes and pricing mechanisms such as reverse auctions and/or marketplaces (Hartmann 2002). In addition, strategic alliances with suppliers and joined innovation processes help not only to minimize costs but also to jointly develop innovative products (A.T. Kearney 2004).

However, the local optimization in procurement can lead to goal conflicts with other areas in the value chain: long-term purchasing contracts with high volumes to reach minimum prices can reduce the flexibility in the value chain. Typical "battles" in the value chain are that the purchasing department has to fulfil volume commitments agreed with the supplier especially at the end of the year and purchases more raw material volume as required in the value chain. The effect is the build-up of unnecessary inventory and capital employed. Some authors postulate a strategic reorientation of procurement research towards a stronger cross-functional orientation in the value chain (van Weele/Rozemeijer 1996).

Supply Chain Management

Supply chain management is next step in supply-oriented concepts towards cross-functional processes with focus on production and distribution decisions. Main motivation for supply chain management was the bullwhip effect. The bullwhip effect was observed already in the 1950s and 1960s by the MIT: small changes in consumer demand led to significant variance in production and inventories on the following retailer and manufacturer steps of the supply chain (Alicke 2003, pp. 99-130). Time delays in information and material flows between the participants in the supply chain have been identified as main causes for the bullwhip (Corsten 2001, p. 87).

The bullwhip effect motivated research and practice to focus on cross-company supply chain optimization of information and material flows between companies. Several authors specify a set of objectives related to cross-company supply chain optimization:

- *"minimize total supply chain costs to meet given demand"* (Shapiro 2001, p. 8)
- *"reduce lead times, reduce inventories and increase delivery reliability with the overall objective to increase the service level for the end consumer and reduce costs across all value chain steps in the supply chain"* (Corsten 2001, p. 95)
- *"increase competitiveness of entire supply chains instead of single companies by fulfilling a pre-specified, generally accepted customer service level at minimum costs"* (Stadtler 2004a, p. 9)
- *"maximize the overall value generated"* (Chopra/Meindl 2004, p. 6). Besides, Chopra and Meindl point out that a supply chain should be measured by the entire profitability and not by the profitability of individual stages.

Most of the authors except Chopra/Meindl share the objective to minimize costs in the inter-company supply chain between companies with given demand and customer service level. Chopra/Meindl support the objective of value maximization, where it is later proposed to distinguish this objective with the term *"value chain management"*.

Definitions for *supply chain management* reflect these objectives. The term *supply chain management* was first created by Oliver and Webber (1982). Since then, various definitions in literature can be found:

- supply chain management is the *"flow of material, information and fund across the entire supply chain, from procurement to production to final distribution to the consumer"* (Silver et al. 1998)
- supply chain management can be defined as *"the integrated planning, coordination and control of all material and information flows in the supply chain to deliver superior consumer value at less cost to the supply chain as a whole whilst satisfying requirements of other stakeholders in the supply chain"* (reviewed by Lütke Entrup 2005, based on van der Vorst 2000)
- Mentzer et al. reviewed SCM definitions and concluded three shared characteristics of SCM definitions as a management philosophy (Mentzer et al. 2001, p. 6):
- *"a system approach viewing supply chain as a whole and to manage the total flow of goods inventory from the supplier to the ultimate customer;*
- *a strategic orientation toward cooperative efforts to synchronize and converge intra-firm and inter-firm operational and strategic capabilities into a unified whole; and*
- *a customer focus to create unique and individualized sources of customer value, leading to customer satisfaction"*
- supply chain management *"involves the management of flows between and among stages in a supply chain to maximize total supply chain profitability"* (Chopra/Meindl 2004, p. 6).

Except of the latest definition of Chopra/Meindl, all definitions share the aspect of cross-company management, the focus on volume management to fulfil customer needs.

Significant savings could have been realized in practice thanks to supply chain management for example minimizing inventory values by postponing final assembly to the latest stage of the supply chain as in the case of Hewlett-Packard (Lee/Billington 1980), by improving delivery accuracy to nearly 100% as in the case of Ericsson (Frerichs 1999) and better utilizing production resources. Several key supply chain management research results are presented in the following in more detail.

Supply Chain Planning Matrix: the Supply Chain Planning (SCP) Matrix provides a framework for supply chain management (Rohde et al. 2000, reviewed among others by Fleischmann et al. 2004, pp. 87-92) illustrated in fig. 14.

	Procurement	Production	Distribution	Sales
long-term	• materials program • supplier selection • cooperations	• plant location • production systems	• physical distribution structure	• product program • strategic sales planning
mid-term	• personnel planning • material requirements planning • contracts	• master production scheduling • capacity planning	• distribution planning	• mid-term sales planning
short-term	• personnel planning • ordering material	• lot-sizing • machine scheduling • shop floor control	• warehouse replenishment • transport planning	• short-term sales planning

flow of goods ↔ information flows

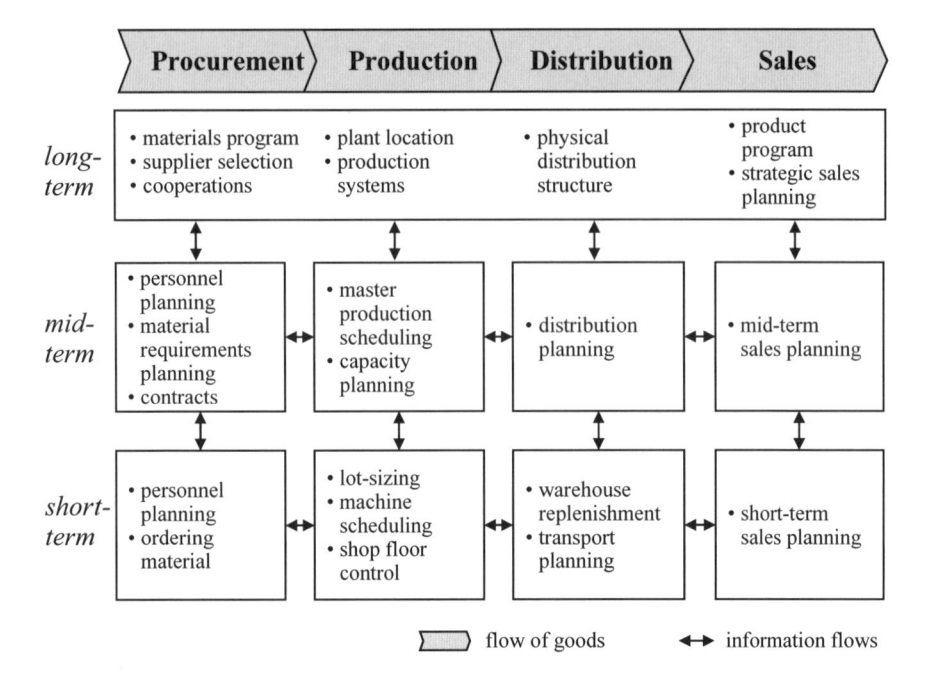

Fig. 14 Supply chain planning matrix

The supply chain planning matrix provides an integrated management framework by planning horizon (strategic, tactical and operative) and supply chain process (Fleischmann et al. 2004, pp. 87). Strategic decisions are related to plant locations or physical distribution centers also called strategic network planning or network design (Goetschalckx 2004). Tactical decisions are related to planning of volumes in sales, distribution, production and procurement also called master planning (Miller 2002; Rohde/Wagner 2004; Pibernik/Sucky 2005). Short-term decisions are related to short-term planning and scheduling of production. This operative and transactional level is related to the traditional focus of logistics and/or MRP I and MRP II concepts. Overall the supply chain planning matrix is related to the term *advanced planning* emphasizing and enhancement of planning not only on the operative level but also on a tactical and strategic level. Hence, a primary research area is related to advanced planning systems (APS) support advanced planning processes.

Advanced Planning Systems: information systems in supply chain management play a critical role to support companies effectively in decision making, handling complex supply chain problems and data (Gunasekaran/Ngai 2004). APS research focuses on the planning systems extending the scope of traditional ERP systems limited to operations

(Bartsch/Bickenbach 2002; Knolmayer/Mertens et al. 2002; Dickersbach 2004; Günther 2005). While ERP systems focus on the operational and transactional level of order processing and scheduling as well as on-line inventory control (Mandal/Gunasekaran 2002), APS are used specifically for demand and supply network planning and integration of production planning and production scheduling (Betge/Leisten 2005). APS are subject to dedicated research evaluating capabilities of developed software packages (Zeier 2002; Lütke Entrup 2005). Key research deliverable is the mapping of APS software modules to the supply chain planning matrix as shown in fig. 15 (Meyer et al. 2004, pp. 110):

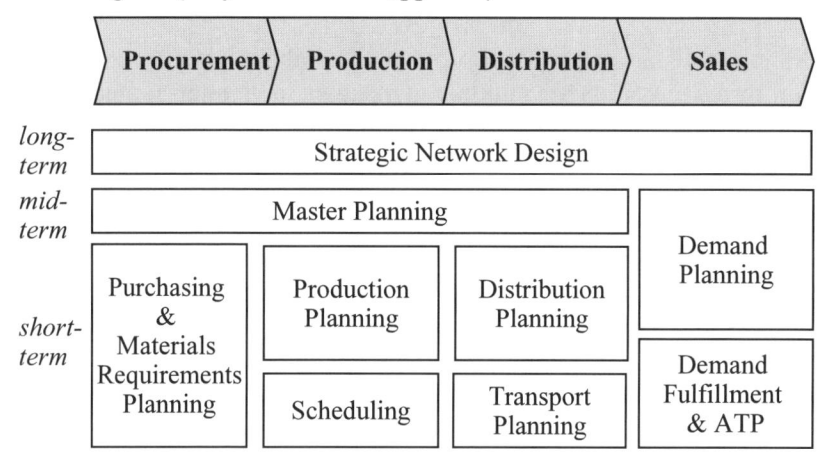

	Procurement	Production	Distribution	Sales
long-term	Strategic Network Design			
mid-term	Master Planning			Demand Planning
short-term	Purchasing & Materials Requirements Planning	Production Planning	Distribution Planning	
		Scheduling	Transport Planning	Demand Fulfillment & ATP

Fig. 15 APS software modules covering the SCP-Matrix

Here, it can bee seen that system modules are not directly matched to process structures defined in the Supply Chain Planning Matrix. Also, the asymmetry between market facing parts of procurement and sales are not intuitive. However, APS extend the perspective on business applications extending the classical tasks of ERP and transactional systems to a management and planning level. With APS implemented in multiple industries and validated specifically in the process industry (Schaub/Zeier 2003) or also for Small and Medium Enterprises (SME) (Friedrich 2000), importance will further grow.

Supply Chain Collaboration and Negotiation: since supply chain management across companies is a key objective, several authors focus on the management of the interface and collaboration between company supply chains towards a cross-industry supply chain: the idea is that a collaboration between all companies from natural resource (e.g. metals) to end consumer product (e.g. cars) can lead to lower inventories, lowest costs and highest efficiency (Zimmer 2001; Hieber 2001). This cross-company supply chain managements requires a transparent sharing of available inventories, capacities and demand across all companies. Prices and value aspects are not relevant in this view. This is build on the assumption

- that no competition in supply chain between multiple customers for a limited supplier capacity exists,
- no conflict of interests between buyers and sellers in negotiation exists,
- and market constellations and purchasing powers have no influence on the collaboration e.g. large OEM corporations would not use their purchasing power to achieve minimum prices at their SME suppliers.

Main results are negotiation protocols, collaboration rules and collaboration forms to coordinate multiple companies in an inter-company supply chain. However, it is shown that the ideal world is hard to achieve in practice. *"It is difficult or maybe even impossible, to get a large network consisting of independent companies to agree and implement a centralized planning and control solution"* (Holström et al. 2002, reviewed by Pibernick/Sucky 2005, pp. 77). Companies are not always willing to open the books entirely and share company-internal information e.g. inventories, capacities or cost structures with customers and suppliers in order to protect competitive information. Power in the supply chain for example in the automotive industry with few large OEMs and many mid-size tier suppliers do have an influence on negotiations as well as profitability for the single participants in the supply chain (Maloni/Benton 1999). Recent authors recognize the aspect that companies rather negotiate in a competitive constellation than cooperating with its business partners and propose appropriate negotiation protocols (Homburg/Schneeweiss 2000; Dudek 2004). Since a centralized planning task for the entire intercompany supply chain comprising multiple legal entities is rarely realistic in practice, Dudek has developed a non-hierarchical negotiation-based scheme to synchronize plans between two independent supply chain partners with offers and counter-proposals to minimize total costs; prices and competition among limited supply is not considered (Dudek/Stadtler 2005).

Special SCM Concepts: in addition, some industry-specific terms have been developed in the context of supply chain management in the last years:

- *Just In Time (JIT):* time-exact delivery to the customer's production having no own inventory (specifically practiced in the automotive industry).

- *Vendor Managed Inventory (VMI):* supplier manages the inventory at the customer site to ensure delivery capability (practiced among others in the chemical and electronic industry)
- *Efficient Consumer Response (ECR)* and *Collaborative Planning, Forecasting and Replenishment (CPFR):* both are operations models in the consumer goods industry to ensure delivery capability and avoid stockouts based on an automated replenishment of outlets using product inventory, historic and/or planned sales information at the point-of-sales (POS). CPFR focuses on a close cooperation between retailer and manufacturer. ECR focus on the customer-facing reaction on customer responses in logistics, sales and promotions.

All concepts can be related to the supply chain planning matrix; most of them are a re-branded description of short-term and operative supply chain planning problems. Concluding, SCM reached the highest level of cross-functional and cross-company orientation of management concepts in the value chain with the emphasis on supply.

Conclusions: Supply-oriented Management Concepts

Supply-oriented concepts have in common to minimize supply costs in order to fulfil given demand. Sales prices and sales quantity decisions are not subjects of research. Supply-oriented research with its definitions and frameworks contributes to main parts of the work's theoretical background. The study needs to combine the research results with management concepts focusing on demand and on values.

2.2.4 Concepts Comparison

Comparing the presented management concepts in the value chain it can be concluded that concepts focus either on values or volumes and/or certain steps in the value chain as illustrated in fig. 16.

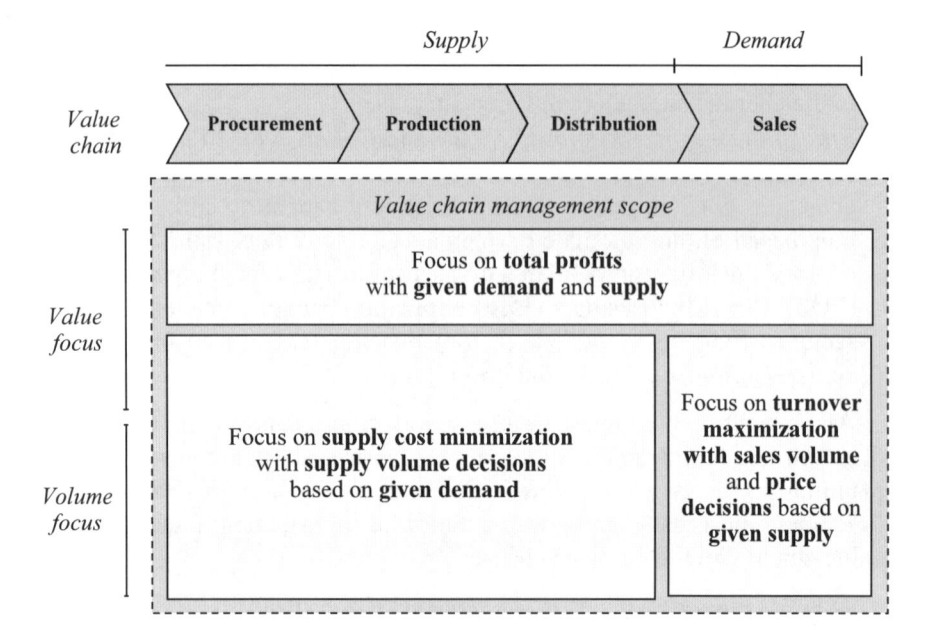

Fig. 16 Comparison of management concepts in the value chain

- Supply management concepts focus on supply decisions in order to minimize costs with a given demand
- Demand management concepts focus on sales volume and price decisions to maximize turnover based on a given and/or unlimited supply
- Value management concepts focus on total profit analysis with given demand and supply

There is a lack of having an integrated concept of managing volumes and values across the entire value chain. The specialized concepts with focus either on demand and supply decisions or on value analysis have to be combined to an integrated approach. This integrated approach is required to manage a global commodity value chain end-to-end by values and volumes.

Some authors already postulate to extend the focus of supply chain management towards integration with demand management and in some parts with value management

- to coordinate purchasing and production with customers by using quantity discounts on both ends of the value chain to decrease costs (Munson/Rosenblatt 2001),

- to integrate logistics into marketing to successfully manage different channels in the consumer goods and retail sector (Alvarado/Kotzab 2001),
- to decide supply chain positioning in a global context driven by demand rather than by production (Sen et al. 2004),
- to integrate supply chain and pricing decisions in Marketing (Christopher/Gattorna 2005),
- to tailor customer experiences to increase customer loyalty and growth by synchronizing supply chain and marketing decisions (Pyke/Johnson 2005),
- to synchronize manufacturing, inventory and sales promotions specifically in industries with seasonal demand (Karmarkar/Lele 2005),
- to synchronize procurement, manufacturing with sales pricing considering specifics such as perishable items, setup costs and demand uncertainty (Yano/Gilbert 2005),
- to synchronize new product development with the supply base (Asgekar 2004),
- to decide integrated financial planning and evaluation of market opportunities with production planning using real options (Gupta/Maranas 2004).

Some scholars suggested using *demand chain management* instead of SCM (Williams et al. 2002; Heikkilä 2002) expressing to shift the focus of the chain towards demand incl. (prospective) customers (Van Landeghem/Vanmaele 2002) and the needs of the marketplace, *before* integrating the supplier and manufacturer perspective. Specifically, time-to-market pressure requires to better link product development, sourcing and sales driving the focus shift towards the ends of the value chain in procurement and sales (Kennedy Information 2005). This shift is suitable for demand-driven industries with a flexible and less cost-intensive supply as in the case of mobile devices described by Heikkilä (2002) or lightning manufacturing (Childerhouse et al. 2002). The shift from supply chain towards demand management can be also observed in spending for supporting SCM software where understanding end-user demand became key priority instead of operations efficiency (Frontline Solutions 2005 reviewing an AMR Research "Supply Chain Management Spending Report 2005-2006").

However, a focus shift from supply to demand would again not consider the overall profitability of the value chain leaving out supply volumes and values supply specifically in procurement. Concluding, a focus on either demand or supply is not sufficient and both have to be managed in an integrated way together with the resulting values. Therefore, the different management concepts have to be combined in an integrated value chain management framework and approach.

2.3 Integrated Value Chain Management

In the following integrated value chain management is defined and a framework is developed as synthesis of management concepts presented in subchapter 2.2. Key methods used in value chain management such as optimization or simulation are presented at the end of the chapter.

2.3.1 Value Chain Management Definition and Framework

Having defined the *value chain*, Porter does not provide a definition for *value chain management* (Porter 1985). The term *value chain management* is used in recent research (McGuffog/Wadsley 1999; Teich 2002; Jörns 2004; Kaeseler 2004; Al-Mudimigh et al. 2004) and in industry practice (Trombly 2000; Harvard Business Review 2000; bitpipe 2007) compared to Porter's initial publishing on the value chain. In addition, a recent dedicated journal "International Journal of Value Chain Management" has been launched (Inderscience 2007).

Teich (2002) provides a comprehensive work on *"extended value chain management"*. He defines *Extended Value Chain Management (EVCM)* as *"the holistic consideration of the value chain where starting at the customer and depending on the situation in production and procurement orders are generated at the same time under consideration of previous production steps"* (Teich 2002, p. 2). He argues *"that previous isolated concepts focused either on advanced planning and scheduling in production or on supply chain management for procurement planning"* (Teich 2002, p. 2). Teich's definition of value chain management covers procurement and production aspects with focus on volumes and schedules. Value in the value chain as a consideration of sales and prices are not covered in the definition. His focus is rather the cooperation of different *competence cells* within a value chain network specifically for small and medium enterprises to improve overall value chain network planning. The concept is used by some authors e.g. to automate finding and negotiations of suppliers within a pool of competence cells (Neubert et al. 2004, p. 177)

Kaeseler provides a more comprehensive definition of value chain management from a consumer goods industry perspective (Kaeseler 2004, pp. 228-229). *Value Chain Management* is an essence of *Supply Chain Man-*

agement and *Efficient Consumer Response (ECR)* with SCM as a *"renaissance of production and logistics planning"* and ECR as *"customer orientation and marketing in retail"*. To overcome the separation of these concepts, Kaeseler proposes Value Chain Management as a *"holistic redesign of processes from the retail customer to purchasing from the manufacturer including Sales, Marketing, Logistics, Production and Purchasing"* (Kaeseler 2004, pp. 229). However, Kaeseler limits the concept on the *volume* management problems in the value chain e.g. avoidance of the bullwhip effect, planning of seasonal demand as well as managing returns and variants in the product portfolio. The *value* management aspect is not covered including purchase and sales prices.

Jörns describes *Value Chain Management* as a superset of the management concepts SCM, *Supplier Relationship Management* (SRM), *Customer Relationship Management* (CRM) and *Enterprise Management*. This perspective reflects a broader scope of VCM compared to SCM without providing an integrated framework (Jörns 2004, pp. 35-36).

Practice-oriented articles as from Trombly (2000) formulate the objective of value chain management to be *"full and seamless interaction among all members of the chain, resulting in lower inventories, higher customer satisfaction and shorter time to market"*. Public websites offer additional definitions for value chain management such as *"the optimization of value chain interactions. Each internal and external operation and the links between these operations are reviewed in a systematic and standard way in order to optimize speed, certainty and cost effectiveness"* (bitpipe 2007). Again the term *"value chain management"* is used in practice mirroring objectives, content and concepts already addressed in supply chain management.

Al-Mudimigh et al. (2004) are among the few authors distinguishing between *supply chain management (SCM)* and *value chain management (VCM)*: they argue that SCM is recognized and practiced in many industries and has reached high popularity *"becoming a way of improving competitiveness by reducing uncertainty and enhancing customer service"*. For VCM in comparison so far *"there is little evidence of the development of an accompanying theory in literature"*. They propose a VCM model from suppliers to end-user in order to *"reduce defects in inventories, reduce the processed time to market and improve customer satisfaction"*. The VCM concept is centered on the value for the customer with four pillars: VCM vision, process management, partnership approach, IT integrated infrastructure and agility and speed. They argue for a broader perspective on the value chain, however, conclude with similar results and concepts compared already in SCM to focus on collaboration and customer service. Aspects of quantitative value-added and volumes and value management throughout a value chain from sales to procurement are not considered.

Concluding, existing definitions use *value chain management* as alternative term for *supply chain management* focusing on supply volume decisions to fulfil a given demand and minimize costs. Especially, value and sales decisions are not covered in an integrated framework.

To continue, an appropriate definition of integrated value chain management has to combine the characteristics of simultaneously managing volumes and values throughout the entire value chain in order to ensure companies' profitability. Therefore, value chain management has to be defined in this work.

> Value chain management is the integration of
> demand, supply and value decisions from sales to procurement
> using strategy, planning and operational processes.

This value chain management definition relies on a three-level structure for strategic, tactical and operative company control introduced by Anthony (1965) and used in controlling and supply chain management literature (Rohde et al. 2000).

The key aspect is *integration* of decisions on each level across the company value chain with the defined interfaces to suppliers and customers. But why integrate decisions within the value chain? Why strategic supplier and procured product prices and volume decisions should for example be integrated with sales price or market strategy decisions? The answer is simple: to achieve a *global optimum* in the value chain instead of a *local optimum* in only one area of the value chain. A company for example can reach a local optimum in procurement negotiating very low raw material prices for high fixed contracts volumes. This local optimum will not lead to a global optimum, if sales volumes are more volatile and fixed procured raw material remains as excess inventory on stock. A company targeting a local optimum in distribution minimizes inventory and capital costs leading to lost sales or limited capabilities to hedge risk of volatile raw material prices with inventories and hence no global optimum in overall value. Shapiro et al. support the idea of having one optimum in the value chain stating that a value chain is a *"single mathematical model with an optimal solution"* (Shapiro et al. 1993 reviewed by Schuster et al. 2000).

Integrated decisions also require *simultaneous* decision making instead of iterative or even isolated decision making. Fulfilment of this postulation was nearly impossible to achieve in former years without real-time information technology and decision support methods. Thanks to information technology and operations research method advances, the objective to synchronize decisions in real-time even in larger organizations is feasible today.

The new aspect in *value chain management* becomes clear comparing it to a quotation of Alan Greenspan related to better management of *supply chains*: *"New technologies for supply chain management and flexible manufacturing imply that business can perceive imbalances in inventories at an early stage – virtually in real time – and can cut production promptly in response to the developing signs of unintended inventory build up"*[2] (Datta/Betts et al. 2004, p. 4). Compared to this postulated direction of supply chain management to increase production flexibility in order to follow volatile demand and suppliers (Aprile et al. 2005), value chain management heads for an opposite direction: it is not about fully increasing production flexibility and responsiveness in production to avoid inventories; it is about better stabilizing production utilization by better integrating value and volume decisions in procurement and sales.

The value chain management concept is detailed in a framework being presented in fig. 17.

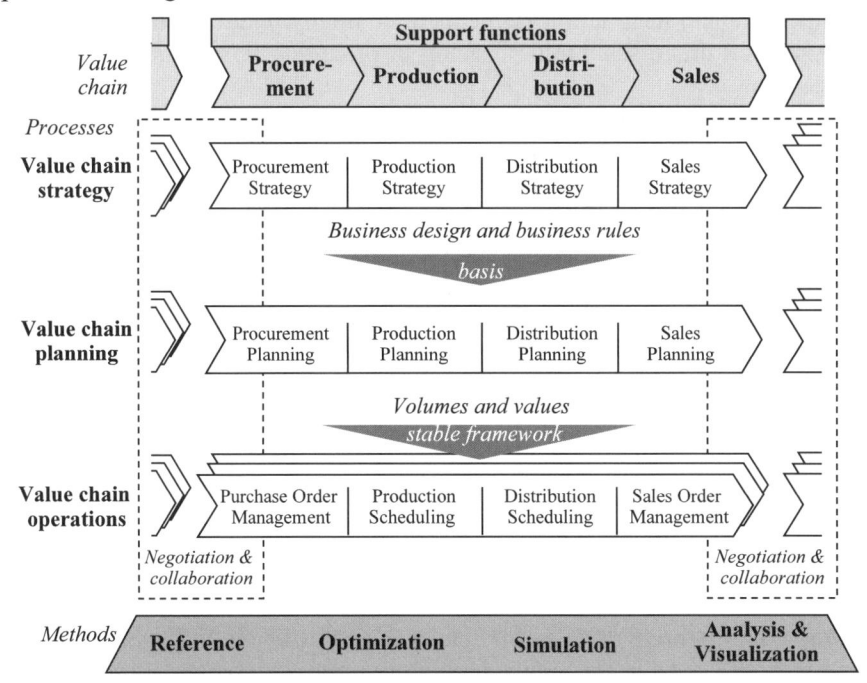

Fig. 17 Value chain management framework

---

[2] Alan Greenspan Testimony to the U.S. Senate Committee on Banking, Housing and Urban Affairs, 13. February 2001.

The framework is mainly based on the supply chain management framework of Rohde et al. (2000). Rohde's work is gradually enhanced to address the aspects of synchronized decision making within the value chain and the integration of supply, demand and value management concepts as shown in fig. 17. The framework is structured into the areas *value chain*, *processes and methods*.

The area *value chain* provides the framework structure by procurement, production, distribution and sales. The framework requires having these steps under a central control; typically, this is a company organization with clear interfaces to customer and supplier organizations. The framework supports the idea of having a network of individually managed value chains interacting with each other based on clearly defined interfaces and legal agreements. The framework does not support the idea towards one cross-company industry value chain, where individual companies cooperate and share e.g. plans, inventories and value results transparently based on an agreed central planning control authority. This would assume having only a situation of collaboration between companies without considering competitive and negotiation elements in company relations such as request for proposal processes, multi-sourcing or price and service negotiations to name a few.

Value chain *processes* are differentiated into strategy, planning and operations according to the structure proposed by Anthony (1965), pp. 15-18. The strategy, planning and operations processes are further detailed in section 2.3.2.

Different *methods* are applied in the value chain management processes for decision support. Reference, optimization, simulation and analysis and visualization methods are distinguished as further detailed in section 2.3.3.

2.3.2 Value Chain Strategy, Planning and Operations

The value chain management processes are presented in a process overview initially and then further detailed with respect to process characteristics and compared within the framework.

Value Chain Strategy

Value chain strategy focuses on synchronized decision on business design and business rules in the value chain as summarized in the following definition.

> Value chain strategy is the integration of business design and business rule decisions in the value chain.

Business design comprises traditional company network design decisions on production and distribution sites or production resource capacity design. The term *business design* also includes market strategy decisions in sales and procurement as well as product strategy and life cycle decisions. Shapiro criticizes in supply chain strategy studies that these are often too narrowly defined not covering the company strategy as a whole (Shapiro 2004, pp. 855-856).

Business rules define upper and lower boundaries and service levels agreed in contracts or given by physical structures of the value chain. The objective is to integrate business design and business rule decisions throughout the global value chain network already on the strategic level to enable global value optima in planning and operations. The scope of the value chain strategy is illustrated in fig. 18.

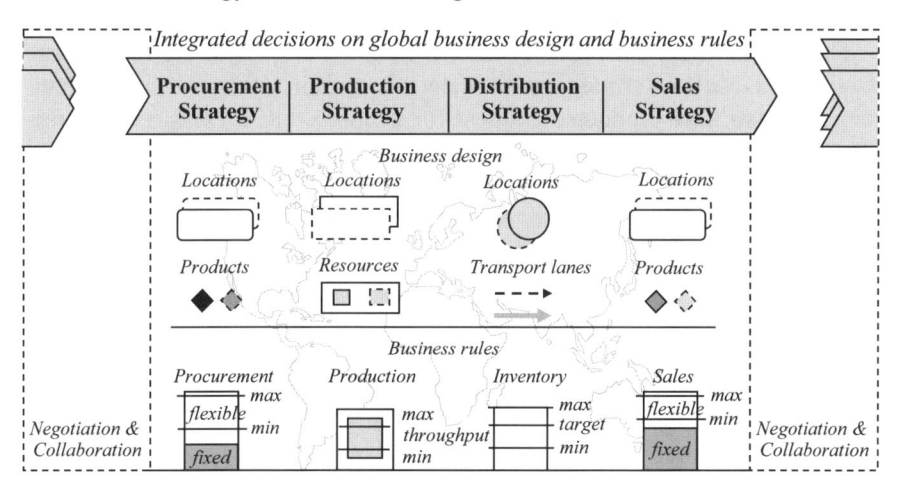

Fig. 18 Value chain strategy

The *sales strategy* needs to decide what product to be sold in which sales market representing the sales location in the value chain network. New markets needs to be evaluated for their attractiveness and the own competitive position with respect to existing products or the capabilities in the development of new products for the respective demand. Sales business rules include decisions on the strategic share of contracted business volumes vs. flexible spot business volumes. These business rules often depend on sales channels and frame contracts with customers. The sales strategy can be matched with classical marketing mix decisions on products, prices, promotion and communication, as well as sales channel decisions.

The *distribution strategy* needs to support the sales strategy in distribution location and transportation design decisions specifically to balance the market requirements of lead times and delivery capability with distribution costs. Examples for distribution strategy projects are regularly found in practice specifically when restructuring a comprehensive distribution network (Sery et al. 2001). Hence, distribution business rules are mainly related to inventory and transportation boundaries effecting the delivery service and support of sales strategies.

The *production strategy* is the most investment-critical decision affecting the opening of new production sites and specifically investments and divestments in resource capacities and technologies. The production strategy is mainly covered by typical supply chain network design models focusing on production site and resource network design decisions (Lakhal et al. 2001). Production business rules are related to the flexibility of the resources with terms of throughputs, multi-purpose capabilities or changeovers to name a few.

The *procurement strategy* needs to decide strategic sourcing regions and suppliers as well as strategic raw materials and products included in current and also new products. Request for proposal (RFP) and reverse auction processes as well as contract negotiations are key elements of the strategic sourcing process. As a mirror compared to the sales strategy, again the company needs to decide, how much volume is procured based on fixed contracts and much volume flexibility is required in order to benefit from lower prices or to reduce the risk not to be able to sell the corresponding volumes of finished products. Procurement strategies in large corporations are often coordinated by a corporate procurement unit in order to bundle corporate-wide volumes for shared products to achieve better prices.

As already mentioned, *negotiation and collaboration* in value chain strategy is firstly related to contract negotiations with customer and suppliers to agree on business rules. Secondly, acquisitions and divestitures – representing a network change in the company value chain network – are important areas of negotiation and collaboration. Thirdly, joined product strategies and development with customers and suppliers – e.g. agreeing on specifications and standards – are important areas of negotiation and collaboration.

Value Chain Planning

Value chain planning is defined in the following.

> Value chain planning is the integration of volume and value decisions in the value chain based on the value chain strategy.

Volume and values in the defined business design with the given business rules are optimized jointly in sales, distribution, production and procurement plans as illustrated in fig. 19.

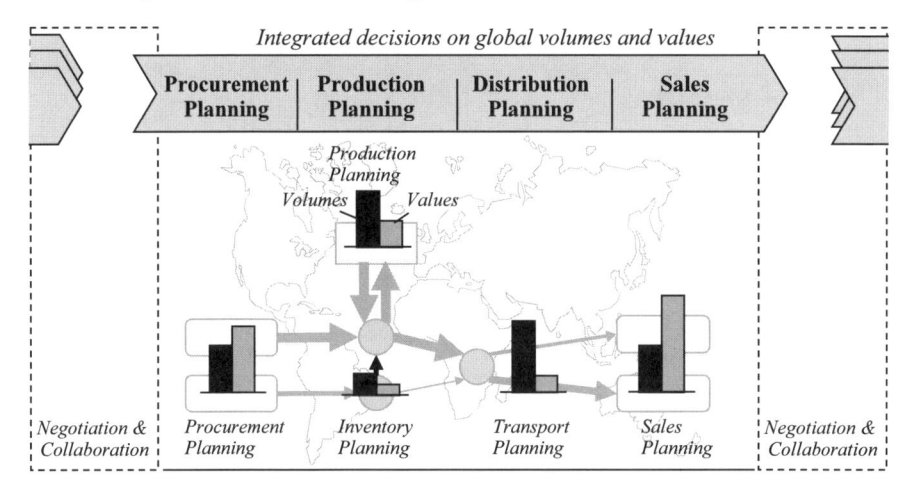

Fig. 19 Value chain planning

Volume and values in all global network nodes are planned as well as the transportation volumes and values between the nodes. Main difference compared to traditional supply chain and master planning approaches is the joined planning of volumes and values throughout the global value chain network with the intention to manage the overall profitability of the company ex-ante based on planned volumes and values for the chosen planning buckets e.g. months. Specifically, the integration of sales volume and price planning with supply planning decisions is an aspect in the value chain planning process different to traditional supply planning as shown in fig. 20.

- Demand is forecasted with price and quantity in a first step and aggregated to a total demand volume with an average price.
- Then, consolidated demand is matched with available supply by volume and value. If demand exceeds supply, sales volumes needs to be lower than the supply. If demand is not profitable since prices are too low in selective businesses, the company also reduces sales volumes where possible to ensure profitability.
- Result is a sales plan to be disaggregated on the individual customer basis. Sales volumes different to demand volumes are possible if sales flexibility in spot businesses exists compared to sales contracts that need to be fulfilled.

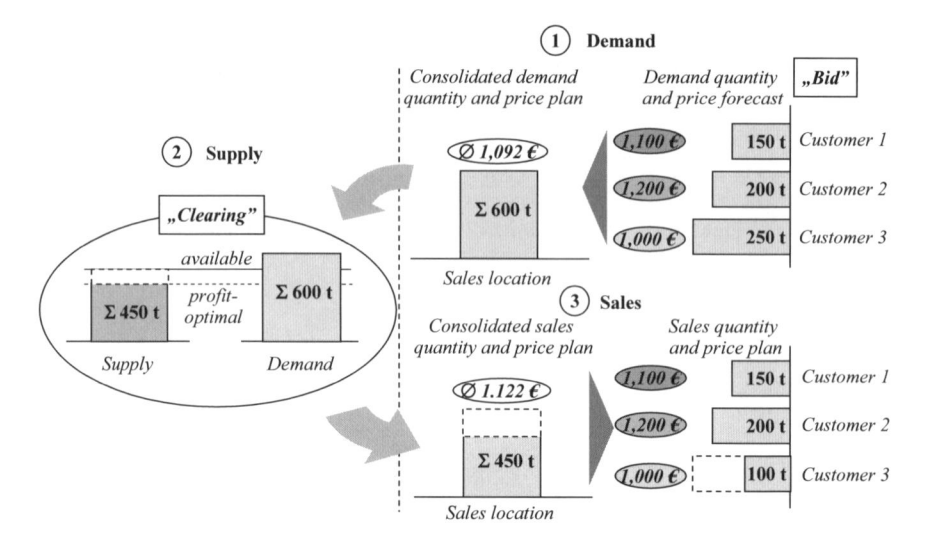

Fig. 20 Integration of sales and supply decisions in the value chain

In this case, the aggregate average sales price increases due to the reduced volumes, since low-price spot customers are rejected. Thinking one step ahead, this sales planning process has many similarities to auction and financial market clearing processes: the demand forecast of the customers has the character of an *ask bid*. The volume and price clearing mechanism is not based on multiple *offers* as in double auctions or many-to-many exchanges, but is comparable to single-sided auctions. Multiple customers compete among a single product supply of the company. The company uses the competition to utilize supply in a profitable way. The result is – again similar to financial markets – that demand forecast bid not fulfilling the clearing conditions are not successful and not supplied.

Distribution planning covers planning of inventories and transportation volumes and values. Both needs to comply with volume boundaries from the value chain strategy to ensure delivery capability and comply with structural and delivery constraints. Distribution planning is one core competence for retailers focusing on buying, distributing and selling without having own production.

Production planning decides on production volumes and values by site and production resource. Production planning normally considers total volumes only, while production scheduling in operations decides on the respective schedule. However, cases exist where production lead times and change-over constraints may require also considering the sequence of products in production master planning.

Procurement planning, finally, decides on spot and contract procurement volumes and values based on the negotiated and/or offered market respectively supplier prices. Procurement planning is based on the sourcing strategy and frame contracts agreed with suppliers. Here, the discrepancy between local optima and the global optimum in the value chain often gets transparent: procurement tends to bundle volumes in fixed contracts to minimize procurement costs. This can lead to the situation that volumes are not consumed due to a lack of sales; however, the company must take the material leading to high and undesired inventories especially at the end of the year.

Negotiation and collaboration in planning is a key aspect of recent research. The negotiation aspect may be less formalized since main negotiations of frame contracts already happened on the strategic level. However, contracts can also be and become more short-term in case of increasingly volatile prices and markets. Here, negotiations specifically on prices and volumes can become integral part of the planning process. If an agreement is achieved, collaborative planning focuses on exchanging planning information to improve planning quality to jointly lower inventory and ensure delivery service. Collaborative planning requires a further integration of planning processes with respect to organization, process and information technologies.

Overall the integrated planning of volumes and values in the value chain planning process continuously reacts on changes on procurement and sales markets and ensures ex-ante the profitability of the company. Therefore, limited supply chain planning processes further evolve by integrating procurement and sales volume and value planning into the process. The company value chains transforms into a marketplace where the company operates as market maker clearing supplier offering in procurement with customer demand in sales through the value chain. This recognition is an interesting change of perspective on the role of large industry companies with many suppliers and many customers: these companies do not have to participate in marketplaces hosted by third party providers but they have a large marketplace already inside their company with suppliers and customers participating.

Value Chain Operations

The volume and value plan is the stable framework for value chain operations as formulated in the following definition.

> Value chain operation is the integration of order schedule decisions in the value chain based on the value chain plan.

Customer order schedules need to be integrated with deliveries, production orders and procurement orders. Volumes and values are already defined. Therefore, the focus is on a time schedule of orders considering production and distribution lead times. Fig. 21 illustrates the main task in value chain operations also now focused on a geographical region such as Europe. The individual schedules of sales orders and purchase orders have to be integrated with distribution and production schedules.

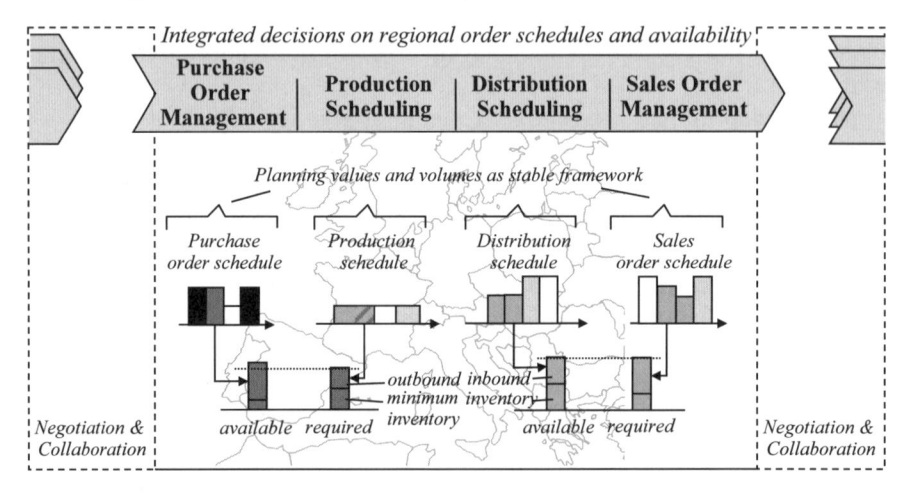

Fig. 21 Value chain operations

The purchase orders, sales and distribution order quantities can be higher or lower each day depending on the available number of transportation units e.g. trucks or ships. The production quantity, however, each day is limited by production capacity and cannot be so easily changed day-by-day. These different volume structures need to be matched by integrating order schedules and availabilities of materials.

Sales order management deals with order entry, order change, availability check and confirmations to the customer. Availability check as a concept and as part of Advanced Planning Systems (APS) is also summarized under the term *Available-To-Promise* (Kilger/Schneeweiss 2004; Pibernick 2005). The availability has to be checked against the sales plan as stable framework for the overall period and the physically available material at the specific point in time.

Distribution scheduling covers warehouse scheduling incl. picking and packing as well as transport scheduling. Transportation route optimization and bundling of transportation volumes have to match the customer order schedule.

Production scheduling of resources and detailed production orders as well as change-overs and throughputs is one of the most challenging problems specifically when multi-purpose resources and production changes have to be considered. Production scheduling can be decoupled from orders using inventories and make-to-stock production.

Purchase order management needs to ensure stable replenishment with raw materials or other procured products for production or trading purpose executing negotiated contracts or spot plans.

Negotiation and collaboration in value chain operations is focused on electronic and automated exchange of orders and further business documents like as invoices, quality certificates or delivery documents using electronic shops, portals or marketplaces.

Special concepts such as VMI or CPFR share the characteristic to be volume and supply-focused as in supply chain management. Although the terms may differ, the detailed processes and tasks match the overall value chain management framework, since the anatomy of the value chain is considered not to be different.

Process Characteristics and Comparison

The processes can be further systematized and compared by process level, decision supported, time buckets, planning horizon, frequency and granularity (s. table 5).

Table 5 Value chain management process characteristics and attributes

Characteristic	Strategy	Planning	Operations
Level	Strategic	Tactical	Operative
Decision	Business design Business rules	Volumes Values	Schedule
Time bucket	Year, quarter	Month, week	Day, real time
Horizon	Years (1-10)	Months (1-12)	Days (1-90)
Frequency	Yearly, quarterly	Monthly, weekly	Daily, continuously
Granularity	High aggregation	Medium aggregation	Detailed

The *value chain strategy* process focuses on long-term strategic business design and business rule decisions. Decisions are based on yearly and quarterly buckets with a horizon of multiple years. This process is conducted or updated yearly with a new or an updated strategy; in case of very dynamic markets, a review could also be quarterly. In decision making a high aggregation level is used not focusing on single customers or articles but rather entire markets and product lines or technologies.

In comparison, the *value chain planning* process is the bridge between the strategic and the operative level deciding all volumes and values in the network. The planning process is conducted by default on a monthly basis, in businesses with short manufacturing lead times also on a weekly basis. Decisions are based on monthly respectively weekly buckets for the next 1 to 12 months at a medium aggregation level. The volume and value decision has to be made on the tactical level. The long horizon of the strategy process does not allow predicting the future volumes and values exactly being influenced by many internal and external factors like raw material prices, changes in demand patterns or geopolitical factors or natural catastrophes. The short horizon on the operations level does not allow a stable volume and value plan, since geographical distances and production resources structure have limited flexibility to react on short-term order scheduling.

Operations processes are on the operative level focusing on order scheduling for a specific day or point in time. The schedules have a shorter horizon than the planning processes focusing on days. The schedule is monitored and updated continuously – daily to weekly. Orders are managed on the most detailed level for single customer respectively suppliers and articles.

Key framework characteristic is the linkage between strategy, planning and operations: the strategy process defines the network to be planned as well as business rules to be considered as constraints in planning. Agreed volume and value plans are the stable framework for operations schedule requiring participants to meet the agreed plans. It is important to mention that decisions are clearly associated only to one process. For example, annual budget plans of volumes and values often are used for individual or organizational target setting. Given the strategic character, these volumes should support business rules or business design decisions e.g. investment decisions in locations or production resources as well as market entry strategies or strategic alliances with suppliers, but they are less suitable for target setting specifically when operating in a volatile business environment. Therefore, actual volume and value decisions as well as target setting should be made in the tactical planning process. Same is true for operations, where it is not be the objective to optimize the overall *volumes* but the *schedule* of already agreed volumes and values in the plan. This is often a complex operations research problem, however, the volume and value optimization potential and degree of freedom is given by the plan.

As shown in the framework, there is *one* strategy and *one* planning process as well as *multiple* operations processes for volumes and values.

Typically, multiple functions-oriented processes can be found, where the same volumes and values are planned several times from different perspectives. Here, all functional units in sales, controlling, marketing, supply chain management, logistics, production and procurement should agree on *one* strategy and *one* planning process. Theses processes interact with the respective *multiple* processes of *multiple* customers and *multiple* suppliers. This is also important to mention, since collaborative supply chain management concepts often rely on the assumption that the company collaborates only with *one* supplier or *one* customer not considering the *competition* of multiple customers and suppliers for company products and production resource capacities as well as procurement volumes, respectively. This is a main obstacle to collaboration requiring 1:1 partnerships while the real world is a many-to-many market system.

Decisions in value chain processes and the processes itself have always a conceptual and quantitative basis, which is complex and comprehensive considering the entire value chain. Several methods have been developed to support decision-making as shown in section 2.3.3.

2.3.3 Value Chain Management Methods

Different *methods* exist to support value chain management decisions in strategy, planning and operations that are applied in respective decision support *models*. A basic definition of *method* and *model* can be found in a review by Teich (2002), pp. 219-220.

Method is based on the Greek term *methodos* meaning *way towards something* or *way or process of examination*. A method can be defined as "*systematic approach with respect to means and objectives that leads to technical skills in soling theoretical and practical tasks.*" Methods and methodological approaches are characteristic for scientific work and solution of theoretical as well as practical problems. Primary decision support method categories are shown in fig. 22 (Specker 2001, p.39) reviewed by Nienhaus (2005): *reference, simulation, optimization* as well as *analysis and visualization*.

54   2 Value Chain Management

```
                    ┌─────────────────────────┐
                    │  Value Chain Management │
                    │    Method Categories    │
                    └─────────────────────────┘
         ┌──────────────┬────────┴────────┬──────────────────┐
   ┌───────────┐  ┌───────────┐   ┌──────────────┐   ┌──────────────┐
   │ Reference │  │ Simulation│   │ Optimization │   │ Analysis and │
   │           │  │           │   │              │   │ Visualization│
   └───────────┘  └───────────┘   └──────────────┘   └──────────────┘
```

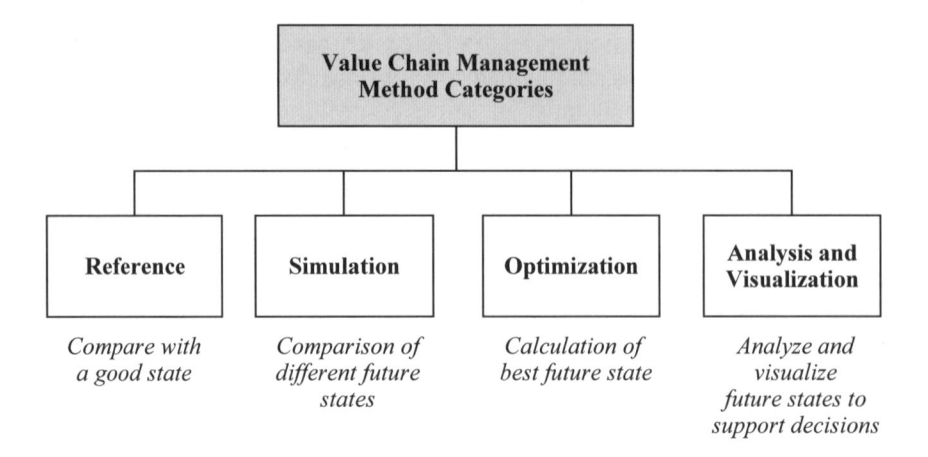

Compare with   *Comparison of*   *Calculation of*   *Analyze and*
a good state   *different future*   *best future state*   *visualize*
                        states   *future states to*
                                                                          support decisions

Fig. 22 Value chain management method categories

Reference

The *reference* method develops good states as comparison for decision support on concept design (Nienhaus 2005, pp. 24). Reference models – in industry also often called *best practices* – can be found e.g. for processes, organization, performance management or information technology (IT) concepts. Business *process* reference models have been developed in the context of process-supporting applications specifically Enterprise Resource Planning (ERP) applications (Brenner/Keller 1994; Keller/Teufel 1997; Curran/Keller 1998). These process models used specific process modeling methods such as the *Event-driven Process Chain* (EPC) or Petri networks. ERP application suppliers such as SAP developed process reference models to support the introduction and training of their software in a business-oriented way and use the reference for optimization of processes. These reference models provide processes combined with IT and organization reference, since processes are modeled together with IT functions and organizational roles or units. However, reference processes are often on a very detailed transaction level limited to operations and administration processes in the company. The aspect of volume and value management in the value chain and concentration on these fundamentals is often overwhelmed by a significant complexity and number of processes in the reference models.

The *Supply Chain Operations Reference* (SCOR®) model is a reference model for supply chain planning and operations *processes* as well as *performance management* developed by the cross-industry organization Supply Chain Council (SCC) started in 1996 (Supply Chain Council 2006; reviewed by Sürie/Wagner 2004, pp. 41-49). The SCOR® model structures the value chain in make (production), source (procurement) and deliver (sales & distribution) processes as well as the planning and operations level. The SCOR® model also includes a set of best-practices supply chain measures called Key Performance Indicators (KPIs) to share common definitions. The SCOR® model is specialized on supply chain management excluding value and pricing in sales and procurement as well as the strategy level in the value chain.

Specialized *performance management reference* exclusively concentrate on key performance indicators and reference definitions. In addition, integrate performance management framework such as the balanced scorecard structure performance indicators into different performance categories such as customers, processes, human resources and financials (Kaplan/Norton 1997; Zimmermann 2003). Several KPIs such as production utilization, delivery reliability, inventory ranges and planning quality are key measures in supply chain management (Nienhaus et al. 2003) and also in value chain management. However, these KPIs need to be extended to cover the entire value chain including the value aspect of the management. Consistent KPI definitions in Sales, Marketing, Controlling, Supply Chain Management, Production and Procurement are required. Process reference model in this work influences the Value Chain Management Framework with respect to Strategy, Planning and Operations Processes.

Simulation

Simulation methods compare different future states serving as basis for sensitivity analysis and system design decisions. Simulation can be used as prescriptive method in decision support (Tekin/Sabuncuoglu 2004) and is used for example in the area of production and logistics (Rabe 1998). Material flow simulation in physical logistics facilities are one example, where simulation of future running operations is used to design capacities and material flows as decision support for an investment. Simulation methods in value chain management can be used to compare different scenarios in strategy, planning and/or operations e.g. to simulate decision outcome including uncertainty of volumes and prices. Simulation results are analyzed with respect to sensitivity considering risks, validity and optimization criteria (Kleijnen 2005a). Kleijnen distinguishes *spreadsheet simulation*, *system dynamics (SD)*, *discrete-event simulation* and *business games* (Kleijnen 2005b, p.82):

- *spreadsheet simulation* provides simple and easy to use test beds to simulate e.g. focused production and distribution systems (Enns/Suwanruji 2003)
- *system dynamics (SD)* developed by Forrester (1961) initially under the term "industrial dynamics" consider entire industry systems from an ag-

gregate perspective and simulate change of key system parameters based on quantitative cause-effect relations between the parameters; in supply chains, system dynamics is used e.g. to simulate cause-effect relations between orders, production and inventory quantities (Angerhofer/Angelides 2000, Reiner 2005)

- *discrete-event simulation* simulates individual events such as arrivals of customer orders incorporating uncertainties
- *business games* includes human behavior into simulation letting human participants interact based on a defined game or business setup as for example in game theory

Simulation methods are embedded in simulation tools supporting to model simulation problems and partly supporting comprehensive visualization of simulation results (Fu 2002; Mason 2002).

Uncertainty in value chain management is a key motivation to use simulation comparing different scenarios, e.g. of demand quantities and prices, in order to simulate capacity planning in the automotive industry (Eppen et al. 1989)

Optimization

Optimization methods calculate one best future state as optimal result. Mathematical algorithms e.g. SIMPLEX or Branch & Bound are used to solve optimization problems. Optimization problems have a basic structure with an objective function $H(X)$ to be maximized or minimized varying the decision variable vector X with X subject to a set of defined constraints Θ leading to $\max(\min)H(X), X \in \Theta$ (Tekin/Sabuncuoglu 2004, p. 1067). Optimization can be classified by a set of characteristics:

- *Local vs. global optimization* addresses the computation and characterization of global optima (i.e. minima and maxima) of non-convex functions constrained in a specified domain. Global optimization focuses on finding a global optimum of the objective function f subject to the constraints S (Floudas et al. 2005, pp. 1185-1186) ensuring that no other global optimum exists within other local optima; in value chain management, a global value optimum should be reached instead of local optima in the individual functions procurement, distribution, production and sales.
- *Single v. multiple objectives* is related to having a single objective to be maximized or minimized or if multiple also competing objectives have to be balanced; in value chain there can be a single global objective e.g. to maximize profit or multiple objectives addressing different stakeholders such as customers, employees and the public. Multi-objective optimization often requires a subjective evaluation of objectives e.g.

customer satisfaction vs. profits. Therefore, it is easier and more pragmatic to optimize one objective and to ensure the compliance with other objectives in constraints.
- *Discrete vs. continuous space* is related to the possible values of the decision variables: deciding production quantities for instance is reflected by a continuous decision variable while deciding to make a change-over or not is a binary decision requiring a discrete decision reflected by integer variables in this case 0 or 1.
- *Deterministic vs. stochastic:* an optimization problem can be based on deterministic parameters assuming certain input data or reflect uncertainty including random variables in the model; in value chain management deterministic parameters are the basic assumptions; extended models also model specifically uncertain market parameters such as demand and prices as stochastic parameters based on historic distributions; in chemical commodities, this approach has some limitations since prices and demand are not normally distributed but depend on many factors such as crude oil prices (also later fig. 37).

Optimization models are also classified by the mathematical problem to be solved:

- Linear Programming (LP) for continuous variables based on the SIMPLEX algorithm
- Mixed Integer Linear Programming (MILP) including continuous and integer variables using e.g. the Branch & Bound Algorithm for finding a solution near to optimum defined by the optimization tolerance called MIP gap
- Quadratic programming (QP) is a special problem including a product of two decision variables in the objective function e.g. maximization of turnover max $p \cdot x$ with p and x both variable requiring a concave objective function and that can be solved if the so-called Kuhn-Tucker-Conditions are fulfilled, e.g. by use of the Wolf algorithm (Domschke/Drexl 2004, p.192)
- Constraint Programming (CP) is a further optimization approach where relations between variables are stated in form of constraints in order to better solve specifically hard bounded integer optimization problems such as production scheduling
- Genetic Algorithms (GA) are used in case of large combinatorial problems and can be applied e.g. for example in complex value chain network design decisions (Chan/Chung 2004)

Where mathematical programming promises exact optimal solutions, *heuristics* can find solutions that come close to optimal solutions. The advantage of heuristics used to lie in simplicity and speed of solutions finding a solution that is close or even match the optimal solution (Schuster et al. 2000, pp. 176). However, today, exact optimization is capable also to solve many complex industry-scale optimization problems in acceptable time thanks to the advance of computer technology and progress has made in improving optimization algorithms since 1950s: large scale problems e.g. of 10 million constraints and 19 million variables can be solved within 1.5 hours (Bixby 2005). Therefore, optimization is widely used in practice e.g. in production scheduling, transportation route optimization or strategic network design problems. Challenges in practices are more the level of specialized knowledge required to operate optimization systems in industry application (Schuster et al. 2000).

Analysis and Visualization Methods

Analysis and visualization methods focus on direct decision support to bridge the gap between comprehensive data results from simulation or optimization towards focused condensation, analysis and visualization supporting action-orientation and decision making. They also target to support the modeling of value chain structures and networks to make processes and network structures transparent and ease the understanding of planning as well as supporting to use optimization and simulation methods without having a profound know-how in these methods (Ünal et al. 2002)

Key Performance Indicators (KPIs) in supply chain balanced scorecards and performance management are one example for analysis methods. Beamon (1998) and Chan (2003) distinguish *qualitative* performance measures such as customer satisfaction, on-time delivery, fill rate or flexibility as well as *quantitative* measures based on costs in distribution, manufacturing and inventory or warehousing.

Besides combined methods exist such as search algorithms or simulated annealing that are applied to analyze optimization or simulation results as presented in the following.

Simulation-based Optimization as Combined Method

Presented methods can be combined to provide advanced decision support. *Simulation-based optimization* combines simulation and optimization in order to use simulation no longer as descriptive but as a prescriptive method and decision support (Tekin/Sabuncuoglu 2004). Tekin and Sabuncuoglu provide a classification on advanced simulation-based optimization methods (Tekin/Sabuncuoglu 2004, p. 1068) as illustrated in fig. 23.

```
                          Optimization
                            Problems
                               │
              ┌────────────────┴────────────────┐
              ▼                                 ▼
            Local                             Global
         Optimization                      Optimization
              │
      ┌───────┴───────┐                • Evolutionary Algorithms
      ▼               ▼                • Tabu Search
                                       • Simulated Annealing
   Discrete       Continuous           • Bayesian/Sampling Algorithms
 Decision Space  Decision Space        • Gradient Surface Methods
```

- Ranking and Selection   • Response Surface Methodology
- Multiple Comparison   • Finite Difference Estimates
- Ordinal Optimization   • Perturbation Analysis
- Random Search   • Frequency Domain Analysis
- Simplex/Complex Search   • Likelihood Ratio Estimates
- Single Factor Method   • Stochastic Approximation
- Hooke-Jeeves Pattern Search

Fig. 23 Simulation-based optimization method classification

In addition to the basic methods such as SIMPLEX, other key methods for value chain management are the response surface methodology (RSM) to find a global optimum in a multi-dimensional simulation result "surface" (Merkuryeva 2005) or simulated annealing applied in the chemical production to find optima e.g. for reaction temperatures (Faber et al. 2005).

Several simulation-based optimization models in the context of supply chain management can be found e.g. in the area of supply chain network optimization (Preusser et al. 2005) or to simulate rescheduling of production facing demand uncertainty or unplanned shut-downs (Tang/Grubbström 2002; Neuhaus/Günther 2006). A basic approach of simulation-based optimization is presented by Preusser et al. 2005, p. 98 illustrated in fig. 24.

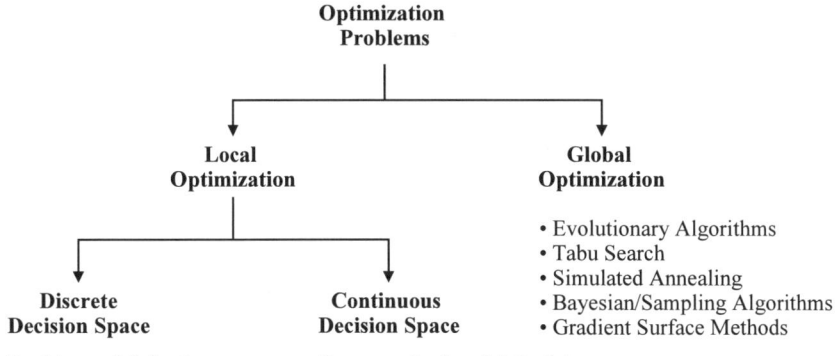

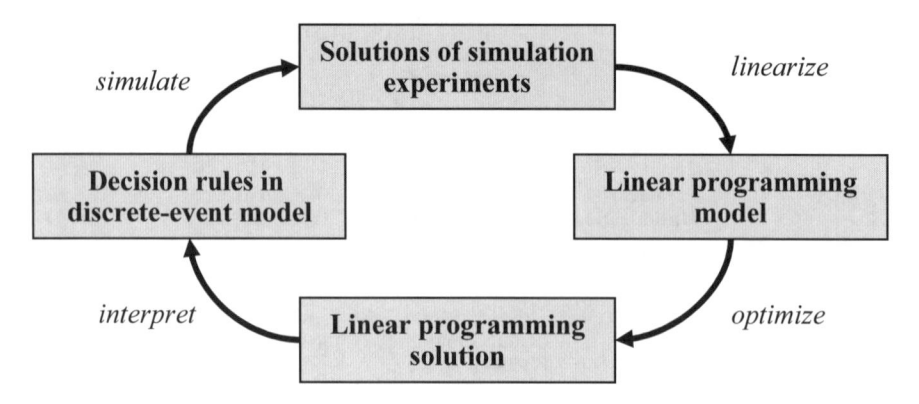

Fig. 24 Interaction between simulation and optimization

By combining simulation and optimization, benefits of both methods can be combined e.g. to simulated different input data scenarios – such as price scenarios – and analyze the resulting optimal plans in comparison. This approach is specifically relevant for planning volatile and uncertain prices of chemical commodities.

Methods used in Models

The introduced methods can be used in a value chain planning *model*. A *model* – derived from the Latin word *modellus* meaning *measure* – is a focused representation of reality focusing on problem-relevant aspects and their functional relations (Teich 2002, p. 219). The model applies reference, optimization, simulation and/or analysis and visualization methods to support decisions based on formulated requirements.

2.4 Conclusions

Integrated value chain management framework is an essence of so far separated concepts in the value chains either focusing on managing supply, demand or values:

- Value chain management is the integration of strategy, planning and operations decisions in the value chain to reach a global value optimum
- In this context, value chain planning is the integration of volume and value decisions based on the value chain strategy transforming the company into a marketplace clearing supplier offers in procurement with customer demand in sales

- Value chain management is based on models using appropriate methods like reference, simulation, optimization and/or analysis and visualization.

The value chain management framework is used as conceptual basis for developing a global value chain planning model for the specific scope of a global commodity value chain in the chemical industry.

3 Chemical Industry and Value Chain Characteristics

The chemical industry is the application field for the study and the development of a global value chain planning model. General characteristics of the chemical industry as application field are described in this chapter. Particularities of chemical commodities are described in more detail being relevant for the considered case.

The considered global commodity value chain is specified applying a value chain typology. The typology is used also to define the work scope and to derive the value chain planning requirements.

3.1 Chemical Industry Characteristics

The chemical industry is presented in an overview with chemical value chain structures, industry specifics, market structures and trends before focusing on commodities.

3.1.1 Chemical Industry Overview

The chemical industry is one of the key global industries with chemical product sales of € 1,776 billion globally in 2004 (CEFIC 2005, p. 3). Industries can be classified as mainly process, discrete or service industries between natural resources and the final end consumer need as shown in fig. 25.

The chemical industry is a sub-industry of the process industry. The process industry is characterized by production in processes that can be convergent as well as divergent. The process industry consists of firms that *"add value by mixing, separating, forming and/or chemical reactions by either batch of continuous mode"* (Wallace 1992 reviewed by Dennis/Meredith 2000, p. 683). Products in process industries can be intermediates and finished products at the same time sold or used for others products. Other sub-industries in the process industries are oil and gas, steel and metals, pulp and paper or pharmaceuticals as well as parts of consumer goods such as food production.

64   3 Chemical Industry and Value Chain Characteristics

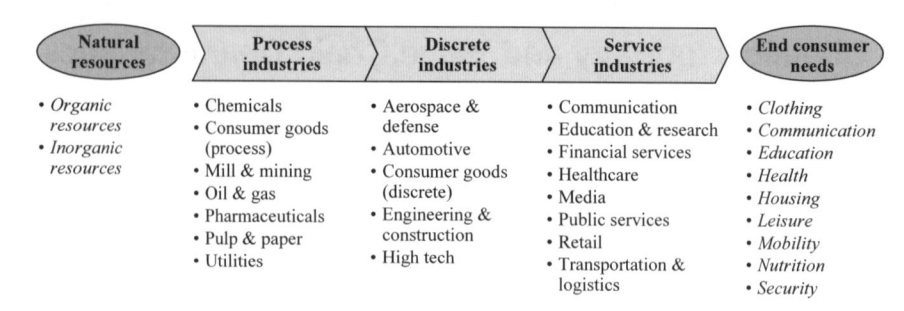

Natural resources	Process industries	Discrete industries	Service industries	End consumer needs
• *Organic resources* • *Inorganic resources*	• Chemicals • Consumer goods (process) • Mill & mining • Oil & gas • Pharmaceuticals • Pulp & paper • Utilities	• Aerospace & defense • Automotive • Consumer goods (discrete) • Engineering & construction • High tech	• Communication • Education & research • Financial services • Healthcare • Media • Public services • Retail • Transportation & logistics	• *Clothing* • *Communication* • *Education* • *Health* • *Housing* • *Leisure* • *Mobility* • *Nutrition* • *Security*

Fig. 25 The chemical industry as part of the process industry

The manufacturing pendant to *process industry* is the *discrete industry* e.g. automotive or engineering industry, where discrete products are assembled using other discrete components. Here, production is convergent, since multiple input components are assembled to one produced product resulting e.g. in built-to-order planning problems in the automotive industry (Meyr 2004a).

Thirdly, the *service sector* covering multiple services is characterized by intangible services not requiring a physical production. Industries and specific companies are often not fully classifiable into these categories if mixed business model exist.

The chemical industry as part of the process industry sector can be perceived as a raw material supplier for other process as well as discrete industries.

The term *chemistry* has roots in the Greek term *khumeia* meaning *pouring together-*, the Egypt term *khemein* meaning *preparation of black powder* and the Arabic term *al-kimia* leading to alchemy as *the art of transformation.* Chemistry developed over ca. 1.300 years driven by key discoveries and innovations, which can be structured in three periods: the ancient period (until 7th century) characterized by trial and error, the middle age (7th- 17th century) characterized by the alchemists and the modern times (after 17th) characterized by scientific chemical research (N.N. 2006g; N.N. 2006h; N.N. 2006i).

The current structure of the chemical industry can be characterized by the different products starting at with oil and gas and with further refinements on the following steps with petrochemicals, basis chemicals, polymers, specialties and active ingredients as shown in fig. 26.

3.1 Chemical Industry Characteristics 65

	Oil & Gas	Petro-chemicals	Basic Chemicals	Polymers	Specialties	Active Ingredients

Product categories

- Olefins
  - Ethylene
  - Propylene
  - Butadien
- Polyolefines
  - PE
  - PP
- Industrial gases

- Intermediates
  - Butanediol
  - THF
  - HMDA
- Inorganics
  - Ammonia

- Performance polymers
  - Polycarbonate
  - ABS/SAN
  - PMMA
- Performance chemicals
  - Pigments
  - Dispersions
  - Coatings

- Specialty chemicals
  - Additives
- Fine chemicals
  - Pharma intermediates
  - Vitamins
  - Flavors & Fragrances
- Agro-chemicals

Applications

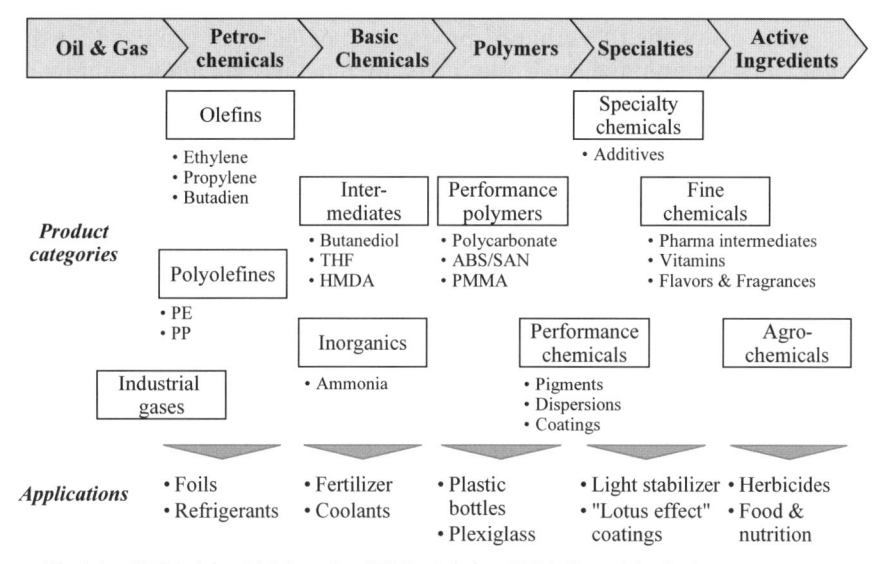

- Foils
- Refrigerants
- Fertilizer
- Coolants
- Plastic bottles
- Plexiglass
- Light stabilizer
- "Lotus effect" coatings
- Herbicides
- Food & nutrition

Abbreviations: PE: Polyethylene; PP: Polypropylene; THF: Tetrahydrofuran; HMDA: Hexamethylenediamine; ABS: Acrylonitrile Butadiene Styrene; SAN: Styrene Acrilonitrile; PMMA: Polymethyl Methacrylate

Fig. 26 Chemical products in the chemical industry value chain

These products are used in multiple applications cross-industries e.g. in packaging, cooling, coatings, as well as food and nutrition. Product life cycles are often longer compared to other industries and products, e.g. semi-conductors posing different requirements on forecasting semiconductor demand (Mallik/Harker 2004). Products developed decades ago are still important raw materials sold to the market today. The chemical industry serves many other industries as raw material supplier and often serves as a good indicator for the overall economic development. The chemical industry has some specifics to be detailed in the following:

- The chemical product tree and the "Verbund" production
- Every product is a finished product
- Commodity products vs. specialty products
- Batch, campaign and continuous production processes
- Global vs. regional vs. local markets

The Chemical Product Tree and the "Verbund" Production

The chemical value chain shown in fig. 26 results into a product tree over multiple steps: starting from the oil refinery and a steam-cracker, chemical products are processed over multiple steps with increasing variety and complexity by adding further substances or additives. The chemical product tree is often reflected in the production structure of chemical production plants also called "Verbund" production: neighbored products are arranged in factories at the same site linked by pipelines leading to highly integrated production sites as shown illustratively in fig. 27:

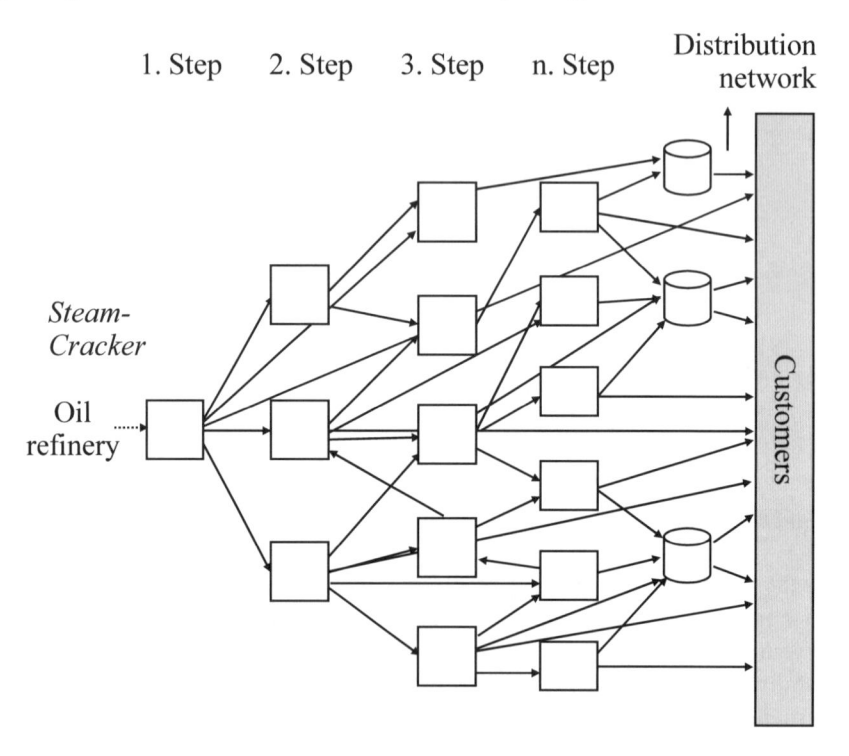

Fig. 27 Multi-stage structure of chemical industry production

Managing and planning these complex networks including production, material flows, inventories but also procurement and sales is a challenging task.

Every Product is a Finished Product

As illustrated in fig. 27, products produced in a chemical production network are by default "finished" products, meaning they can be sold to customers instead of being used as intermediate products in the next production step. This principle leads to additional complexity since production demand for a product is composed of secondary demand caused by the subsequent production step as well as market demand or sales opportunities for this product. On the other hand, this also provides the opportunity to better utilize production assets by pushing excess production quantity to the market if the price is sufficiently attractive.

Commodities vs. Specialties

A key product classification scheme in the chemical industry is the differentiation of specialty and commodity products. Kline (1976) provides a segmentation of the chemical industry into commodities, specialties and fine chemicals shown in fig. 28.

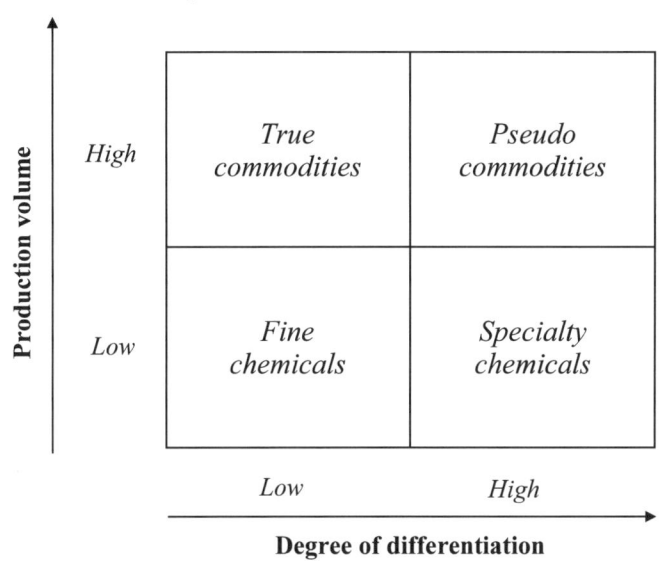

		Low	High
Production volume	High	True commodities	Pseudo commodities
	Low	Fine chemicals	Specialty chemicals
		Degree of differentiation	

Fig. 28 Chemical industry segmentation example

This classification correlates with the chemical value chain and the product tree. Products produced in early stages of the product value chain are rather commodity-type products, while products produced in the very late stage of the value chain are rather specialty-type products. Commodity and specialty classification is often not straight-forward and can depend on a set of characteristics as shown in table 6:

Table 6 Differentiating characteristics of commodities vs. specialties

Characteristics	Commodity	Specialty
Product type	Standard	Special
Product lifecycle	Mature	Early stages
Product variants	Few	Many
Main buying criterion	Price	Unique Product Properties
Volumes	High (bulk)	Small (bags)
Unit value	Low	High
Unit margins	Low	High

Commodity vs. specialty is not only related to product properties from a company-internal perspective but also to the business associated with this product. The management of commodities is less focused on product complexity as in the case of specialties, e.g. related to product variants, packaging and small volumes. It is more related to manage large volumes and values as well as prices. Consequently, the differentiation of commodities and specialties impacts the management of the value chain significantly.

Continuous, Campaign and Batch Production Processes

Chemical production is a further area of characteristics and specifics in the chemical industry. Chemical products are produced in production processes including a reaction of chemicals. These production processes can be differentiated in continuous, campaign and batch production processes as illustrated in fig. 29.

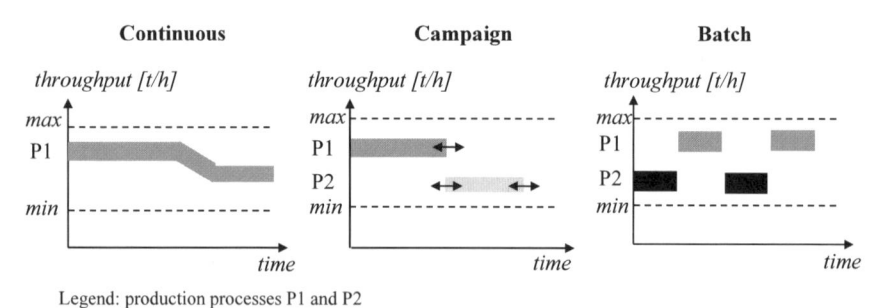

Fig. 29 Production process types

Production processes differ with respect to production time and throughput. Continuous processes have a variable production time and variable throughput during the process. Continuous processes run on single-purpose assets with one product continuously produced not requiring regular change-over decisions.

Campaign processes have also variable production time. Different to continuous production, campaign production is related to multi-purpose assets, where different processes and products can run on the same production resource and change-over decisions between campaigns need to be taken. Finally, batch processes have a defined lot size, start and end time of production as well as throughput.

Batch production is also related to multi-purpose resources. The integration of batch schedules across resources for related products is one of the most challenging production scheduling tasks. Commodity products are rather produced in continuous and campaign production mode with high volumes, while specialty products are rather produced in campaign and batch mode with smaller lot sizes and overall lower volumes.

Global vs. Regional vs. Local Markets

A third overview characteristic for the chemical industry is the geographical orientation differentiated into global, regional and local as shown in fig. 30.

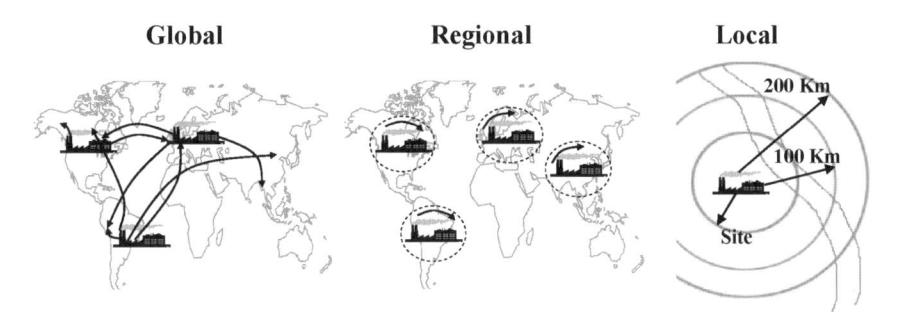

Fig. 30 Global, regional and local networks

Global networks are designed to serve a global market structured by the different continents. World-scale assets at the globally-oriented production sites are designed to serve global demand. The management of global material flows specifically based on container shipment is a key task and often organized in global business units. Secondly, regional network are designed for separated regions such as NAFTA, EMEA and Asia. Similar production structures are located in the respective region and designed to serve this region. The value chain management for these businesses is also often structured into regional business units. Thirdly, local networks are designed around a specific site in an area of hundreds of kilometers meaning with distances. Local networks focus on integrated site management including partners and material flows. The geographical network orientation has a significant influence on value chain management.

The chemical market with respective players, trends and products are described in the following as basis for a better understanding of the specific application field.

3.1.2 Chemical Market and Development

Chemical market characteristics and development is important to understand requirements and drivers of this industry to be addressed by research and practitioners. The market overview is structured in different topics:

- *Chemical market overview:* provide understanding for market structure and development by products, applications, regions and market players
- Chemical industry trends: provide overview on current trends and challenges in the industry

Chemical Market Overview

The chemical industry is one of the largest global industries with an annual sales value of € 1,776 billion in 2005. The chemical industry in Europe counts for 2.5% within 24.5% overall industry contribution to the total GDP in the EU 15. Traditionally important markets for the chemical industry are Europe and the United States counting for 60% of global sales value in 2004 as shown in fig. 31 (CEFIC 2005).

Global Chemical Sales by Regions - 2004, in Bil. € -

Total Chemical Sales € 1,776 Bil. = 100%

Other 11%
Asia 29%
Europe 37%
US 23%

EU-15[1]: 559
EU-10[2]: 27
Rest of Europe[3]: 70
United States: 415
Japan: 186
China: 137
Rest of Asia: 183
Latin Amer.: 100
Other[4]: 98

1) First 15 countries of European Union
2) New 10 countries joined European Union
3) Other European countries e.g. Switzerland, Norway and other in Central & Eastern Europe
4) incl. Canada, Mexico, Africa & Oceania
Source: CEFIC (2005)

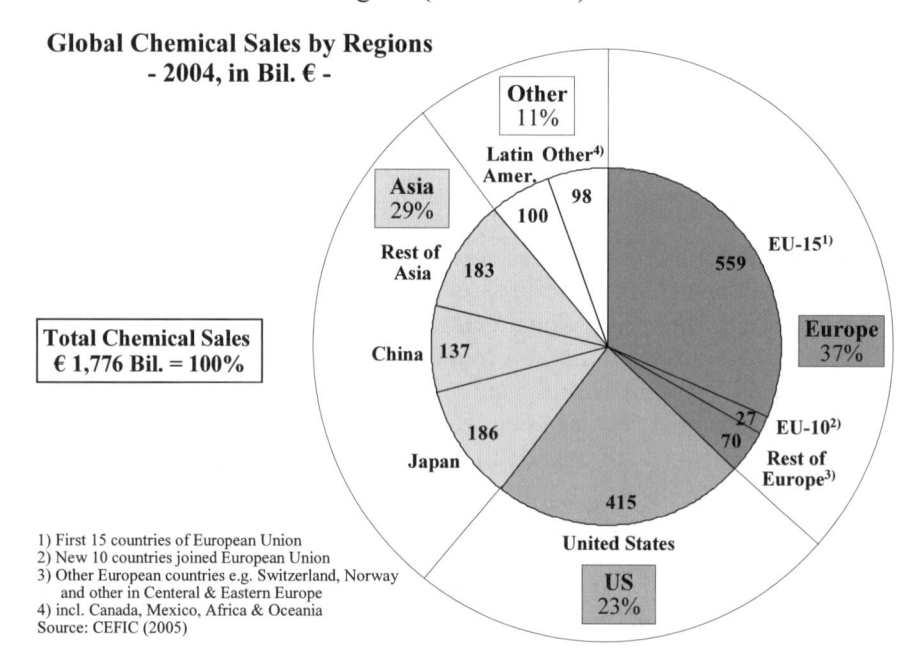

Fig. 31 Global chemical market by regions

However, Europe and the US face lower growth rates close to GDP growth while Asia is growing dynamically and already count for 29% of global chemical sales. Chemical companies operating in these markets face the situation that large part of the production capacities are located in the traditional markets of North America and Europe, while the demand and growth opportunities are shifting to Asia.

This in-balance between demand and supply is reflected in the increase of global trade driven by *globalization*. Expansion of world trade for

3.1 Chemical Industry Characteristics 71

chemicals is driven by opening of markets with less protectionism and lowering of trade barriers such as import tariffs or restrictions on the regulatory side but also by significant decline of transportation costs thanks to standardized container shipment. Considering the global balance of sales, imports and exports in 2004, Europe reached the highest level of trade import and export volumes compared to its sales within the region and compared to trade in other regions (COMTRADE 2005, p. 23) as shown in fig. 32.

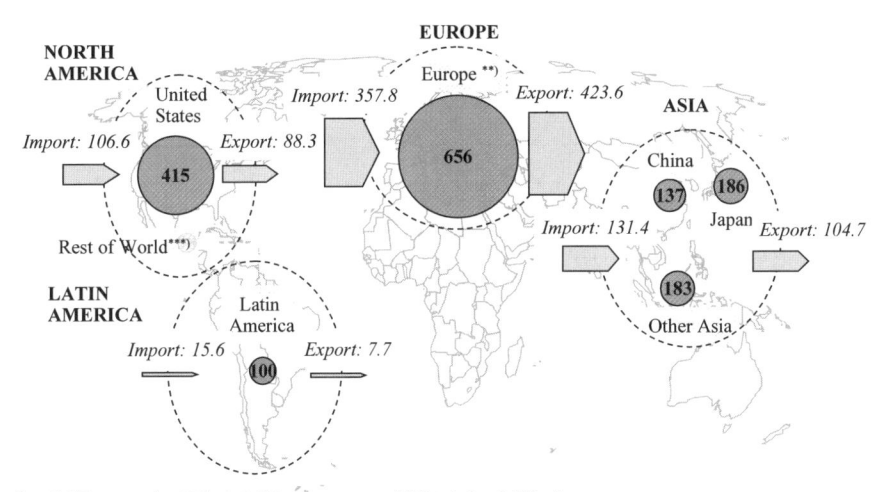

Size of bubble corresponds to 2004 sales in billion Euro; arrows equal 2004 trade flows in billion Euro
**) Including EU-25, Switzerland, Norway, other Central and Eastern European countries
***) Including Canada, Mexico, Oceania & Africa
Source: ACC, CEFIC Analysis

Fig. 32 Global sales and value flows in the chemical industry

Globalization in the chemical industry is characterized by regional growth differences. High growth rates exist in emerging markets in Asia and Eastern Europe and lower growth rates in traditional mature markets such as the EU and NAFTA, where the majority of the chemical industry capacities are located. These differences will drive further trade between traditional producing regions and emerging demanding regions. This constellation is a key driver for global trade between these regions and would foster new investments and increase in capacities in the growing markets such as Asia with the core countries China, Japan, as well as Korea.

Along with globalization, the industry has generated large corporations of significant size acting around the global. The global top 50 chemical producers in 2004 had sales of 587 billion dollars with a profit margin of 8.1% and research and development spending of 2.1% both against sales (Short 2005). Still, the chemical industry is a very fragmented industry not much consolidated: the first three companies count for only estimated 5%

global market share, the Top-50 companies count for 27% market share as shown in fig. 33.

Rank	Company	Region	Revenue Mil. $, 2004	Estimated Market Share in %
1	Dow Chemical	US	40.161	
2	BASF	EU	38.189	5%
3	DuPont	US	30.130	
4	Royal Dutch/Shell	EU	29.497	
5	ExxonMobile	US	27.781	12%
6	Total	EU	24.928	
7	BP	US	21.209	21%
8	Bayer	EU	18.088	
9	China Petroleum & Chemical	CN	16.730	27%
10	Mitsubishi Chemical	JP	16.274	
..				
30	BOC	US	7.095	
..				
50	Celanese	US	5.069	

Source: Short (2005), CEFIC (2005)

Fig. 33 Company ranking in the chemical industry

Deans et al. (2002) confirm that the chemical industry is still in the second of four phases in industry consolidation phases towards an industry endgame with few very large corporations. Further global consolidation driven by internal organic growth as well as by external growths using mergers and acquisitions is expected.

Chemical Industry Trends

With the beginning of the 21st century, the chemical industry changes driven by several trends (see for example Staudigl 2004):

- *Globalization:* as shown increase of world trade driven by emerging markets especially in Asia is a main trend not only in the chemical industry (Laudicina 2004). Besides managing global material flows, companies face new markets with suppliers, customers, but also new competitors from emerging markets.
- *Consolidation:* as shown further consolidation of the industry leads will drive the occurrence of increasingly large and complex corporations that needs to be managed (Deans et al. 2002, pp. 13-17)

- *Commoditization and margin pressure:* product portfolios former being specialties are confronted with commoditization, standardization leading to margin pressure. 121 process industry managers reported in 2002 that cost reductions e.g. by restructuring, outsourcing and optimization of production networks have highest priority in 2003 (A.T. Kearney 2003).
- *Innovation:* recently several innovation areas emerged such as biotechnology, nanotechnology, energy technologies as gene technology leaving the research laboratories; new products are expected to be using these basis technologies for new applications as well as substituting former products.
- *Legislation:* specifically EU legislation targets to ensure health of consumers controlling toxic impact of chemicals; corporations are confronted with precise documentation and test procedures requiring systems support to handle complexity. Globally, *trade policies* of the GATT and WTO has well as compatibility of standards and compliances are further conditions to be considered (Delfmann/Albers 2000, pp. 18)
- *Sustainability:* overall objective for human beings formulated by the United Nations in the 1990s is to ensure sustainable development for future generations; chemical companies have already started to translate this objective into their industry practice with respects to products developed and sold, energy and natural resource efficiency in their processes, climate protection, corporate social responsibility for the workforce as well as stakeholders in production and consuming areas; sustainability as an objective also already inspired operations research and supply chain literature (see for example Zhou et al. 2000; Al-Sharrah et al. 2002)

Budde et al. (2002) conclude that the chemical industry companies have to address globalization, increasing raw material prices and increased competition by focusing on core competencies, regional and global consolidation but also on better pricing e.g. using an industry pricing strategy (Budde et al. 2002).

In addition to overall industry trends, the chemical industry has some specific value chain and supply chain requirements (Grunow/Günther 2001, Poesche 2001, A.D. Little 2003, Nienhaus et al. 2003, Shah 2005). The economic importance of supply chain and value chain management is significant since supply chain costs can represent as 60%-80% of a typical chemical manufacturer's costs (Gibson 1998 reviewed by Garcia-Flores/Wang 2002). Moreover, value chain management addresses the overall improvement of the value-add between turnover and procurement costs. Therefore, some chemical industry-specific requirements for supply chain management are

- decrease supply chain costs by better using "economies of scale" specifically in production by running longer campaigns and avoiding change-overs (A.D. Little 2003),
- decrease inventories and capital employed; for the related pharmaceutical industry inventory value in global operating companies can reach up to 20-40% of turnover (Boeken/Kotlik 2001)

Hence, value chain management and specifically global value chain planning of commodities plays an important role for chemical companies due to the direct relation to globalization, consolidation as well as commoditization. Specifics of chemical commodities are presented in the following.

3.1.3 Specifics of Chemical Commodities

Commodity as a term is derived from the French term *commodité* meaning *convenience* in terms of quality and service based on the former Latin word *commoditas* meaning the *appropriate measure of something* (N.N. 2006j).

Commodities are mass products produced and sold in high volumes with standardized quality and few variants. Primary commodities such as natural resources can be defined as *"materials in their natural state"* (Baker 1992) produced in large volumes and available from many sources (Champion/Fearne 2000).

The price is typically the key buying criterion for customers since service and product properties are of standardized quality and a less differentiating buying factor for customers.

Commodities are originally subject to economic research and financial market analysis (Meadows 1970; Labys 1973; Labys 1975; Hallwood 1979; Guvenen 1988). Natural resource commodities such as metals, agricultural products or oil and gas are subjects to research with the focus on effective and efficient market mechanisms from a macro-economic and financial market perspective. These commodities are mainly traded on many-to-many exchanges with double auction pricing mechanisms clearing offer and demand bids to determine market prices (Bourbeau et al. 2005; Xia et al. 2005). Market price transparency allows to analyze and trying to predict future prices using statistical models, e.g. as demonstrated for copper by Nielsen/Schwartz (2004). Compared to natural resource commodities, industry commodities markets are less perfect, little many-to-many exchange exists, mainly single-sided auctions or bilateral negotiations are applied as market pricing mechanisms.

Chemical commodity products are typically produced and sold in high volumes at low unit value to mass markets in comparison to specialties sold in lower volumes at higher unit value to specialized markets. Typical product categories with commodity character in the chemical industry are petrochemicals, basis chemicals and parts of polymers, while agriculture or nutrition products are rather specialties. However, also specialty products exist within commodity product categories, since value-adding substances can be attached to a commodity product to modify the material's properties required by applications like color, inflammability, flexibility or resistance against hot or cold temperatures to name a few. Finished commodity products sold to the market mainly require commodity products as key raw materials that are produced on earlier stages of the chemical product tree. Naturally, every commodity product used to be a specialty when it was launched initially. Hence, commodity products and the respective markets are often more mature and exist for quite some time compared to specialty products. In case of overcapacities, commodity products can become subject to aggressive price competition and suppliers try to improve their cost position e.g. by optimizing the production network (Ferdinand/Haeger 2001).

The production network for commodity products are often multi-level involving multiple steps, where on each step products flow into the subsequent steps or they are sold to the market. Petrochemicals, e.g. as shown in fig. 34 with an example of Kuwait's petrochemical industry, are a good example (Al-Sharrah et al. 2001, pp. 2110). The relation between oil and gas-near products on the left side and further processed products such as plastics like polystyrene get transparent. A main task is to plan these networks and also look for simplification in material flows (Al-Sharrah et al. 2003). These chemicals are produced in large volumes in continuous or campaign production modes with certain flexibility in throughput and utilization between a minimum and maximum output level. Polystyrene is an example for a chemical material used for end user application e.g. in refrigerators, packaging or consumer electronics (Franke 2005).

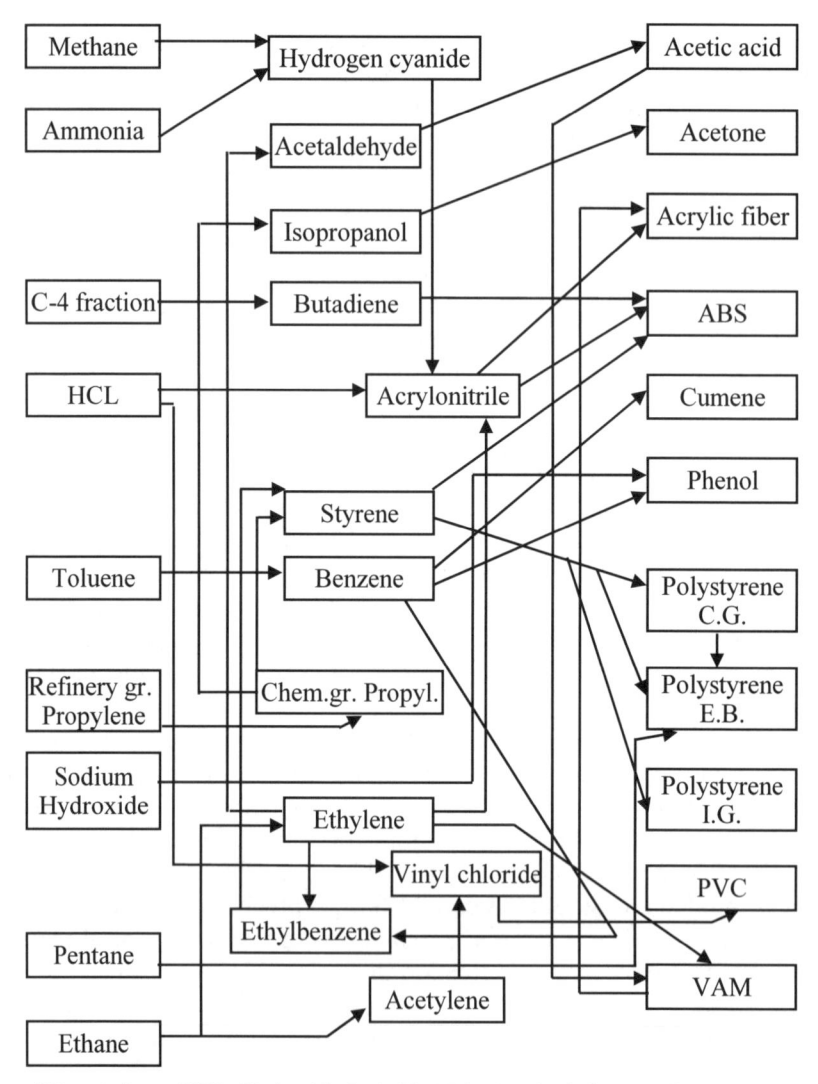

Abbreviations: HCL: Hydrochloric Acid; ABS: Acrylonitrile Butadiene Styrene; PVC: Polyvinyl Chloride; VAM: Vinyl Acetate Monomer

Fig. 34 Petrochemical industry example from Kuwait

Production processes for chemical commodities exist often already for decades and are continuously enhanced as shown in the following example from the 1970s. Commodity production processes this time already have been rather complex composed by multiple reactions and interim steps as shown in the following example of Caprolactam production, an intermediate product for Polyamide (Sittig 1972, p. 139) in fig. 35.

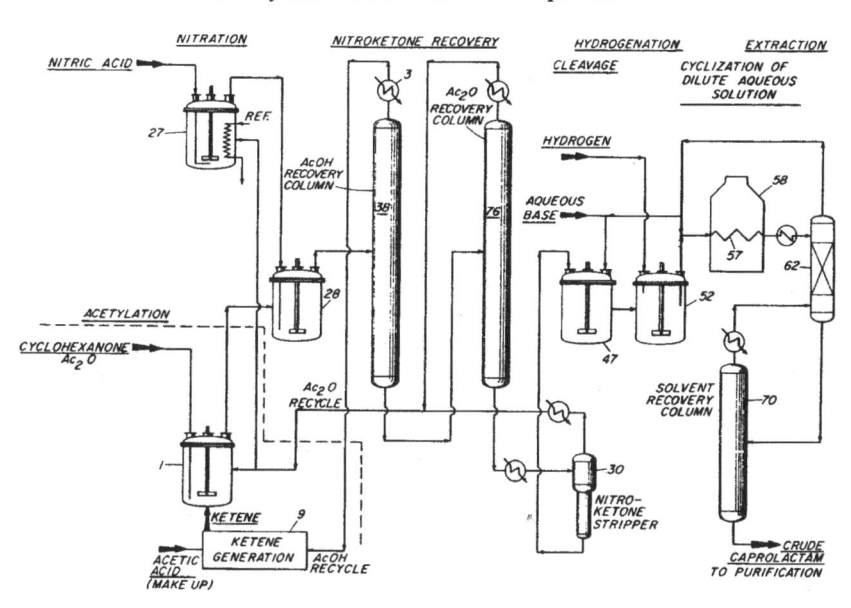

Continuous Production Process for Caprolactam Production via Nitrocyclohexanone and Aminocaproic Acid

Patent: Sheehan, D.; Vellturo, A.F.; Gay, W.A.; Hegarty, W.P.; Threlkeld, D.D.; US Patent 3,562,254, February 9, 1971

Fig. 35 Example of a chemical commodity production process

Commodity production planning requires to aggregate the process-internal units such as reactors, dryers or tanks into a an aggregate asset planned as a whole with dedicated interfaces of raw material input and production output as shown in the left and right part of the process example.

Typical management problems given volatile raw material and sales prices are driven by bottleneck steps in the network: e.g. Styrene is an example in the network shown in fig. 34 for a product used in multiple subsequent products. In this case, value chain planning across multiple steps from sales to raw material is required to decide the optimal use of Styrene on the subsequent steps not only considering this relation but the entire value chain network including raw material volumes and prices required to produce Styrene.

Prices for chemical commodities are volatile and can change regularly as shown in a further example for two polymers in fig. 36.

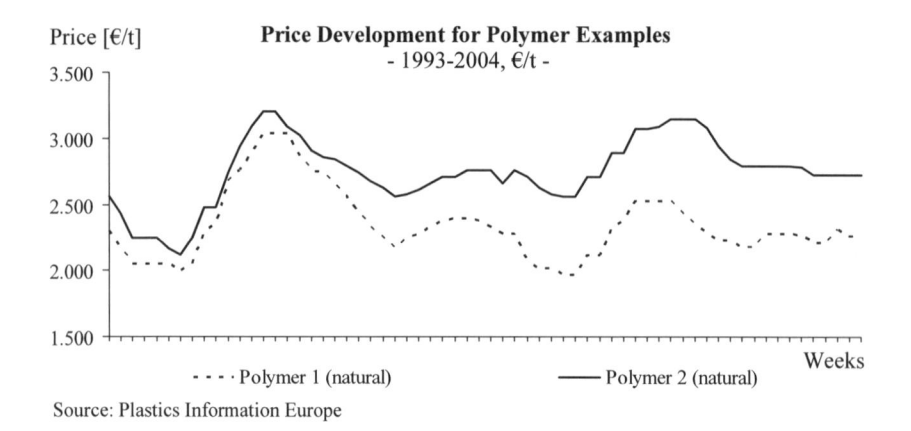

Price Development for Polymer Examples
- 1993-2004, €/t -

- - - - Polymer 1 (natural) ——— Polymer 2 (natural)

Source: Plastics Information Europe

Fig. 36 Example of chemical commodity price development

Main price driver for chemical commodities is the development of oil prices influenced by many parameters as shown in the fig. 37 (s. Al-Sharrah et al. 2003, p. 4680). Not only direct demand and supply for crude-oil but also the development of substitutes such as natural gas or other energy forms such as nuclear power can have an influence on oil prices according to Al-Sharrah et al. as shown in fig. 37.

Slowing World Economic Growth
Rising World (excluding OPEC) Oil Production
Natural Gas Substitution for Oil
Oil Conservation
OPEC Capacity Additions
OPEC Downstream Discounting to Gain Market Share

↓

Oil prices

↑

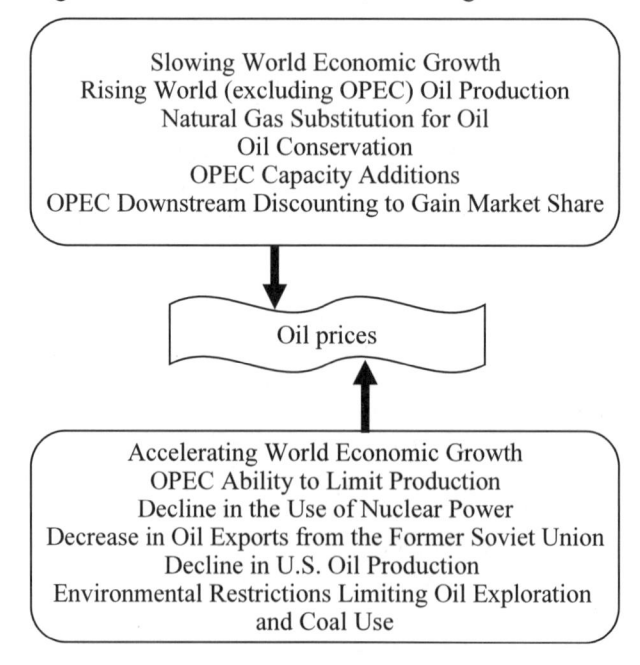

Accelerating World Economic Growth
OPEC Ability to Limit Production
Decline in the Use of Nuclear Power
Decrease in Oil Exports from the Former Soviet Union
Decline in U.S. Oil Production
Environmental Restrictions Limiting Oil Exploration and Coal Use

Fig. 37 Selected variables determining oil prices in the short range

Since many influences exist, oil prices are volatile in a short range that price management of commodity chemicals dependent on crude oil require regular attention. Several authors investigate the relationship between crude oil prices and the prices of subsequent products such as Kerosene and Naphtha (Asche et al. 2003) as well as discuss optimal markup pricing strategies for petroleum refining (Considine 2001).

Chemical commodity prices are also analyzed regularly and published e.g. in journals and papers. For most of chemical products, no many-to-many exchanges as for natural commodities exist. Prices are rather negotiated bilaterally between supplier and customer based on contracts or spot business. Spot and contract pricing is mainly done bilaterally with some specific instruments established such as the "European Contract Price" (ECP) in Europe where market participants can agree on a quarterly contract that is oriented in general at the price of the two leading suppliers in the respective industry (Rainer/Jammernegg, 2000, pp. 118). The right balance between spot and contract has impact on the profit variability as shown by Seifert et al. (2002).

Prices are analyzed in regular market surveys where producers, consumers and merchants across a region are contacted to gather current price level. Results are published in magazines as shown in the following example from the ECN magazine (Todd 2004) or in web-based analysis services. Here, the typical differentiation in spot and contract gets transparent as shown in fig. 38.

■ **BULK CHEMICAL PRICES**

	European spot €/tonne	$/tonne	Change on last week	European contract €/tonne	$/tonne	US contract $/tonne
Naphtha	na	296-303 (cif)	▼ 10.5	na	na	na
Ethylene	na	863-888 (cif)	▲ 110.5	580 (Q1)	742	667 (Dec)
Propylene[1]	580-600 (cif)	na	▲ 15	475 (Q1)	608	557 (Jan)
Butadiene	na	500-520 (fob) (nom)	▼ 22.5	520 (Q1)	640	640 (Jan)
Benzene	na	570-576 (fob)	▼ 7	416 (Q1)/465 (Feb)	516/580	592 (Feb)
Toluene*	na	500-515(fob) (nom)	▼ 15	333 (Q4)	392	na
Xylenes	na	580-600 (fob)	▲ 25	na	na	473-479 (Jan)
Paraxylene	na	670-685 (fob)	▼ 27.5	575 (Feb)	722	634 (Jan)
Orthoxylene	na	670-680 (cif) (nom)	◆ nc	445 (Q1)	558	562 (Jan)
Styrene[2]	na	790-800 (fob) (nom)	▼ 30	716.5-741.5 (Q1)	915-947	1055-1100(Jan)
Methanol	180-185 (fob)	na	▲ 9	190 (Q1)	235	255 (Jan)
MTBE	na	341-349 (fob)	▼ 5	na	na	na
Ammonia	na	280-290(CFR) (nom)	▼ 5	na	na	320 (CFR) (1H Feb)

NOTES *TDI grade; [1]Indicates polymer grade; [2]Lower figure for barge price, higher figure for free delivery inland; [3]Initial contract settlement

Fig. 38 Bulk chemical price examples

Commodity markets are also characterized by more intense competition in supply and demand with multiple offering suppliers and multiple demanding customers. This causes the fact that a customer can change to a different supplier and a supplier can supply alternative customers more easily compared to specialty markets. Specialty markets are also often characterized by close cooperation between customer and supplier e.g. using just-in-time delivery in the automotive industry requiring a close integration and collaboration.

Concluding, due to price and volume volatility, margins and profitability are also volatile as already shown in fig. 1. Hence, managing chemical commodity value chains limited to volume management is not enough to ensure profitability (also Franke 2005). This also holds true increasingly for subsequent industries buying chemical commodities e.g. in the molding industry: here volatile raw material prices for polymers such as PE and PP impacts directly profitability of the molders (Hofmann 2004).

Chemical Commodity Characteristics Relevant for Value Chain Management

Initial characteristics relevant for chemical commodity value chain management are:

- Raw material prices are volatile e.g. on a daily, weekly or monthly basis if not contractually fixed
- Raw material volumes are volatile depending on available supply and on the companies' consumption rates in production, which can be stable but also dynamic, e.g. if higher production utilization requires more raw material
- Production and distribution quantities can vary from a minimum utilization to full capacity utilization
- Sales prices can change frequently e.g. on a daily, weekly or monthly basis if not contractually fixed
- Sales volumes vary driven by changing demand, but the company also has a certain flexibility to cut or push sales quantities compared to customer demand, for example if customer demand exceeds available company supply.

This overview is further detailed and structured in the following subchapter, where the characteristics of a global commodity value chain as well as the model scope is defined.

3.2 Global Commodity Value Chain in the Chemical Industry

A global commodity value chain can be characterized by a multiple set of attributes in a typology to formalize the planning problem. Purpose of this subchapter

- is to provide a typology to formally describe a value chain network
- to apply the typology to specify the scope of the work

The defined scope determines the applicability of developed planning requirements and the planning model limited to the selected attributes. For example, the value chain for commodity production is focused on campaign and continuous production modes; batch production is out of the scope that planning requirements and consequently, planning model are not developed for batch production problems.

3.2.1 Global Value Chain Network Overview

The global value chain network for commodities in the chemical industry is composed by locations, resources and transportation lanes as illustrated in fig. 39

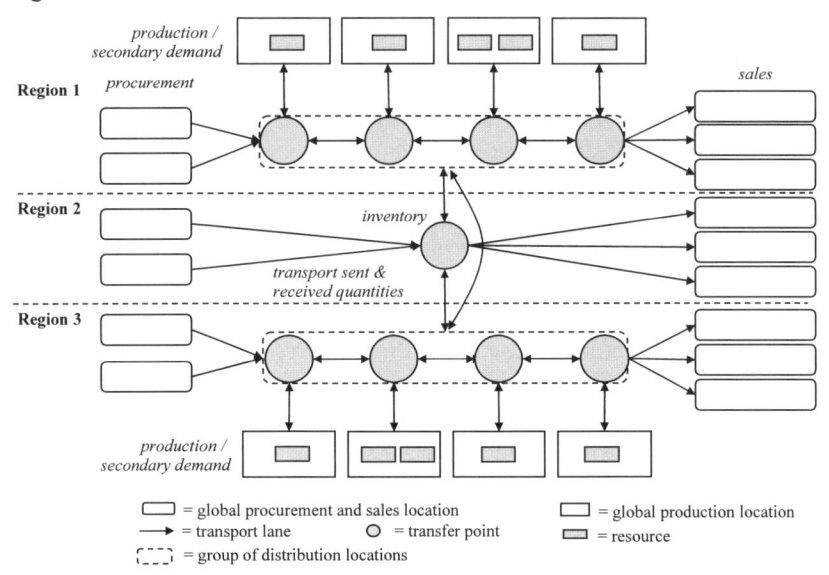

Fig. 39 Global value chain network structures

The value chain network consists of procurement, production, distribution and sales locations connected by transportation lanes. These locations belong to the global region they are located in. Transports between global regions can take more than one month. The structuring of value chain networks into locations and lanes can be found in APS as well as case-specific literature (Siprelle et al. 2003; Dickersbach 2004).

Sales locations cluster one or multiple customers or marketplaces based on geographical or market segmentation criteria.

Distribution locations are single or groups of storage facilities, warehouses, distribution centers or logical inventory management points e.g. for modal split between transportation means (container terminals, cross-docking-stations, rail-truck-terminals, etc.). *Transfer point (TP)* as a characteristic name for global distribution locations is chosen in order to include also distribution locations with modal split of different transportation modes. The transfer points are also a decoupling point between sales and production holding inventories (Lee, 2001, p. 195) according to the defined distribution strategy and business rules e.g. make-to-stock (MTS), make-to-order (MTO), etc.

A *production location* comprises one or multiple production plants where production resources are located. Production resources are single units or groups of production units aggregated to production lines or assets. Having the structure of chemical commodity value chain network as a network of chemical production processes in mind presented in fig. 34 (Al-Sharrah et al. 2001), production locations include respective resources and transportation lanes between production locations to model relations in chemical "Verbund" structures.

Procurement locations, finally, comprise one or multiple suppliers or marketplaces, products are procured from.

Transportation lanes represent the global highways to manage material flows between all locations in the network.

The specific value chain network is characterized in the following based on a value chain typology. Several authors developed typologies and characteristics to classify industrial value chains with focus on supply chain and production (Loos 1997; Delfmann/Albers 2000; Zeier 2002; Schaub/Zeier 2003, Meyr/Stadtler 2004).

Existing typologies are extended towards a value chain typology also considering aspects of sales and procurement value characteristics. The typology classifies the value chain by overall network as illustrated in fig. 40:

3.2 Global Commodity Value Chain in the Chemical Industry

Network Characteristics		
• Geographical topography • Legal position	• Geographical configuration • Spatial dispersion	• Value creation focus • Value creation steps

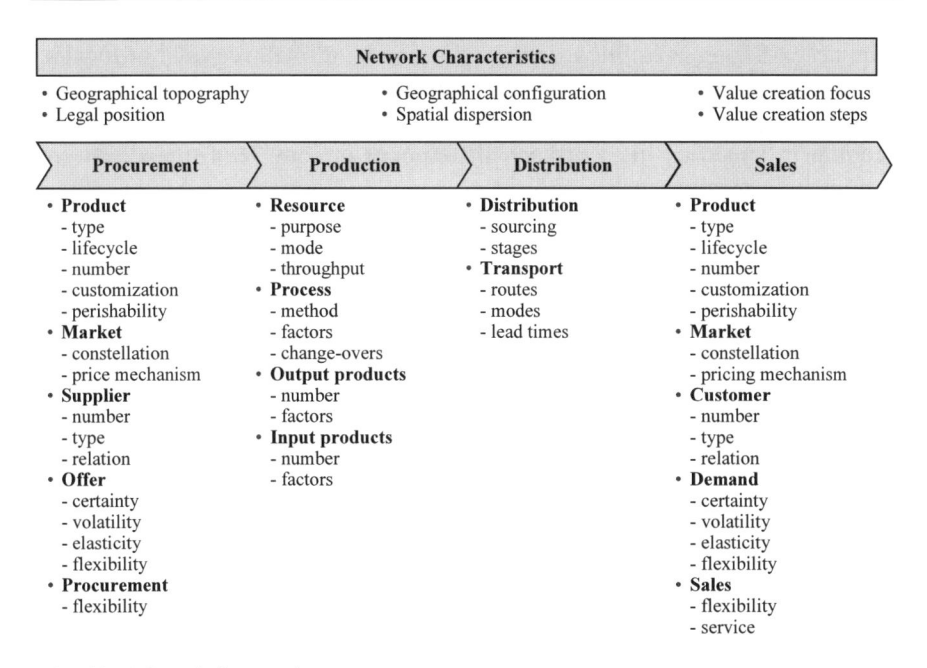

Procurement	Production	Distribution	Sales
• **Product** - type - lifecycle - number - customization - perishability • **Market** - constellation - price mechanism • **Supplier** - number - type - relation • **Offer** - certainty - volatility - elasticity - flexibility • **Procurement** - flexibility	• **Resource** - purpose - mode - throughput • **Process** - method - factors - change-overs • **Output products** - number - factors • **Input products** - number - factors	• **Distribution** - sourcing - stages • **Transport** - routes - modes - lead times	• **Product** - type - lifecycle - number - customization - perishability • **Market** - constellation - pricing mechanism • **Customer** - number - type - relation • **Demand** - certainty - volatility - elasticity - flexibility • **Sales** - flexibility - service

Fig. 40 Value chain typology

The characteristics are introduced now in detail and used to define the problem scope.

3.2.2 Network Characteristics

The value chain network can be characterized by the criteria listed in table 7. Attributes within work's scope are underlined and explained in table 7.

Table 7 Network characteristics

Characteristics	Attributes
Geographical topography	global, regional, local
Legal position	intercompany, intracompany
Geographical configuration	multinational, international, classic global, complex global
Spatial dispersion	concentrated, host-market, specialized, vertical integration
Value creation focus	production, distribution
Value creation steps	single-step, multi-stage

The network's *geographical topography* can be global, regional or local as already illustrated in fig. 30. A global network with global distribution locations in procurement, production, distribution and sales is considered leading to specifics like currency differences or long lead times between continents to name a few.

The *legal position* in the network distinguishes between intercompany and intracompany networks. Intracompany networks combine value chain networks of multiple companies and focus on cross-company optimization. Delfmann/Albers propose *supply chain perspective* as alternative time (Delfmann/Albers 2000, p. 35) differentiating between *focal company* and *bird's eye* as shown in fig. 41:

"Focal company"   **"Bird's eye"**

intercompany perspective   *intracompany perspective*

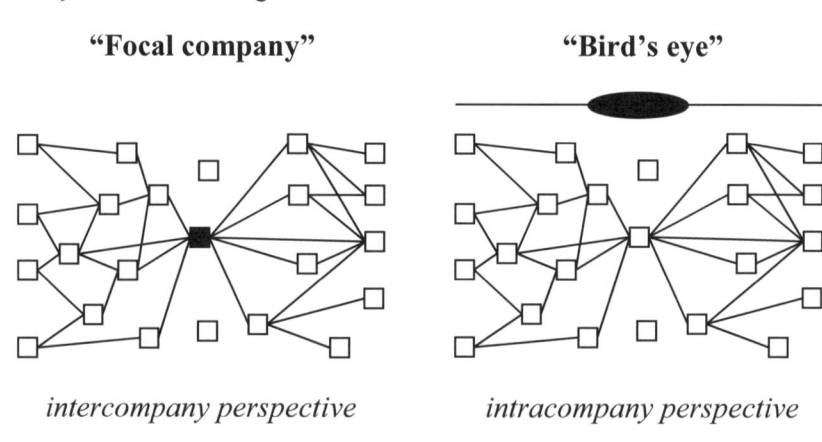

Fig. 41 Intercompany vs. intracompany perspective

Here, the scope is on an *intercompany* value chain network for one *focal company* that can make central planning decisions for its own facilities and tries to optimize the internal global value chain network with clear interfaces to multiple customers and multiple suppliers.

Delfmann and Albers (2000) discuss further specifics of global supply chain management and network characteristics. They review characteristics such as *geographical configuration* and production *spatial dispersion* in global supply chains developed by Dicken (1998).

The *geographical configuration* classifies global networks into four categories (Delfmann/Albers 2000, pp. 19-20)

- *multinational:* a decentralized federation with many key assets and decentralized decisions
- *international:* a coordinated federation with many decisions and responsibilities decentralized but controlled by the central headquarter
- *classic global*: centralized hub with centralized assets and decisions

- *complex global*: distributed network of specialized resources and capabilities with a complex coordination and cooperation environment and decision making

The considered scope is focused on the classic global with mainly centralized assets and decisions, since also considered production resources are treated as virtually global sources.

Besides, the production *spatial dispersion* distinguishes four cases illustrated in fig. 42 (Dicken 1998 reviewed by Delfmann/Albers 2000, pp. 44-45).

(a) Globally concentrated production

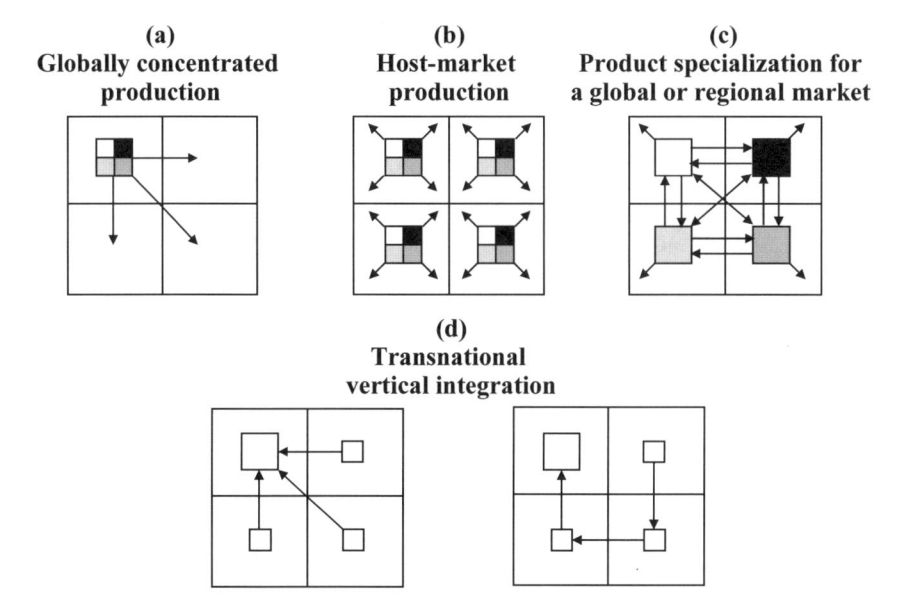

(b) Host-market production

(c) Product specialization for a global or regional market

(d) Transnational vertical integration

Fig. 42 Production unit spatial dispersion

- Production at single location; all products are produced and exported to world market
- Each production unit produces for its home regions all demanded products, no export to other regions
- Each production unit in each region specialized only on one product to serve the world market and to reach economies of scale
- Each production unit performs a separate operation in production and ships its output to a final assembly plant in another region or according to a chain like sequence.

In the considered case, each production is managed as a global source, Therefore, production is *globally concentrated* and there is lack of relationship between the production site and the region where it is located.

The network's *value creation* focus can lay on production and/or distribution. Retailers and traders have pure distribution focus. Manufacturing companies create value in production and distribution, which is the scope in this case.

Finally, the value chain network can have a single *value-creation step* or multiple *value-creation steps* in production and distribution where raw materials are processed through several production and distribution steps before being sold to the market. In the work, a multi-stage value chain network is considered.

3.2.3 Sales Characteristics

First parts of the sales characteristics are listed in table 8, attributes in the scope are underlined.

Table 8 Sales characteristics – part I

Characteristics	Attributes
Product	
- type	commodity, specialty
- life cycle	short, middle, long
- number	low, medium, high
- customization	standard, variants, customer-specific
- perishability	fast perishable, medium perishable, not perishable
Market	
- constellation	monopoly, oligopoly, polypoly
- price mechanism	exchange, auction, negotiation

The *product* type can be commodity or specialty. Commodity products are considered with a defined standard quality, where price is the key buying criterion. The *product life cycle* for chemical commodities can be relatively long meaning that the products are in the market partly for decades. Examples for short life cycle commodities on the other hand are semiconductors that are also mainly sold over price, but are shortly out-dated due to technology advances. The *number of products* is medium and does not reach the complexity of specialty product portfolios, where often more than 1,000 products need to be handled by a company. The *product customization* is standardized with some variants with respect to product properties but not related to a specific customer. *Product perishability* is not a constraint for most of chemical commodities different to specialties such as food additives or fresh food production requiring incorporating shelf live in planning and systems (Günther et al. 2005).

The *sales market constellation* for these commodities is relatively mature leading to an oligopoly constellation with few customers and few suppliers. *Price mechanisms* are bilateral negotiations between customers and suppliers; no formal exchanges or single-sided auctions are considered from the selling company perspective. The second part of the sales characteristics is shown in table 9.

Table 9 Sales characteristics – part II

Characteristics	Attributes
Customer	
- number	single, few, many
- type	internal, external
- relation	contract, spot
Demand	
- certainty	forecasted, stochastic, unknown
- volatility	stable quantity, volatile quantity, stable price, volatile price
- elasticity	inelastic (0), relatively inelastic (<1), unitary elastic (=1), relatively elastic (>1)
Sales	
- flexibility	flexible quantity, fixed quantity, flexible price, fixed price
- service	standard, differentiating

The *customer number* is few mainly smaller than 500 customers compared to mass business with often more than 1 million customers or consumers. *Customer types* are external and company-internal customers buying on basis of transfer price agreements that are delivered with priority. Therefore, the *customer relation* is spot and contract-based with sales flexibility for a spot relation and fixed sales for contract relations. Customers can also have mixed spot and contract agreements depending on the product.

With respect to *demand certainty*, demand is forecasted with bid character and is not stochastic following for example a normal distribution pattern, since demand is influenced by the price development. With respect to *demand volatility*, demand prices and quantities are not stable but monthly volatile. The total *demand elasticity* is smaller or equal to 1 with respect to average prices. That means that average prices for total demand can change, if more or less sales quantity is sold in the market.

Consequently, *sales flexibility* exists with respect to total sales quantities and average prices for spot sales, while contract sales quantities and prices are fixed. *Sales-related services* such as technical services – e.g. application or product introduction support – or commercial services – e.g. sales force support or customer service support – or logistics services – e.g. delivery services – or product-related services – e.g. brochures or product information – can be standard and/or differentiating. Standards means that service level meet the market standards and customer expectations that sales-related services have no additional influence on the customer decision and/or prices. Differentiating means that sales-related services provided with the product are influencing the buying decision and/or prices e.g. services are charged separately. In this work, sales-related services are considered as standard having no influence on sales volumes or prices.

3.2.4 Distribution Characteristics

Distribution characteristics are related to inventory and transportation and are listed and underlined in table 10.

Table 10 Distribution characteristics

Characteristics	Attributes
Inventory	
- sourcing	single-sourcing, multi-sourcing
- stages	single-stage, multi-stage
Transportation	
- routes	standard routes, variable routes
- modes	single, multiple dedicated, multiple alternatively
- lead times	single-period, multi-period

Inventory sources in the global value chain network are multiple and it can be supplied from multiple distribution locations. Also, single-sourcing constellation exists. With respect to *inventory stages*, the global network includes multi-stage distribution locations resulting in multi-echelon inventory planning problems for example in the origin region and again in the destination region. The special case of single-stage inventory holding does also apply.

Transportation routes are standard routes predefined in the value chain strategy. *Transportation modes* are related to the means of transportation such as truck, rail, ship or air freight. Transportation mode can be single dedicated, meaning only one transport mode such as standard truck is used for the entire value chain network. Alternatively, multiple transportation modes are used e.g. standard truck, dangerous good truck, rail, ship or air freight either dedicated or alternatively by transportation lane and/or product. Dedicated means that each transportation lane has a dedicated transportation mode. Alternatively, means that multiple transportation modes are used for the same transportation lane. In a global network, multiple transportation modes are used e.g. ships for transcontinental shipments and truck and/or rail for ground transportation. In this work, the mode is clearly dedicated by transportation lane. *Transportation lead times* are multi-period for transcontinental shipments and single-period for local or regional transportation.

3.2.5 Production Characteristics

Production characteristics are related to resources, processes and products as shown in table 11 (see also Schaub/Zeier 2003).

Table 11 Production characteristics

Characteristics	Attributes
Resource	
- purpose	single-purpose, multi-purpose
- mode	continuous, campaign, batch
- throughput	variable, static
Process	
- method	synthetic, analytic, regrouping, process
- factors	labor, assets, material, energy
- change-overs	flying, process, stop
Output products	
- number	single, few, many
- factors	static, variable
Input products	
- number	single, few, many
- factors	static, variable

Production resource purposes and *modes* are single-purpose continuous production and multi-purpose campaign production resources, where multiple processes run on the same resource. *Production throughputs* in both cases are variable.

Process methods are process-based. *Production factors* and intensive in asset, material and energy. *Change-overs* between processes are either flying during the process by a simple change of additives to the process or based on a change-over process leading from one finished product campaign to the next campaign producing off-spec products out of required quality specifications. A complete stop of the resource is not required for a change-over between campaigns.

Output products can be one or multiple. *Output factors* are mainly static; some cases exist where output share relations of output products are variable meaning that the relation between multiple output products produced in the same process can be varied within certain boundaries.

Input products are single to few and factors are mainly stable. *Input factors* are reflected in the recipe. Recipe in the chemical industry is a synonym for the bill-of-material in discrete parts manufacturing and includes all input products with their respective input fraction required to produce one unit of one or several output products in a production process. In chemical production, the degree of raw material consumption rates and hence the recipe factors can depend on the processing mode of the equipment, which can be employed at different utilization or throughput levels. In this case, the recipe is not composed of static input factors but of recipe functions, which express the relationship between the input consumption and the process quantity produced.

3.2.6 Procurement Characteristics

Procurement characteristics structure is a mirror of the sales characteristics except the sales-related services provided to customers (s. table 12).

Table 12 Procurement characteristics

Characteristics	Attributes
Product	
- type	commodity, specialty
- life cycle	short, middle, long
- number	low, medium, high
- customization	standard, variants, customer-specific
- perishability	fast perishable, medium perishable, not perishable
Market	
- constellation	monopoly, oligopoly, polypoly
- price mechanism	exchange, auction, negotiation

Table 12 (continued) Procurement characteristics

Characteristics	Attributes
Supplier	
- structure	single, <u>few</u>, many
- type	<u>internal</u>, <u>external</u>
- relation	<u>contract</u>, <u>spot</u>
Offer	
- certainty	<u>forecasted</u>, stochastic, unknown
- volatility	stable quantity, <u>volatile quantity</u>, stable price, <u>volatile price</u>
- elasticity	<u>inelastic (0)</u>, relatively inelastic (<1), unitary elastic (=1), relatively elastic (>1)
Procurement	
- flexibility	<u>Flexible quantity</u>, <u>fixed quantity</u>, flexible price, <u>fixed price</u>

Procured *products* are also commodities with a long *life cycle*; the *number of products* is relatively small compared to the number of finished products. *Customization* is limited to standard raw materials. Raw materials considered are not *perishable*.

Market constellation is also an *oligopoly* with few suppliers and few buyers. *Price mechanisms* considered are also bilateral negotiations.

With respect to *supplier structure* and *type*, few suppliers are used and suppliers are internal and external; *business relations* with suppliers are spot and contract.

With respect to *offer certainty* and *volatility*, the offer is forecasted and volatile by quantity and price. With respect to *elasticity*, the offer is inelastic meaning that the price does not change if the company's procurement quantity differs from the offer quantity.

Procurement flexibility exists for spot quantities, while contract quantities are fixed. Prices are fixed in both cases.

3.3 Conclusions

Relevant characteristics of the chemical industry and the considered global value chain network have been presented in more detail. Results can be summarized:

- The chemical industry has a significant importance with respect to volumes and economic values. Value chain planning methods applied on this basis can have significant influence and lead to respective improvements.

- The globalization is a key trend in the chemical industry especially between traditional industry markets in Europe and NAFTA and emerging markets in Asia. Planning and managing these flows is a further area, where value chain planning can provide significant decision support to overall volume and value optimization.
- Price and quantity volatility of commodities in procurement and sales require integrated volume and value decisions to ensure profitability.
- Planning the considered global value chain network has to address equally specifics in sales, distribution, production and procurement to reach a global optimum. A typology extending so far supply-focused typologies by procurement and sales characteristics has been presented as a holistic basis for the value chain planning problem.

4 Value Chain Planning Requirements and State of the Art Analysis

Planning requirements for the specified value chain are elaborated in this chapter based on the value chain management framework established in chapter 2. Planning requirements are gathered from industry cases, research literature analysis and practice studies. A state of the art analysis of recent literature is conducted for these requirements in order to present recent concepts and applicable ideas and to specify research gaps. Requirements collection and coverage by state of the art literature is summarized at the end of the chapter also as input for the model development in the subsequent chapter.

4.1 Value Chain Planning Requirements

Value chain planning requirements are structured along the value chain and value chain planning framework. Requirements are presented in requirements packages and numbered from R1 to R13 across the value chain areas.

4.1.1 Requirements Gathering Overview

Requirements are structured into the areas planning process, value planning, sales planning, distribution planning, production planning and procurement planning according to the value chain planning framework:

- *Planning Process:* detailing the global value chain planning process requirements incl. interaction between regional and global level
- *Value Planning*: detailing the requirements to plan monthly values consistent to the company profit and loss statement
- *Sales Planning*: detailing the requirements to plan monthly sales volumes and values addressing commodity business characteristics of price-quantity relations and price volatility as well as uncertainty

- *Distribution Planning*: detailing the requirements for planning transportation and inventory volumes and values addressing the aspect of a global value chain
- *Production Planning*: detailing the planning requirements for a chemical commodity production with continuous and multi-purpose resources
- *Procurement Planning*: detailing the planning requirements for procurement of raw materials and products for a commodity business by volume and values

4.1.2 Planning Process Requirements

Planning a global value chain on a monthly basis is based on the value chain planning framework introduced in chapter 2 and shown again as an excerpt in fig. 43

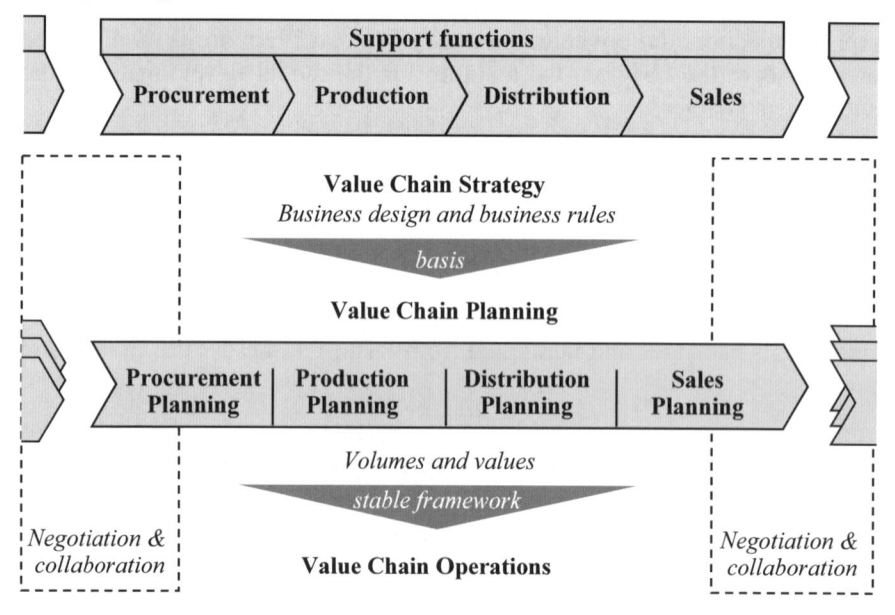

Fig. 43 Framework for value chain planning

Value chain planning is based on the business design and rules defined in the value chain strategy. Value chain planning sets the stable volume and value framework for value chain operations. Conceptually, value chain planning covers all areas in the value chain from sales to procurement interfacing with customer and supplier markets. However, a global value chain requires a dedicated process specifying the process steps as well as the interaction between decentralized regional planning and centralized global planning as shown in the following in requirement R1.

R1 - Global monthly value chain planning process: The global value chain planning process requirements are gathered from industry practice addressing the fact that global chemical companies operate in global regions such as NAFTA, EMEA and Asia and have to increasingly manage global business and volume and value flows within and between these global regions.

The planning process defines, when and in which sequence planning activities are conducted in the organization. Since a global planning problem across several regions like the EU, NAFTA or Asia is considered, the planning process has to define, which activities are done on global and which on regional level. The balance between market proximity and customer or supplier know-how as well as contact within the region has to be balanced with the objective of finding a global optimum across all regions. A global value chain planning process should distinguish between the regional and the global level and the different elements in the value chain as illustrated in fig. 44

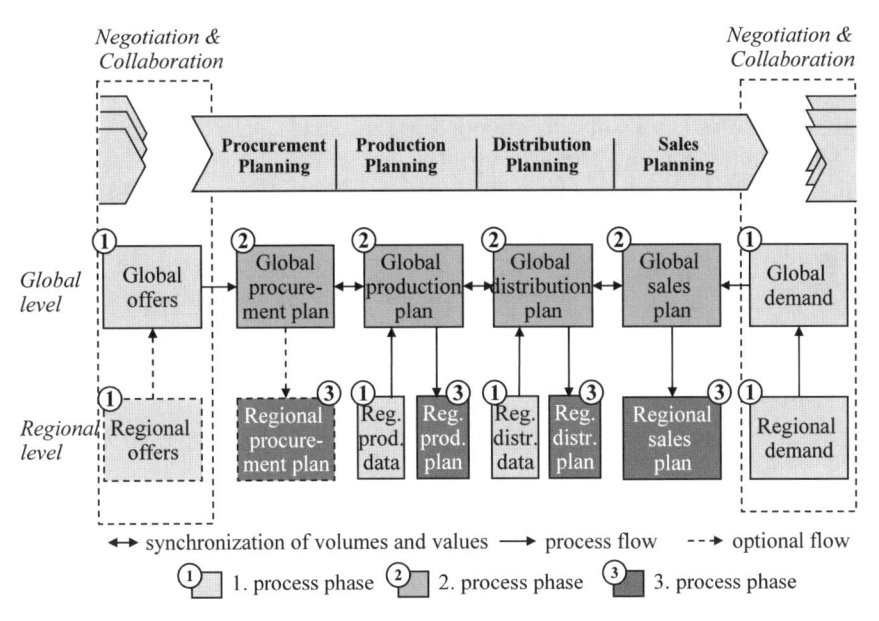

Fig. 44 Global value chain planning process

The rolling planning process starts with a *first phase* (①) typically in the first half of the period. The regions update the regional demand forecast by price and quantity that is aggregated to a global demand. In analogy, offers for procured products can be forecasted on the regional level with price and quantity depending on the numbers of procured products. In case of few strategic raw materials, offers are gathered and updated directly on a global level. Demand and offer data can be generated based on contract negotiation or formal collaborative planning processes together with customers and suppliers, respectively, or anticipated internally inside the procurement and sales organization based on market intelligence. In parallel, regional production and distribution data are updated inside the organization. Production data comprise capacity, shut-down or current resource allocation information. Distribution data comprise actual inventory, transportation quantity and transit inventory information. The due date for the first phase depends mainly on availability of market price information for products and raw materials that influence demand and offer prices and quantities between company and customers.

The global plan is created in the *second phase* (②) of the planning process typically in the third quarter of the month. The sales, distribution, production and procurement plans are integrated by volume and value on global level. Optionally, alternative planning scenarios are prepared together with the basis plan. *One* global planning meeting has to decide open issues in the plan related for example to profitability, utilization or shortage situations. Key for planning a global network is of course to consider global demand, coordinate distribution & sales to global markets and manage inventories (Jackson/Grossmann 2003, p. 3046)

The finalized plan is then communicated to regional organizations in sales, production and supply chain management during the *third phase* (③) in the fourth quarter of the period. Regional organizations create a regional sales plan and optionally a regional procurement plan, distributing global volumes and values on a detailed regional level. Global and regional plans serve as stable framework for order scheduling in value chain operations. The planned volumes and values have to be matched by orders within the respective period.

Value chain planning models should support the described planning process by

- having the right level of aggregation for planning on regional and global level
- integration all volume and value decisions on global level from sales and procurement in a simultaneous step
- generating volume and value results realizable on regional level and in value chain operations as stable framework

4.1.3 Value Planning Requirements

Value chain planning differs from *supply chain planning* by simultaneously planning future *volume* and *values* across the value chain on a tactical level. Value planning in this context refers to plan future values – turnover, costs and profits - consistent to company's profit and loss statement. So far, value and volume planning are often separated disciplines as shown in chapter 2: Controlling focuses on values for budget planning and EBIT forecasting to contribute to corporate reporting processes, while supply-oriented functions focus primarily on volumes and secondly, on costs while demand-oriented functions focus on sales volumes and turnover. Value planning now requires a cooperation of all functions on a tactical level to optimize profits future-oriented based on planned volumes and values as described in R2. Besides this includes also a future-oriented planning of working capital such as inventory values mainly influenced by tactical value chain planning illustrated in R3.

R2 - Profit planning according to profit & loss statement: The value planning requirements are derived from standard concepts to manage values as presented in subchapter 2.2. The purpose is to plan values consistent to standard profit and loss statements. This requires matching actual cost and price parameters with planned volumes across the value chain. Given the global value chain processes described previously, value planning intends to plan global profits according to the profit & loss statement on a tactical level for 6 to 12 months. The value plan has to match with companies' profit & loss statement categories sales/revenue, gross profit, earnings before interest and tax (EBIT) and earning before tax (EBT) as illustrated in the waterfall chart in fig. 45, also called *pocket margin waterfall* by some authors (Marn/Rosiello 1992). Value categories in the value chain have to be matched with the respective categories in the P&L structure. Purpose is to plan and optimize the impact of prices and costs on overall profitability. In particular, only costs measurable in the company's financial books are applied; no penalty costs are used as found in theoretical optimization models and implemented in standard APS systems but actual costs to reach comparability of value results with company's P&L as shown in fig. 45.

98   4 Value Chain Planning Requirements and State of the Art Analysis

Value parameters in value chain planning

| Net turnover | Sales costs (var.) | Transportation costs (var.) | Warehousing costs (var.) | Changeover costs (var.) | Production costs (var.) | Procurement costs (var.) | Profit I | Production costs (fix.) | Profit II | Interests/ capital costs | Profit III |

Value categories in profit & loss statement

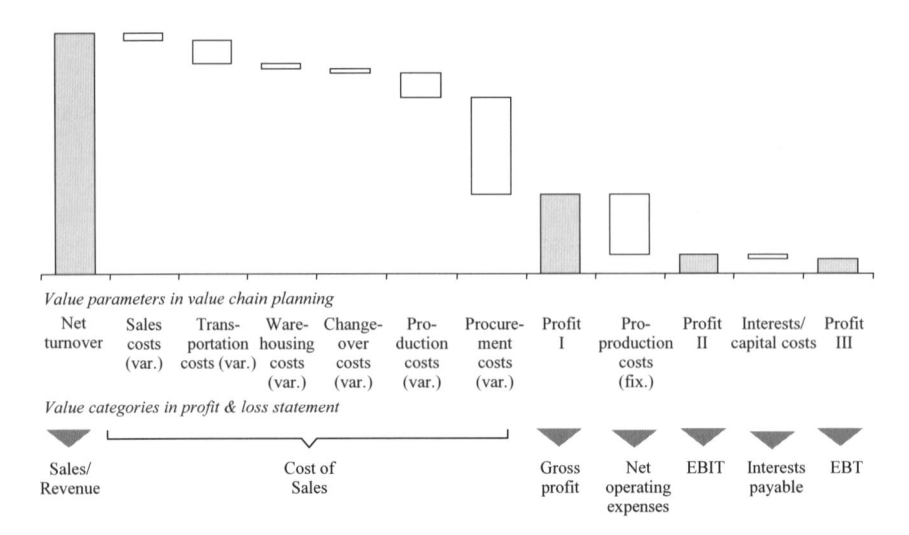

| Sales/ Revenue | Cost of Sales | Gross profit | Net operating expenses | EBIT | Interests payable | EBT |

Fig. 45 Value planning consistent with profit and loss statement

In this work, value parameters matched with P&L structures should be focused on the key cost and turnover blocks in the value chain excluding administrative and support costs or also financial results. Therefore, the intention of value planning is not to replace accurate profit and loss reporting but to focus on the key value parameters in the value chain influencing the company profitability:

- Net turnover composed of the product of net prices and net sales volume having customer rebates already deducted
- Cost of sales covering all key variable costs in the value chain such as variable sales costs for export financial and insurances services applied as percentage on turnover, variable transportation and warehousing costs driven by logistic quantity, variable change-over costs occurring for production change-overs e.g. exceptional machinery cleaning not covered by production shifts already included in production fixed costs, variable production costs e.g. for energy or other auxiliary materials depending on production quantity and mainly procurement costs for products and raw materials purchased often accounting for more than 60% of turnover depending on the value-add level
- Profit I is the approximation of the contribution margin I, which is subject to analysis to evaluate short-term profitability
- Production fixed costs account for e.g. depreciation of assets as well as fixed costs for shift personnel; of course companies have more fixed costs specifically in administration and overhead, which are out-of-scope here but could be integrated in a further extension of the value

chain management idea including also support functions; basically, fixed costs are not decision-relevant in tactical value chain planning but are included in order to get transparency also on the long-term profitability of the entire value chain network; it is characteristic that production fixed costs are *not* allocated to products with a unit cost rate that is dependent on production quantities but are treated as a resource-related cost block
- Profit II is then the equivalent of the contribution margin II used to evaluate long-term profitability
- Important elements in company's value chain planning is the management of working capital and the consideration of opportunity capital costs as well as influencing key value indicators such as Return on Capital Employed (ROCE) as introduced in section 2.2.1; inventory values are besides accounts receivables the key position in company's working capital; planning and optimization the future inventory value is an important task in value chain planning specifically if the inventory value depends on volatile raw material prices. Capital costs considered are opportunity costs of invesing capital in inventory instead of investing in an alternative investment with a defined interest rate. Accounts receivables could be also included in the value chain planning model, since customer payment terms that are often country-specific can be applied on planned sales; this would be a further extension of the value chain planning philosophy, but excluded here in this scope
- Profit III tries to match the EBT level not considering taxes; on a tactical value chain planning level, taxes are not decision-relevant; for a global value chain strategy and network design decisions, taxes are of course an important parameter to consider when deciding on sites and locations in the value chain network

A global value plan has to be calculated on the basis of the corporate base currency requiring all values measured in other currencies to be transformed into the basis currency applying exchange rate plans (Delfmann/Alberts 2000) and also applying interest rates to discount period cash flows to a net present value of the tactical value plan (see also Eppen et al. 1989, p. 520 for an example in the automotive industry).

Now, future inventory value planning as a specific chemical commodity value planning requirement reflecting the volatility of working capital and capital costs influenced by volatile raw material prices is described.

R3 - Future inventory value planning: inventory values are a crucial aspect in value planning: on the one hand, inventory value leads to capital costs for the company. On the other hand, inventory value is capital employed influencing key value management indicators such as return on capital employed (ROCE). The same profit with higher inventories leads to a lower interest rate for shareholders. Commodity inventory value is mainly influenced by the volatile costs of raw materials included. The inventory value increases if raw material prices increase. The raw material price plan determines the planning of future inventory values and capital costs considering recipes, production costs and location mapping throughout the value chain. Hence, future inventory planning has to ensure, that inventory values in the value chain plan are not based on past evaluations but on future raw material price forecasts.

4.1.4 Sales Planning Requirements

Sales planning has to reflect the bidding process presented in subchapter 2.3. Fig. 20 illustrates the paradigm shift from demand fulfilment towards sales plan achievement, where demand forecast captures the role of a price-quantity bid that is cleared based on available supply and a certain sales flexibility. The sales planning mechanism is further described in the following detailed requirements.

R4 - Contract and spot sales quantity planning: demand is not monolithic to be fulfilled in this mechanism, but differentiated in *contract* and *spot*. *Contract demand* is based on negotiated agreements between company and customer, where sales quantities and prices are fixed for a defined period, e.g. applying the ECP contract mechanism. Contract demand quantities and prices are fulfilled as forecasted. *Spot demand* is also forecasted by quantity and price. The spot price can be bilaterally negotiated, requested directly by the customer or set by the company with the customer then reacting with a demand quantity bid. In all cases, prices are negotiated bilaterally between company and customer. Competitor behavior has influence on overall market prices and available supply; however, in bilateral negotiations between the company and its customers, this business relationship is confidential and not transparent to competitors to formulate reactions. Therefore, considering competitor behavior is not a value chain planning requirement in this scope. Besides, double auctions as pricing mechanism applied in exchanges with multiple buyers and customers submitting offer and ask bids cleared in one market price are not considered in this context. Fig. 46 illustrates the principle of fixed contracts and flexible spot demand and sales.

4.1 Value Chain Planning Requirements   101

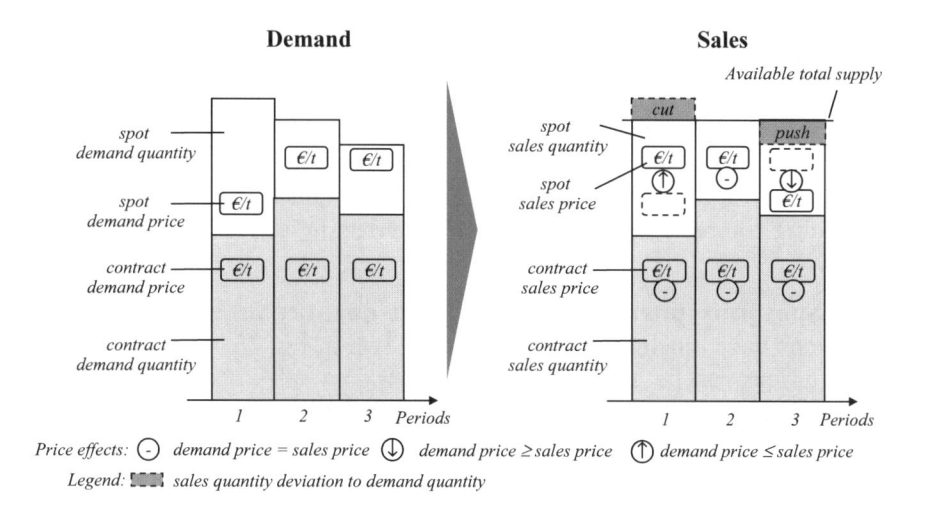

Fig. 46 Principle of contract and spot demand and sales

Spot sales quantity is flexible and can be lower or higher than the demand quantities for various reasons as shown in fig. 46. Primarily, spot sales are lower than the demand quantity, if spot demand quantity exceeds available supply and the company has to make volume quotation decisions. Secondly, spot sales are reduced if spot demand prices are too low compared to raw material costs forcing the company to make a loss when supplying the customer. Hence, the spot demand has bid character as in single-sided auctions competing for limited supply, where the bid is supplied depending on supply and profit situation and of course on customer relation or strategic considerations of the company. Hence, buyers and sellers are not forced to stick to volumes. Spot sales opportunities are flexible specifically for months 2-12, where customers get early notice that they won't be supplied at a respective price level in the coming months. It is also important to mention that different customers pay different prices for the same product (see also Dolan 1995). This is a key difference to past approaches found in research and practice. For example Jänicke (2001) presented a chemical multi-purpose planning problem that was not feasible using optimization since demand exceeded supply and not the entire forecast could be fulfilled. Demand not supplied was penalized and sometimes a backlog of demand still not supplied has been tracked. Here, the mechanism is more oriented at financial markets, where insufficient ask bids to buy company stocks do not lead to a transaction, if they are too low compared to other market participants.

Therefore, sales planning will always have a flexible spot part, where demand can exceed supply and a certain demand share facing the risk not to be supplied based on the flexibility the supplier has.

Summarizing, demand is not a given input quantity to be fulfilled in the traditional supply chain management sense but is defined more differentiated as a mix of fixed contract demand to be supplied and spot demand providing company a degree of freedom in making active sales target decisions.

R5 - Spot price planning based on price-quantity functions: spot sales decisions have inherent price effects as shown in fig. 46, where higher average prices can be achieved when cutting spot sales quantities or lower average prices are required when pushing additional quantities into the market. Again, a monopolistic market situation is not assumed, where the company can influence or dominate market prices. Additionally, we are not considering transparent exchange markets e.g. for energy and crude-oil where market price-quantity relations can be observed and analyzed (Considine 2001). In our case, the "price" is a result of the spot sales quantity decision made by the company. Since the price is an average price across several customer demands grouped in one sales location, it is logical that the average price increases, when sales quantities are lower than the demand quantity. In this case, it is assumed that customers with lower prices are cut first. Hence, the average price across the remaining customers increases.

R6 - Price uncertainty consideration in planning: Spot demand quantity and prices are uncertain in commodity business specifically in the considered planning horizon of 3-12 months. Since price is the main buying criterion in commodity business, mid-term demand quantity is mainly influenced by the price level. If spot demand quantity and prices depend on each other, uncertainty can be limited to one parameter while the other parameter is kept constant. The spot demand price is considered as uncertain in this problem leading to different turnover scenarios for the same sales quantity. Lababidi et al. (2004) presenting a petrochemical case that had to consider uncertainty in market prices and raw material costs in supply chain optimization.

4.1.5 Distribution Planning Requirements

Distribution planning covers transportation and inventory planning in the global value chain network from a company perspective. Distribution planning has to balance volumes and flows in and between the respective sales, production, distribution and procurement locations. Significant lead times between global regions are a specific planning problem in global distribution including not only transportation costs but also capital employed in transit inventories on the ship with significant lead times. Besides, local inventory counting for additional capital employed has to be managed ensuring defined delivery capability in the transfer points. Planning problems related to global distribution from a carrier or port perspective such as container flow optimization (Willems et al. 2002) or container terminal optimization (Grunow et al. 2004) are not in the scope.

R7 - Global material flow planning: Global material flows between all location types have to be planned on a monthly level including material balances in production, procurement and sales as well as inventory balances in distribution locations considering lower and upper volume limits on the lanes and in the distribution locations as well as respective costs (Jang et al. 2002). Material flows have to be planned on transportation lanes connecting the locations. Global material flow planning also has to cover a multi-stage value chain with several production and distribution steps including the material flow planning of consumed raw materials as well as produced finished and intermediated products (see for example Schuster et al. 2000, pp. 172 for a case study from process industry).

R8 - Multi-period transport and transit inventory planning: in a global distribution network, long lead times are a key challenge in cross-regional material flows (Bogataj/Bogataj 2004). Unlike lead times in production to be scheduled on a detailed operative level to match order dates (Spitter et al. 2005), global transportation lead times require a dedicated planning also on a tactical monthly level. In global ocean-based transport networks, transportation costs can be as high as 20% of the purchasing costs (Jetlund/Karimi 2004). Transportation quantities have to consider the multi-period transportation time on transcontinental transportation lanes. Long transportation time leads to time gaps between sent and received transportation quantities and to significant transit inventories as illustrated in fig. 47 in a simplified example.

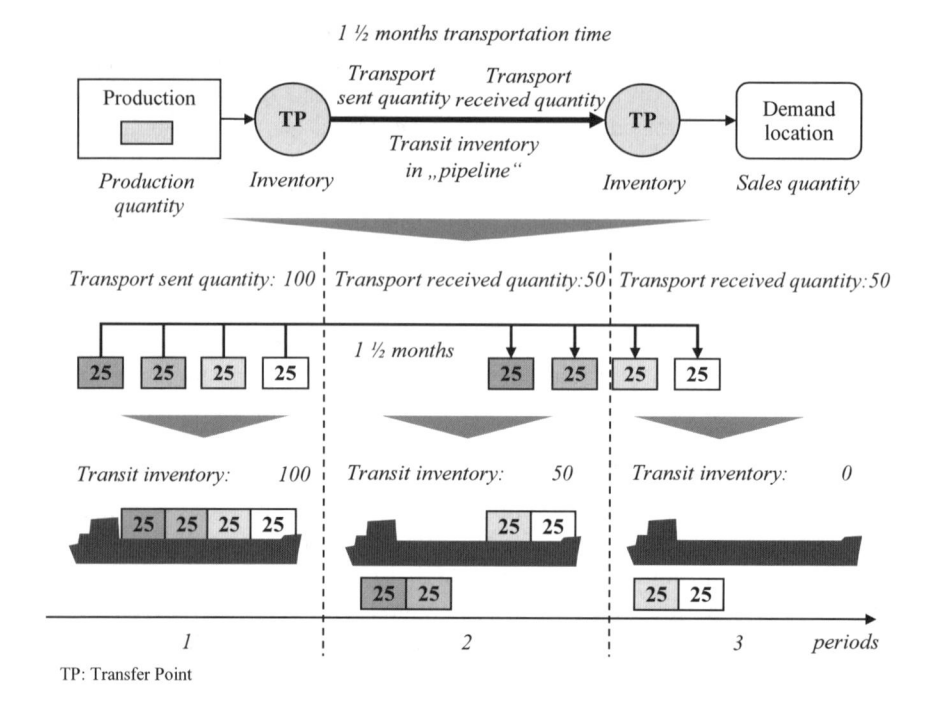

Fig. 47 Principle of multi-period transportation and transit inventories

Transit inventories cause additional capital costs in addition to the stationary inventories in warehouse locations that need to be considered in value chain planning.

R9 - Static and dynamic inventory planning: Inventory quantities are planned in distribution locations statically or dynamically applying inventory management rules defined by the value chain strategy. Inventory has to be managed for each product and distribution location or transfer point in the value chain network. The goal conflict between inventory holding costs and capital employed and to ensure delivery capability has to be solved not only for finished product but also for raw materials procured as shown in an example for coal imports (Shih, 1997). Static inventory planning is based on static quantity boundaries as illustrated in fig. 48.

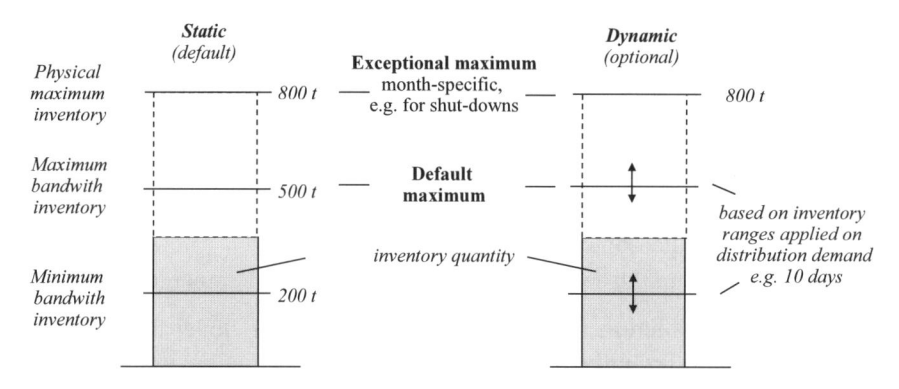

Fig. 48 Principle of static and dynamic inventory planning

The inventory management boundaries taken into account that inventory is not a constant parameter but change continuously over time due to the asynchronous pattern of demand – e.g. customer orders, own consumption or transfers between warehouses - and supply – e.g. arrival of supplier deliveries or end of production campaigns. Therefore, inventory management on a tactical monthly level has to account for a certain bandwidth, the monthly ending inventory falls into. The minimum and maximum bandwidths are determined in the value chain strategy taking into account different inventory drivers for example line fill and heels inventory, safety stock, cycle inventory, planning error inventory, quality and offspec inventory to name a few.

Additionally, the physical maximum inventory determined by physical storage capacity should be applied in exceptional months specifically for the first planning month if actual inventories to be considered in the plan are higher than the maximum bandwidth inventory. Minimum and maximum inventory boundaries are regular components in standard supply chain planning models (see for example Chen et al. 2003, p. 1881).

Dynamic inventory management applies inventory ranges measured in days dynamically on the total distribution demand for a distribution location (Alicke 2003, pp. 72-74). Inventory ranges ensure that inventory boundaries follow the planned business. This is a critical requirement especially for new product launches during the planning horizon or in case of strong future sales growths in a certain region, where inventories have to be built up to support the sales targets.

4.1.6 Production Planning Requirements

Production planning is a key part in planning since it impacts utilization of capital-intensive assets and the overall offered supply. Production planning requirements are comprehensive addressing two key tasks for planning commodity production

- Determine production quantity and time
- Determine campaign sequence and change-overs of campaigns

Typically, production master planning on a tactical level is limited to determine quantities only. However, production campaign sequence can influence significantly production quantity, if change-overs require significant time and reducing the available capacity. This can be the case for the long-running commodity production campaigns on multi-purpose resources with change-over time up to several days. In this case, production planning also has to consider campaign sequences and change-overs to determine a feasible production quantity. Production planning requirements are initially related to production quantity determination and will then be detailed for change-over planning.

R10 - Variable production processes, input and output planning: Production processes have variable run times and throughputs as well as multiple input and output products as illustrated in fig. 49.

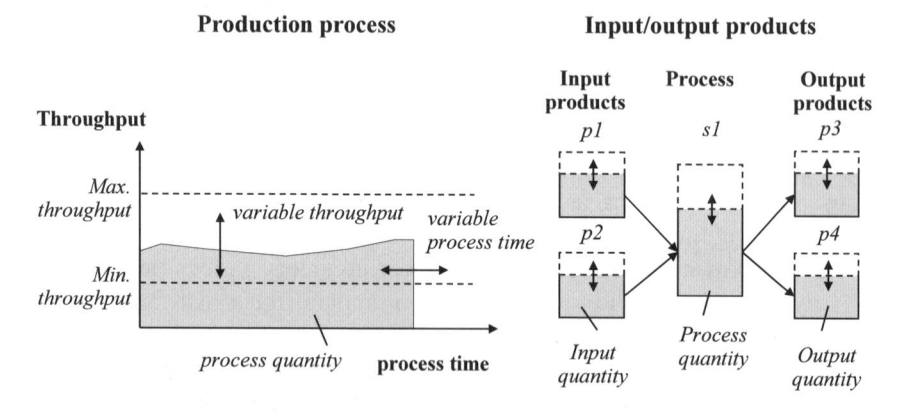

Fig. 49 Variable production processes, input and output

Production planning has to determine run time and throughputs of production processes in order to derive input and output quantities for related input and output products (see also Franke 2005). Production processes can run between a minimum and maximum utilization (Sürie 2005b, p. 213). Production processes apply for continuous single purpose assets as well as campaign multi-purpose processes to produce finished but also intermediate products (see also Berning et al. 2004, p. 914). In addition, production planning has to consider for planned maintenance idle time to be bridged with inventory or supplied by alternative production plants or suppliers (Pistikopoulos et al. 2001).

The raw material in production is not constant but variable depending on the throughput. In this case, the raw material recipe is not a constant factor. Instead recipe functions have to be used expressing the relation between input quantity of raw material and output quantity produced. Examples for recipe functions from industry practice are shown in the fig. 50.

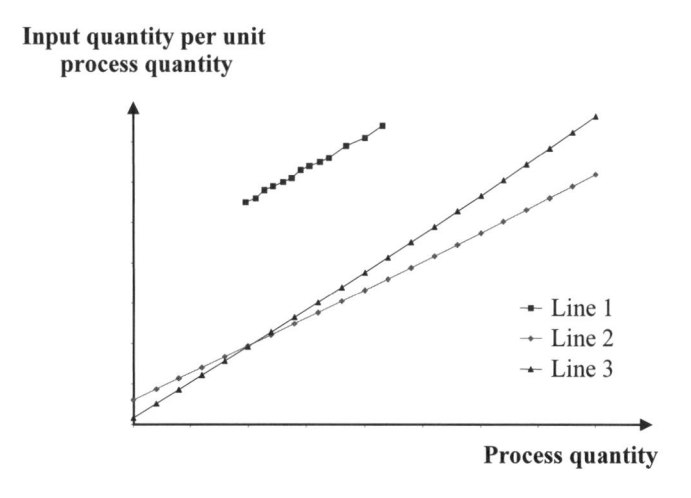

Fig. 50 Raw material recipe function principle

This effect can be compared to the gas consumption of a car requiring more gas per 100 km being run at a higher average speed. Selective papers address the specifics of variable raw material consumption e.g. in the case of fuel consumption of container ships (Jetlund et al. 2004, p. 1271). Hence, the problem to balance raw material consumption and volatile raw material costs with sales quantities and prices has to be solved in value chain planning.

R11 - Process throughput smoothing: Production processes with variable throughput provide planning flexibility to run a resource between minimum and maximum throughput level (Franke 2005). However, these resources require certain throughput stability over time in order to ensure process stability and product quality. Process throughput smoothing should support the planner to limit dynamic throughput changes resource-specific within a planning period. Extreme throughput changes between minimum and maximum throughputs in short time should be avoided, if chemical production processes are less flexible with respect to throughput changes.

R12 - Campaign and change-over planning: Commodity production is based on continuous or campaign production mode. Campaigns are long-running taking weeks or months. For multi-purpose production, campaign changes generally require a sequence-dependent change-over process with an offspec product produced (Franke 2005). This change-over process may take significant time and may lead to profit loss caused by the offspec product that can be sold only at a lower price to the market compared to the finished product as well as impacting the total amount of available capacity (Hill et al. 2000). This problem is similar to the lot sizing problem with sequence dependent setup costs (Fleischmann/Meyr 1997), however, it has to be ensured that minimum run times and change-over times do not lead to infeasibility in case of discrete planning periods as in the case in monthly planning (Koçlar/Süral 2005). Monthly production planning is often limited to quantities, while production scheduling considers change-overs and campaign sequences. In the discussed cases, campaign sequence and change-overs have significant influence on volumes and values and have to be considered simultaneously in the monthly planning.

4.1.7 Procurement Planning Requirements

Procurement planning is the interface towards the supplier market. Procurement planning has the same critical importance as sales planning in a commodity value chain, since companies' profitability is mainly determined by the value-added between procurement costs and sales turnover as illustrated in chapter 1. The monthly planning of required procurement volumes and costs given volatile raw material offer prices is detailed in the following. Procurement planning requirements mirror sales planning requirements now from a buyer perspective with focus on contract and spot differentiation in procurement planning.

R13 - Contract and spot procurement planning: procurement planning has to be differentiated into spot and contract in analogy to contract and spot demand. Raw materials are procured either based on fixed contracts or on the spot market (see also Seifert et al. 2001). Spot and contract prices can differ as illustrated by an example of Reiner/Jammernegg (2005), pp. 119 in the fig. 51.

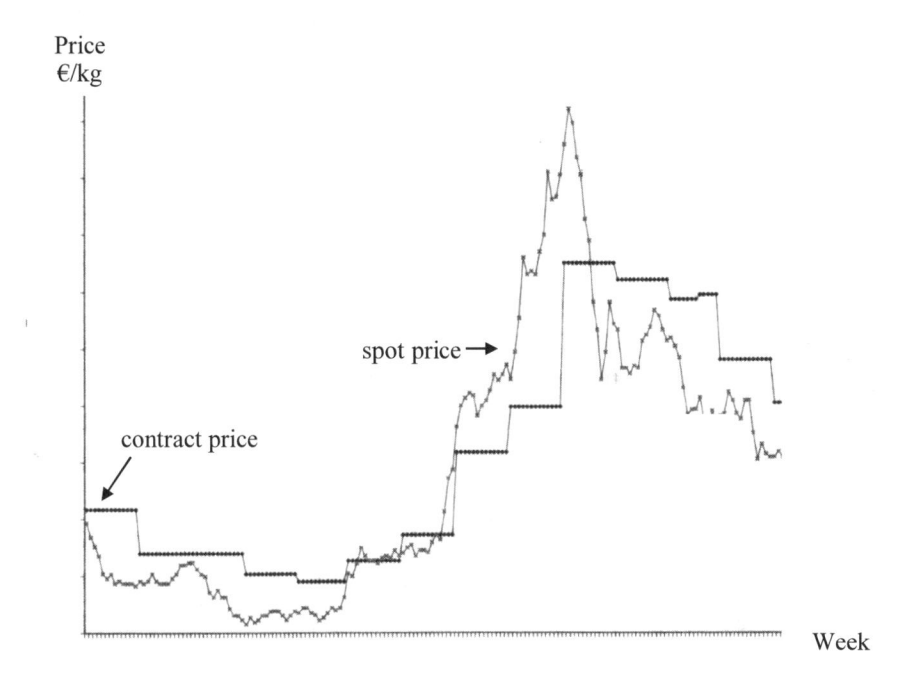

Fig. 51 Contract and spot procurement example

In analogy to the demand side, procurement contracts are fixed by quantity and price with the objective to ensure a basis volume of raw materials. Spot procurement supports company's flexibility requirements and the company can decide the spot procurement quantity with certain flexibility around the offered quantity. Price levels for contracts and spot business differ and are volatile in each period. Typically, companies operate with few key strategic suppliers for a respective product or raw material. Therefore, price-quantity models like in sales planning are less applicable. More often is the case that specifically commodity-type raw materials are procured on many-to-many exchanges, which is out of the scope in our case as described in section 3.2.6. If products are supplied by internal business units, transfer prices are applied following the contract procurement principles.

4.2 Literature Review and State of the Art Analysis

State of the art literature is analyzed to evaluate the coverage of value chain planning requirements in related models. The review helps to identify concepts presented in literature that can be used in a planning model as well as identify gaps in current models.

4.2.1 State of the Art Analysis Overview

Models in literature with relation to the scope of this work are reflected by the key words in the title *planning, global, commodity* and *chemical industry* in the context to value chain management. Given the comprehensive scope of the value chain planning problem, literature analysis is grouped into these four groups:

- [1] *Planning-related:* models related to general planning and value chain management focusing on tactical master planning, hierarchical planning, sales & operations planning and advanced planning of value chain and/or supply chain networks
- [2] *Global-related:* models related to a global scope and value chain management and optimization problems addressing global requirements
- [3] *Commodity-related:* models related to value chain management and the commodity-specific requirements such as demand and procurement uncertainty and volatility
- [4] *Chemicals-related:* models related to value chain management and the chemical industry specific requirements

In table 13, an overview of the four groups and related literature is shown:

Table 13 Literature for the state of the art analysis

Literature group	Literature	Comment
[1] Planning-related	Alicke (2003) Fleischmann/Meyr (2003) Minner (2003) Fleischmann et al. (2004) Meyr (2004b) Rohde/Wagner (2004) Wagner (2004) Pibernick/Sucky (2005) Günther (2005) Genin (2005)	Models focusing on overall tactical and integrated master planning and process including APS, hierarchical planning, general demand and distribution planning models as well as practice-oriented S&OP processes

Table 13 (continued) Literature for the state of the art analysis

Literature group	Literature	Comment
[2] Global-related	Arntzen et al. (1995) Scharlacken/Harland (1997) Vidal/Goetschalckx (2001) Goetschalckx et al. (2002) Nagurney (2003) Chakravarty (2005) Kazaz et al. (2005)	Models focusing on global network design and allocation problems as well as global production planning
[3] Commodity-related	Seifert et al. (2001) Asche et al. (2003) Cheng et al. (2003) Gupta/Maranas (2003) Lababidi et al. (2004) Cheng et al. (2004) Chen/Lee (2004) Jammernegg/Paulitsch (2004) Reiner/Jammernegg (2005) Christopher/Gattorna (2005) Charnsirisakskul et al. (2006)	Models focusing on volatile and uncertainty in demand and procurement as characteristic for commodity business
[4] Chemicals-related	Loos (1997) Timpe/Kallrath (2000) Grunow (2001) Trautmann (2001) Berning et al. (2002) Kallrath (2002a) Kallrath (2003) Grunow et al. (2003a) Grunow et al. (2003b) Günther/van Beek (2003b) Berning et al. (2004) Levis/Papageorgiou (2004) Yang G. (2005)	Models focusing on chemical industry-specific planning problems with focus on production planning and scheduling as well as distribution planning

Requirements coverage in the respective section is discussed in the following.

4.2.2 Planning-related Literature

Integrated planning models in the context of value chain planning can be found in the *planning-related* literature group under key words such as *master planning* (Alicke 2003, Rohde/Wagner 2004; Pibernik/Sucky 2005), *demand planning* (Meyr 2004b, Wagner 2004), *distribution planning* (Fleischmann et al. 2004) and *inventory planning* (Minner (2003) as well as *advanced planning systems* incl. *supply network planning* (Günther 2005), *hierarchical planning* (Fleischmann/Meyr 2003) or *aggregate production planning* (APP) (Wang/Liang 2004). Practice-oriented articles and studies present planning processes under the term *sales & operations planning* (S&OP) (Genin et al. 2005).

Supply network planning (SNP) intends to minimize costs by planning transportation, inventory and production quantities for discrete planning periods $t = 1,...,T$ with a given demand forecast. The supply network plan intends to calculate a feasible and cost-minimized supply plan on the tactical level for defined time buckets including procurement quantities, production quantities, inventory quantities and transportation quantities to fulfil the demand. Supply network planning relies on inventory and material flow balances between the locations in the network. Günther (2005) describes an *advanced planning process* and the respective APS (Günther (2005), pp. 13) illustrated in fig. 52.

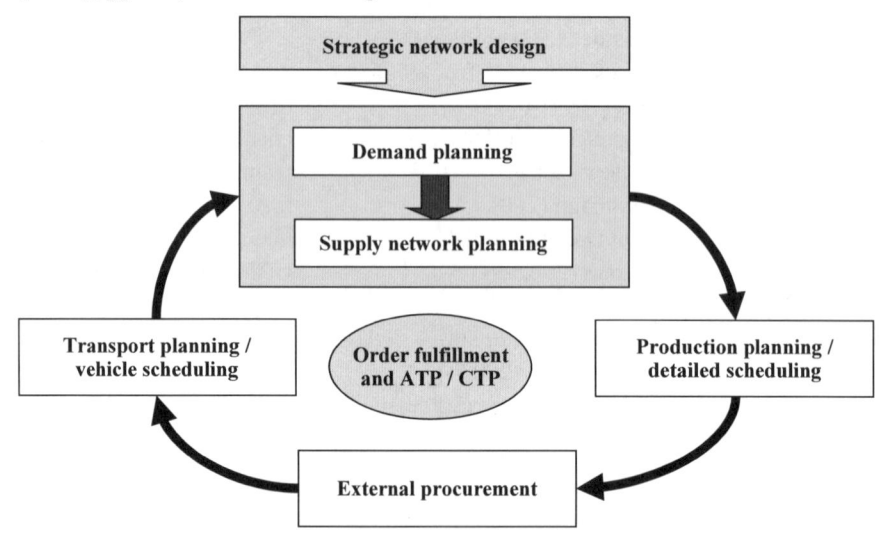

Fig. 52 Typical planning cycle of APS

The challenge in supply planning is that specifically the available production quantities per month can depend on the schedule of the products on a specific resource if change-overs consume significant time so that the overall capacity error in the rough-cut master plan would not be acceptable. Therefore, supply network planning includes also the aspect of hierarchical planning, where production quantities based on a discrete monthly time bucket are defined first at an aggregate product level and then disaggregated into a schedule for the production of specific product variants at individual resources e.g. equipment units.

Critical problem and focus in supply network planning and also in the industry-practice sales & operations planning processes is the demand forecast and the respective forecast accuracy. A demand forecast exceeding available supply can cause a shortage situation destabilizing the volume balances. Inaccurate demand forecasts in practice lead to higher supply costs than planned specifically into excess inventories. Therefore, demand planning methods intend to forecast future demand as good as possible also using historical data and statistical forecast methods (Wagner 2004; Meyr 2004b). They do not address flexible spot demand and the option to not fully supply demand.

Finally, distribution and transportation planning is reviewed for example by Alicke (2003), Minner (2003) or Fleischmann (2004) and addresses also the aspect of transit inventories. Specific inventory models focus on setting static inventory boundaries especially considering uncertainty in demand and supply (Krevera et al. 2005; Alicke 2003). They address the aspect to extend static inventory management towards dynamic inventory boundaries using inventory ranges. This approach, however, is not further detailed in a specific model.

Evaluating Literature against Requirements

Concluding, planning-related literature covers parts of the planning process and provides model input for distribution and transportation planning. Specifically, they cover

- the aggregation of volume plans in one master plan focused on production and distribution based on given demand
- hierarchical planning to combine production volume and production sequence planning
- demand planning methods as well as distribution planning to calculate material balances and inventories
- analogy to sales and operations planning processes in practice

Specific areas with gaps considering formulated value chain planning requirements

- Focus on supply volume planning to fulfil given demand, reach a feasible plan and minimize supply costs also using subjective penalties instead of actual cost parameters from controlling; future-oriented profit-maximization according to profit and loss statement and inventory value planning not covered so far

114 4 Value Chain Planning Requirements and State of the Art Analysis

- Focus on demand forecasting and forecast accuracy rather than sales target achievement based on a differentiation of contract and spot sales
- Global aspects such as global and regional planning, global lead times or exchange rates are less covered

Concluding, planning-related literature so far addresses many requirements areas by covering formulated requirements partly (s. table 14).

Table 14 Requirements coverage by planning-related literature

Value Chain Planning Requirements	Coverage
R1: Global monthly value chain planning process	◔
R2: Profit planning according to profit & loss statement	◔
R3: Future inventory value planning	○
R4: Contract and spot sales quantity planning	◔
R5: Spot price planning based on price-quantity functions	○
R6: Price uncertainty consideration in planning	○
R7: Global material flow planning	◔
R8: Multi-period transport and transit inventory planning	◔
R9: Static and dynamic inventory planning	◕
R10: Variable production processes, input and output planning	◕
R11: Process throughput smoothing	○
R12: Campaign and change-over planning	◕
R13: Contract and spot procurement planning	◒

Legend: Evaluation: from 5 = fully covered to 1 = not covered

Planning-related models, however, are not specific enough to cover global, chemical-industry and commodity-related aspects of the value chain planning problem. Specifically, future inventory value planning, price-quantity functions and uncertainty as well as process throughput smoothing are specific requirements not covered in planning-related literature focusing on master planning and supply network planning.

4.2.3 Global-related Literature

Models with a *global* focus can be found mainly for strategic network design problems, where location decisions in a global company network need to be optimized (Arntzen et al. 1995; Vidal/Goetschalckx 2001; Goetschalckx et al. 2002). These models consider exchange rate, import tariffs and tax rate differences as global specifics in network design decisions. Recent papers develop also global planning models on a more tactical level (Chakravarty 2005; Kazaz et al. 2005). Some authors address the aspect of global transportation planning and the impact of lead times (Tyworth/Zeng

1998; Bogataj/Bogataj 2004; Ham et al. 2005 and Zhang 2005). Scharlacken/Harland (1997) proposes in additional a global planning process.

Hwarng et al. (2005) point out on the one hand the importance of consolidating distribution points in complex supply chains and analyze on the other hand the impact of simplifying demand and lead time assumptions. They argue to simulate the complicated interactions in a supply chain

Chakravarty (2005) develops a global optimization model for global network design decisions incorporating sales quantity and price decisions. The author uses demand curves, where demand quantity is a function of price and turnover is decided using quadratic optimization. The value scope of the model is profit optimization incorporating variable sales prices and quantities as supply quantities and costs. It is similar to the considered problem more on a network design-level rather than on a monthly planning level for a chemical industry value chain. In addition, the assumption of a monopolistic market constellation, with the company able to influence demand by price setting reflected in the demand curves is not valid in this work.

Evaluating Requirements Coverage

Global models are focused mainly on global network design, transfer price and tax optimization on a more strategic level.

- Models address the aspect of global and regional design in planning without addressing the monthly global value chain planning process on a tactical level
- Global models target to support strategic invest decisions and consequently follow also the requirements of value planning to have actual costs and turnover as decision basis as it is done in classical investment calculation including taxes
- Global material flow and transport planning is also an integral part of global models not on a tactical level but addressing requirements of lead time gaps
  Specific areas with a lack of value chain integration
- Global models since being more strategic oriented less addressing chemical supply chain specifics required for tactical production planning such as change-overs or recipes
- Except of one example, prices in procurement and sales are given and not an active decision factor; purpose is to minimize costs for taxes and the network requiring profits and turnovers to calculate taxes

Concluding, the areas mostly impacted by the global scope such as global material flow planning and multi-period transport and transit inventory planning are covered best by global models (s. table 15).

Table 15 Requirements coverage by global-related literature

Value Chain Planning Requirements	Coverage
R1: Global monthly value chain planning process	◐
R2: Profit planning according to profit & loss statement	◐
R3: Future inventory value planning	○
R4: Contract and spot sales quantity planning	○
R5: Spot price planning based on price-quantity functions	○
R6: Price uncertainty consideration in planning	○
R7: Global material flow planning	◕
R8: Multi-period transport and transit inventory planning	◐
R9: Static and dynamic inventory planning	○
R10: Variable production processes, input and output planning	◔
R11: Process throughput smoothing	○
R12: Campaign and change-over planning	○
R13: Contract and spot procurement planning	◔

Legend: Evaluation: from 5 = fully covered to 1 = not covered

Since global models are more focused on strategic network design problems than tactical planning, tactical aspects such as price planning and price uncertainty, inventory planning or chemical production-specific planning of campaigns and change-overs are not covered.

4.2.4 Commodity-related Literature

Commodity-related models focus on demand volatility and uncertainty in volumes and prices as with sales quantity flexibility. Several authors proposed models to handle demand uncertainty in general focusing on quantities (Cheng et al. 2003; Gupta/Maranas 2003; Cheng et al. 2004; Chen/Lee 2004). Uncertainty is reflected by demand quantity scenarios and/or probabilities. Proposed models maximize expected or robust profit. Process industry-specific models use simulation to address demand uncertainty and to determine optimal inventory levels (Jung et al. 2004).

Gupta/Maranas (2003) as one example for a demand uncertainty model present a demand and supply network planning model to minimize costs. Production decisions are made "here and now" and demand uncertainty is balanced with inventories independently incorporating penalties for safety stock and demand violations. Uncertain demand quantity is modeled as normally distributed random variables with mean and standard deviation. The philosophy to have one production plan separated from demand uncertainty can be transferred to the considered problem. Penalty costs for unsatisfied demand and normally distributed demand based on historical data cannot be applied in this commodity case since spot demand is flexible and demand price uncertainty for chemical commodities does not mainly follow historical patterns but principally depends on raw material and crude oil price developments in the future.

As further example, Chen/Lee (2004) present a multi-company demand and supply network planning model to maximize profits with demand uncertainty and pricing decisions. Demand uncertainty is modeled with quantity scenarios and probabilities. A two-phase optimization strategy is developed to reach robust plans. Both approaches can be transferred to handling of price uncertainty and price scenarios. Pricing decisions, however, are modeled with fuzzy logic considering satisfaction levels of buyer and seller assuming collaboration and preference transparency between both parties. This assumption cannot be made in the spot sales commodity business considered.

Lababidi et al. (2004) incorporate uncertainty and stochastic market prices and raw material costs for a petrochemical case. They modeled market price and raw material price uncertainty as given and analyzed the effects on production utilization. They initially observed that prices can have significant influence on production plans and utilization.

Evaluating Requirements Coverage by Commodity-related Literature

Commodity-related models focus either on the demand or on the procurement side addressing respective requirements:

- Differentiating spot and contract business specifically in procurement; and integrating uncertainty and volatility using stochastic distribution functions and scenarios
- Addressing opportunities for dynamic pricing e.g. in relation with inventories
- Addressing the objective of profit maximization instead of cost minimization
  Specific areas with a lack of value chain integration
- Commodity-oriented models focus more on the market interfaces in sales and procurement and consider less complexity in the supply chain determining volumes and values in the value chain; integration with production planning and chemical-specifics often not modeled
- Global aspects are less combined with commodity-characteristics

Commodity-related models support requirements in sales and procurement as shown in table 16.

118   4 Value Chain Planning Requirements and State of the Art Analysis

Table 16 Requirements coverage by commodity-related literature

Value Chain Planning Requirements	Coverage
R1: Global monthly value chain planning process	○
R2: Profit planning according to profit & loss statement	◑
R3: Future inventory value planning	○
R4: Contract and spot sales quantity planning	◑
R5: Spot price planning based on price-quantity functions	◑
R6: Price uncertainty consideration in planning	◑
R7: Global material flow planning	○
R8: Multi-period transport and transit inventory planning	○
R9: Static and dynamic inventory planning	◑
R10: Variable production processes, input and output planning	○
R11: Process throughput smoothing	○
R12: Campaign and change-over planning	○
R13: Contract and spot procurement planning	◑

Legend: Evaluation: from 5 = fully covered to 1 = not covered

4.2.5 Chemicals-related Literature

Chemical-industry related literature addressing value chain management focuses on production and supply chain management as well as selectively procurement. Companies in the oil and chemical industries have been leaders for almost 50 years in the development and use of linear and mixed integer programming models to support decision-making at all levels of planning (Shapiro 2004).

Several industry studies analyze the status, requirements and areas of supply chain management also considering the chemical industry (Chakravarty 2005; Kazaz et al. 2005). Scientific research focuses on production (Günther/van Beek 2003b). Subjects to research are the production and logistics characteristics and planning requirements in the chemical industry (Loos 1997; Kallrath 2002a), detailed scheduling models especially for batch production (Blömer 1999; Neumann et al. 2000; Trautmann 2001; Neumann et al. 2002) and in some cases continuous production (Zhou et al. 2000) or hierarchical production planning (Hauth 1998) or multi-site production and supply network planning problems in complex company networks providing production integration planning methods (Timpe/Kallrath 2000; Berning et al. 2002; Kallrath 2003; Grunow et al. 2003a; Grunow et al. 2003b; Berning et al. 2004; Levis/Papageorgiou 2004; Yang 2005; Timpe/Kallrath 2000). A chemical industry-related production and distribution planning model is presented by Grunow (2001).

4.2 Literature Review and State of the Art Analysis 119

Further research focuses on the shipment planning for crude oil (Nygreen et al. 2000; Cheng/Duran 2004; Persson/Göthe-Lundgren 2005).

Integrated production and distribution network design and planning are addressed by Grunow (2001) and Timpe/Kallrath (2000). Production scheduling for batch and campaign production and integration of production plans across plants considering sequence and production mode constraints are primary subjects of research. The specific aspect of variable raw material consumption by resources depending on throughput level has not been addressed until now. Timpe/Kallrath (2000) addresses the aspect of material losses in production in the raw material recipe.

While production and distribution are intensively investigated due to the complexity and cost-importance of capital-intensive production assets in the chemical industry, procurement and demand management in the chemical industry value chain is less investigated.

Procurement planning in general and spot and contract procurement planning in the chemical industry in particular are recently investigated by Stadtler (2004b), Marquez/Blanchar (2004), Seifert et al. (2004) and Reiner/Jammernegg (2005), who develop a risk-hedging model and compare different procurement strategies including speculation inventories. Stadtler (2004b) presents general tasks of purchase planning integrated in overall supply chain management on the order level. Methods for BOM-explosion and calculating secondary demand – the demand for products to be consumed in production - are discussed. Recent papers discuss procurement strategies on spot and contract markets. Marquez/Blanchar (2004) present extended procurement strategies based on real options to optimize contract portfolios considering in-transit and warehouse inventories. Seifert et al. (2004) underline the importance of spot procurement next to contract procurement and show the advantage of a fraction of demand being based on spot market procurement.

Demand-oriented models investigating demand and classical forecasting of demand quantities in the chemical industry can be found for example in practice-oriented industry cases (Franke 2004).

Evaluating Requirements Coverage

Chemicals-related literature with respect to value chain management has built up comprehensive knowledge and results in the area of production planning, scheduling and distribution as well as in procurement. Therefore, literature covers the following requirements

- Production planning in the chemical industry with processes, variable utilization, comprehensive recipes and multiple input and output products has been in the focus of research in the last years; specifically optimization of production schedules and change-overs across resources

120   4 Value Chain Planning Requirements and State of the Art Analysis

and sites have been intensively investigated specifically for batch production; special aspects of commodity production such as throughput smoothing or variable recipes have been investigated less
- Distribution planning including transports and inventories are also investigated in the context of production-distribution systems providing methods for material balances or inventory calculations
- Contract and spot procurement planning confronted with volatile prices specifically in the area of petrochemicals
  Specific areas with less requirements coverage
- Value planning and the integration of company's profit and loss structure with supply chain management is not addressed; often artificial penalty costs are applied in models to steer results instead of actual cost parameters from controlling
- The demand and procurement side is treated often as given and monolithic; models do not analyze the integration of sales and procurement with production and distribution throughout the chain by volume and value
- The global aspect so far is less addressed in chemical-industry related models.

Concluding, chemical-related literature covers mainly parts of the distribution and production requirements.

Table 17 Requirements coverage by chemical-related literature

Value Chain Planning Requirements	Coverage
R1: Global monthly value chain planning process	◓
R2: Profit planning according to profit & loss statement	○
R3: Future inventory value planning	○
R4: Contract and spot sales quantity planning	○
R5: Spot price planning based on price-quantity functions	○
R6: Price uncertainty consideration in planning	○
R7: Global material flow planning	◐
R8: Multi-period transport and transit inventory planning	◐
R9: Static and dynamic inventory planning	◐
R10: Variable production processes, input and output planning	●
R11: Process throughput smoothing	◓
R12: Campaign and change-over planning	●
R13: Contract and spot procurement planning	◐

Legend: Evaluation: from 5 = fully covered to 1 = not covered

The results of the state of the art analysis are summarized in the following.

4.3 Conclusions

Considering the specific global value chain planning requirements for commodities in the chemical industry, related research on global models focuses on network design problems, research on chemical supply chain models focuses on production and distribution while commodity-oriented models accentuate demand and procurement aspects. So far, models presented in the academic literature focus either on demand or on supply aspects. A value chain planning model integrating sales and supply decisions by volume and value in a price-volatile chemical commodity business could not be found so far, although this planning problem is of high importance not only in the chemical commodity industry. The research gaps are illustrated in table 18.

Table 18 Requirements coverage summary

Value Chain Planning Requirements	[1]	[2]	[3]	[4]
R1: Global monthly value chain planning process	◐	◐	○	◕
R2: Profit planning according to profit & loss statement	◐	◐	◐	○
R3: Future inventory value planning	○	○	○	○
R4: Contract and spot sales quantity planning	◐	○	◐	○
R5: Spot price planning based on price-quantity functions	○	○	◐	○
R6: Price uncertainty consideration in planning	○	○	◐	○
R7: Global material flow planning	◐	●	○	◐
R8: Multi-period transport and transit inventory planning	◐	◐	○	◐
R9: Static and dynamic inventory planning	●	○	◐	◐
R10: Variable production processes, input and output planning	●	◕	○	●
R11: Process throughput smoothing	○	○	○	◕
R12: Campaign and change-over planning	●	○	○	●
R13: Contract and spot procurement planning	◕	◕	◐	◐

Legend: [1]: Planning-related; [2]: Global-related; [3]: Commodity-related; [4]: Chemicals-related; Evaluation: from 5 = fully covered to 1 = not covered

The coverage shows that models rather focus on specific requirements areas and functions in value chain planning. It turns out that some requirements such as future inventory planning and process throughput smoothing are less investigated than others.

In the following an integrated global value chain planning model for chemical commodities supporting end-to-end value planning of volumes and values is developed to close the research gap.

5 Global Value Chain Planning Model

The global value chain planning model is developed based on the requirements formulated in chapter 4. This chapter is structured into a model overview providing structures and elements of the model and subsequently in the different parts model basis, value planning, sales planning, distribution planning, production planning and procurement planning.

5.1 Model Overview and Structure

The global value chain planning model is structured in parts mapping the value chain planning requirements structure as shown in fig. 53.

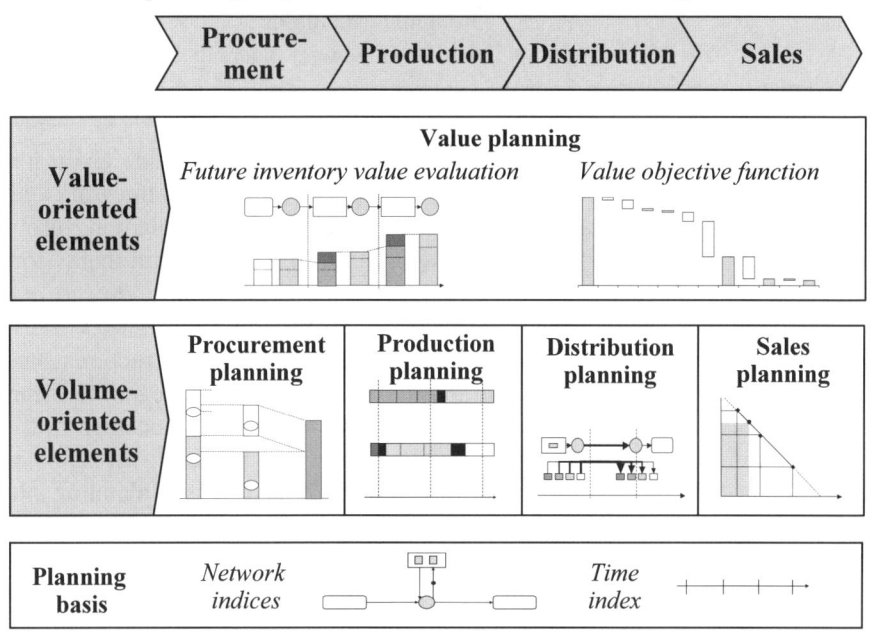

Fig. 53 Global value chain planning model-overview

Each model part – e.g. the sales planning part – is composed of single model elements such as objective functions, constraints or decision variables explained in the respective sections in mode detail.

Planning requirements formulated in chapter 4 are covered by the respective model parts shown in the model capability overview in table 19:

Table 19 Model capabilities overview

Model part	Planning Requirements/Model Capabilities
5.2 Planning basis	Global monthly value chain planning process
5.3 Value planning	Profit planning consistent with profit & loss statement
	Future inventory value planning
5.4 Sales planning	Contract and spot sales planning
	Spot price planning based on price-quantity functions
	Price uncertainty consideration in planning
5.5 Distribution planning	Global material flow planning
	Multi-period transport and transit inventory planning
	Static and dynamic inventory planning
5.6 Production planning	Variable production processes, input and output planning
	Process throughput smoothing
	Campaign and change-over planning
5.7 Procurement planning	Spot and contract procurement planning

All model parts share the same *planning basis* across the value chain initially described in subchapter 5.1 including the planning framework and basis planning objects as well as the basis indices for the planning problem. The planning basis translates the planning process requirements formulated in subchapter 5.2 into a *planning framework, planning objects and planning indices* supporting the process. The *planning framework* translates the planning process requirements into basis planning structures such as planning buckets, horizon and granularity as well as aggregation. *Planning objects* and *basis indices* are the specific planning dimensions in the value chain plan e.g. by products and locations. Given the global scope of the planning problem, the appropriate aggregation level of planning objects is an important instrument to limit planning complexity. This is elaborated in 5.2.2.

Value planning described in subchapter 5.3 consolidates all values in a consistent profit and loss statement view and maximizes global profit. In addition, value planning addresses the requirements of planning future inventory values across the value chain network.

Sales planning described in subchapter 05.4 supports spot and contract sales management and planning of sales price effects using price-quantity functions.

Distribution planning described in subchapter 5.5 handles multi-period transportation time and transit inventories as global material flow planning. Moreover, static and dynamic inventory planning is supported.

Production planning of quantities and campaigns described in subchapter 5.6 has to consider the variable production processes with multiple input and output and throughput smoothing as the planning of change-overs between campaigns.

Procurement planning of spot and contract procurement quantities is the final planning model element described in subchapter 5.7.

The model is composed of *model elements* used in the different model parts:

- *Indices* and *index sets*: indices and index sets – combinations of indices – being the basis planning objects for input, control data and decisions variables e.g. products
- *Input* and *control data*: given input data and control data defined by the planner and/or given by the value chain strategy bounding the optimization model e.g. demand forecast as input data and sales control boundaries as control data
- *Preprocessing*: additional parameters required for the optimization model based on input and control data being calculated in preprocessing
- *Decision variables*: decision variables representing the planning decisions of the planner and being decided in the optimization model e.g. production volumes
- *Objective function*: objective function to maximize profit incl. considered values
- *Constraints*: constraints being used to bound decision variables in model
- *Postprocessing*: planning indicators being calculated after optimization

Concluding, the model architecture integrates the value and volume focus as well as all functional management areas in the value chain from sales to procurement and bridges the former separation between value, supply and sales management concepts described in subchapter 2.2. The model architecture reflects the value chain management philosophy to integrate volume and value decisions across the chain for the considered tactical level of value chain planning.

5.2 Planning Basis

The planning basis is the foundation for the planning process and the entire value chain planning model. The planning basis comprises definitions and structures shared throughout the model. The planning basis covers a planning framework defining planning bucket, horizon, frequency and granularity to support the planning process requirements formulated in chapter 4. Then the planning objects and indices are defined including the aggregation of planning objects in order to address the requirements of global planning. As a result, key model indices can be formalized at the end of the chapter.

5.2.1 Planning Framework

The planning framework defines core structures in planning to support the decision of planning volumes and values on the tactical level as intermediate layer between strategy and operations as formulated in the planning process requirements in 0.

The planning framework consists of planning bucket, granularity, horizon and frequency. Characteristics and possible attributes of the global value chain planning problem are shown in table 20.

Table 20 Planning framework

Characteristics	Attributes
Planning bucket	week, <u>month</u>
Planning horizon	from 1 to <u>12 months</u>
Planning frequency	weekly, <u>monthly</u>
Planning granularity	detailed, <u>aggregated</u>

The planning model is flexible to support different attribute configurations and provide degrees of freedom to modify the planning framework attributes over time e.g. shortening or extending the planning horizon. Underlined in the tables are the attributes that will be applied in the planning model to match the planning process requirements formulated in process requirements in section

The planning bucket defines the discrete periods for planning. Here, the plan is structured into monthly buckets and all planning results refer to *month* as basis period.

The planning horizon defines the number of future periods planned. Here, planning is required for *12 months*. The 12 months horizon allows anticipating planned shut-downs or identifying shortage situations requiring additional procurement early in advance. Shorter planning horizons such as 3 or 6 months can also be well motivated e.g. if future demands and procurement planning quality can only be achieved within this timeframe. However, 3 or 6 months can be too short in a global network with long lead times in transportation. Moreover, planning models based on optimization tend to reduce volumes in the final periods since no demands for following periods exist. This is an additional argument for having a longer horizon. A very short horizon of few months makes only sense for weekly planning buckets.

Finally, the planning granularity can be *detailed* or *aggregated*. Detailed granularity means that the most detailed level of all objects is planned, such as single customers, articles, storage facilities or production units. Since we have a global planning problem, aggregation is required to limit planning complexity for all participants involved in the planning process and to combine detailed decisions to aggregate planning decisions for larger units that are robust against changes on the detailed level.

5.2.2 Planning Objects and Basis Indices

A central element in the planning framework is the definition of planning objects and potential aggregation levels. Fig. 54 illustrates planning object hierarchies for prod that can be found in industry practice.

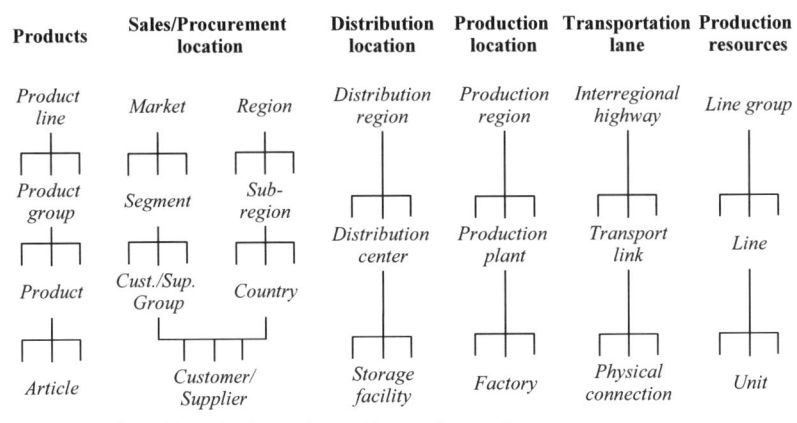

Products	Sales/Procurement location		Distribution location	Production location	Transportation lane	Production resources
Product line	Market	Region	Distribution region	Production region	Interregional highway	Line group
Product group	Segment	Sub-region				
Product	Cust./Sup. Group	Country	Distribution center	Production plant	Transport link	Line
Article	Customer/ Supplier		Storage facility	Factory	Physical connection	Unit

⊓ = hierarchy, lower element(s) part of upper element

Fig. 54 Planning objects hierarchies

A *product hierarchy* comprises product line, product group, product and article. Product line and product group combine products by common characteristics on two aggregation levels. A product is the direct input or output of a production process; articles include also packaging information. Therefore, one product can be filled into multiple articles.

Sales & procurement location hierarchies have two aggregation paths: a market-oriented and a geographical aggregation path. Both paths meet on a single customer respectively supplier level as lowest level of detail. The geographic hierarchy path aggregates customers by country, sub-region and region like "Germany", "Central Europe" and "EMEA" across several markets and segments. Geographical aggregation of course groups countries by their homogeneity e.g. with respect to currencies and import duties (Pontrandolfo et al. 2002, p. 1301). The market-oriented path aggregates customers by industry characteristics across several regions by market, segment, customer or supplier groups. For example, the automotive industry on the market level may have a segment of truck manufacturers and the premium truck OEMs may be clustered into one customer group. Market-oriented aggregation supports also differentiation of internal and external customers with internal customers having transfer prices and other transfer rules than those of external customers.[3] Geographical and market-oriented hierarchies can also be used in mixed forms.

The *distribution location hierarchy* has three levels with a distribution region, distribution center and storage facilities. A distribution region aggregates all inventories laying in different locations of the same region such as total inventories in EMEA. A distribution center is a distribution location with one or multiple storage facilities or cross-docking facilities between two different or identical modes like truck-rail or ship-ship. Distribution centers are often differentiated into regional DCs serving as hubs and customer-near local DCs e.g. as in the case of depot and hub transportation networks found for mail and parcel services (Wasner/Zäpfel 2003). Storage facilities can be dedicated warehouses or single tanks or silos for bulk material representing a single physical storage unit.

The *production location hierarchy* follows a similar logic as distribution locations do: Production regions consolidate all production resources within one geographical region to a virtual production region. A production plant combines one or multiple factories at the same site. Finally, a factory is a dedicated physical production block inside the plant holding the production resources.

---

[3] The determination of transfer prices between internal business units is out of the scope; models to determine transfer prices in supply chains are described for example by Gjerdrum et al. (2001).

A *transportation lane hierarchy* differentiates interregional highways, transportation lanes and physical connections between physical storage units. Interregional highways link regions or markets. Transportation links connects locations like plants and distribution centers on the tactical level. Physical connections such as pipelines or conveyer belts link factories and storage facilities in the same location.

The *production resource hierarchy* differentiates line group, line and unit. A line group combines multiple production lines with identical processes and technologies to one virtual resource. A line combines all production units used in one production process to one resource. A unit is a component in a production line like a reactor or dryer.

Theses hierarchies and levels again can be found in the chemical industry practice, but may differ by wording or aggregation levels in different industries or even in other companies. Key is that object and hierarchies are an important aspect in planning in order to limit planning complexity and to ensure decision significance.

The appropriate aggregation level for value chain planning has to be determined by finding the right balance between level of detail and planning complexity. In tactical planning it has to be ensured that aggregation does not lead to inaccurate volume and value planning. For example planning product groups instead of single groups would be not accurate enough on the tactical level since production planning requires the product information for determining product-dependent throughputs and recipes.

While some objects like production and distribution locations match the tactical level of value chain planning with distribution center or plant, aggregation has to be validated by aggregation rules considering the focus of value chain planning on volumes and values as illustrated in the following.

Planning Object Aggregation

Value chain planning objective is to plan volumes and values on a monthly level. Aggregation of planning objects has to find the right level of detail

- that volumes and values are accurately planned within a certain tolerance and
- that planning complexity is limited and volume variances between single objects can be leveled out on an aggregated level.

Considering the different planning objects, the aggregation decision is not a straight-forward decision and the mentioned criteria are not clearly measurable. Fig. 55 shows the criteria matching roughly value management process levels and the respective allocation of planning object hierarchies.

	Product line	Market/ Region	Distribution region	Production region	Interregional highway	Line group	Low
Strategic	— Product line —	Market/ Region —	Distribution region —	Production region —	Interregional highway —	Line group —	Low
	Product group						
Tactical	— Product —	Segment/ Subregion —	Distribution center —	Production plant —	Transport link —	Line —	Medium
		C./S.Group Country					
Operative	— Article —	Customer/ Supplier —	Storage facility —	Factory —	Physical connection —	Unit —	High

Process level — *Volume & value accuracy/ level of detail & complexity*

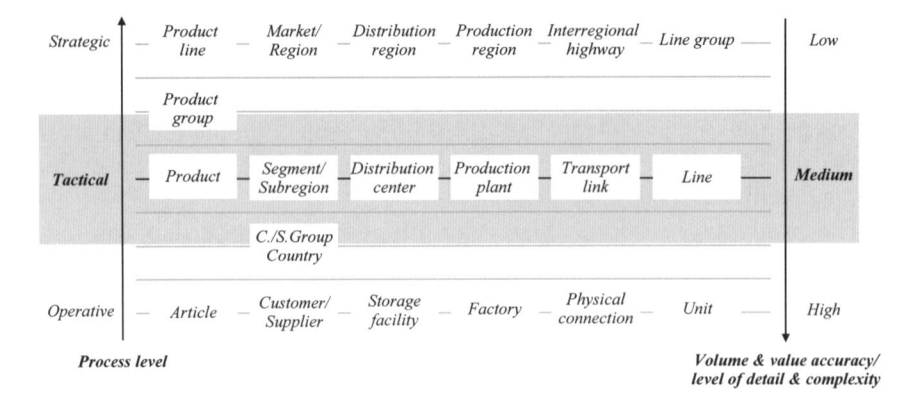

Fig. 55 Aggregation level by planning objects

Tactical volumes and value planning is done on the *product* level instead of a detailed article level also including packaging information or an aggregate product group level clustering several products. Main reason is that product quantities have to be integrated across procurement, production, distribution and sales. Product groups that cluster multiple similar products would not meet these criteria, since product group demand cannot be matched with product group inventories because the specific product matters to the customer. The packaging information given by the article is mainly required on regional and operations level within customer orders or to support filling and packaging decisions. Hence, articles are used in regional demand planning on a customer level. Globally, article demand is aggregated on a product level to limit complexity and to have a common planning basis.

Location and transportation lane aggregations have to consider, whether distribution volumes and values can be accurately planned between locations. *Sales location* aggregation requires transportation time and cost differences being in a certain tolerance interval. The European Union (EU) could form for example one sales location, since transportation time varies between 1-3 days and the transportation costs for ground transportation are in similar ranges. In addition, sales locations have to differentiate internal and external EU customers, since sales planning business rules and transfer pricing vs. market pricing differ. Therefore, a mixed aggregation considering geographical and market segment criteria is more appropriate. *Distribution location* aggregation of multiple distribution centers to one distribution region may reduce the planning complexity of inventories. However, material flows between distribution centers or mapping of sales quantities on locations are not accurate enough. For that reason, distribution locations are planned on a distribution center level. A *production location* is planned on a production plant level at the same site, with the same arguments of the distribution location aggregation. *Procurement locations* do not need to consider transportation cost differences, because the supplier normally covers the transportation costs. However, transportation time, price and business rule differences between procurement locations need to be considered; therefore, an aggregation on a sub-region/segment level is appropriate. *Transportation lane* aggregation is a result of the location aggregation decisions, since the transportation link connects procurement, production, distribution and sales locations. Finally, *production resources* aggregation has to ensure that production quantities and costs are accurately planned. Line groups of similar technologies may not be accurate enough, if product-resource allocation and throughputs differ between lines in the same line group. The line level covering an entire production process is a more appropriate aggregation level, while single units like dryers or reactors are too detailed for the tactical planning level. Table 21 shows aggregation results with the chosen aggregation level underlined.

Table 21 Aggregation results

Planning object	Aggregation level
Product	Product line, product group, <u>product</u>, article
Sales location	Market/region, <u>segment / sub-region</u>, customer cluster/country, customer
Distribution location	Distribution region, <u>distribution center</u>, storage facility
Production location	Production region, <u>plant</u>, factory
Procurement location	Market/region, <u>segment / sub-region</u>, customer cluster / country, customer
Transportation lane	Interregional highway, <u>transportation link</u>, physical connection
Resource	line group, <u>line</u>, unit

The planning objects are now formalized as basis indices for the planning model.

Basis Indices

The model basis comprises *indices* used across the planning model. Fig. 56 illustrates the basis indices:

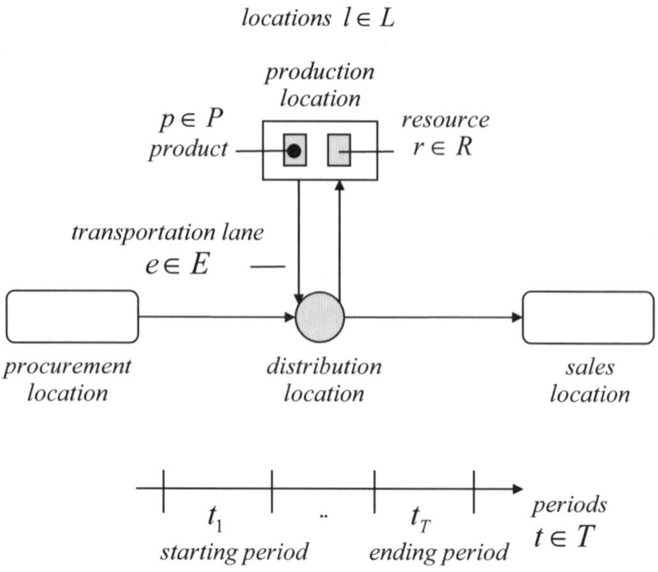

Fig. 56 Basis indices

Locations $l \in L$ are the nodes in the value chain network like sales, distribution, production or procurement locations.

Resources $r \in R$ are production units that produce finished or intermediate products as output an $d_t, \forall t \in T$ d $e \in E$ require intermediate or raw material products as input. A resource is related to one location.

Transportation lanes are the edges within the network and connect the respective locations.

Products $p \in P$ are finished products sold to the market, intermediate products used and produced in production and raw materials procured according to the chemical industry principle "every product is a finished product".

Periods $t \in T$ are discrete planning buckets as defined in the planning framework. Default bucket is one month. The planner defines a starting period $t_1 \in T$ and an ending period $t_T \in T$. The number of period days and period hours $h_t, \forall t \in T$ is defined according to the calendar.

Indices and planning basis are shared across the optimization model that is detailed in its different elements in the following.

5.3 Value Planning

The planning objective is to plan global value chain *volumes* and *values*. Initially, the value planning model with the objective function to maximize global profit is presented. The objective function also includes a relaxation concept for hard constraints leading to potential plan infeasibility. The future-oriented inventory value planning concept based on volatile raw material prices is presented at the end of the subchapter.

5.3.1 Value Objective Function

The value objective function maximizes profit consolidating all values considered in value chain planning. The global scope requires consolidating values on one currency basis applying exchange rates for values in foreign currencies as described in the following.

Value Input Data

Value input data are given parameters to be entered by the planner in the model provide by controlling or finance functions in the company and often determined by financial markets.

Each location in the network has a defined location currency e.g. USD in a US-based location. All value parameters related to this location are defined in this location currency called *foreign currency (fc)* in the model. Secondly, the company has a *base currency (bc)* for global consolidation of values in all regions. A monthly exchange rate forecast is the basis for deriving exchange rate factors used in the model. The currency exchange rate factor is the exchange rate of the foreign currency compared to the base currency. The exchange rate factors are defined for periods $t \in T$ and by locations $\chi_{lt}^L, \forall l \in L$, resources $\chi_{rt}^R, \forall r \in R$ and transportation lanes $\chi_{et}^{T}, \forall e \in E$. The location exchange rate factor χ_{lt}^{L} is the monthly exchange rate factor of the location-specific foreign currency to the base currency. The resource exchange rate factor χ_{rt}^{R} is identical to the respective location exchange rate factors of the resource's location. Due to several resource-specific value parameters, the resource exchange rate factor is defined explicitly for easy application in the model. Transportation lane exchange rate factors have to be defined explicitly, since a transportation lane connects two locations that can have different location currencies. The transportation lane currency depends on the leading currency for the transportation costs of the respective transportation lane.

The capital cost rate φ reflects the company-specific interest rate applied to calculate capital costs on working capital like inventories and outstanding liabilities or used for net present value calculation. In case of market financed corporations, the weighted average cost of capital (WACC) is used as opportunity capital cost rate. WACC considers the mixed financing structure of a company consisting of equity and debt capital[4].

Value Objective Function Decision Variables

The value objective function is oriented at the company's profit and loss definitions. Guiding principle is to only use value parameters that can be found in the cost controlling of the company "signed" by controlling. Penalty costs and without currency and weighting factors being applied to steer optimization results but having no actual financial impact – as it can be often found in supply chain optimization models - do not meet this requirement.

A second principle in value chain planning is that volume-related objectives like *high service level* or *high utilization* are managed in constraints applying appropriate boundaries and are not integrated into a multi-objective functions. Reason is that financial and non-financial objectives should not be mixed up e.g. by applying subjective weighting factors.

z is the objective variable and represents the discounted profit on earnings-before-tax level excluding resource fixed costs. Note that some aggregate (redundant) decision variables are introduced to improve the readability of the model formulation. z is composed of the value parameters as postulated by the value planning requirement in section 4.1.3. y_{t}^{S} is the net

---

[4] $WACC = \left(\dfrac{E}{K}\right) \cdot y + \left(\dfrac{D}{K}\right) \cdot b(1 - X_{c})$,

with E = total equity, K = capital employed, y = expected costs or return on equity, D = total debt, b = expected costs or interests on debt, X_c = company tax rate (N.N. 2006k).

sales turnover, v_t^{Ssc} related sales costs withdrawn form the net sales turnover. Withdrawn distribution cost variables in the objective function comprise warehousing costs v_t^{lwc} and transportation costs v_t^{Ttc} as well as opportunity capital costs for local inventory v_t^{Icc} and transit inventory v_t^{Ttcc}. Production cost variables are the variable production costs v_t^{Pvpc} and specific costs for campaign change-overs v_t^{Pcc}. Finally, procurement costs v_t^{Sc} for raw materials and other products procured are withdrawn. All variables are defined per monthly period $\forall t \in T$.

Value Objective Function

The value objective function maximizes profit z. z sums up all considered monthly turnovers and costs on the planning base currency across all planning periods. Monthly values are discounted with a net present value factor to reflect the net present value of later planning periods compared to early planning periods in the tactical planning horizon of up to 12 months. One can argue that – unlike investment decisions in the value chain strategy with a horizon of several years – that the net present value is of less importance on a tactical level. However, given significant volumes and value decisions with the horizon of 12 months, it does make a difference if certain volumes and values are realized several periods earlier or later.

$$\max z = \sum_{t \in T} \left\{ \left[y_t^S \right. \right. \quad \text{+ net sales turnover} \tag{1}$$
$$-v_t^{Ssc} \quad \text{- sales costs}$$
$$-v_t^{lwc} \quad \text{- warehousing costs}$$
$$-v_t^{Ttc} \quad \text{- transportation costs}$$
$$-v_t^{Icc} \quad \text{- inventory capital costs}$$
$$-v_t^{Ttcc} \quad \text{- transit inventory capital costs}$$
$$-v_t^{Pvpc} \quad \text{- variable production costs}$$
$$-v_t^{Pcc} \quad \text{- change-over production costs}$$
$$\left. -v_t^{Bc} \right] \quad \text{- procurement costs}$$
$$\left. / \left[(1 + \frac{\varphi \cdot d_t}{365})^t \right] \right\} \quad \text{net present value factor}$$

The net present value factor of a period t considers the period-independent capital cost rate WACC[5] φ, the number of period days d_t and the total days per year. Sub-calculations of turnover and costs applying ex-

---

[5] Hence WACC is applied two times in the model: to calculate inventory capital costs and to discount period profits. This approach is used in payment plans, where interests for investments paid in each period are also discounted with an interest rate to calculate the net present value.

change rate factors are detailed in the respective sales, distribution, production and procurement subchapters.

The economic values in the objective function are treated and structured from an operations research perspective as variables calculated bottom up considering underlying volume decision variables. These result variables are integrated in the model to make the objective function more readable and easier to communicate to stakeholders such as planners, top-management, marketing and/or controlling.

In order to ensure the consistent view on the economic values compared to the controlling view, additional controlling indicators are calculated in a postprocessing phase.

Value Indicator Postprocessing

As postulated in value planning requirements, value planning results are structured by:

- the gross contribution margin defined as model parameter *profit I* z_t^I,
- earnings before interests and tax (EBIT) defined as model parameter *profit II* z_t^{II},
- and earnings before tax (EBT) defined as model parameter *profit III* z_t^{III}, $\forall t \in T$.

z_t^{III} requires considering also fixed production costs v_t^{Pfpc} deducted from z_t^{II}. The additional terminology of profit I, profit II and profit III is chosen, since calculated values do not cover all values included in EBIT or EBT e.g. additional administrative fixed costs. The indicators profit I, profit II and profit III rather are approximations of the official controlling indicators to support focused value chain planning decisions. The calculations of z_t^I, z_t^{II} and z_t^{III} are presented in eq. 2.

		(2)
y_t^S	+ net sales turnover	
$-v_t^{Ssc}$	- sales costs	
$-v_t^{Iwc}$	- warehousing costs	
$-v_t^{Ttc}$	- transportation costs	
$-v_t^{Pvpc}$	- variable production costs	
$-v_t^{Pcc}$	- change-over production costs	
$-v_t^{Sc}$	- procurement costs	
z_t^I	profit I	
$-v_t^{Pfpc}$	- fixed production costs	
z_t^{II}	profit II	
$-v_t^{Icc}$	- inventory capital costs	
$-v_t^{Ttcc}$	- transit inventory capital costs	
z_t^{III}	profit III	

Altogether, the model supports the company to optimize monthly profits based on volume decisions consistent as far as possible to company's profit and loss structures. Ideally, it is fully consistent with the company's profit and loss statement requiring integrating costs for support areas such as further overhead costs or capital costs on receivables. This would be a long-term vision, where further research should be directed to.

The value objective function includes also a relaxation concept introduced in the following.

Relaxation Concept

Relaxation of hard constraints is critical for optimization-based planning models used in industry practice with more than even 100,000 constraints and specifically for hard integer programming problems (Fisher 2004). Hard constraints set hard minimum and maximum boundaries for decision variables that have to be fulfilled. It may occur that no solution exists fitting all constraints at the same time. Planners have difficulties to identify manually constraints leading to infeasibility. Value chain planning model infeasibility is mainly caused by volume-related constraints of material flows e.g. by bounding sales quantities, inventories, transportation quantities, production and procurement quantities. Examples in literature for relaxation methods to e.g. transportation problems is presented by Klose/Lidke (2005)

Relaxation of hard boundaries enables to find a solution by adding continuous relaxation variables Δ^{min} and Δ^{max} to the hard constraints measuring the deviation to the minimum and maximum boundaries respectively. Relaxation for sales, inventory and transportation constraints is used, where minimum and maximum quantities have to be met. Relaxation, however, should only be possible, if no feasible solution exists. Therefore, relaxation will be penalized with very high costs in the objective function.

Relaxation Control Parameter

Three relaxation penalties are defined as control parameters: κ^θ is a penalty applied if the model can only be solved with relaxation. κ^θ is applied independently on how many constraints or quantities have to be relaxed. κ^ρ is a penalty per relaxed quantity unit and κ^ψ is a penalty per relaxed constraint. κ^ρ and κ^ψ are required to control the relaxation result: Either few constraints with high number of relaxed quantities or many constraints with few relaxed quantities are relaxation result options. The planner tends to have fewer constraints relaxed where boundaries have to be checked and adapted. On the other hand, the planner prefers to avoid extreme changes of boundaries in one case but adapt boundaries slightly in many cases. κ^ρ and κ^ψ support the planner to set these preferences for the relaxation case.

The penalties κ^θ, κ^ρ and κ^ψ have to be set high enough to make relaxation unattractive compared to the overall profit in order to ensure constraints being only relaxed in the case with no feasible solution. As alternative to a manual setting, these parameters can also be determined dynamically in a preprocessing phase, e.g. the total demand forecast turnover for κ^θ, the maximum demand forecast price per ton for κ^ρ and the maximum demand forecast turnover for κ^ψ.

Relaxation Variables

The relaxation variables are defined in the following: θ is the binary infeasibility switch variable. θ is 1 if the model needs to be relaxed or 0 if a feasible solution exists. ρ counts the total volume of relaxed volumes composed by the single relaxed sales volumes ρ^S, relaxed inventory volumes ρ^I and relaxed transportation volumes ρ^T. ψ counts the total number of relaxed constraints composed by the number of relaxed sales constraints ψ^S, the number of relaxed inventory constraints ψ^I and the number of relaxed transportation constraints ψ^T.

The relaxation variables focus on the front-end of the value chain in sales and distribution excluding production and procurement due to the commodity value chain characteristics with long production lead times and less flexibility in the backend. Of course, it is possible to have relaxation variables for all constraints and areas of the value chain. However, this would lead to higher complexity for the planner as well as longer solution times with more integer variables. Therefore, relaxation is kept limited.

Relaxation Terms and Constraints

The value objective function is extended by the relaxation terms penalizing the model infeasibility. The term (3) is withdrawn from the profit z in the objective function.

$-\theta \cdot \kappa^\theta$ Total model infeasibility penalty   (3)
$-\rho \cdot \kappa^\rho$ Total relaxation ton penalty
$-\psi \cdot \kappa^\psi$ Total relaxation constraint penalty

The binary model infeasibility variable is set to one, if the number of relaxation tons is not zero, meaning, there exists a case, where the model needs to be relaxed.

$$\theta^I \leq \rho \leq M \cdot \theta^I \qquad (4)$$

M is a sufficiently big number used in these logical constraints. M can be defined manually by the planner or determined dynamically in a preprocessing phase. M has to exceed the possible total sum of relaxation tons in sales, inventory and transportation in the model. Hence, the sum of demand forecast, maximum inventory and transportation quantity is a suitable value for M.

The relaxation ton counter ρ sums relaxation ton counters in sales, inventory and transportation. The individual relaxation ton counters are presented in more detail in the respective sales, transportation and inventory planning subchapters.

$$\rho = \rho^S + \rho^T + \rho^I \qquad (5)$$

The relaxation constraint counter ψ sums relaxation ton counters in sales, inventory and transportation. The individual relaxation ton counters are presented in more detail in the respective sales, transportation and inventory planning sections.

$$\psi = \psi^S + \psi^T + \psi^I \qquad (6)$$

Relaxation results are considered in postprocessing to determine overall model results.

Relaxation Postprocessing

Relaxation postprocessing determines the feasibility cases communicated to the planner as shown in table 22:

Table 22 Model feasibility cases

Feasibility case		Feasibility	θ^I
I.	Solution found without relaxation	Feasible	0
II.	Solution found only with relaxation	Feasible	1
III.	No solution found even with relaxation	Infeasible	0 or 1

Case I is the desired model result: all constraints are met, no relaxation is required. The model is solved and all value and volume results are processed and communicated to the planner. Case II requires relaxation to make the model feasible. Planning results do not represent a solution that is desired in reality, profit results are meaningless due to the relaxation penalties withdrawn from the objective value. Hence, the planner does not get the planning results but the list of relaxation cases that occurred. The list enables the planner to review input and control data of the specific constraint. Case III occurs, if the model is infeasible due to the constraints that have no relaxation variables. This case is the most difficult one for the planner to solve. A theoretical solution would be to relax all hard constraints; an 80-20-solution in practice is to use relaxation only for the infeasibility cases occurring most often. In practice, these cases can be found in sales, inventory and transportation. There, control boundaries can be easier adapted to the model and in practice be compared to production constraints like maximum and minimum throughputs or change-over rules.

Automated relaxation already is an integrated feature of newest version of optimization tools that a manually programmed relaxation concept would not be necessary. However, a problem-specific relaxation concept can control, which constraints are subject to relaxation that are suitable to be relaxed from a planners perspective. Therefore, a manually programmed relaxation concept still will be an important element even if optimization tools provide relaxation as standard feature.

5.3.2 Future Inventory Value Planning

Future capital costs considered in the objective function rely on future capital values – in this scope future inventory values. The planning of future inventory values in all future periods and in all network locations is a complex task. As described in the requirements, future inventory value is determined by the future product values of the products on stock. These product values change, if the included material costs of the product change, which is regularly the case due to volatile raw material prices. The task now is to calculate the *future* inventory value throughout the value chain network and product steps considering the raw material price forecast for the planning horizon. The problem is illustrated in fig. 57.

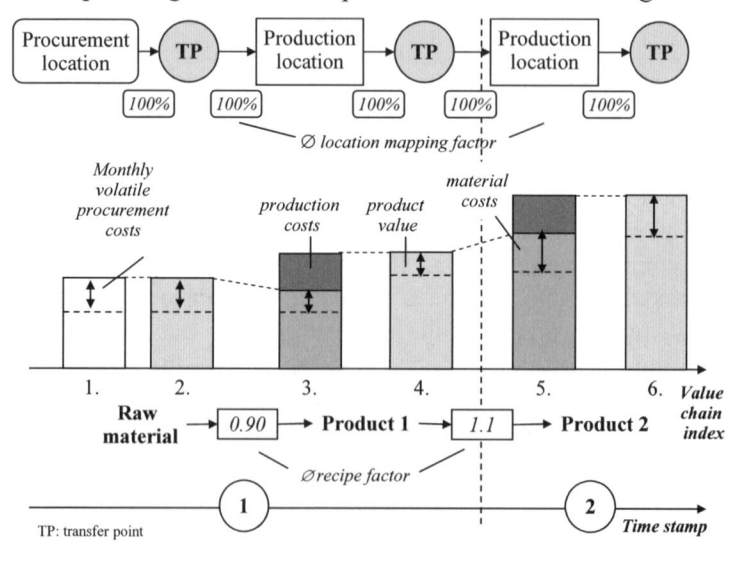

Fig. 57 Future inventory planning principle

A raw material is procured from a procurement location in the first period. It has a monthly volatile procurement price being also the inventory value at the transfer point of the respective product in the respective month. Subsequently, the raw material is used with produced products, in the example of fig. 57 in product 1 with a recipe factor of 0.9. In addition, production of product 1 requires additional production costs. Hence, the inventory value of the product 1 consists of the raw material costs based on the recipe and the production costs.

In a global value chain network, products are not always composed of materials from the same location. A location mapping factor defines, which share of material from a defined location is included in the subsequent product.

Besides, products in a global multi-stage network can have a lead time caused by transportation or inventory ranges until they are used in the subsequent steps. This lead time has to be considered when calculating future inventory values of products in the value chain network: a raw material product procured at a certain price can require several periods, until it is included in a final product sold in distant markets. Therefore, the inventory value change related to the procured raw material is effective certain periods after the raw material has been procured.

In order to reflect these lead times, the concept of a *timestamp* is introduced. *Timestamp* is used in computer science documenting the system time when a certain event or transaction occurs e.g. for logging events (N.N. 2007). In the context of future inventory value planning, the timestamp marks the period, when the first raw material has reached a certain stage in the value chain network included into a specific product. In the example illustrated in fig. 57, the raw material is processed in the same period to be converted into product 1. Therefore, all four value chain steps indexed from one to four occur in the same period and have the same timestamp one. Conversion into product 2, however, requires additional time caused by production lead times, safety inventory and/or transportation time, that the steps indexed with five and six have a time stamp of two. The timestamp reflects that the inventory value of product 2 is not based on the raw material costs from the same period but based on the raw material costs from the previous period in order to reflect the lead time. Consequently, value chain indices and timestamps are defined for all steps and can cover multiple periods reflecting that raw materials in a global complex multi-stage value chain network can take several months, until they are sold as part of a finished product to the market.

Summarizing, the product value consists of material costs and average production costs considering fixed and variable costs. Material costs are calculated based on the product value of ingoing products applying recipe and location mapping factors. The timestamp considers the time gap in the value chain between a raw material and the final product. The first raw material has a timestamp of 1. All subsequent products in the network have the same or a higher timestamp driven by time required for transportation or keeping inventory.

Index and Index Sets

The objective of future inventory planning is to determine the future material costs and product values for all product-location combinations in the value chain network defined in the index set $\{p,l\} \in I^{VC1}, \forall p \in P, l \in L$. The value chain index $\iota \in I$ is introduced indicating the position sequence of the respective value chain step – procurement, production or transportation. $\iota \in I$ has to be an ordered set that will determine the calculation sequence of the product values starting with the raw material procurement from a supplier in a procurement location and ending with the final sales location of the final finished product. A value chain step is defined for the index set $\{\iota, p_1, p_2, l_1, l_2\} \in I^{VC2}$ including $\iota \in I$, input and output product $p_1, p_2 \in P$ and the starting and ending location $l_1, l_2 \in L$. The subset of all target product-location combinations is created, for which material costs and product values are calculated, including the value chain index $\{\iota p_2 l_2\} \in I^{VC4}$, $\forall \iota \in I$, $\{p_2, l_2\} \in I^{VC1}$ required during the calculation and excluding the index $\{p_2 l_2\} \in I^{VC3}$, $\forall \{p_2, l_2\} \in I^{VC1}$.

Control Data

Future product values are determined by several control data. The average production cost rate $\phi^{VCpc}_{\iota p_1 p_2 l_1 l_2}$, the weighted average location mapping factor $\phi^{VClmf}_{\iota p_1 p_2 l_1 l_2}$ and the average recipe factor $\phi^{VCrf}_{\iota p_1 p_2 l_1 l_2}$, all defined $\forall \{\iota, p_1, p_2, l_1, l_2\} \in I^{VC2}$. All factors are illustrated with value domains in table 23.

Table 23 Value chain step cases

Value chain step		$\phi^{VCpc}_{\iota p_1 p_2 l_1 l_2}$	$\phi^{VClmf}_{\iota p_1 p_2 l_1 l_2}$	$\phi^{VCrf}_{\iota p_1 p_2 l_1 l_2}$
Procurement	($p_1=p_2$, $l_1=l_2$)	0	100%	100%
Transportation	($p_1=p_2$, $l_1 \neq l_2$)	0	≤ 100%	100%
Production	($p_1 \neq p_2$, $l_1=l_2$)	> 0	100%	> 0%

Procurement steps are initial steps in the value chain and require to link raw materials with the subsequent products. Procurement steps have no production costs. Since one raw material product is considered as p_1 and p_2 and one procurement location as l_1 and l_2, related factors are all 100%.

5.3 Value Planning

Transportation value chain steps have no production costs either. Product p_1 is equal to p_2, while l_1 and l_2 differ to reflect transportation between locations. Hence, recipe factors are 100% and the location mapping factor is 100% for single sourcing or lower than 100% for multi-sourcing.

Finally, production is determined by identical locations l_1 and l_2 and different products p_1 and p_2. Production steps have non-negative production costs and a non-negative recipe determining the share of p_1 in p_2.

Finally, the timestamp $\eta_{pl}^{VC}, \forall \{p,l\} \in I^{VC1}$ is defined to indicate the average lead time measured in planning periods compared to the first raw material initialized with timestamp 1. Increase of the timestamp is caused by transportation e.g. between different continents, holding inventories or the further production processing in the value chain.

Input and Calculated Data in Preprocessing

Input data are the starting material costs $c_{plt_1}^{VCmc}$ and product values $c_{plt_1}^{VCpv}$ for all product-location combinations $\{p,l\} \in I^{VC1}$ in the starting period $t_1 \in T$. These initial values are given in the location-specific currency. In addition, the latest procurement contract offer prices for $c_{plt}^{Bc} \ \forall \{p,l\} \in I^{B2}, t \in T$ are used as raw material value basis across all periods. All other values are determined in the calculation as illustrated in fig. 58.

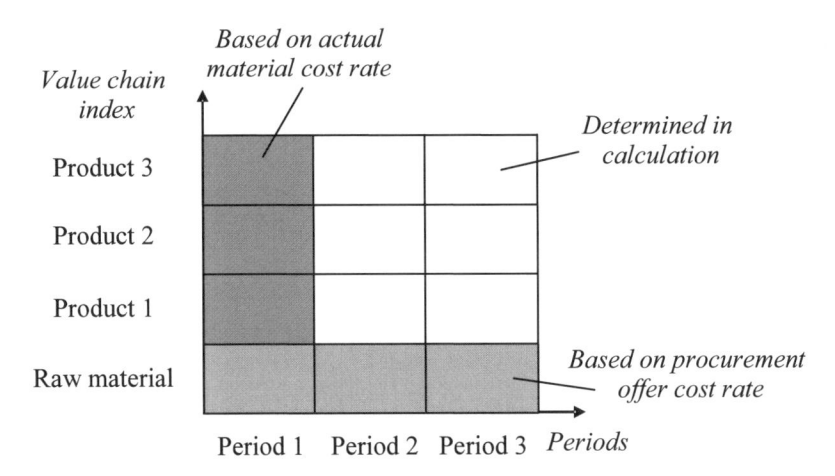

Fig. 58 Product value calculation structure

Calculated parameters in a preprocessing step are the indexed material costs $c_{tp_2l_2t}^{VCimc}$ and the indexed product value rate $c_{tp_2l_2t}^{VCipv}$, both defined $\forall \{t,p_2,l_2\} \in I^{VC4}, t \in T$ and the final material costs c_{plt}^{VCmc} and product value rate c_{plt}^{VCpv} $\forall \{p,l\} \in I^{VC1}$, $t \in T$. All parameters are measured in the location-specific currency.

Value Chain Preprocessing

The first step in preprocessing is the initialization of the material cost rate and product value rate with the actual values for the first period.

$$c_{plt}^{VCmc} = c_{plt_1}^{VCmc}, \ c_{plt}^{VCpv} = c_{plt_1}^{VCpv} \quad \forall \{p,l\} \in I^{VC1}, \ t = t_1 \in T \tag{7}$$

Secondly, all material costs and product values for raw materials are initialized with their contract procurement offer cost rate in the procurement locations.

$$c_{plt}^{VCmc} = c_{plt}^{Bc}, \ c_{plt}^{VCpv} = c_{plt}^{Bc} \qquad \forall \{p,l\} \in I^{B2}, \ t = t_1 \in T \tag{8}$$

Now, indexed material costs for all subsequent products and locations are calculated along the value chain within the indexed step sequence applying location mapping, recipe factors and product value rates as currency relations between starting location l_1 and ending location l_2.

$$c_{tp_2l_2t}^{VCimc} = \sum_{\{t,p_1,p_2,l_1,l_2\} \in I^{VC2}} \left(\phi_{tp_1p_2l_1l_2}^{VCrf} \cdot \phi_{tp_1p_2l_1l_2}^{VClmf} \cdot c_{plt-(\eta_{p_2l_2}^{VC} - \eta_{pl_1}^{VC})}^{VCpv} \cdot \frac{\chi_{l_1t}^L}{\chi_{l_2t}^L} \right) \tag{9}$$

$$\forall \{t,p_2,l_2\} \in I^{VC4}, \ t \in T$$

Then, indexed material costs can be used to calculate indexed *product value* rates for all other products and locations along the value chain within the index sequence summing up material costs and average production cost rates considering location exchange rate factor ratios.

$$c_{tp_2l_2t}^{VCipv} = c_{tp_2l_2t}^{VCimc} + \sum_{\{t,p_1,p_2,l_1,l_2\} \in I^{VC2}} \left(\phi_{ip_1p_2l_1l_2}^{VCpc} \cdot \frac{\chi_{l_1t}^L}{\chi_{l_2t}^L} \right) \tag{10}$$

$$\forall \{t,p_2,l_2\} \in I^{VC4}, t \in T$$

Final material cost rates and product value rates are determined based on the indexed material cost and product value rates. Multiple indexed material cost and product value rates occur, if cyclic material flows exist in the value chain. In order to apply index-independent cost and value rates in the model for future inventory planning, the maximum value and cost rates are determined for all products, locations and periods across all value chain steps i.

$$c_{plt}^{VCmc} = \max_{\{t,p,l\} \in I^{VC4}} \{c_{tplt}^{VCimc}\} \quad (11)$$

$$c_{plt}^{VCpv} = \max_{\{t,pl\} \in I^{VC4}} \{c_{tplt}^{VCipv}\}$$

$$\forall \{p,l\} \in I^{VC1}, t \in T$$

The product value rate for future inventory planning is equal to the product values at all transfer point locations.

$$c_{plt}^{Iv} = c_{plt}^{VCpv} \qquad \forall \{p,l\} \in I^{I2}, t \in T \quad (12)$$

Finally, future inventory planning is integrated in the overall optimization process as preprocessing phase. Alternatively, it can be run independently before the optimization to ensure usage of the most recent future product values for calculating capital costs in the optimization.

The presented approach for future inventory planning can be only a first proposal in the specific scope of this work with significant potential for further research.

5.4 Sales Planning

The sales planning model part comprises the integration of sales with supply decisions by volume and value as illustrated by fig. 20: the demand forecast for flexible spot volumes is no longer given to be fulfilled but has bid character to be cleared with an active sales quantity considering all forecasted bids by volumes and prices. The sales planning part formalizes this mechanism and presents an approach to integrate price-quantity functions and active sales decisions into the overall value chain planning model.

5.4.1 Sales Index Sets, Control and Input Data

Global demand and sales is planned for all valid global product-location combinations $\forall \{p,l\} \in I^{S2}$ of products $p \in P$ and sales locations $\{l\} \in I^{S1}$, $\forall l \in L$ for the medium-term planning horizon covering periods $t \in T$. The global demand forecasts are aggregated from a single customer level to sales location level provided by regional sales or marketing. Demand is aggregated from a single customer level to sales location level clustering multiple customers e.g. by a defined region such as EMEA or NAFTA. Based on the requirements as illustrated in fig. 46, the demand plan consists of the cumulated contract demand quantity q_{plt}^{Sc} and the average contract price p_{plt}^{Sc} as well as the cumulated spot demand quantity q_{plt}^{Ss}, the average spot price p_{plt}^{Ss} based on the individual customer forecasts defined for $\forall \{p,l\} \in I^{S2}$, $t \in T$.

The total turnover achieved from spot sales depends on the company's decisions on spot prices and sales quantities for each period and product-location combination. As explained in 0, the company receives demand quantity and price bids from its spot market customers. Clearly, a higher average price can be achieved if only best-price customer bids are accepted, i.e. spot sales quantities are reduced accordingly. The derivation of price-quantity functions is based on the following main assumptions:

- The relationship between spot sales price and spot sales quantity can be modeled as a linear function within the feasible minimum and maximum quantities defined by the management of the company. Of course, the price-quantity relationship could also be modeled using a non-linear function depending on the actual price-quantity-bids the company receives. In this work the linear function showed a sufficient statistical fit based on the real data provided by the industry case.
- External factors affecting the spot demand quantity e.g. competitor actions, are not considered, i.e. spot sales demand only depends on spot sales price for each period and product-location combination.

The relationship between spot sales price and spot sales quantity is expressed by the period-specific parameter spot demand price elasticity ε_{plt}^{Ss} also defined $\forall \{p,l\} \in I^{S2}$, $t \in T$. The spot demand elasticity ε_{plt}^{Ss} typically is not directly forecasted but requires further analysis. An example to determine ε_{plt}^{Ss} is presented in section 5.4.2.

The respective spot price-quantity with the average spot sales price p_{plt}^{Ss*} and spot sales quantity x_{plt}^{Ss} and the spot turnover curve with spot demand turnover y_{plt}^{Ss} and spot sales turnover y_{plt}^{Ss*}, all defined $\forall \{p,l\} \in I^{S2}$, $t \in T$ are illustrated in fig. 59.

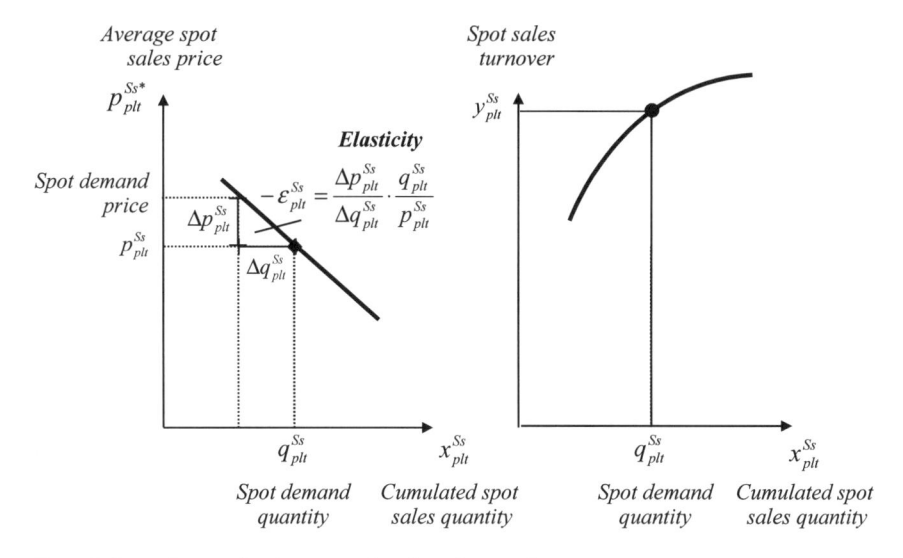

Fig. 59 Spot demand price-quantity function and turnover curve

The left curve reflects the effect of sales decisions on average prices: spot sales quantities lower than the spot demand quantity lead to average prices higher than the average forecasted price for an elasticity > 0 as illustrated in the sales planning requirements in figure 38.

The price-quantity and turnover functions of the form $p(x) = Ax + B$ for spot sales are derived from the spot demand quantity q_{plt}^{Ss}, the spot demand price p_{plt}^{Ss} and the elasticity ε_{plt}^{Ss}.

$$p_{plt}^{Ss*}(x_{plt}^{Ss}) = A \cdot x_{plt}^{Ss} + B \tag{13}$$

$$\text{given } A = \frac{\left(p_{plt}^{Ss*} - p_{plt}^{Ss}\right)}{\left(x_{plt}^{Ss} - q_{plt}^{Ss}\right)} \text{ and } -\varepsilon_{plt}^{Ss} = \frac{\left(p_{plt}^{Ss*} - p_{plt}^{Ss}\right)}{\left(x_{plt}^{Ss} - q_{plt}^{Ss}\right)} \cdot \frac{q_{plt}^{Ss}}{p_{plt}^{Ss}}$$

$$\Rightarrow A = -\varepsilon_{plt}^{Ss} \cdot \frac{p_{plt}^{Ss}}{q_{plt}^{Ss}}$$

$$\text{given } p_{plt}^{Ss*}(q_{plt}^{Ss}) \Rightarrow p_{plt}^{Ss} = -\varepsilon_{plt}^{Ss} \cdot \frac{p_{plt}^{Ss}}{q_{plt}^{Ss}} q_{plt}^{Ss} + B$$

$$\Rightarrow B = (1 + \varepsilon_{plt}^{Ss}) \cdot p_{plt}^{Ss}$$

$$\text{then } p_{plt}^{Ss*}(x_{plt}^{Ss}) = -\varepsilon_{plt}^{Ss} \cdot \frac{p_{plt}^{Ss}}{q_{plt}^{Ss}} \cdot x_{plt}^{Ss} + (1 + \varepsilon_{plt}^{Ss}) \cdot p_{plt}^{Ss}$$

$$\forall \{p,l\} \in I^{S2}, t \in T$$

148 5 Global Value Chain Planning Model

The respective turnover function $y^{Ss}_{plt}(x^{Ss}_{plt})$ can be derived using the price-quantity function $p^{Ss*}_{plt}(x^{Ss}_{plt})$.

$$y^{Ss}_{plt}(x^{Ss}_{plt}) = p^{Ss*}_{plt}(x^{Ss}_{plt}) \cdot x^{Ss}_{plt} \qquad (14)$$

$$\text{with } p^{Ss*}_{plt}(x^{Ss}_{plt}) = -\varepsilon^{Ss}_{plt} \cdot \frac{p^{Ss}_{plt}}{q^{Ss}_{plt}} \cdot x^{Ss}_{plt} + (1+\varepsilon^{Ss}_{plt}) \cdot p^{Ss}_{plt}$$

$$\Rightarrow y^{Ss}_{plt}(x^{Ss}_{plt}) = -\varepsilon^{Ss}_{plt} \cdot \frac{p^{Ss}_{plt}}{q^{Ss}_{plt}} \cdot (x^{Ss}_{plt})^2 + (1+\varepsilon^{Ds}_{plt}) \cdot p^{Ss}_{plt} \cdot x^{Ss}_{plt}$$

$$\forall \{p,l\} \in I^{S2}, \, t \in T$$

The turnover function is used in the model when optimizing profit including the respective turnover.

Sales Control Data

Sales control data are managed by the planner executing business rules defined in the sales strategy. The sales strategy has to define for a sales location – e.g. a certain market – the minimum and maximum spot sales quantity x^{Ss}_{plt} to be reached. These boundaries should reflect the respective business strategy e.g. to ensure minimum sales required to stay in the market and to ensure continuous customer relations or maximum sales possible reflecting opportunities to push additional quantities into the market in the case of very dynamic growth e.g. experienced in specific regions and countries such as China. Contract sales is fixed and fulfilled as demanded. Spot sales flexibility is defined with relative and absolute boundaries: $R^{Ss\,min\,s}_{pl}$ and $R^{Ss\,max\,s}_{pl}$ are the minimum respective maximum shares of the spot demand plan that have to be fulfilled. $R^{Ss\,min\,a}_{pl}$ and $R^{Ss\,max\,a}_{pl}$ are the absolute spot sales boundaries. All boundaries are defined $\forall\{p,l\} \in I^{S2}$ and applied across all planning periods.

5.4.2 Price Elasticity Analysis

Spot demand price elasticity is not a forecasted parameter but needs to be derived analytically. As specified in the value chain characteristics in subchapter 3.2 the company does not have a monopoly in the market and sales decision of the company do not influence the market price. Therefore, elasticity is not determined from a macro-economic perspective considering market prices but from a micro-economic perspective analyzing the specific spot demand forecasts the company receives. Table 24 provides the detailed steps of the algorithm for determining elasticity and the price-quantity functions for spot sales demand using a simple numerical example.

Table 24 Algorithm to determine price-quantity function

Algorithmic steps	Parameter	Unit	A	B	C	D
1. List individual customer clusters $k \in K$ with spot demand quantity q_{pkt}^{Ssk} and price forecast p_{pkt}^{Ssk}	Quantity	[t]	100	200	100	200
	Price	[€/t]	100	90	80	70
2. Sort price forecasts in non-increasing order giving ranks $f \in F$	Rank		1.	2.	3.	4.
3. Determine cumulated spot demand quantity $\hat{q}_{pkft}^{Ssk}$ for rank $f \in F$	Σ Quantity	[t]	100	300	400	600
4. Determine average spot demand price $\bar{p}_{pkft}^{Ssk}$ for rank $f \in F$	Ø Price	[€/t]	100	93.3	90	83.3
5. Determine cumulated quantity share of rank $f \in F$	Δ Quantity	[%]	17	50	67	100
6. Determine average price ratio $\left(\bar{p}_{pkft}^{Ssk}\right):\left(p_{plt}^{Ss}\right)$ of rank $f \in F$	Δ Price	[%]	120	112	108	100
7. Linear regression for price ratios with respect to quantity shares	Regression			y = -0.24 x + 1.24 R^2=1.00		
8. Determine price elasticity	Elasticity			$\varepsilon = 0.2407$		

Given are spot demand quantity q_{pkt}^{Ssk} and price forecast p_{pkt}^{Ssk} for product and customer cluster combinations grouped into the index set $\{p,k\} \in I^{S4}$, $\forall p \in P$, $k \in K$ with clusters of customers $k \in K$ in the sales location $l \in I^{S1}$ (step 1)[6]. Next, all price forecasts p_{pkt}^{Ssk} are sorted in non-increasing order giving ranks $f = 1,..,F, f \in F$ (step 2). Then the cumulated spot demand quantity $\hat{q}_{pkft}^{Ssk}$ for each rank $f \in F$ is determined (step 3). In step 4, the corresponding average spot demand price forecast for cumulated

---

[6] In practice, the smallest customers are not planned individually but are grouped into a cluster e.g. called "other customers"; therefore, single customer forecasts are considered on a customer cluster level, where a large customer forms a single customer cluster and small customers are grouped.

sales quantity $\hat{q}_{pkft}^{Ssk}$, $\forall \{p,k\} \in I^{S4}$, $f \in F$, $t \in T$ is determined for each rank starting with the best price assuming only this customer cluster should be served. In the following steps 5 and 6, the cumulated quantity share $(\hat{q}_{pkft}^{Ssk}):(q_{plt}^{Ssk})$ and the average price ratio $(\overline{p}_{pkft}^{Ssk}):(p_{plt}^{Ss})$ of each rank $f = 1,..,F, f \in F$ are determined. In step 7 a linear regression for price ratios with respect to quantity shares is carried out giving the price-quantity function. Finally, the spot demand elasticity is obtained as the negative slope of the regression function (step 8).

This proposed algorithm requires a sufficient number of individual customer bids or forecasts within one sales location and thus relies on effective support by the local sales and marketing units. If the number of price-quantity bids is not sufficient and the regression is not accurate enough, elasticities cannot be directly used for decision making. In this case, elasticity is assumed to be 0 meaning no price effects are included in the model and calculated profits are lower and more cautious than in reality. If all customers have the same spot prices, the average price is equal to the individual prices and the elasticity is equal to 0 meaning that no average price effects occur in case of volume reductions.

The elasticity is derived by a linear regression as illustrated in fig. 60 using the example above. If all customers have the same spot prices, the average price is equal to the individual prices and the elasticity is equal to 0 meaning that no average price effects occur in case of volume changes.

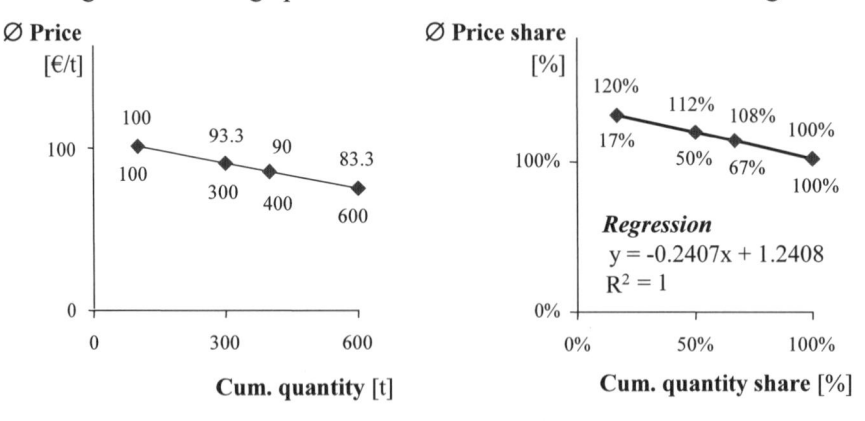

Fig. 60 Elasticity analysis example

The gradient g_{plt}^{Ss} $\forall \{p,l\} \in I^{S2}$, $t \in T$ of the approximated price-quantity share function represents the approximated negative elasticity. The gradient is determined by the spot demand quantity q_{plt}^{Ss}, the spot demand price

p_{plt}^{Sc}, the spot sales quantity x_{plt}^{Ss} and the spot sales price p_{plt}^{Ss*}, which will be used later as decision variables in the model defined $\forall \{p,l\} \in I^{S2}$, $t \in T$.

$$g_{plt}^{Ss} = \left(\frac{p_{plt}^{Ss*}}{p_{plt}^{Ss}} - \frac{p_{plt}^{Ss}}{p_{plt}^{Ss}} \right) : \left(\frac{x_{plt}^{Ss}}{q_{plt}^{Ss}} - \frac{q_{plt}^{Ss}}{q_{plt}^{Ss}} \right) \qquad \forall \{p,l\} \in I^{S2}, t \in T \qquad (15)$$

$$= \frac{p_{plt}^{Ss*} - p_{plt}^{Ss}}{x_{plt}^{Ss} - q_{plt}^{Ss}} \cdot \frac{q_{plt}^{Ss}}{p_{plt}^{Ss}} = -\varepsilon_{plt}^{Ss}$$

The analysis method requires a sufficient number of individual customer cluster demands within one sales location and thus relies on effective support by the regional sales and marketing units. In the investigated application from the chemical industry, it could be observed that price elasticity were volatile over time and ranked mainly between 0.1 and 0.5 depending on products and locations as it will be presented in the case evaluation in chapter 6 in more detail. The linear regression is applicable but not always sufficient in terms of number of customer clusters considered and statistical correlation reflected by correlation coefficient R^2. Alternatively, a quadratic regression of the sales turnover curve could be applied. This concept, however, does not create the same basis for understanding in the sales and marketing organization of the company since elasticity is the parameter known in sales and marketing to discuss and understand price-quantity dynamics in the market rather than discussing quadratic regression parameters that cannot be well understood and translated into direct price-quantity-relations.

5.4.3 Turnover Approximation Preprocessing

Since both spot price and quantity are modeled as variables, the resulting optimization problem of maximizing turnover is quadratic. In the following, we show how a linear approximation of the turnover function can be achieved (see also Habla 2006). This approach is based on the concavity property of the turnover function and the limited region of sales quantity flexibility to be considered. Approximation parameters are determined in a preprocessing phase based on the sales input and control data. The preprocessing is structured in two phases as shown in table 25:

Table 25 Turnover approximation preprocessing phases and steps

Phase I: Determine spot sales boundaries	Step 1: Determine theoretic maximum spot sales quantity
	Step 2: Determine overall spot sales quantity boundaries
Phase II: Determine turnover approximation parameters	Step 3: Determine partial quantity points
	Step 4: Determine partial spot sales quantities
	Step 5: Determine partial spot sales turnovers
	Step 6: Determine partial spot turnover gradients

Phase I: Determine Spot Sales Boundaries

Effective minimum spot sales quantity $X_{plt}^{Ss\,min}$ and maximum spot sales quantity $X_{plt}^{Ss\,max}$ $\forall \{p,l\} \in I^{S2}$, $t \in T$ have to be determined in advance comparing the relative and absolute minimum and maximum spot sales boundaries and the theoretic maximum spot sales quantity $q_{plt}^{Ss\,max}$, $\forall \{p,l\} \in I^{S2}$, $t \in T$ of the price-quantity function.

Step 1: Determine Theoretic Maximum Spot Sales Quantity

The theoretic maximum spot sales quantity $q_{plt}^{Ss\,max}$ is zero point of the price-quantity function.

$$p_{plst}^{Ss}(x_{plt}^{Ss}) = -\varepsilon_{plt}^{Ss} \cdot \frac{p_{plt}^{Ss}}{q_{plt}^{Ss}} \cdot x_{plt}^{Ss} + (1+\varepsilon_{plt}^{Ss}) \cdot p_{plt}^{Ss} \qquad (16)$$

$$\Rightarrow p_{plst}^{Ss}(q_{plt}^{Ss\,max}) \stackrel{!}{=} 0 \Leftrightarrow q_{plt}^{Ss\,max} = \frac{1+\varepsilon_{plt}^{Ss}}{\varepsilon_{plt}^{Ss}} \cdot q_{plt}^{Ss}$$

$$\forall \{p,l\} \in I^{S2}, \ s \in S, \ t \in T$$

The maximum spot sales quantity assumes that the sales price can be reduced to zero. This is of course a theoretic assumption rarely found in practice. From a model perspective it is important to determine the zero point in order to evaluate, if defined absolute and relates sales quantity boundaries are still associated with positive sales prices.

Step 2: Determine Overall Spot Sales Quantity Boundaries

The minimum spot sales quantity is the lower sales boundary. Since this boundary can be defined as relative and/or absolute limit, the effective limit applied is the maximum of the absolute minimum sales quantity and the minimum spot sales quantity share applied on the spot demand.

$$X_{plt}^{Ss\,min} = \max\{R_{plt}^{Ss\,min\,a}, R_{plt}^{Ss\,min\,s} \cdot q_{plt}^{Ss}\} \quad \forall \{p,l\} \in I^{S2}, \ t \in T \qquad (17)$$

5.4 Sales Planning

The maximum spot sales quantity is the minimum of absolute maximum sales quantity, the maximum sales share applied on the spot demand and theoretic maximum sales quantity.

$$X_{plt}^{Ss\,max} = \min\{R_{plt}^{Ss\,max\,a}, R_{plt}^{Ss\,max\,s} \cdot q_{plt}^{Ss}, q_{plt}^{Ss\,max}\} \quad (18)$$

$$\forall \{p,l\} \in I^{S2},\ t \in T$$

Minimum and maximum spot sales quantities by period are the effective boundaries applied in the optimization as illustrated in fig. 61.

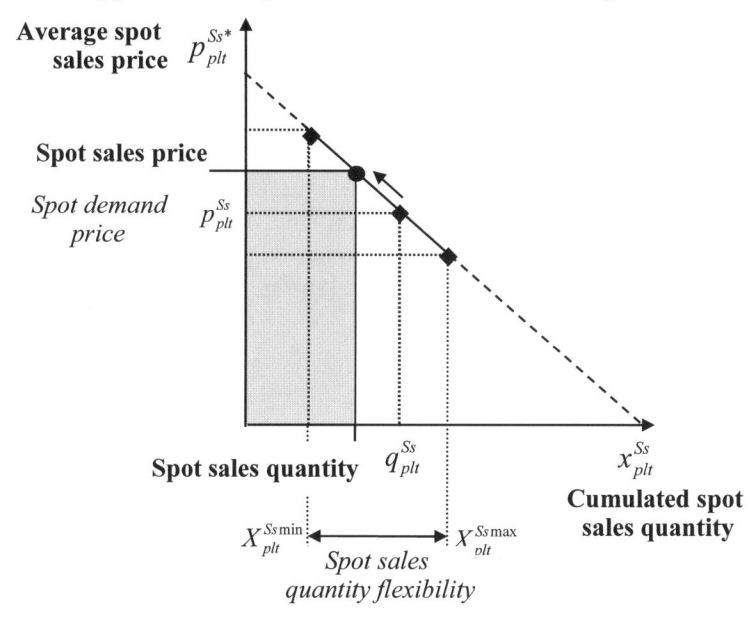

Fig. 61 Price-quantity function with sales flexibility boundaries

Spot sales quantity decisions upon the demand quantity lead to price changes within the limited interval of sales flexibility between $X_{plt}^{Ss\,min}$ and $X_{plt}^{Ss\,max}$. Summarizing, the company has a certain spot sales flexibility allowing the company to optimize volumes and values in the value chain specifically in production with this given flexibility.

Phase II: Determine Turnover Approximation Parameters

The turnover approximation approach illustrated in figure 54 is based on partial quantity points subdividing the turnover curve into multiple sections, for which turnover is linearly approximated. As explained in the previous section, $X_{plt}^{Ss\,min}$ and $X_{plt}^{Ss\,max}$ are given as management-defined control parameters, which indicate the minimum and maximum spot sales that needs to be considered, respectively. The set of partial quantity points $i \in N$ has four elements by default: 0, $X_{plt}^{Ss\,min}$, q_{plt}^{Ss} and $X_{plt}^{Ss\,max}$, where q_{plt}^{Ss} indicates the total quantity of all forecasted customer quantities. The algorithm for determining the price-quantity function is described in section 0. Note that $X_{plt}^{Ss\,max} > q_{plt}^{Ss}$ expresses the possibility of gaining additional spot market quantity at decreased sales prices. In the case of $X_{plt}^{Ss\,max} = q_{plt}^{Ss}$ only forecasted demand is considered. The three non-zero points are fixed and indexed by i^{min} for $X_{plt}^{Ss\,min}$, i^{mid} for q_{plt}^{Ss} and i^{max} for $X_{plt}^{Ss\,max}$ with $i^{min}, i^{mid}, i^{max} \in N$. The approximation can be improved by adding additional partial quantity points i^+ between i^{min}, i^{mid} and i^{mid}, i^{max}, respectively. Partial spot sales quantities $\tilde{q}_{iplt}^{Ss}$ $\forall \{p,l\} \in I^{S2}$, $t \in T$ are determined at each partial quantity point $i \in N$. Corresponding partial spot turnovers $\tilde{y}_{iplt}^{Ss}$, $\forall \{p,l\} \in I^{S2}$, $i \in N$, $t \in T$ are calculated for each partial spot sales quantity $\tilde{q}_{iplt}^{Ss}$ using the exact turnover function. Partial spot turnover $\tilde{y}_{jplt}^{Ss}$ in the partial quantity section $j = 1..N-1$ between two partial quantity points $i \in N$ is approximated based on the turnover gradient τ_{jplt}^{Ss}, $\forall \{p,l\} \in I^{S2}$, $j = 1..N-1$, $t \in T$ of the linear connection. The principle of linear turnover approximation is illustrated in fig. 62

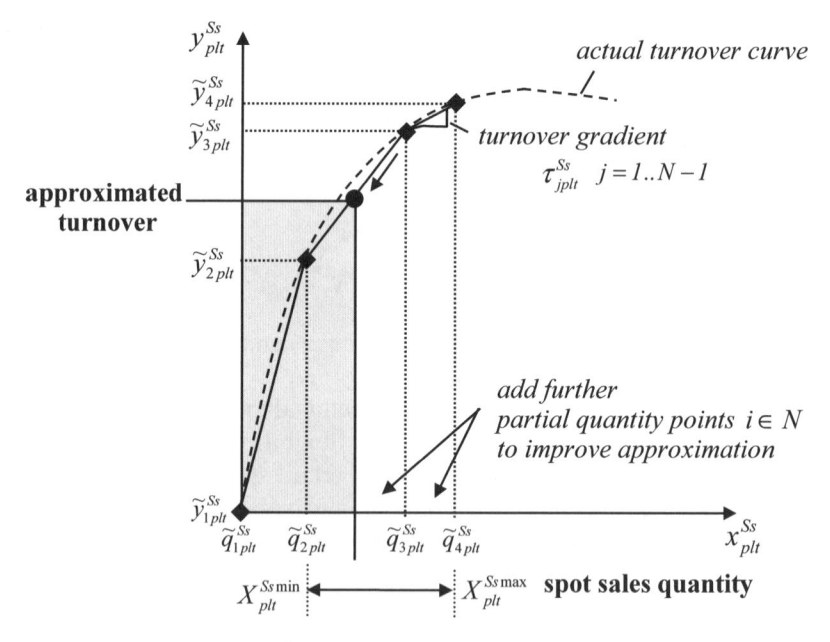

Fig. 62 Piecewise linear turnover approximation approach

Since the turnover curve is concave[7] and the piecewise linear turnover gradients decrease monotonically, no integer variables are required to decide, which partial quantity section is filled first. The objective function to maximize turnover will ensure to fill the partial quantity sections from left to right[8].

Step 3: Determine Partial Quantity Points

The partial quantity points i^{min}, i^{mid}, i^{max} depend on the number of additional partial quantity points i^{add} added to improve the approximation accuracy.

$$i^{min} = 2, \; i^{max} = 4 + (2 \cdot i^{add}), \; i^{mid} = \frac{(i^{min} + i^{max})}{2} \quad (19)$$

$$\forall i^{min}, \; i^{mid}, \; i^{max} \in N$$

The set of partial quantity points are now defined as $i \in N : \{1, i^{min}, ..., i^{mid}, ..., i^{max}\}$.

Step 4: Determine Partial Spot Sales Quantities

Partial spot sales quantities are defined first for the partial quantity points $i = 1$, i^{min}, i^{mid} and i^{max} as cornerstones for the turnover approximation. The zero point, minimum and maximum sales boundaries as well as the spot demand forecast are assigned as partial spot sales quantities to these cornerstones.

$$i = 1: \; \tilde{q}^{Ss}_{iplt} = 0, \; i = i^{min}: \; \tilde{q}^{Ss}_{iplt} = X^{Ss\,min}_{plt} \quad (20)$$

$$i = i^{mid}: \; \tilde{q}^{Ss}_{iplt} = q^{Ss}_{plt}, \; i = i^{max}: \; \tilde{q}^{Ss}_{iplt} = X^{Ss\,max}_{plt}$$

$$\forall \{p, l\} \in I^{S2}, \; i \in N, \; t \in T$$

If further partial quantity points are added, additional partial sales quantities are evenly determined between minimum, demanded and maximum spot sales quantity.

$$i^{min} < i < i^{mid}: \tilde{q}^{Ss}_{iplt} = X^{Ss\,min}_{plt} + \frac{(i - i^{min})}{(i^{mid} - i^{min})} \cdot (q^{Ss}_{plt} - X^{Ss\,min}_{plt}) \quad (21)$$

---

[7] A function f on the interval C is concave, if
$$f\left(\frac{x+y}{2}\right) \geq \frac{f(x) + f(y)}{2}, \; \forall x, y \in C.$$

[8] For a review on linear approximation for non-linear functions see Kallrath (2002b), p. 125.

$$i^{mid} < i < i^{max} : \tilde{q}_{iplt}^{Ss} = q_{plt}^{Ss} + \frac{(i - i^{mid})}{(i^{max} - i^{mid})} \cdot (X_{plt}^{Ss\,max} - q_{plt}^{Ss})$$

$$\forall \{p,l\} \in I^{S2}, \; i \in N, \; t \in T$$

Now, partial spot sales quantities are defined for all partial quantity points on the x-axis of the turnover approximation, and the partial turnovers are determined for all partial spot sales quantities.

Step 5: Determine Partial Spot Sales Turnovers

Partial spot sales turnovers at the partial quantity points are determined using the exact turnover function.

$$\tilde{y}_{iplt}^{Ss}(x_{plt}^{Ss}) = -\varepsilon_{plt}^{Ss} \cdot \frac{p_{plt}^{Ss}}{q_{plt}^{Ss}} \cdot \tilde{x}_{iplt}^{Ss\,2} + (1 + \varepsilon_{plt}^{Ss}) \cdot p_{plt}^{Ss} \cdot \tilde{x}_{iplt}^{Ss} \qquad (22)$$

$$\forall \{p,l\} \in I^{S2}, \; i \in N, \; t \in T$$

In case of constant prices with $\varepsilon_{plt}^{Ss} = 0$, the turnover function is simplified to the term $p_{plt}^{Ss} \cdot \tilde{x}_{iplt}^{Ss}$ being a linear optimization problem, since only $\tilde{x}_{iplt}^{Ss}$ is variable.

Step 6: Determine Partial Spot Sales Turnover Gradients

Turnover gradients are calculated for the linear connection of the sections between two neighbored partial quantity points. The special case of a section size 0 has to be handled.

$$\tilde{q}_{iplt}^{Ss} - \tilde{q}_{i-1,plt}^{Ss} = 0 : \tau_{jplt}^{Ss} = 0 \qquad (23)$$

$$\tilde{q}_{iplt}^{Ss} - \tilde{q}_{i-1,plt}^{Ss} > 0 : \tau_{jplt}^{Ss} = \frac{\tilde{y}_{iplt}^{Ss} - \tilde{y}_{i-1,plt}^{Ss}}{\tilde{q}_{iplt}^{Ss} - \tilde{q}_{i-1,plt}^{Ss}}$$

$$\forall \{p,l\} \in I^{S2}, \; i > 1, \; i \in N, \; j = 1..N-1, \; t \in T$$

Now, the turnover approximation based on partial quantity points, partial spot sales quantities and partial spot turnover is fully defined. Concluding, thanks to this preprocessing phase, the spot sales parameters used in the model can be reduced to only four parameters:

- the minimum and maximum spot sales boundaries $X_{plt}^{Ss\,min}$ and $X_{plt}^{Ss\,max}$,
- the partial spot sales quantities $\tilde{q}_{iplt}^{Ss}$ and
- the turnover gradient τ_{jplt}^{Ss}.

5.4.4 Sales Decision Variables and Constraints

Sales decision variables are the spot sales quantity x_{plt}^{Ss}, the spot sales turnover y_{plt}^{Ss} and the respective total sales quantity x_{plt}^{S}, $\forall \{p,l\} \in I^{S2}$, $t \in T$. Additionally, the partial spot sales quantities $\tilde{x}_{jplt}^{Ss}$ and the approximated partial spot sales turnovers $\tilde{y}_{jplt}^{Ss}$ are required for turnover approximation $\forall \{p,l\} \in I^{S2}$, $j = 1..N-1$, $t \in T$. Relaxation variables $\Delta_{plt}^{S\min}$ and $\Delta_{plt}^{S\max}$, $\forall \{p,l\} \in I^{S2}$, $t \in T$ are used for hard constraints to relax them in case of model infeasibility as introduced in the relaxation concept in 0. They represent the sales minimum relaxation quantity and sales maximum relaxation quantity required to open the hard constraints. The binary sales relaxation case variable δ_{plt}^{S}, $\forall \{p,l\} \in I^{S2}$, $t \in T$ is 1 if the related constraint is relaxed, otherwise it is 0. δ_{plt}^{S} is used to count all sales relaxation cases.

Sales constraints limit partial and total spot sales quantities and calculate sales quantities and turnover. Partial spot sales quantities have to fit into the respective section between partial spot sales quantities.

$$\tilde{x}_{jplt}^{Ss} \leq \tilde{q}_{iplt}^{Ss} - \tilde{q}_{i-1,plt}^{Ss} \qquad \forall \{p,l\} \in I^{S2}, \, i \in N, \, z_o, \qquad (24)$$
$$j = 1,..,N-1, \, j = i-1, \, t \in T$$

The total spot sales quantity is the sum of the partial spot sales quantities.

$$x_{plt}^{Ss} = \sum_{j=1}^{N-1} \tilde{x}_{jplt}^{Ss} \qquad \forall \{p,l\} \in I^{S2}, \, t \in T \qquad (25)$$

The total spot sales quantity is limited through the minimum and maximum boundaries including relaxation variables.

$$X_{plt}^{Ss\min} - \Delta_{plt}^{S\min} \leq x_{plt}^{Ss} \leq X_{plt}^{Ss\max} + \Delta_{plt}^{S\max} \qquad \forall \{p,l\} \in I^{S2}, \, t \in T \qquad (26)$$

A constraint is counted as relaxation case with δ_{plt}^{S} equal to 1, if constraint's minimum or maximum boundaries are relaxed and relaxation variables are not 0.

$$\delta_{plt}^{S} \leq \Delta_{plt}^{S\min} + \Delta_{plt}^{S\max} \leq M \cdot \delta_{plt}^{S} \qquad \forall \{p,l\} \in I^{S2}, \, t \in T \qquad (27)$$

The sales relaxation ton counter ρ^{S} sums up all positive and negative relaxation quantities.

$$\rho^S = \sum_{t \in T} \sum_{\{p,l\} \in I^{S2}} \Delta_{plt}^{S\max} + \Delta_{plt}^{S\min} \tag{28}$$

The sales relaxation constraint counter ψ^S sums up all binary variables δ_{plt}^S.

$$\psi^S = \sum_{t \in T} \sum_{\{p,l\} \in I^{S2}} \delta_{plt}^S \tag{29}$$

The total sales quantity is the sum of contract sales and spot sales quantity.

$$x_{plt}^S = x_{plt}^{Ss} + q_{plt}^{Sc} \qquad \forall \{p,l\} \in I^{S2}, \, t \in T \tag{30}$$

Partial spot sales turnover is the product of partial quantity and partial turnover gradient.

$$\tilde{y}_{jplt}^{Ss} = \tau_{jplt}^{Ss} \cdot \tilde{x}_{jplt}^{Ss} \qquad \forall \{p,l\} \in I^{S2}, \, j=1,..,N-1, \, t \in T \tag{31}$$

The spot sales turnover is the sum of the partial spot sales turnovers.

$$y_{plt}^{Ss} = \sum_{j=1}^{N-1} \tilde{y}_{jplt}^{Ss} \qquad \forall \{p,l\} \in I^{S2}, \, t \in T \tag{32}$$

The total sales turnover is the sum of contract turnover and spot sales turnover.

$$y_{plt}^S = y_{plt}^{Ss} + \left(q_{plt}^{Sc} \cdot p_{plt}^{Sc} \right) \qquad \forall \{p,l\} \in I^{S2}, \, t \in T \tag{33}$$

Altogether, the constraints decide spot sales quantity and turnover while contract sales quantity and turnover are fulfilled as demanded.

The total net sales turnover y_t^S per period sums spot sales turnover y_{plt}^{Ss} as well as contract turnover by product and location $\forall p \in P, l \in L$ multiplied with the location exchange rate factor χ_{lt}^L of the period.

$$y_t^S = \sum_{\{p,l\} \in I^{S2}} \left[y_{plt}^{Ss} + (q_{plt}^{Sc} \cdot p_{plt}^{Sc}) \right] \cdot \chi_{lt}^L \qquad \forall t \in T \tag{34}$$

Sales costs in the base currency are calculated applying the sales cost share rate on sales turnover.

$$v_t^{Ssc} = \sum_{\{p,l\} \in I^{S2}} \left[y_{plt}^{Ss} + (q_{plt}^{Sc} \cdot p_{plt}^{Sc}) \right] \cdot c_{pl}^{Ssc} \cdot \chi_{lt}^L \qquad \forall t \in T \tag{35}$$

5.4.5 Sales Indicator Postprocessing

Sales indicators are calculated after the optimization in a postprocessing phase. Sales indicators focus on decision support for the planner to quickly analyze the overall sales planning result and to specifically evaluate the quality of the turnover approximation results.

Turnover approximation evaluation compares approximated spot sales turnover $y_{plt}^{SsApprx}$ with the exact calculated spot sales turnover y_{plt}^{SsCalc} for the same spot sales quantity decision $\forall \{p,l\} \in I^{S2}$, $t \in T$. The approximated spot sales turnover is equal to the spot sales turnover determined in the model.

$$y_{plt}^{SsApprx} = y_{plt}^{Ss}, \qquad \forall \{p,l\} \in I^{S2}, t \in T \qquad (36)$$

The exact spot sales turnover is determined using the spot sales quantity x_{plt}^{Ss} within the exact turnover function.

$$y_{plt}^{SsCalc} = -\varepsilon_{plt}^{Ss} \cdot \frac{p_{plt}^{Ss}}{q_{plt}^{Ss}} \cdot (x_{plt}^{Ss})^2 + (1+\varepsilon_{plt}^{Ss}) \cdot p_{plt}^{Ss} \cdot x_{plt}^{Ss} \qquad (37)$$

$$\forall \{p,l\} \in I^{S2}, t \in T$$

Two accuracy indicators are defined:

- XTG^S as maximum relative turnover gap
- TTG^S as total relative turnover gap.

XTG^S determines the maximum turnover gap between the approximated turnover and the calculated turnover across all product-locations and period combinations.

$$XTG^S = \max_{\{p,l\} \in I^{S2}, t \in T} \{ \frac{y_{plt}^{SsCalc} - y_{plt}^{SsApprx}}{y_{plt}^{SsCalc}} \} \qquad (38)$$

XTG^S analyzes turnover gaps for each individual business by product and location and shows the case with the highest gap between actual and approximated turnover.

TTG^S compares the total approximated turnover with the total calculated turnover to identify the overall error.

$$TTG^S = \frac{\sum_{\{p,l\} \in I^{S2}, t \in T} y_{plt}^{SsCalc} - y_{plt}^{SsApprx}}{\sum_{\{p,l\} \in I^{S2}, t \in T} y_{plt}^{SsCalc}} \qquad (39)$$

A good approximation should achieve values smaller than 0.001 for both indicators.

Sales result indicators are the relative sales level SL^S and the value-added level VA^S. The sales level is defined as the ratio of total sales quantity to total demand quantity.

$$SL^S = \frac{\sum_{\{p,l\} \in I^{S2}, t \in T} x^S_{plt}}{\sum_{\{p,l\} \in I^{S2}, t \in T} \left(q^{Ss}_{plt} + q^{Sc}_{plt}\right)} \qquad (40)$$

The relative sales level aggregates the sales volume plan into one indicator to show the tendencies of the sales plan. For example, relative sales levels smaller than 1 indicate the planner that some sales locations exist receiving less volumes than demanded to be analyzed in more detail.

The value-added level measures the ratio between total turnover and total procurement costs. Total procurement costs v^B_{plt} are presented in more detail in subchapter 5.7.

$$VA^S = \frac{\sum_{\{p,l\} \in I^{S2}, t \in T} y^S_{plt}}{\sum_{\{p,l\} \in I^{B2}, t \in T} v^B_{plt}} \qquad (41)$$

A higher value-added level leads to higher utilization and volumes, if production and distribution costs in-between are relatively small and/or stable compared to turnover and procurement volumes and values.

5.5 Distribution Planning

Distribution planning covers transportation and inventory planning within the network, as well as the material balance calculation between sales, production and procurement. Global transportation planning considers the lead times between continents resulting in transit inventories differentiation of sent and received transportation quantities as shown in the requirements in section 4.1.5. Inventories are managed at the defined transfer point locations either with static or dynamic boundaries.

5.5.1 Transportation Index Sets, Control and Input Data

Global transportation planning covers sent and received transportation quantities as well as transit inventories by transportation lane $e \in E$. The differentiation of sent and received transportation quantities is required due to long transportation lead times between continents causing that sent transportation quantities in one period can arrive in different periods. Exact vessel scheduling would require defining the exact points in time of departure and arrival in the port (Jetlund/Karini 2004, p. 1272). In monthly planning from a chemical company perspective, the scheduling of single vessels is not in focus given regular container vessel routes.

Transportation lanes have a transportation time $d_e^T, e \in E$ measured in days. A transcontinental transportation lane connecting NAFTA with Asia for example can require more than 30 days of transportation time. A normed period transportation time d^{Tn} of 30 days per period is defined. The normed period transportation time represents the planning bucket month. Since sent and received transportation quantities depend on transportation time, subsets of transportation lanes depending on the transportation time $d_e^T, e \in E$ and the normed transportation time d^{Tn} as illustrated in table 26 are created.

Table 26 Transportation lane index sets depending on transportation time

Index set	Index set description	Transportation time
1. $\{e\} \in I^{T1}$	in-period transportation lanes	$d_e^T = 0$
2. $\{e\} \in I^{T2}$	between-period transportation lanes	$0 < d_e^T \leq d^{Tn}$
3. $\{e\} \in I^{T3}$	cross-period transportation lanes	$d_e^T > d^{Tn}$
4. $\{e\} \in I^{T4}$	between-/cross-period transportation lanes	$d_e^T > 0$

The transportation time criterion is used to group transportation lanes uniquely into one of the shown three index sets. Transportation lanes with transportation time longer than 0 are additionally grouped in index set 4. Grouping of transportation lanes will be used to later distinguish different transportation cases leading to different equations to calculate transportation sent and received quantities.

The grouping approach accepts a certain error on the monthly planning level compared to the exact operations level. On the operations level, all transportation lanes – also location-internal transfers e.g. in pipelines – have a transportation time > 0. Conceptually, it is required to make a clear cut between planning and operations and to define a planning tolerance interval e.g. 10% of the total period time – in this case 3 days –, where transportation times are set equal to 0. Otherwise, the planner always would miss 3% of volume in the same planned period due to the transportation time lag of 3 days leading to complexity in the plan.

In addition to the grouping of transportation lanes in index sets, all starting and ending locations are grouped into the index sets $l_1 \in I^{T5}$, $\forall l_1 \in L$ and $l_2 \in I^{T6}$, $\forall l_2 \in L$. Transportation lanes, starting and ending locations are grouped $\{e, l_1, l_2\} \in I^{T7}$, $\forall e \in E$, $l_1, l_2 \in L$ generally and product-specific $\forall \{p, e, l_1, l_2\} \in I^{T8}$, $\forall p \in P$, $\{e, l_1, l_2\} \in I^{T7}$. Finally, all product-transportation lane index sets of between and cross-period product transportation lanes are grouped with $\{p, e, l_1, l_2\} \in I^{T9}$, $\forall \{p, e, l_1, l_2\} \in I^{T8}$ with $d_e^T > 0$. Index sets are used to define the transportation control data introduced in the following.

Transportation Control Data

Transportation is controlled with minimum and maximum total transportation quantities $R_e^{Te\min}$ and $R_e^{Te\max}$ for the transportation lane $e \in E$ and product-specific minimum and maximum product transportation quantities $R_{pel_1l_2}^{Tp\min}$ and $R_{pel_1l_2}^{Tp\max}$ for all product-transportation lane combinations $\forall \{p, e, l_1, l_2\} \in I^{T8}$. Here, transportation business rules e.g. contractually agreed with global carriers in the value chain strategy and procurement strategy can be applied such as minimum transportation quantities per months or capacity limits. The product-specific transportation cost rates $c_{pel_1l_2}^{Ttcr}$ $\forall \{p, e, l_1, l_2\} \in I^{T8}$ per transported unit in the transportation lane-specific currency is applied to calculate transportation costs. The cost rate is product-specific, e.g. due to difference in transportation modes applicable for the product for the same transportation lane.

Transportation Input Data

Transcontinental transportation and transit inventory planning during the initial planning periods need considering transportation quantities and transit inventories already on the way. The carry-over transportation receive quantity $x^{Tcarryrecv}_{pel_1l_2t}$ and the carry-over transit inventory quantity $x^{Tcarrytrans}_{pel_1l_2t}$ are required for all cross- or between-period transportation lanes $\{p,e,l_1,l_2\} \in I^{T9}$, since they affect transportation planning and material balances during the initial planning periods. Considering carry-over quantities is commonly known for modeling inventory balances, where the start inventory of the first period needs to be taken into account. Now, carry-over quantities have to be also considered for planning transportation quantities and transit inventories.

5.5.2 Transportation Variables and Constraints

Transportation planning has to decide on sent transportation quantities $x^{Tsent}_{pel_1l_2,t}$ and received transportation quantities $x^{Trecv}_{pel_1l_2t}$ $\forall \{p,e,l_1,l_2\} \in I^{T8}$, $t \in T$. In addition, transit inventories for $x^{Ttrans}_{pel_1l_2t}$ on ships result for between- and cross-period transportation lanes $\forall \{p,e,l_1,l_2\} \in I^{T9}$, $t \in T$, since these are the lanes, where transit inventory needs to be accounted for. Hard transportation constraints can be relaxed with the minimum and maximum relaxation quantity variables $\Delta^{T\min}_{pel_1l_2t}$ and $\Delta^{T\max}_{pel_1l_2t}$, $\forall \{p,e,l_1,l_2\} \in I^{T8}$. The binary variable $\delta^{T}_{pel_1l_2t}$, $\forall \{p,e,l_1,l_2\} \in I^{T8}$, $t \in T$ counts the transportation relaxation cases.

Transportation value variables are transportation costs $v^{Ttc}_{pel_1l_2t}$ for $\forall \{p,e,l_1,l_2\} \in I^{T8}$, $t \in T$ in the transportation-lane specific currency as transit inventory value $v^{Ttv}_{pel_1l_2t}$ and transit inventory capital costs $v^{Ttcc}_{pel_1l_2t}$, $\forall \{p,e,l_1,l_2\} \in I^{T8}$, $t \in T$.

Transportation Constraints

The first transportation constraints bound transportation sent quantities for the entire transportation lane across all products.

$$R^{Te\min}_{e} \leq \sum_{\{p,e,l_1,l_2\} \in I^{T8}} x^{Tsent}_{pel_1l_2t} \leq R^{Te\max}_{e} \qquad \forall e \in E, t \in T \qquad (42)$$

Secondly, product-specific sent transportation quantity boundaries have to be considered or relaxed with the relaxation variables.

$$R^{Tp\min}_{pel_1l_2} - \Delta^{T\min}_{pel_1l_2t} \leq x^{Tsent}_{pel_1l_2t} \leq R^{Tp\max}_{pel_1l_2} + \Delta^{T\max}_{pel_1l_2t} \qquad (43)$$

$$\forall \{p,e,l_1,l_2\} \in I^{T\Pr odStartEnd}, t \in T$$

Transportation relaxation cases are determined for all transportation boundary constraints using a logical constraint formulation.

$$\delta^T_{pel_1l_2t} \leq \Delta^{T\min}_{pel_1l_2t} + \Delta^{T\max}_{pel_1l_2t} \leq M \cdot \delta^T_{pel_1l_2t} \qquad \forall \{p,l\} \in I^{12}, t \in T \qquad (44)$$

The transportation relaxation ton counter ρ^T sums up all positive and negative relaxation quantities

$$\rho^T = \sum_{t \in T} \sum_{\{p,e,l_1,l_2\} \in I^{T8}} \Delta^{T\max}_{pel_1l_2t} + \Delta^{T\min}_{pel_1l_2t} \qquad (45)$$

The transportation relaxation constraint counter ψ^T sums up all binary variables $\delta^T_{pel_1l_2t}$.

$$\psi^T = \sum_{t \in T} \sum_{\{p,e,l_1,l_2\} \in I^{T8}} \delta^T_{pel_1l_2t} \qquad (46)$$

The following constraints determine the sent transportation quantity depending on the transportation time and the respective transportation lane cases introduced at the beginning of the section. Fig. 63 illustrates the different cases depending on transportation time and on the impact on received transportation quantity calculation.

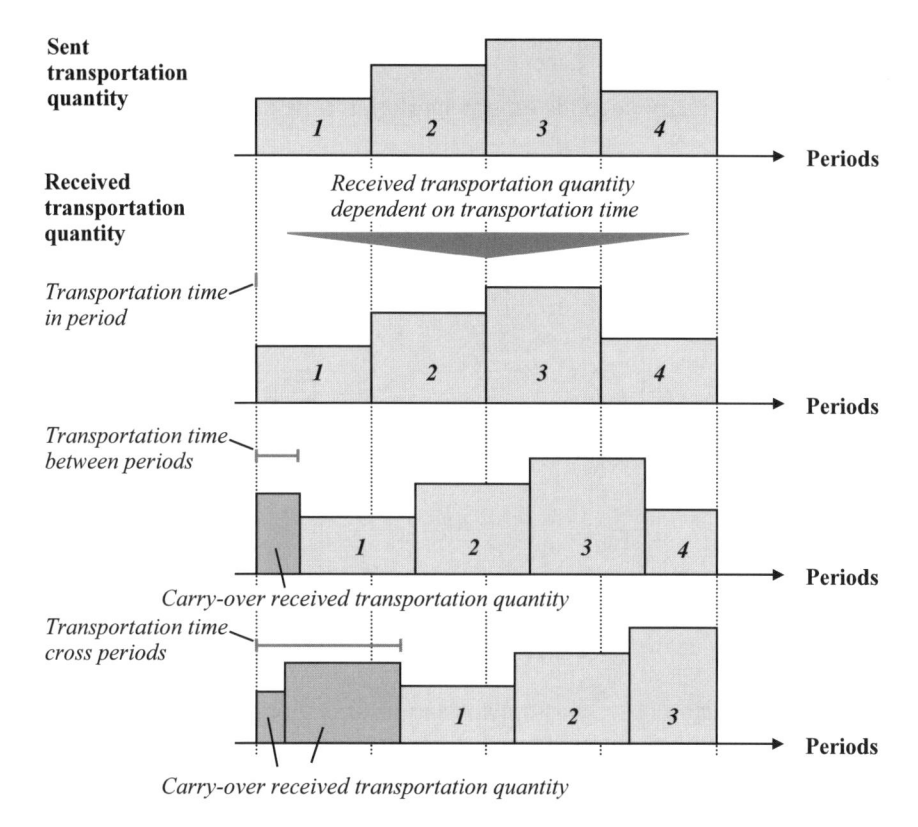

Fig. 63 Principle of calculating received transportation quantity

The simplest case is the in-period case with transportation time equal to 0. Here, the received transportation quantity is equal to the sent transportation quantity meaning that the entire quantity shipped in one period arrives fully in the same period.

$$x^{Trecv}_{pel_1l_2t} = x^{Tsent}_{pel_1l_2t} \qquad \forall \{p,e,l_1,l_2\} \in I^{T8}: e \in I^{T1}, t \in T \qquad (47)$$

If transportation time is between periods, received transportation quantity calculation differs for the starting period and for all other periods. Received transportation quantity for the starting period is composed of carry-over received transportation quantity already on the way and a share of the sent transportation quantity from the first period. Received transportation quantities for all other periods are composed by a share of sent transportation quantities from the two periods $t - \lfloor (d_e^T / d^{Tn}) \rfloor$ and $t - \lceil (d_e^T / d^{Tn}) \rceil$ with d_e^T being the transportation time for the transportation lane e measured in days and d^{Tn} being the normed transportation time for a planning period by default 30 days.

The quantity share depends on transportation time and normed transportation time.

$t = t_1$
$$x_{pel_1l_2t}^{Trecv} = x_{pel_1l_2t}^{Tcarryrecv} + \left[(x_{pel_1l_2t}^{Tsent} \cdot (1 - \frac{d_e^T}{d^{Tn}}) \right], \quad (48)$$

$$\forall \{p,e,l_1,l_2\} \in I^{T8} : e \in I^{T2}, t \in T$$

$t > t_1:$
$$x_{pel_1l_2t}^{Trecv} = \left[(x_{pel_1l_2t - \left\lfloor \frac{d_e^T}{d^{Tn}} \right\rfloor}^{Tsent} \cdot (1 - (\frac{d_e^T}{d^{Tn}} - \left\lfloor \frac{d_e^T}{d^{Tn}} \right\rfloor)) \right]$$

$$+ \left[(x_{pel_1l_2t - \left\lfloor \frac{d_e^T}{d^{Tn}} \right\rfloor}^{Ts} \cdot (\frac{d_e^T}{d^{Tn}} - \left\lfloor \frac{d_e^T}{d^{Tn}} \right\rfloor)) \right]$$

$$\forall \{p,e,l_1,l_2\} \in I^{T8} : e \in I^{T2}, t \in T$$

The cross-period case with transportation times longer than the normed transportation time requires three differentiations. The carry-over received transportation case is not only required for the first planning period but also for subsequent periods due to the long shipment times.

$t \leq t_1 + \left\lfloor \frac{d_e^T}{d^{Tn}} \right\rfloor:$
$$x_{pel_1l_2t}^{Trecv} = x_{pel_1l_2t}^{Tcarryrecv}, \quad (49)$$

$$\forall \{p,e,l_1,l_2\} \in I^{T8} : e \in I^{T3}, t \in T$$

$t_1 + \left\lfloor \frac{d_e^T}{d^{Tn}} \right\rfloor < t \leq t_1 + \left\lceil \frac{d_e^T}{d^{Tn}} \right\rceil:$
$$x_{pel_1l_2t}^{Trecv} = x_{pel_1l_2t}^{Tcarryrecv}$$
$$+ \left[(x_{pel_1l_2t - \left\lfloor \frac{d_e^T}{d^{Tn}} \right\rfloor}^{Tsent} \cdot (1 - (\frac{d_e^T}{d^{Tn}} - \left\lfloor \frac{d_e^T}{d^{Tn}} \right\rfloor)) \right],$$

$$\forall \{p,e,l_1,l_2\} \in I^{T8} : e \in I^{T3}, t \in T$$

$t > t_1 + \left\lceil \frac{d_e^T}{d^{Tn}} \right\rceil:$
$$x_{pel_1l_2t}^{Trecv} = \left[(x_{pel_1l_2t - \left\lfloor \frac{d_e^T}{d^{Tn}} \right\rfloor}^{Tsent} \cdot (1 - (\frac{d_e^T}{d^{Tn}} - \left\lfloor \frac{d_e^T}{d^{Tn}} \right\rfloor)) \right]$$

$$+\left[(x_{pel_1l_2t-\left\lceil\frac{d_e^T}{d^{Tn}}\right\rceil}^{Tsent})\cdot(\frac{d_e^T}{d^{Tn}}-\left\lfloor\frac{d_e^T}{d^{Tn}}\right\rfloor))\right]$$

$$\forall\{p,e,l_1,l_2\}\in I^{T8}: e\in I^{T3}, t\in T$$

The following numerical examples illustrate the calculation results for the different transportation time cases (s. table 27).

Table 27 Numerical example for global transportation quantity calculation

transportation time [d]	sent in t=1	sent in t=2	carry-over in t=1	carry-over in t=2	Received in t=1	Received in t=2	Received in t=3	Received in t=4	Received in t=5	Received in t=6	Total
0	100	50	0	0	100	50	0	0	0	0	150
10	100	50	50	0	117	67	17	0	0	0	200
30	100	50	50	0	50	100	50	0	0	0	200
45	100	50	50	50	50	100	75	25	0	0	250
60	100	50	50	50	50	50	100	50	0	0	250
70	100	50	50	50	50	50	67	66	17	0	250

The transportation time is varied from 0 days to 70 days. The normed transportation time is set to 30 days. A quantity of 100 is sent in period 1, a quantity of 50 is sent in period 2. Carry-over transportation quantity of 50 exists for transportation time longer than 0 in the first period, for transportation time longer than 30 days also for the second period. The received quantities are calculated for the periods 1 to 6 based on the calculation rules introduced. It gets obvious that depending on the transportation time, the share of sent quantities allocated to a period differ. The importance of carry-over quantities to be considered in the first planning periods especially for long transportation time in transcontinental shipment gets transparent. This extends the scope of distribution planning models considering only carry-over inventory for the first period to calculate inventory balances towards carry-over transportation quantities not only for the first but also for further periods depending on the transportation time.

Sent and received transportation quantities are the basis to calculate transit inventories for the between and cross-period case. Transit inventory is the balance of carry-over or transit inventory from the previous period plus new sent transportation quantity minus received transportation quantity leaving the "pipeline".

$$t=t_1: x_{pel_1l_2t}^{Ttrans} = x_{pel_1l_2t}^{Tcarrytrans} + x_{pel_1l_2t}^{Tsent} - x_{pel_1l_2t}^{Trecv} \qquad (50)$$

$$t > t_1: x_{pel_1l_2t}^{Ttrans} = x_{pel_1l_2t-1}^{Ttrans} + x_{pel_1l_2t}^{Tsent} - x_{pel_1l_2t}^{Trecv}$$

$$\forall \{p,e,l_1,l_2\} \in I^{T9}, t \in T$$

Transportation costs in the respective transportation lane currency are the sent transportation quantity multiplied with the product-specific transportation cost rate.

$$v_{pel_1l_2t}^{Ttc} = x_{pel_1l_2t}^{Tsent} \cdot c_{pel_1l_2}^{Ttcr} \qquad \forall \{p,e,l_1,l_2\} \in I^{T8}, t \in T \qquad (51)$$

Monthly transportation costs sums up all transportation costs by product and transportation lane combinations applying the transportation lane-specific exchange rate factor.

$$v_t^{Ttc} = \sum_{\{p,e,l_1,l_2\} \in I^{T8}} (v_{pel_1l_2t}^{Ttc} \cdot \chi_{e,t}^{TL}) \qquad \forall t \in T \qquad (52)$$

The transit inventory value is the transit inventory quantity multiplied by the product value rate of the destination location.

$$v_{pel_1l_2t}^{Ttv} = x_{pel_1l_2t}^{Ttrans} \cdot c_{pl_2t}^{Iv} \qquad \forall \{p,e,l_1,l_2\} \in I^{T9}: \{l_2\} \in I^{T6}, t \in T \qquad (53)$$

Detailed transit inventory capital costs are measured for each period in the transportation lane-specific currency.

$$v_{pel_1l_2t}^{Ttcc} = v_{pel_1l_2t}^{Ttv} \cdot \frac{\phi \cdot d_t}{365} \qquad \forall \{p,e,l_1,l_2\} \in I^{T9}, t \in T \qquad (54)$$

Sent and received transportation quantities are the basis for balancing material flows in all procurement, production and sales locations as presented in the following.

Monthly capital costs for transit inventories are calculated based on the transportation lane and product-specific transit inventory value in the basis currency of the end location and applying the interest rate equation.

$$v_t^{Ttcc} = \left[\sum_{\{p,e,l_1,l_2\} \in I^{T9}} (v_{pel_1l_2t}^{Ttv} \cdot \chi_{l_2t}^{L}) \right] \cdot \frac{\phi \cdot d_t}{365} \qquad \forall t \in T \qquad (55)$$

Concluding, the transportation planning model realized the planning requirements for a global value chain network with respect to global transportation send and received quantities as well as transit inventory planning.

5.5.3 Inventory Index Sets, Control and Input Data

Inventory Index Sets

Inventory is managed in distribution locations $\{l\} \in I^{I1}, \forall l \in L$ called transfer points as defined in the value chain network presented in section 3.2.1. The product and transfer point combinations are defined in the index set $\{p,l\} \in I^{I2}$, $\forall p \in P$, $l \in I^{I1}$. Transfer points are the logical inventory management locations as defined in the planning object aggregation in section 5.2.2. A transfer point can combine multiple physical separated warehousing locations where inventory is physically distributed but managed as being logically one virtual location.

Inventory Control and Input Data

Inventory quantity is managed within defined minimum and maximum inventory management bandwidth as shown in fig. 64

	Absolute values	*Ranges*	
Physical maximum inventory	$R_{pl}^{\text{Im}ax}$	Maximum bandwidth inventory limit	$\sigma_{plt}^{\text{Im}ax}$
Maximum bandwidth inventory	$R_{pl}^{Ibw\max a}$	$R_{pl}^{Ibw\max r} \cdot x_{plt+1}^{Dd}$	
Inventory end quantity	x_{plt}^{I}		
Minimum bandwidth inventory	$R_{pl}^{Ibw\min a}$	$R_{pl}^{Ibw\min r} \cdot x_{plt+1}^{Dd}$	
		Minimum bandwidth inventory limit	$\sigma_{plt}^{\text{Im}in}$

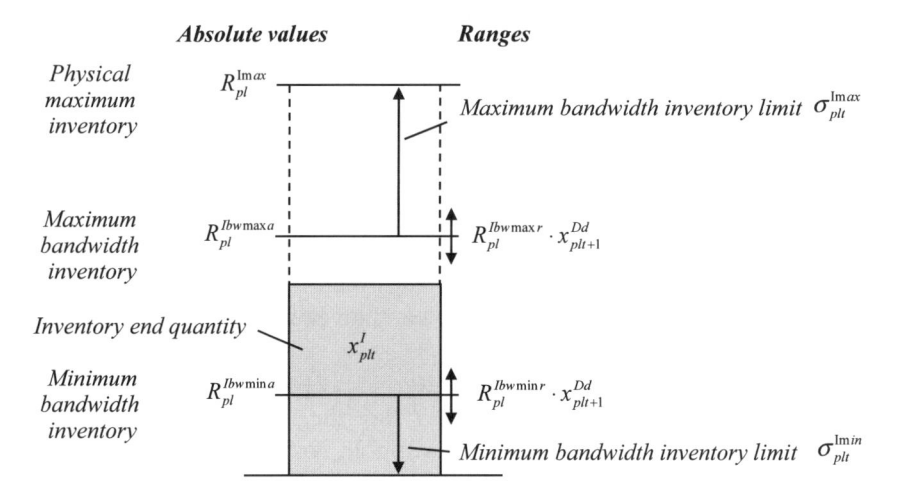

Fig. 64 Inventory management boundaries

Minimum bandwidth inventory boundary can be defined statically as absolute quantity $R_{pl}^{Ibw\min a}$, $\forall\{p,l\} \in I^{I2}$ or dynamically as inventory range $R_{pl}^{Ibw\min r}$, $\forall\{p,l\} \in I^{I2}$ measured in days applied on the future total distribution demand for the transfer point. While absolute boundaries ensure a stable inventory baseline, inventory range boundaries support a dynamic adoption of inventories to the business situation. Especially, minimum bandwidth inventory for new products can be easier managed and built up using ranges applied on distribution demand instead of fixed absolute quantities.

The minimum bandwidth inventory boundary is set for all planning periods. Exceptionally, the minimum bandwidth inventory can be reduced down to 0 in a specific period controlled by the binary parameter σ_{plt}^{Imin}, $\forall \{p,l\} \in I^{12}$, $t \in T$ defined as minimum bandwidth inventory limit switch. The minimum bandwidth inventory includes the safety stock to ensure delivery capability, physical line fill inventory in the resources during production, as well as minimum unavoidable working level inventory occurring due to the operating mode.

The maximum bandwidth inventory is also defined statically as absolute quantity $R_{pl}^{Ibw\max a}$ or as inventory range $R_{pl}^{Ibw\max r}$ in analogy to minimum inventories $\forall \{p,l\} \in I^{12}$. Exceptionally, this limit can be increased up to a physical maximum inventory quantity $R_{pl}^{I\max}$, $\forall \{p,l\} \in I^{12}$ in a specific period controlled by the binary maximum inventory switch parameter σ_{plt}^{Imax}, $\forall \{p,l\} \in I^{12}$, $t \in T$. Compared to the maximum bandwidth inventory, the physical maximum inventory quantity corresponds with storage capacity limits in the transfer point.

Minimum and maximum bandwidth inventory boundaries are defined in the value chain strategy based on value chain structure, inventory drivers and statistical inventory formulas. Depending on supply chain and business structures, different inventory quantity flexibility is required: supply chain reasons are for example campaign production. Business reasons are the risk-hedging of raw material price volatility by building up forward raw material inventories in low-price periods to bridge high-price periods. A further reason for higher maximum bandwidth inventories is a missing value chain planning quality with the sales plan being not executed in operations as planned leading to higher carry-over inventories for the planning process in the next period.

The inventory warehousing cost rate c_{pl}^{Iwc}, $\forall \{p,l\} \in I^{12}$ and the product value rate c_{plt}^{Iv}, $\forall \{p,l\} \in I^{12}$, $t \in T$ are the inventory value parameters. The warehousing cost rate is a variable cost factor in the location-specific currency applied on the inventory quantity in the transfer point. Variable warehousing costs are often charged if warehouses are operated by service providers. Company-owned warehouses can also be included in distribution fixed costs that cannot be variablized for optimization purpose. Product value rates are taken from future inventory planning from section 5.3.2 and reflect the future product values considering anticipated future raw material price development.

Inventory management requires the starting inventory within the first planning period called carry-over inventory $x_{plt_1}^{I}$ $\forall \{p,l\} \in I^{12}$, $t_1 \in T$.

5.5.4 Inventory Variables and Constraints

Inventory planning has to decide inventory ending quantities x_{plt}^{I}, $\forall \{p,l\} \in I^{12}$ in each planning period $t \in T$. Inventory relaxation variables are used in analogy to sales and transportation relaxation: $\Delta_{plt}^{\text{Im}in}$ and $\Delta_{plt}^{\text{Im}ax}$ are the minimum and maximum inventory relaxation quantities $\forall \{p,l\} \in I^{12}$, $t \in T$. The binary variable δ_{plt}^{I} indicates, whether an inventory constraint is relaxed or not $\forall \{p,l\} \in I^{12}$, $t \in T$. In addition, the product-location specific average warehousing costs v_{plt}^{Iwc}, average inventory value v_{plt}^{Iv} and the related average capital costs v_{plt}^{Icc} are determined. These value variables are calculated for average inventory, since values have to take into account the inventory quantities and development within the period, not the ending inventory.

Inventory Constraints

Inventory boundary constraints have to combine absolute and range boundaries considering limit switch parameters and relaxation variables. The absolute minimum and maximum inventory boundaries are defined in the following constraint.

$$x_{plt}^{I} \geq \left[(1-\sigma_{plt}^{\text{Im}in}) \cdot R_{pl}^{Ibw\min a}\right] - \Delta_{plt}^{\text{Im}in} \quad \forall \{p,l\} \in I^{12}, t \in T \quad (56)$$

$$x_{plt}^{I} \leq \left[(1-\sigma_{plt}^{\text{Im}ax}) \cdot R_{pl}^{Ibw\max a}\right] + (\sigma_{plt}^{\text{Im}ax} \cdot R_{pl}^{\text{Im}ax}) + \Delta_{plt}^{\text{Im}ax}$$

Lower inventory boundary is 0, if the minimum inventory limit switch $\sigma_{plt}^{\text{Im}in}$ is 1. Upper inventory boundary is equal to the maximum bandwidth inventory, if the maximum inventory limit switch $\sigma_{plt}^{\text{Im}ax}$ is 0, otherwise the maximum absolute inventory quantity is applied as upper limit. The constraint is relaxed with $\Delta_{plt}^{\text{Im}in}$ of $\Delta_{plt}^{\text{Im}ax}$, if no feasible solution exists due to hard inventory constraints.

Inventory range boundaries got a very similar structure also considering limit switch variables and relaxation. Inventory ranges are applied to the distribution demand x_{plt+1}^{Dd}, $\forall \{p,l\} \in I^{12}$, $t \in T-1$, the transfer point has to fulfil in the following period. This ensures sufficient built up of inventory for the distribution demand in the next period.

$$x_{plt}^{I} \geq \left[(1-\sigma_{plt}^{\text{Im}in}) \cdot R_{pl}^{Ibw\min r} \cdot \frac{x_{plt+1}^{Dd}}{d_{t+1}}\right] - \Delta_{plt}^{\text{Im}in} \tag{57}$$

$$x_{plt}^{I} \leq \left[(1-\sigma_{plt}^{\text{Im}ax}) \cdot R_{pl}^{Ibw\max r} \cdot \frac{x_{plt+1}^{Dd}}{d_{t+1}}\right] + (\sigma_{plt}^{\text{Im}ax} \cdot R_{pl}^{\text{Im}ax}) + \Delta_{plt}^{\text{Im}ax}$$

$$\forall \{p,l\} \in I^{12}, t \in T-1$$

These equations have to be adapted for the final planning period with no distribution demand existing for the following period out-of the planning horizon. It is assumed that the ranges are applied on the distribution demand for the final period. Hence, they remain stable compared to the period before the last period.

$$x_{plt}^{I} \geq \left[(1-\sigma_{plt}^{\text{Im}in}) \cdot R_{pl}^{Ibw\min r} \cdot \frac{x_{plt}^{Dd}}{d_t}\right] - \Delta_{plt}^{\text{Im}in} \tag{58}$$

$$x_{plt}^{I} \leq \left[(1-\sigma_{plt}^{\text{Im}ax}) \cdot R_{pl}^{Ibw\max r} \cdot \frac{x_{plt}^{Dd}}{d_t}\right] + (\sigma_{plt}^{\text{Im}ax} \cdot R_{pl}^{\text{Im}ax}) + \Delta_{plt}^{\text{Im}ax}$$

$$\forall \{p,l\} \in I^{12}, t \in T: t = T$$

Inventory relaxation cases are determined for all inventory boundary constraints using a logical constraint equation.

$$\delta_{plt}^{I} \leq \Delta_{plt}^{\text{Im}in} + \Delta_{plt}^{\text{Im}ax} \leq M \cdot \delta_{plt}^{I} \qquad \forall \{p,l\} \in I^{12}, t \in T \tag{59}$$

The inventory relaxation ton counter ρ^I sums up all relaxation quantities.

$$\rho^I = \sum_{t \in T} \sum_{\{p,l\} \in I^{12}} (\Delta_{plt}^{\text{Im}ax} + \Delta_{plt}^{\text{Im}in}) \tag{60}$$

The inventory relaxation constraint counter ψ^I sums up all binary variables δ_{plt}^I.

$$\psi^I = \sum_{t \in T} \sum_{\{p,l\} \in I^{12}} \delta_{plt}^I \tag{61}$$

Warehousing costs are determined based on average inventory quantity applying the warehousing cost rate in location-specific currency.

5.5 Distribution Planning

$$t = t_1 : v_{plt}^{Iwc} = \frac{(x_{plt_1}^I + x_{plt}^I)}{2} \cdot c_{pl}^{Iwc} \quad (62)$$

$$t > t_1 : v_{plt}^{Iwc} = \frac{(x_{plt}^I + x_{plt-1}^I)}{2} \cdot c_{pl}^{Iwc}$$

$$\forall \{p,l\} \in I^{12}, t \in T$$

The average inventory quantity is approximated with the starting plus ending inventory quantity per period divided by two assuming a linear relation between starting and ending inventory. The average inventory quantity differs in the first instance compared to all other periods: carry-over inventory is the starting inventory during the first period, while the ending inventory of a previous period is the starting inventory of the considered period in all other cases.

Monthly warehousing costs consolidate product and location-specific warehousing costs on the basis currency.

$$v_t^{Iwc} = \sum_{\{p,l\} \in I^{12}} (v_{plt}^{Iwc} \cdot \chi_{lt}^L) \quad \forall t \in T \quad (63)$$

Average inventory values are determined in analogy to warehousing costs on the average inventory quantity applying the product value rate by location and period.

$$t = t_1 : v_{plt}^{Iv} = \frac{(x_{plt_1}^I + x_{plt}^I)}{2} \cdot c_{plt}^{Iv} \quad (64)$$

$$t > t_1 : v_{plt}^{Iv} = \frac{(x_{plt}^I + x_{plt-1}^I)}{2} \cdot c_{plt}^{Iv}$$

$$\forall \{p,l\} \in I^{12}, t \in T$$

Inventory capital costs in the foreign currency are calculated on inventory values using the interest rate term.

$$v_{plt}^{Icc} = v_{plt}^{Iv} \cdot \frac{\phi \cdot d_t}{365} \quad \forall \{p,l\} \in I^{12}, t \in T \quad (65)$$

Inventory capital costs per period in the base currency are calculated summing up product-location specific inventory value and applying the interest calculation term.

$$v_t^{Icc} = \left[\sum_{\{p,l\} \in I^{12}} (v_{plt}^{Iv} \cdot \chi_{lt}^{L}) \right] \cdot \frac{\phi \cdot d_t}{365} \qquad \forall t \in T \qquad (66)$$

The presented inventory model matches the requirements formulated in section 4.1.5 managing inventories statically and dynamically within defined boundaries defined in the distribution strategy.

5.5.5 Distribution Balance Index Sets, Variables and Constraints

Distribution Balance Index Set

Distribution balances need to calculate all volume balances in all value chain network locations between sales, distribution, production and procurement. Material flows have to be balanced for all product-location combinations in the index set $\{p,l\} \in I^{VC1}$.

Distribution Balance Variables

The variables distribution supply x_{plt}^{Ds} and distribution demand x_{plt}^{Dd}, $\forall \{p,l\} \in I^{VC1}$, $t \in T$ are used to balance incoming and outgoing material flows in a value chain network location with transportation quantities as illustrated in fig. 65.

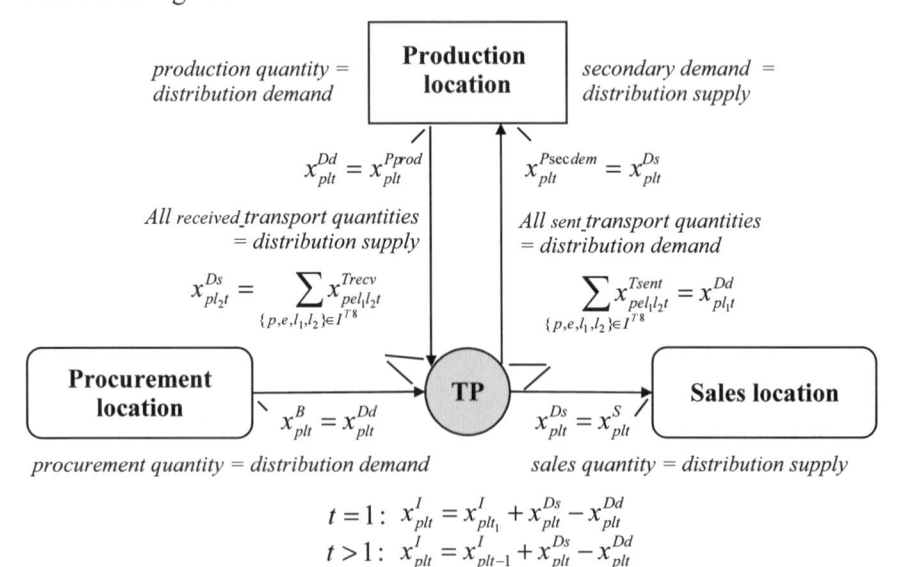

Fig. 65 Principle of distribution balance calculation

5.5 Distribution Planning

The distribution balance constraints shown in fig. 65 are presented in the following.

Distribution Balance Constraints

Product's inventory ending quantity in a transfer point is equal to the carry-over inventory plus all distribution supply minus distribution demand for the product-transfer point combination in the first period. In all other periods, it is equal to the ending inventory of the previous quantity minus distribution demand plus distribution supply.

$$t = t_1 : x^I_{plt} = x^I_{plt_1} + x^{Ds}_{plt} - x^{Dd}_{plt} \qquad (67)$$

$$t > t_1 : x^I_{plt} = x^I_{plt-1} + x^{Ds}_{plt} - x^{Dd}_{plt}$$

$$\forall \{p,l\} \in I^{12}, t \in T$$

The sum of sent transportation quantities of a product is equal to distribution demand of the transportation lane's start location. The transportation lane's start location can be a procurement location, a production location or a distribution location.

$$\sum_{\{p,e,l_1,l_2\} \in I^{T8}} x^{Tsent}_{pel_1 l_2 t} = x^{Dd}_{pl_1 t} \qquad \forall \{p,l_1\} \in I^{VC1} : l_1 \in I^{T5}, t \in T \qquad (68)$$

The sum of received transportation quantities of a product is equal to distribution supply of the transportation lanes' end location. A transportation lanes' end location can be a demand location, a distribution location or a production location.

$$\sum_{\{p,e,l_1,l_2\} \in I^{T8}} x^{Trecv}_{pel_1 l_2 t} = x^{Ds}_{pl_2 t} \qquad \forall \{p,l_2\} \in I^{VC1} : l_2 \in I^{T6}, t \in T \qquad (69)$$

The sales quantity for a product in a sales location is equal to the distribution supply of the product in the sales location.

$$x^{S}_{plt} = x^{Ds}_{plt} \qquad \forall \{p,l\} \in I^{S2}, t \in T \qquad (70)$$

In the following, the production quantity x^{Pprod}_{plt} and secondary demand quantity $x^{Psec\,dem}_{plt}$ of production as part of distribution planning is introduced that will be later presented in more detail in subchapter 5.6. The production output quantity by product and location is equal to distribution demand of the product and production location.

$$x^{Pprod}_{plt} = x^{Dd}_{plt} \qquad \forall \{p,l\} \in I^{P10}, t \in T \qquad (71)$$

The secondary demand quantity for a product in a production location is equal to the distribution supply of the product and the production location.

$$x_{plt}^{Psec\,dem} = x_{plt}^{Ds} \qquad \forall \{p,l\} \in I^{P13},\, t \in T \qquad (72)$$

The procurement quantity by product and procurement location is equal to the distribution demand of the product and the procurement location.

$$x_{plt}^{B} = x_{plt}^{Dd} \qquad \forall \{p,l\} \in I^{B2},\, t \in T \qquad (73)$$

The procurement quantity here being part of distribution planning is presented in more detail in the procurement planning part in subchapter 5.7. Some distribution indicators are determined in addition to the decision variables as further decision support for the planner.

5.5.6 Distribution Indicator Postprocessing

Inventory indicators are of key interest for planners. Higher inventory on the one hand ensures delivery capability and hedges the risk of volatile procurement prices; on the other hand, high inventories increase the capital employed and the capital costs. While transportation quantities are a result of distribution balances, inventory quantities can vary between minimum and maximum bandwidth boundaries. The relative inventory level IL^I measures the percentage of the total inventory ending quantity compared to the total absolute maximum bandwidth inventory.

$$IL^I = \frac{\sum_{\{p,l\} \in I^{I2},\, t \in T} x_{plt}^{I}}{\sum_{\{p,l\} \in I^{I2},\, t \in T} R_{pl}^{Ibw\,\max\,a}} \qquad (74)$$

The maximum bandwidth inventory is used as baseline to measure the inventory development.

In addition, total inventory ranges by quantity IR^I and by value IRV^I measured in days are determined by comparing sales quantities and turnovers with inventory quantities and values respectively. IR^I indicates the range of inventory quantity in relation to entire sales quantity in the value chain.

$$IR^I = \frac{\sum\limits_{\{p,l\}\in I^{I2}, t\in T} x_{plt}^I}{\sum\limits_{\{p,l\}\in I^{S2}, t\in T} x_{plt}^S}$$ (75)

Valued inventory ranges compare total inventory value with total sales turnover.

$$IRV^I = \frac{\sum\limits_{\{p,l\}\in I^{I2}} (v_{plt}^{Iv} \cdot \chi_{lt}^L)}{\sum\limits_{\{p,l\}\in I^{S2}} \left[y_{plt}^{Ss} + (q_{plt}^{Sc} \cdot p_{plt}^{Sc}) \right] \cdot \chi_{lt}^L}$$ (76)

Inventory ranges are indicators to make different businesses comparable. Commodity businesses of high volumes can be compared using the quantity-based inventory range. Specialty businesses with lower volumes of higher value with regard to commodity businesses can be compared with commodity inventory ranges, if sales and inventory values are considered.

5.6 Production Planning

Production planning is the most comprehensive part of the model. Its requirements with variable production processes, input and output products, throughput smoothing and change-over planning of campaigns do not allow a simple quantity-based master planning approach as can be found for tactical planning. Core idea of production planning is to plan input and output quantities on production on *process level* and campaigns and change-overs on *process group level*, as illustrated in fig. 66.

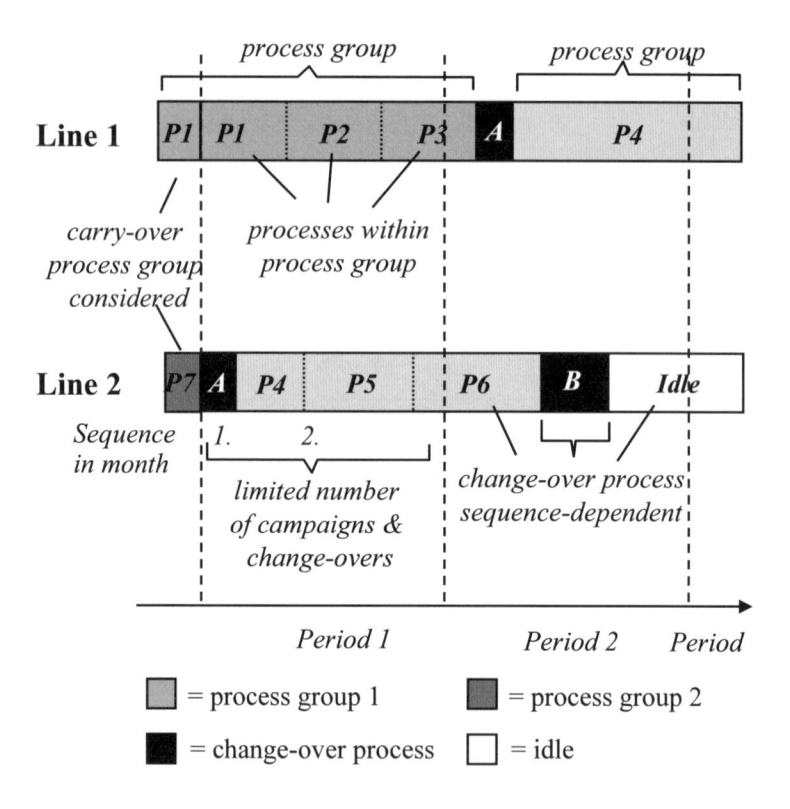

Fig. 66 Production processes and process groups

A limited number of process groups and change-over possibilities per period restrict the number of change-over decisions and the problem complexity. This technique also called *block planning* developed by Günther et al. (2006), where single processes are grouped into a production block and change-overs are calculated between few production blocks instead of many single processes leading to significant reduction of the change-over problem. Block planning can be applied in different applications e.g. in the fresh food production of yogurt, where blocks are formed for yogurt having the same recipe (Günther et al. 2004, p. 10). The approach also allows combining volume and campaign sequence planning in an integrated step instead of more complex two-level and iterative master production scheduling proposed by (Hill et al. 2000).

5.6.1 Production Indices, Index Sets, Control and Input Data

Production Indices

Production planning requires additional indices next to the production resource index $r \in R$. The production process $s \in S$ as core planning object in production is introduced. Production processes can be grouped into process groups $g \in G$. Production campaigns have a dedicated index $c \in C$ numbering the campaigns on the resource.

Production Index Sets

Production has a location subset with the production locations $\{l\} \in I^{P1}$, $\forall l \in L$. In addition, product subsets with all production output products $\{p\} \in I^{P2}$ and input products $\{p\} \in I^{P3}$, $\forall p \in P$ are defined.

Production resources are allocated to production locations $\{r,l\} \in I^{P4}$, $\forall r \in R, \{l\} \in I^{P1}$. Production processes run on production resources defined by $\{r,s\} \in I^{P5}$, $\forall r \in R, s \in S$. Groups of production processes on a resource are defined by $\{r,g\} \in I^{P6}$, $\forall r \in R$, $g \in G$. The triple of production process, process group and resource is defined by $\{r,s,g\} \in I^{P7}$, $\forall \{r,s\} \in I^{P5}$, $\{r,g\} \in I^{P6}$. Multiple input and output products are related to one production process as illustrated in fig. 67.

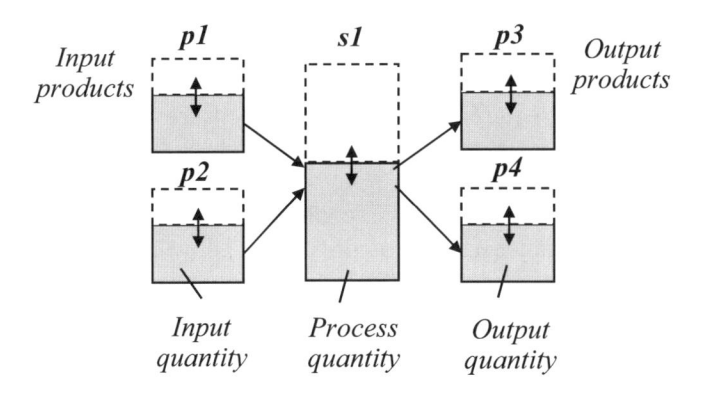

Fig. 67 Process input and output products

Output products created in a production process, are grouped into a resource-related index set $\{r,s,p\} \in I^{P8}$, $\forall \{r,s\} \in I^{P5}$, $p \in I^{Ppo}$ and into resource and location-related set $\{r,l,s,p\} \in I^{P9}$, $\forall \{r,l\} \in I^{P4}$, $\{r,s,p\} \in I^{P8}$. Output product results are aggregated on a location level in the set $\{p,l\} \in I^{P10}$, $\forall p \in I^{P2}$, $l \in I^{Pl}$.

Input products required in a production process have the same index set structure like output products: $\{r,s,p\} \in I^{P11}$ groups all processes and input products according to the resource $\forall \{r,s\} \in I^{P5}$, $p \in I^{P3}$. Combinations of processes, input products, resources and locations are defined by $\{r,l,s,p\} \in I^{P12}$, $\forall \{r,l\} \in I^{P4}$, $\{r,s,p\} \in I^{P11}$. Secondary demand for input products is aggregated on a location level based on the index set $\{p,l\} \in I^{P13}$, $\forall p \in I^{P3}$, $\{l\} \in I^{P1}$.

Output and input product index sets are later used for production and secondary demand quantity planning. Campaign and change-over planning is conducted on a process group and campaign level. $\{r,g_1,g_2\} \in I^{P14}$ is the index set of feasible change-overs between campaigns $g_1, g_2 \in G$, $\forall r \in R$. $\{r,c_1,c_2\} \in I^{P15}$ is the index set of feasible change-overs between campaigns $c_1, c_2 \in C$, $\forall r \in R$. Idle and change-over process groups belong to resource-specific index sets $\{r,g\} \in G^{PIdle}$, $\{r,g\} \in G^{PChange}$, $\forall g \in G, r \in R$.

Production Control Data

Production control data set boundaries and parameters for production operations of resources, processes, output and input products, process groups and change-overs.

Resources are controlled with minimum utilization $U_r^{P\min}$ and maximum utilization $U_r^{P\max}$ as well as a throughput variance parameter tpv_r^{Pr}, $\forall r \in R$. Minimum and maximum utilization boundaries are related to chemical process requirements in order to ensure process stability and product quality or for planning reasons to reach or fix a certain utilization of a resource.

The throughput variance factor controls the throughput smoothing on the resources. Variance factors of full 100% allow flexible throughput in different months, a variance of 20% limits the average throughput to be max. +/-20% higher/lower compared to the average throughput of the previous period as illustrated in fig. 68.

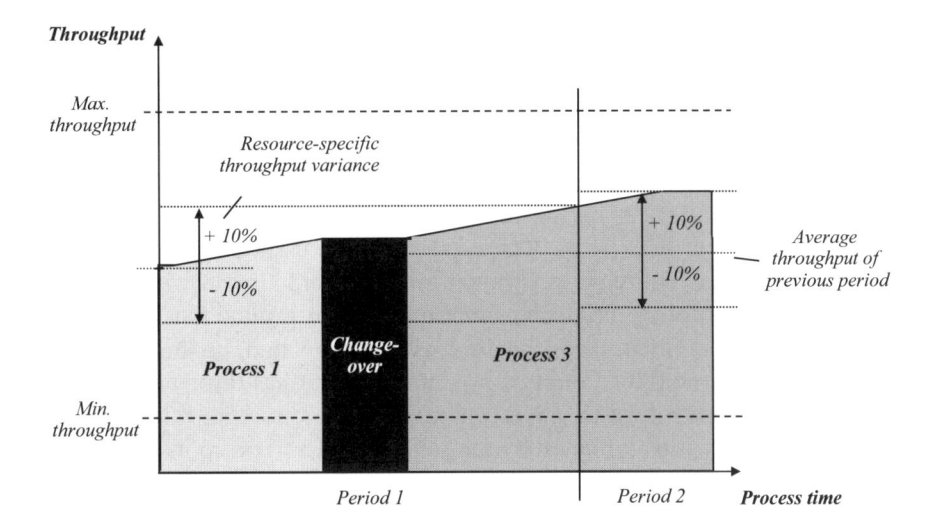

Fig. 68 Throughput smoothing principle

Processes have variable throughputs with minimum process throughput $TP_{rs}^{P\min}$ and maximum process throughput $TP_{rs}^{P\max}$ on a tons per hour basis $\forall \{r,s\} \in I^{P5}$. Minimum and maximum process throughputs bound the process quantity as illustrated in fig. 69.

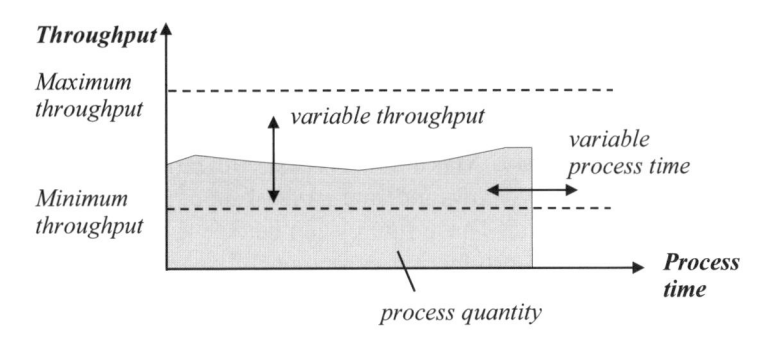

Fig. 69 Minimum and maximum process throughput

Variable production costs c_{rs}^{Pvpc} are related to process quantity on a value per ton basis in resource-specific currency $\forall \{r,s\} \in I^{P5}$.

Resource value fixed production costs c_r^{Pfpc}, $\forall r \in R$ in the resource-specific currency are input data not decision-relevant for optimization, but being used in order to calculate earnings before tax profits. Production fixed costs include the value depreciation of the resource, shift personnel costs and other fixed production-related cost blocks.

Output product quantities are bounded by minimum output share factors $a_{rsp}^{Popt\,min}$ and maximum output share factors $a_{rsp}^{Popt\,max}$ measured as percentage of the total process quantity $\forall \{r,s,p\} \in I^{P8}$.

Input product quantities like raw material consumption rates can be variable depending on utilization of the resource. Input product quantities are determined by linear recipe function with the recipe factors a_{rsp}^{Pipt} and b_{rsp}^{Pipt} on a tons per hour basis $\forall \{r,s,p\} \in I^{P11}$. This is a key issue of the production and the entire supply model including procurement is to decide on the variable raw material consumption rates in production. Both production and procurement planning are highly interrelated, i.e. high production rates determine the amount of raw material that has to be supplied. In the overall context of value chain optimization, production rates have to comply with decisions reflected by the sales model e.g. on spot sales quantities and prices.

In the following, the basic principle of the flexible recipes is presented. To keep the explanations simple, we consider only one single type of end product that is produced from one single raw material on one resource at a specific location during a given period. Required are the maximum process throughput of the resource measured in tons of output per hour and the input of raw material and output of finished products, respectively. In many types of chemical mass production, raw material consumption depends on the utilization rate of the equipment employed. Hence, linear recipe functions can be derived, which indicate the input of raw material required to produce the desired amount of output.

Table 28 shows a numerical example to derive linear recipe functions. Utilization rates (U) are given in steps of 20% assuming that all rates are used with equal probability. Maximum process utilization is given at 60 tons per hour. The next two rows indicate pairs of input and output quantities for each utilization rate. These figures can be derived from the technological parameters of the production equipment. The recipe factor is defined as the ratio of input to output quantities. Note that recipe factors only refer to the main raw material and do not include other input materials. This explains the value of the recipe factor of less than 1.0 for U = 20%. Finally, linear regression is applied with respect to the recipe factors. As a result, a variable consumption factor of $a = 1.29$ and a constant factor of $b = -5.7$ is obtained based on the given utilization rates and the underlying technological parameters.

5.6 Production Planning

Table 28 Recipe function example

Process utilization	Unit	20%	40%	60%	80%	100%
Maximum process throughput	[t/h]	60	60	60	60	60
Process output quantity	[t/h]	12	24	36	48	60
Process input quantity	[t/h]	10	25	41	56	72
Recipe factor (process input /process quantity)	[#]	0.83	1.04	1.14	1.17	1.20
Linear recipe function regression		$x_{rspt}^{Pipt} = 1.29 \cdot x_{rst}^{Pprocess} - 5.7$ $a_{rsp}^{Pipt} = 1.29, b_{rsp}^{Pipt} = -5.7$, $R^2 = 1.00$					

The recipe function factors depend on the process utilization comparing process quantity with maximum process throughput. b_{rsp}^{Pipt} is 0, if the recipe is static and does not change with process utilization. Otherwise the recipe factor increases with increasing process utilization. The example is also illustrated in fig. 70 and compared with a static recipe.

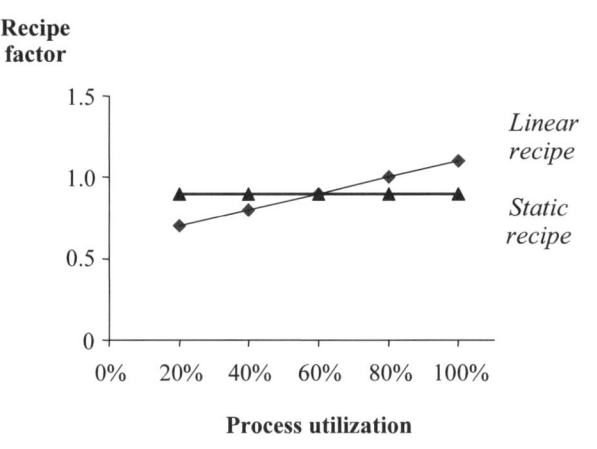

Fig. 70 Static recipe and linear recipe function

Linear recipe functions are one form found in industry. Of course, other forms of recipe functions are possible depending on the consumption pattern analyzed for a specific process. Variable recipe functions have critical importance in value chain planning and for the profitability, since increased raw material consumption rates can squeeze assumed profitability thanks to high sales volumes due to higher raw material consumption costs.

Campaigns are controlled through a resource-specific maximum number of campaigns C_r^{Max}, $\forall r \in R$. Maximum number of campaigns is set in industry practice based on planner experience. For example commodity production tends to have fewer campaigns per month due to long campaign run times and change-over times. In this case, three maximum campaigns per month and resource comprising two finished product campaigns and one change-over campaign are defined. Campaign run-time is bounded with minimum and maximum campaign hours $H_{rg}^{P\min}$ and $H_{rg}^{P\max}$ per period measured in hours $\forall \{r, g\} \in I^{P6}$. Change-overs can have additional change-over costs next to the production fixed costs that already include shifts responsible for cleaning the resource and campaign changes. Change-over costs $c_{rg_1g_2}^{Pcc}$, $\forall \{r, g_1, g_2\} \in I^{P14}$ are applied to the specified change requiring additional cleaning activities not covered by production fixed costs.

While production control parameters are relatively stable, reviewed and updated every three or six months, production input data are monthly updated.

Production Input Data

Production input data information is within the responsibility of the production team in the plant. Main input data is the available production capacity of the resource C_{rt}^{P}, $\forall r \in R, t \in T$ measured in tons in a respective month. Capacity volume refers to the best process on the resource with the highest maximum throughput. This convention is required since multipurpose resources can run different processes with a different maximum throughput. In addition, capacity volume can be influenced by climate conditions: Process throughputs can be different in summer compared to winter terms since weather-related parameters such as humidity and temperature can impact production and reaction conditions leading to different throughputs. Thirdly, the capacity volume is a commitment of production on how much to produce. Therefore, the production management is responsible for capacity achievements, process stability and product quality. So, capacity has also a management objective and responsibility aspect.

Planned shut-down hours H_{rt}^{Pshut}, $\forall r \in R, t \in T$ measured in hours relate to planned maintenance shut-downs occurring in regular yearly cycles and can take days or weeks. The idle status of the resource and the required change-over towards and back from the idle status has to be planned.

The initial process group g_{rt_1}, $\forall r \in R, t_1 \in T$ is the final input data having to be known in order to decide the resource's start-campaign in the first planning period.

5.6.2 Production Variables, Preprocessing and Constraints

Production Decision Variables

Production planning needs to decide production time and volumes as well as campaign sequence and change-overs.

The production process hours $h_{rst}^{Pprocess}$, $\forall \{r,s\} \in I^{P5}$ determine the duration of production process measured in hours. Process group hours h_{rgt}^{Pgroup}, $\forall \{r,g\} \in I^{P6}$, $t \in T$ represents the duration of a process group composed of one or multiple processes.

Production quantities are differentiated in process, input and output quantities. The process quantity $x_{rst}^{Pprocess}$, $\forall \{r,s\} \in I^{P5}$, $t \in T$ is determined by process hours and throughput. Variable production costs $v_{rst}^{P\,var}$, $\forall \{r,s\} \in I^{P5}$, $t \in T$ depend on the process quantity. The sum of all process quantities on a resource is the resource quantity $x_{rt}^{Presource}$, $\forall r \in R$, $t \in T$.

The process quantity is split on one or multiple output products with their output quantities x_{rspt}^{Popt}, $\forall \{r,s,p\} \in I^{P8}$, $t \in T$. The total production quantity by location is aggregated by x_{plt}^{Pprod}, $\forall \{p,l\} \in I^{P10}$, $t \in T$.

The process quantity requires input quantities from one or multiple raw materials or intermediate products x_{rspt}^{Pipt}, $\forall \{r,s,p\} \in I^{P11}$, $t \in T$. The total input quantity by location is the secondary demand $x_{plt}^{P\sec dem}$, $\forall \{p,l\} \in I^{P13}$, $t \in T$.

Campaign and change-over decisions require several binary variables to decide, which process groups run on which campaign. The binary variable α_{rgt}^{Pgroup} decides if a process group is active or not $\forall \{r,g\} \in I^{P6}$, $t \in T$. In analogy, the binary variable α_{rct}^{Pcamp} decides if a campaign is active or not $\forall r \in R$, $c \in C$, $t \in T$. The campaign mode $\alpha_{rgct}^{P\bmod e}$, $\forall \{r,g\} \in I^{P6}$, $c \in C$, $t \in T$ matches active process groups with active campaigns and uniquely assigns a process group to a campaign.

Change-over decisions with discrete planning buckets require deciding the ending campaign of a period becoming the starting campaign of the following period. The problem of campaign planning in time-indexed models is also addressed by Sürie (Sürie 2005a; Sürie 2005b). The binary variable $\hat{\alpha}_{rgt}^{Pend}$ decides, if a process group is on the ending campaign or not $\forall \{r,g\} \in I^{P6}$, $t \in T$. The binary change-over variable $\gamma_{rg_1g_2c_1c_2t}^{Pchange}$, $\forall \{r,g_1,g_2\} \in I^{P14}$, $\{r,c_1,c_2\} \in I^{P15}$, $t \in T$ decides if a change-over between process groups and campaigns takes place or not in the respective period. Related change-over costs $v_{rg_1g_2t}^{Pchange}$ are calculated $\forall \{r,g_1,g_2\} \in I^{P14}$, $t \in T$.

Production Preprocessing

Two parameters are calculated in a preprocessing step based on input and control data to simplify model constraints. $TP_r^{Pbas\max}$ is the maximum throughput basis $\forall r \in R$, determined by comparing all processes on the resource and identifying the maximum throughput out of them.

$$TP_r^{Pbas\,max} = \max_{\{r,s\} \in I^{P5}} \{TP_{rs}^{P\,max}\} \qquad \forall r \in R \qquad (77)$$

The period-specific throughput share $tp_{rt}^P \; \forall r \in R, \; t \in T$ is the capacity volume normed on the available period time deducted by shut-down hours in relation to the maximum throughput basis.

$$tp_{rt}^P = \frac{\dfrac{C_{rt}^P}{h_t - H_{rt}^{PShut}}}{TP_r^{Pbas\,max}} \qquad \forall r \in R, \; t \in T \qquad (78)$$

The throughput share will be later applied on all processes running on the resource, assuming that a higher throughput share compared to the maximum throughput basis impacts all processes on the resource. For example, higher throughputs in winter compared to summer apply to the best process but also to all other processes with lower throughput.

Production Constraints

Production constraints apply to resource, process and process group control data and model campaign and change-over planning. Initial constraints are related to production processes and planning of process times and quantities.

The sum of all process hours needs to fill the entire period and must be equal to the period hours.

$$\sum_{\{r,s\} \in I^{P5}} h_{rst}^{Pprocess} = h_t \qquad \forall r \in R, \; t \in T \qquad (79)$$

The process quantity ranges between minimum and maximum throughputs multiplied with the production time for the specific period. Minimum and maximum throughput boundaries are multiplied with the period-specific throughput share in order to reflect period-specific higher or lower throughput levels.

$$TP_{rs}^{P\,min} \cdot tp_{rt}^P \cdot h_{rst}^{Pprocess} \leq x_{rst}^{Pprocess} \leq TP_{rs}^{P\,max} \cdot tp_{rt}^P \cdot h_{rst}^{Pprocess} \qquad (80)$$

$$\forall \{r,s\} \in I^{P5}, \; t \in T$$

Variable production costs for a process are equal to process quantity multiplied by variable production cost rate per ton.

$$v_{rst}^{P\text{var}} = c_{rs}^{Pvpc} \cdot x_{rst}^{Pprocess} \qquad \forall \{r,s\} \in I^{P5}, t \in T \qquad (81)$$

Monthly variable production costs sum up all variable production costs across all processes and resources evaluated with the resource exchange rate factor.

$$v_t^{Pvpc} = \sum_{\{r,s\} \in I^{P5}} v_{rst}^{P\text{var}} \cdot \chi_{rt}^R \qquad \forall t \in T \qquad (82)$$

The resource quantity is the sum of all process quantities on the resource.

$$x_{rt}^{\Pr} = \sum_{\{r,s\} \in I^{P5}} x_{rst}^{\Pr s} \qquad \forall r \in R, t \in T \qquad (83)$$

Resource quantity divided by capacity volume has to comply with minimum and maximum utilization boundaries.

$$U_r^{P\min} \leq \frac{x_{rt}^{Presource}}{C_{rt}^P} \leq U_r^{P\max} \qquad \forall r \in R, t \in T \qquad (84)$$

Throughput smoothing requires the normed resource quantity per day having to be within throughput variance boundaries related to the resource quantity of the previous period if no shut-down is scheduled in current and previous period.

$$\frac{(1-tpv_r^P) \cdot x_{rt-1}^{Presource}}{h_{t-1}} \leq \frac{x_{rt}^{Presource}}{h_t} \leq \frac{(1+tpv_r^P) \cdot x_{rt-1}^{Presource}}{h_{t-1}} \qquad (85)$$
$$\forall r \in R, t \in T : t > t_1 \wedge H_{rt,t}^{PShut} = 0 \wedge H_{rt,t-1}^{PShut} = 0$$

Process quantity is the basis to determine input and output product quantities. Process output product quantity has range between the output minimum and maximum share of the product related to the process quantity.

$$a_{rsp}^{Popt\min} \cdot x_{rst}^{Pprocess} \leq x_{rspt}^{Popt} \leq a_{rsp}^{Popt\max} \cdot x_{rst}^{Pprocess} \qquad (86)$$
$$\forall \{r,s,p\} \in I^{P8}, \{r,s\} \in I^{P5}, t \in T$$

The process output product quantities of all output products have to be equal to the total process quantity to ensure mass equality between process quantity and output products quantities.

$$x_{rst}^{P5} = \sum_{\{r,s,p\} \in I^{P8}} x_{rspt}^{Popt} \qquad \forall \{r,s\} \in I^{P5}, t \in T \qquad (87)$$

Output product quantity by location and product is the sum of all output production quantities across all resources and processes.

$$x_{plt}^{Pprod} = \sum_{\{r,l,s,p\} \in I^{P9}} x_{rspt}^{Popt} \qquad \forall \{p,l\} \in I^{P10}, t \in T \qquad (88)$$

Input product quantities are calculated based on the linear recipe function with the parameters a_{rsp}^{Pipt} and b_{rsp}^{Pipt} on a tons per day basis.

$$x_{rspt}^{Pipt} = (a_{rsp}^{Pipt} \cdot x_{rst}^{Pprocess}) + (b_{rsp}^{ipt} \cdot h_{rst}^{Pprocess}) \qquad (89)$$
$$\forall \{r,s,p\} \in I^{P11}, \{r,s\} \in I^{P5}, t \in T$$

Product input quantities for single processes are aggregated to secondary demand quantity for an entire production location.

$$x_{plt}^{Psecdem} = \sum_{\{r,l,s,p\} \in I^{P12}} x_{rspt}^{Pipt} \qquad \forall \{p,l\} \in I^{P13}, t \in T \qquad (90)$$

Production constraints will be complete only considering input and output volumes and processes. However, campaign and change-over planning require additional constraints. Campaign and change-over planning is done on an aggregated process group level grouping different processes lacking change-over time and material losses if changed mutually. Process groups hence can reduce the number of campaign decisions. Nevertheless, process groups need to be linked to the planned processes. This is ensured by the next constraint, in which the process group hours have to be equal to the sum of process hours within the process group.

$$h_{rgt}^{Pgroup} = \sum_{\{r,s,g\} \in I^{P7}} h_{rst}^{Pprocess} \qquad \forall \{r,g\} \in I^{P6}, t \in T \qquad (91)$$

The process group hours range between minimum and maximum campaign hours, if a process group is active. This constraint bounds the run time of campaigns per period and activates the process group, if related processes have got a positive run time.

$$\alpha_{rgt}^{Pgroup} \cdot H_{rg}^{P\min} \leq h_{rgt}^{Pgroup} \leq \alpha_{rgt}^{Pgroup} \cdot H_{rg}^{P\max} \quad \forall \{r,g\} \in I^{P6}, t \in T \qquad (92)$$

Scheduled shut down hours have be covered by process group time of the idle process group.

$$H_{rt}^{Pshut} \leq \sum_{\{r,g\} \in I^{P6}, g \in G^{Pidle}} h_{rgt}^{Pgroup} \qquad \forall r \in R, t \in T \qquad (93)$$

Subsequently, active process groups are linked with active campaigns via active campaign modes as basis for change-over decisions as illustrated in fig. 71

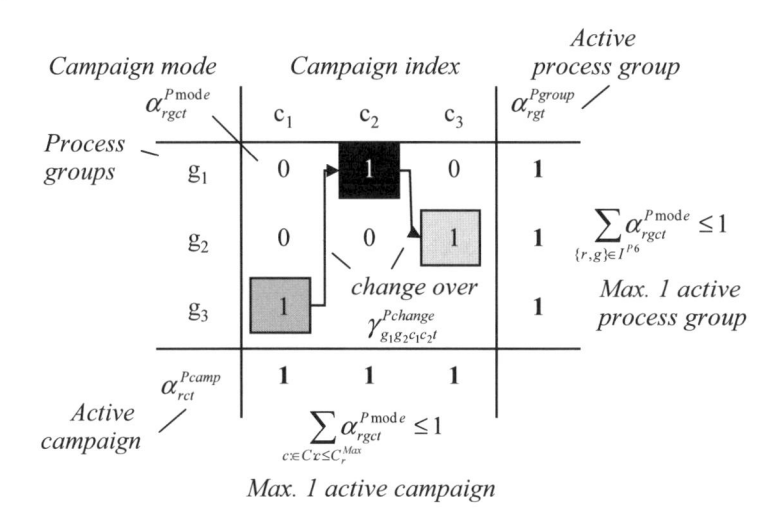

Fig. 71 Campaign and change-over planning example

In the following, the change-over and campaign planning constraints are detailed further. A process group is active, if a respective campaign mode is active.

$$\alpha_{rgt}^{Pgroup} = \sum_{c \in C : c \leq C_r^{Max}} \alpha_{rgct}^{P\,mode} \qquad \forall \{r,g\} \in I^{P6}, t \in T \qquad (94)$$

A campaign is active, if a respective campaign mode is active. Campaigns are bounded resource-specific by the maximum number of campaigns for the resource.

$$\alpha_{rct}^{Pcamp} = \sum_{\{r,g\} \in I^{P6}} \alpha_{rgct}^{P\,mode} \qquad \forall c \in C : c \leq C_r^{Max}, t \in T \qquad (95)$$

The campaign mode for the starting process group g_{rt_1} is active in the first period and first campaign to ensure that g_{rt_1} is the starting campaign for campaign planning.

$$\alpha_{rg_{rt_1}1t_1}^{P\,mode} = 1 \qquad\qquad \forall \{r,g\} \in I^{P6} \qquad (96)$$

The sum of active campaigns must be equal to the sum of active process groups; both cannot exceed the maximum number of campaigns defined for the resources per month.

$$\sum_{c \in C: c \leq C_r^{Max}} \alpha_{rct}^{Pcamp} = \sum_{\{r,g\} \in I^{P6}} \alpha_{rgt}^{Pgroup} \leq C_r^{Max} \qquad \forall r \in R, t \in T \qquad (97)$$

Inactive campaigns are sorted to the end in order to reach an ascending order of active campaigns.

$$\alpha_{rc_2t}^{Pcamp} \leq \alpha_{rc_1t}^{Pcamp} \qquad\qquad \forall \{r,c_1,c_2\} \in I^{P15}, t \in T \qquad (98)$$

A change-over variable is set to 1, if campaign modes for first and second process groups and the respective ordered campaigns both are active.

$$\gamma_{rg_1g_2c_1c_2t}^{Pchange} \leq \alpha_{rg_1c_1t}^{P\,mode} + \alpha_{rg_2c_2t}^{P\,mode} \leq 1 + \gamma_{rg_1g_2c_1c_2t}^{Pchange} \qquad (99)$$
$$\forall \{r,g_1,g_2\} \in I^{P14}, \{r,c_1,c_2\} \in I^{P15}, t \in T$$

Process groups without valid change-overs cannot have active campaign modes when following directly one after another.

$$\alpha_{rg_2c_2t}^{P\,mode} + \alpha_{rg_1c_1t}^{P\,mode} \leq 1 \qquad (100)$$
$$\forall \{r,g_1,g_2\} \notin I^{P14}, \{r,c_1,c_2\} \in I^{P15}, t \in T$$

It is assumed that only one change-over is possible for every process group combination per period. This assumption is valid for commodity production, where products are not produced multiple times in different campaigns within the same period.

$$\sum_{\{r,g_1,g_2\} \in I^{P14}} \gamma_{rg_1g_2c_1c_2t}^{Pchange} \leq 1, \qquad \forall \{r,c_1,c_2\} \in I^{P15}, t \in T \qquad (101)$$

Same constraint logic applies to the campaigns: Only one change-over at the most is possible for campaign combinations in one period.

$$\sum_{\{r,c_1,c_2\} \in I^{P15}} \gamma_{rg_1g_2c_1c_2t}^{Pchange} \leq 1 \qquad \forall \{r,g_1,g_2\} \in I^{P14}, t \in T \qquad (102)$$

In order to ensure campaign planning across periods, the process group being the end campaign of the period has to be determined.

5.6 Production Planning

$$\sum_{c \in C: c \leq C_r^{Max}} \alpha_{rct}^{Pcamp} \geq 1 + c \cdot \alpha_{rgct}^{P\,mode} - \hat{\alpha}_{rgt}^{Pend} \quad (103)$$

$$\forall \{r,g\} \in I^{P6}, \, c \in C : c \leq C_r^{Max}, \, t \in T$$

Exact in one process group is the ending campaign of a period.

$$\sum_{\{r,g\} \in I^{P6}} \hat{\alpha}_{rgt}^{Pend} = 1 \qquad \forall r \in R, \, t \in T \quad (104)$$

It is assumed that change-over process groups should not be ending campaigns, meaning that change-overs are realized *during* the period, not at the end. This assumption has a practical motivation, since the production organization at the end of a month focuses on accurate production accounting for the respective month. Change-overs are avoided if possible during this period to not disturb volume and value accuracy in accounting.

$$\hat{\alpha}_{rgt}^{Pend} = 0 \qquad \forall \{r,g\} \in I^{\text{Pr}\,g}, \, g \in G^{PChange}, \, t \in T \quad (105)$$

The ending campaign of the previous period is the starting campaign of the next period with an active campaign mode.

$$\hat{\alpha}_{rg,t-1}^{Pend} = \alpha_{rgt}^{Pgroup} \qquad \forall \{r,g\} \in I^{P6}, \, t \in T : t > t_1 \quad (106)$$

Change-over costs evaluate the change-overs with the related change-over cost rates.

$$v_{rg_1g_2t}^{Pchange} = \sum_{\{rc_1c_2\} \in I^{P15}} \gamma_{rg_1g_2c_1c_2t}^{Pchange} \cdot c_{rg_1g_2}^{Pcc} \quad \forall \{r,g_1,g_2\} \in I^{P14}, \, t \in T \quad (107)$$

The change-over costs are summed across all change-overs in the basis currency as basis for the objective function.

$$v_t^{Pcc} = \sum_{\{r,g_1,g_2\} \in I^{P14}} v_{rg_1g_2t}^{Pchange} \cdot \chi_{rt}^R \qquad \forall t \in T \quad (108)$$

5.6.3 Production Indicator Postprocessing

Production indicators focus on production utilization and throughput levels in order to indicate how capital-intensive resources with high fixed costs are utilized.

The production utilization level is defined as the total produced quantity divided by the maximum possible production quantity with the given processes on the resource across all resources. The production utilization level provides an overall utilization picture to the planner.

$$UL^P = \frac{\sum_{t \in T} \sum_{r \in R} x_{rt}^{P\,resource}}{\sum_{t \in T} \sum_{\{r,s\} \in I^{P5}} h_{rst}^{Pprocess} \cdot TP_{rs}^{P\max} \cdot tp_{rt}^{P}} \qquad (109)$$

Utilization is defined from the sales perspective to indicate further production quantities available to be sold to the market. Products with lower throughputs than the maximum throughput consequently should not reduce utilization if they are run at their highest maximum throughput level. For detailed analysis, utilization is also defined resource- and period-specific.

$$U_{rt}^{Pr} = \frac{x_{rt}^{P\,resource}}{\sum_{\{r,s\} \in I^{P5}} h_{rst}^{Pprocess} \cdot TP_{rs}^{P\max} \cdot tp_{rt}^{P}} \qquad \forall r \in R, t \in T \qquad (110)$$

The throughput level reflects the usage of the full throughput potential of the resource. Resource quantities are related to the capacity volume with the best throughput as a base line.

$$TP_{rt}^{P} = \frac{x_{rt}^{P\,resource}}{C_{rt}^{P}} \qquad \forall r \in R, t \in T \qquad (111)$$

Final aspects of value planning are production fixed costs. Production fixed costs are not planning-decision relevant but rather used in value planning to calculate the profit III. Hence, monthly production fixed costs per resource c_r^{Pfpc} are consolidated on the base currency in a postprocessing phase.

$$v_t^{Pfpc} = \sum_{r \in R} c_r^{Pfpc} \cdot \chi_{rt}^{R} \qquad \forall t \in T \qquad (112)$$

The monthly production fixed costs in base currency are withdrawn from profit II as shown in eq. 2.

5.7 Procurement Planning

The procurement planning model part needs to meet the requirements to distinguish spot and contract procurement planning including volumes and values integrated in the overall value chain planning.

5.7.1 Procurement Index Sets, Control and Input Data

Procurement planning is based on the index set of procurement locations $l \in I^{B1}$ and the product-procurement location combinations $\forall \{p,l\} \in I^{B2}$. Procurement is also differentiated into spot and contract: q_{plt}^{Bc} and c_{plt}^{Bc} are monthly procurement contract offer quantities and cost rates, q_{plt}^{Bs} and c_{plt}^{Bs} are the respective spot offers $\forall \{p,l\} \in I^{B2}$, $t \in T$. While contract procurement has to be executed as agreed, spot procurement is flexible defined by minimum and maximum quantity share boundaries $R_{pl}^{B \min s}$ and $R_{pl}^{B \max s}$ $\forall \{p,l\} \in I^{B2}$.

5.7.2 Procurement Variables and Constraints

The company decides spot procurement quantities x_{plt}^{Bs}, the sum of contract and spot procurements forms the total procurement total quantity x_{plt}^{B} $\forall \{p,l\} \in I^{B2}$. Applying the offer cost rates leads to total procurement costs v_{plt}^{B} in the location currency $\forall \{p,l\} \in I^{B2}$. Procurement input and control data are illustrated in fig. 72.

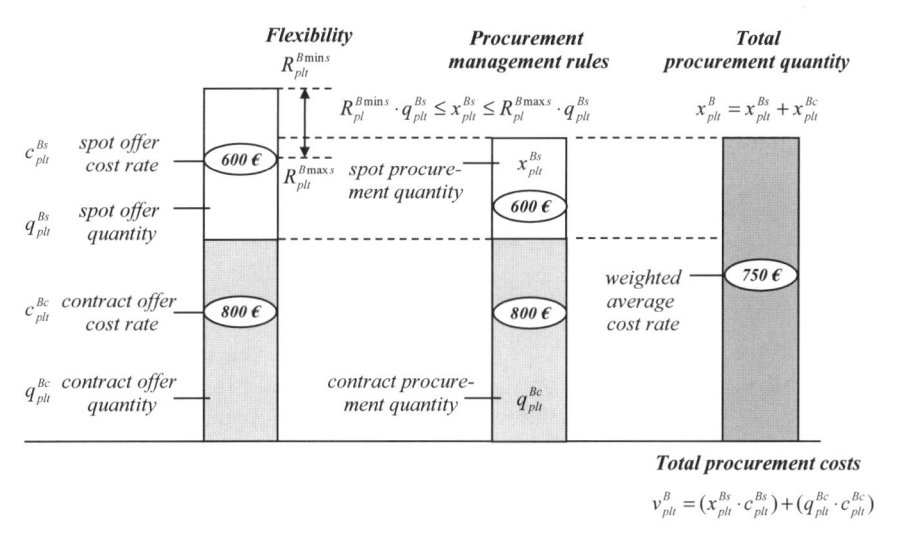

Fig. 72 Procurement planning

Procurement constraints bound the spot procurement quantities and calculate total quantities and costs. The total spot procurement quantity is limited between the minimum and maximum boundaries applying minimum/maximum shares to the offered quantity.

$$R_{pl}^{B\min s} \cdot q_{plt}^{Bs} \leq x_{plt}^{Bs} \leq R_{pl}^{B\max s} \cdot q_{plt}^{Bs} \qquad \forall \{p,l\} \in I^{B2}, t \in T \qquad (113)$$

Total procurement volume is the sum of spot and contract procurement quantities.

$$x_{plt}^{B} = x_{plt}^{Bs} + q_{plt}^{Bc} \qquad \forall \{p,l\} \in I^{B2}, t \in T \qquad (114)$$

Total procurement costs are the sum of spot and contract procurement costs.

$$v_{plt}^{B} = (x_{plt}^{Bs} \cdot c_{plt}^{Bs}) + (q_{plt}^{Bc} \cdot c_{plt}^{Bc}) \qquad \forall \{p,l\} \in I^{B2}, t \in T \qquad (115)$$

Finally, procurement costs are summed for all procured products and procurement locations applying the respective location exchange rate factors.

$$v_{plt}^{B} = \sum_{\{p,l\} \in I^{B2}} v_{plt}^{B} \cdot \chi_{lt}^{L} \qquad \forall t \in T \qquad (116)$$

5.7.3 Procurement Indicator Postprocessing

The procurement level PL^B indicates how much of the total offered quantity is actually procured.

$$PL^B = \frac{\sum_{\{p,l\} \in I^{B2}} \sum_{t \in T} (x_{plt}^{Bs} + q_{plt}^{Bc})}{\sum_{\{p,l\} \in I^{B2}} \sum_{t \in T} (q_{plt}^{Bs} + q_{plt}^{Bc})} \qquad (117)$$

Procurement planning is kept rather simple. However, procurement decisions have key influences on the overall value chain planning as investigated among other things in the following case study evaluation.

5.8 Conclusions

The developed value chain planning model is very comprehensive with its model basis, value, sales, distribution, production and procurement part. The comprehensiveness of the model is a logical consequence of the comprehensiveness of value chain planning requirements based on industry case and literature analysis. Conclusions:

- objective to reach a global optimum in the value chain instead of local optima requires more comprehensive integrated optimization models
- good model design is required to prevent long solution times and handling of infeasibility including
  - creation of relevant index sets to keep the number of constraints and variables minimized to the relevant cases
  - piecewise linear turnover approximation as alternative to exact quadratic optimization
  - block planning in production based on process groups and limiting of maximum campaigns to reduce number of integer variables
  - overall few use of integer variables
  - model-specific relaxation concept to support the planner to easily identifying areas of infeasibility

Model implementation and case study evaluation need to prove that the model supports value chain planning decisions towards global optima that the model is applicable in practice based in industry case data and that solution times are acceptable for application in the global monthly planning process.

6 Model Implementation and Case Study Evaluation

The model is implemented and evaluated with an industry case. The technical implementation is described first. Then, the industry case is introduced and model-relevant case data are presented. Model reaction tests are conducted for various industry case data sets to analyze model applicability, sensitivity and model planning results. Model performance tests are conducted to analyze technical parameters such as solution time or approximation methods quality. The case evaluation inspired several model extension possibilities presented at the end of the chapter.

6.1 Model Implementation

The model is implemented by means of the optimization software *ILOG OPL Studio 3.71*® using the optimization algorithms in *ILOG CPLEX 9.1*® and the database *Microsoft Access 2003*® on a personal computer with an *Intel Pentium 4*® processor, 1,598 Mhz and 256 MB RAM. The optimization software ILOG supports to solve optimization problems of different types such as LP, MILP and CP (Heisig/Minner 1999, p. 419; Skiscim 2001) and provides with Optimization Programming Language (OPL) a dedicated language to model optimization problems (van Hentenryck/Michel 2002).

The system architecture to implement the optimization model is composed by a database part including also a user interface and the optimization system comprising the optimization model, applied algorithms and interfaces to the database. The architecture has to be sufficient to handle comprehensive industry case data and a user friendly one to support the planner in managing data and analyzing results for decision support. The system architecture is illustrated in fig. 73

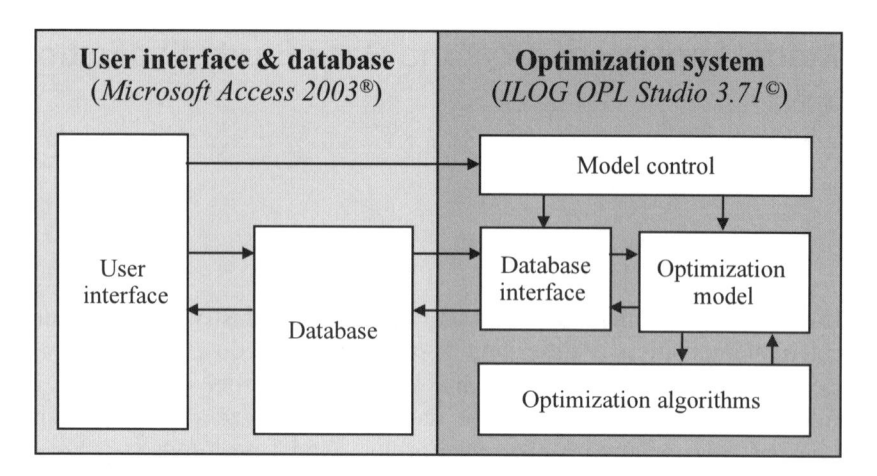

Fig. 73 Optimization model system architecture

Microsoft Access 2003® serves as database system and provides the planner with the user interface.

- *User interface:* planners' interface to the system to manage input and control data, define model control parameters and scenarios, start the optimization and to analyze optimization results and indicators in graphs and dynamic reports.
- Database: central point for all input and control data like optimization results with 50 tables, related queries and user interface forms.

ILOG OPL Studio 3.71® hosts the optimization model and provides separated scripts for preprocessing and postprocessing calculations as well as database interface management.

- *Model control:* this main script controls the database interface, pre- and postprocessing calculations and steers the optimization model. Model results specifically feasibility, relaxation and infeasibility are handled here.
- Database interface: three scripts form the database interface. Two of them include reading and writing procedures between optimization system and database. Data structures used by the optimization system and by the database are defined within a third script.
- Optimization model: decision variables, objective functions and constraints are defined in the optimization model.
- Optimization algorithms: optimization algorithms are integral part of the optimization system running in the background. Once the optimization model is started, optimization algorithms like SIMPLEX or Branch & Bound are automatically applied to solve the model.

The optimization system architecture is supporting the planner to conduct the planning activities integrated within the required monthly value chain planning process as defined in section 4.1.2.

Input data like demand, procurement offers, starting inventories and shipments as well as production capacities gathered in the first half of the planning process are entered or uploaded automatically into the database.

Then, the *basis plan* is calculated using the optimization system. The planner optionally calculates alternative plans when confronted with alternative input data scenarios or applying different control parameter scenarios.

After that, *optimization results* are then analyzed and compared in practice with manual plans, the planner is responsible for. In addition, optimization results reports are prepared for the different stakeholders within the value chain like as sales and marketing, controlling, production and procurement to present results and support management decisions.

The user interface is a critical element for planners' and planning stakeholders' acceptance of a planning system. The developed main user interface is structured

- vertically into input and control data vs. optimization results and
- horizontally into a model header to interactively set model control parameters and display model result indicators and the value chain areas' sales, distribution production and procurement as shown in fig. 74.

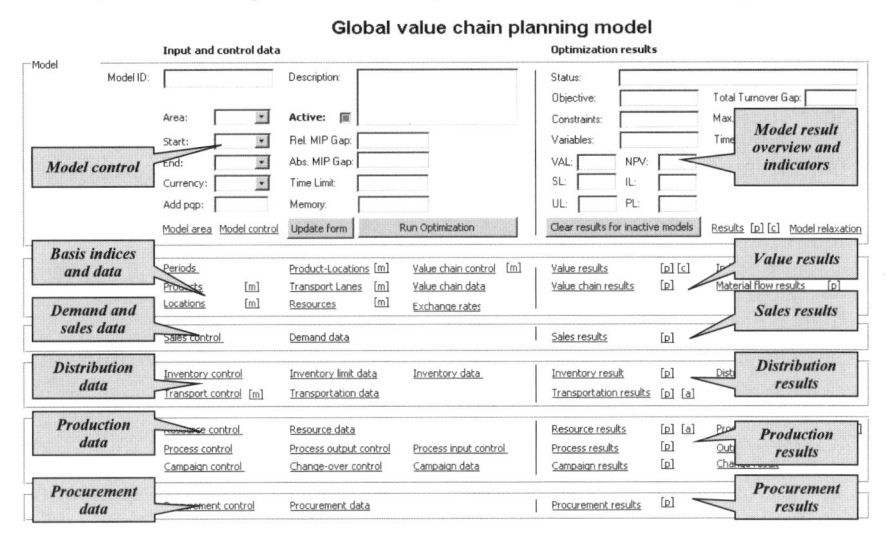

Fig. 74 Optimization model system user interface

User interface objective is to provide direct access to all data and results and to support interactive definition of model control data as well as analysis of key indicators. Specifically, the model control parameters can be set interactively. The most important parameters shown on the left side of the screen header are:

- *ModelID*: model name to keep various plan versions separated.b
- *Active:* activates a defined model; only one active model at a time can be solved. Optimization results are filtered for active models.
- *Area*: definition of a model area allowing the planner to optimize the value chain as a whole or defined sub-models focusing on parts of the value chain like separated products or separated resources.
- *Starting period and ending period*: flexible definition of the planning horizon with starting and ending period within the defined like a month.
- *Currency*: basis planning currency for consolidating all values on same basis.
- *Add pqp:* number of additional partial quantity points applied in piece-wise linear turnover approximation.
- *Relative and absolute MIP gap:* mixed integer programming parameter for controlling optimization accuracy e.g. MIP gap of 1% leads to an algorithm stop, if the objective value cannot be improved within a tolerance interval of 1%.
- *Time and memory limit:* parameters to limit the solution time and system memory used.

Key planning result indicators are displayed on the right side of the header, including

- objective value z and net present value NPV of discounted earnings before tax level (NPV) to evaluate overall value results
- the value-added level VA^S (VAL)
- solution time, constraints and variables for model performance evaluation
- sales level (SL) SL^S, inventory level (IL) IL^I, production utilization level (UL) UL^P, procurement level (PL) PL^B to evaluate overall volume results

The model result indicators support the planner in directly comparing plans on a top level to identify areas for a more detailed analysis.

The optimization system is sufficient for the purpose of model evaluation and testing. In practice, such stand-alone systems often serve as a pilot to prepare implementation of integrated advanced planning systems (APS) into which optimization models can be integrated. APS ensure integration into transaction systems to access actual inventories, resource data or cost information directly. In addition, they are network-capable and globally accessible, a crucial requirement especially in global planning with globally distributed sales and marketing staff contributing own input and market know-how to it.

An APS project requires similar activities like stand-alone optimization systems do, especially the preparation of required basis data and the test and evaluation of optimization models with real industry case data, which is done in the following.

6.2 Case Study Evaluation

The model is evaluated based on an industry case study in order to

- test the model in industry practice against value chain planning requirements
- evaluate model reactions and value chain planning results by volume and values given also different planning scenarios
- specifically evaluate the technical model performance with respect to solution times and accuracy of results

6.2.1 Case Study Overview

The case is provided by a globally operating company producing chemical commodities with annual production volumes exceeding 1 Mio. tons who intents to use the global value chain planning model in their global monthly sales and operations planning process for a planning horizon of 6 to 12 months. The model should also help the planners to better understand the dynamics between the key steps in this value chain network: the profit of a complex value chain network being determined by few parameters: raw material and sales prices and volumes as well as critical bottleneck steps in the network. Therefore, besides in planning, the model is also used for training purpose to show the planners the impact these parameters have on the value chain profit.

The industry case matches the chemical industry characteristics in the scope defined in subchapter 3.1 specifically

- Spot and contract business is an important business differentiation in the case

202   6 Model Implementation and Case Study Evaluation

- The company faces monthly sales and raw material price and volume volatility and operates a global distribution network
- The entire production system is organized as a global multi-stage network with multi-purpose and continuously operated production resources
- Raw material consumption rates in production are variable depending on the degree of capacity utilization

The global value chain network structures introduced in chapter 3 with sales, distribution, production and procurement locations as well as the transportation network matches the case. Now, the considered production resources are introduced in more detail. Production resources are either *continuous* or multi-purpose *campaign* production resources (see also fig. 29): continuous production resources produce one single intermediate product on a dedicated resource in continuous production mode, while campaign production resources produce multiple products on the same resource requiring change-overs between processes. The optimization is tested with an excerpt of the entire company's global value chain network with selected continuous and campaign production resources at four global production locations (see fig. 75).

Legend: ■ =Continuous product model   ■ = Campaign product model   □ = Global Model
           → = Material flow   □ = Continuous resource   □ = Campaign resource

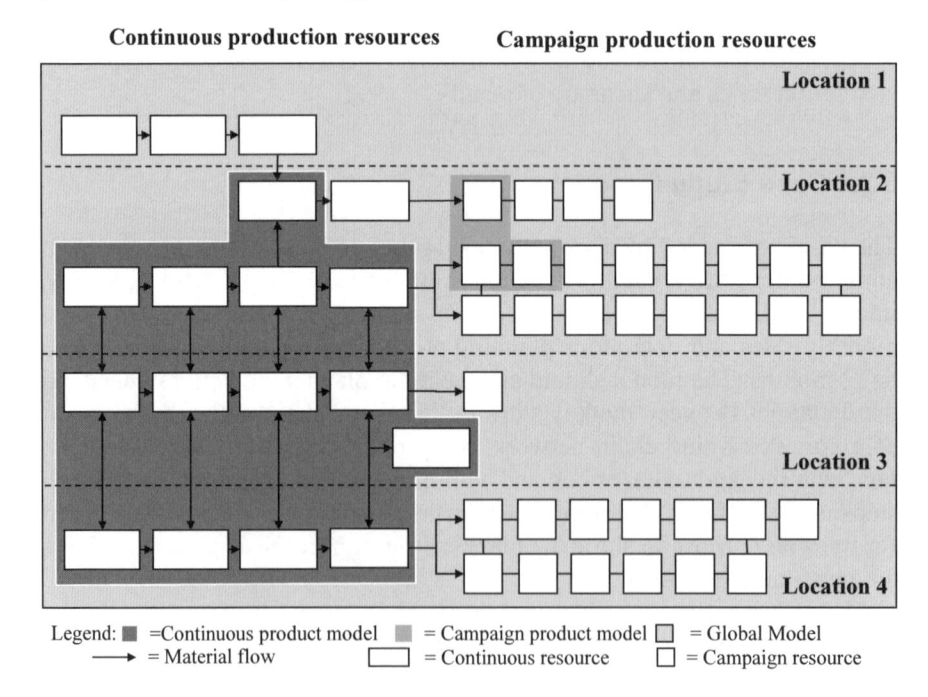

Fig. 75 Production resource structures

Continuous production resources in the location 2, location 3 and location 4 produce the same products that can be exchanged between these locations e.g. in case of shut-downs or shortage situations in a specific market. The continuous production resources supply the subsequent campaign resources. It is also possible to sell intermediate products to the market instead of using it for own campaign production. For example location 3 has one continuous resource not supplying campaign resources since products produced here are exclusively sold to the market.

Three *model areas* can be distinguished. Model areas allow defining separated areas in the value chain network to be optimized separately. Model areas can be defined by clustered resources and/or products that have clear interfaces. Defining model area eases the implementation of a comprehensive value chain planning optimization model for a complex value chain network: the optimization model can be tested for parts of the value chain network with limited data complexity before extending the model to the entire network. Three model areas are defined in the industry case study:

- *Continuous product model (Cont.):* model area clustering continuous production resources and dedicated products with a clear interface to the subsequent campaign resources based on captive demands; model area focus is on balancing raw material consumption and costs, production utilization with volatile and flexible sales.
- Campaign product model (Camp.): model area clustering selected campaign resources with a clear interface to continuous production resources based on captive supply data; model area focuses on campaign planning and change-overs.
- Global model: integrated model including the entire value chain with continuous and campaign production resources.

The model areas have the advantage to build up and test models step by step in order to integrate sub-segments into an end-to-end model. The two model areas *Continuous product model* and *Campaign product model* are evaluated applying the developed planning model. The model scale driven is shown in table 29 or the two model areas investigated of the *Continuous product model* and *Campaign product model*, serving as basis for implementing the *Global model,* which is not presented in this work.

Table 29 Industry case study scale

Indices and index combinations	Unit	Continuous	Campaign
Products	[#]	9	13
Locations	[#]	24	9
Product-location combinations	[#]	71	62
Transportation lanes	[#]	34	10
Transportation lane-product combinations	[#]	67	49
Production resources	[#]	14	3
Production processes	[#]	15	23
Production process groups	[#]	15	14
Maximum campaigns per period and resource	[#]	1	3
Periods	[#]	12	12

Legend: # = number of elements

The model areas have limited complexity considering single indices such as products or resources. Complexity increases combining basis indices like transportation lanes and products. A planning horizon of 12 periods will lead later to optimization models with more than 10,000 decision variables already for this limited scope.

Model Evaluation Overview

The model is evaluated by means of provided case test data. Industry case data are modified by values and selected volume parameters for confidentiality reasons, Therefore, optimization results will not match directly with the actual business. However, the provided data are realistic in order to test sensitivity of the model and to compare model reactions applying different scenarios. Two test types are conducted:

- Model reaction tests focusing on volume and value results
- Model performance tests focusing on solution time and accuracy of results
  The design of model reaction tests follows a set of ideas:
- Model reaction tests focus on analyzing optimization value chain planning results and interpreting the impact of single model parameters on the overall results.
- The experiments always compare the overall profit with the volume indices in sales, distribution, production and procurement in order to compare volume and value results and showing interdependencies
- The experiments cover all areas of the value chain in sales, distribution, production and procurement to demonstrate the influence of a single value chain area on the overall value chain performance

- In each experiment, different scenarios for one parameter are executed to measure the impact on overall profit and the key volume indices
- The parameters modified in each tests are either value or volume parameters with both having impact in the overall volume and value situation in the value chain. The parameters modified are perceived as key parameters in value chain planning, planners are confronted with.

Model reaction tests also demonstrate the applicability of the model in an industry context based on real industry case data.

Model performance tests focus on technical aspects of the model:

- Is the model solution time in an industry case data environment acceptable for the planners and in the planning process? Given the influence of integer variables on solution time, integer values for production changeover parameters are modified to measure the impact on solution times.
- Are the model results accurate enough considering the piecewise linear approximation methods developed? Here, piecewise linear approximation accuracy is modified with additional points added in the approximation and result accuracy as well as model run time compared.

Table 30 provides an overview of the different evaluation experiments conducted by model area and the respective test types.

Table 30 Model evaluation experiment overview

Area	Evaluation experiment	Cont.	Camp.	R.	P.
Basis	Basis plan	■	■	■	■
Values	Exchange rate scenarios	■		■	
Sales	Sales price scenarios	■		■	
	Sales flexibility scenarios	■		■	
	Elasticity scenario evaluation	■		■	■
Distribution	Inventory flexibility scenarios	■	■	■	
	Transportation time scenarios	■		■	
Production	Production variance scenarios		■	■	
	Minimum utilization scenarios	■		■	
	Recipe function scenarios	■		■	
	Minimum campaign time scenarios		■	■	
	Maximum campaign scenarios		■	■	■
Procurement	Procurement price scenarios	■		■	

Legend: Cont. = Continuous product model, Camp. = Campaign product model, R. = Reaction test, P. = Performance tests, ■ = related model area and test type

Basis plan evaluation presents the optimization results of the provided test data: the value plan and the sales, distribution, production and procurement volume plan in an overview. Results of the future inventory value planning are specifically evaluated and the developed elasticity analysis algorithm based on provided demand data as well as present campaign planning results is tested. Subsequently, several what-if-scenario experiments are defined by value chain area, where input or control data scenarios are evaluated to test model reaction and performance.

6.2.2 Basis Plan Evaluation

The basis plan evaluation analyzes optimization volumes and value results across the considered planning horizon of 12 periods. First, solution times for the continuous products and the campaign problem are shown in table 31.

Table 31 Basis plan solution times

Parameters	Unit	Continuous	Campaign
Constraints	[#]	12,745	14,785
Variables	[#]	14,799	15,723
Iterations	[#]	1,003	5,066
Run time	[sec]	5.41	23.98

Solution times are sufficiently fast to be applied in tactical planning where no real time response times are required. Secondly, value results are presented. All value results are indexed focusing on comparing results and to ensure confidentiality of industry data. Initially, the value plan with total profits and single values in sales, distribution, production and procurement is analyzed.

- The considered profit is based on the profit III on the earnings before tax and on a monthly level as shown in 2
- The sales value index represents spot and contract sales net turnovers.
- The distribution cost index combines variable transportation and warehousing costs as well as capital costs for local and transit inventories.
- The production cost index combines variable and fixed production costs.
- The procurement cost index combines spot and contract procurement costs.

Indices reflect the relations of profit, turnover and costs on a normed, sanitized basis in order to focus on relations between value parameters instead of absolute figures.

Fig. 76 shows the total profit index as bar column related to the left vertical axis. The profit index indicates the planned profit per period over the planning horizon of 12 months. Compared to this top value indicator, the detailed turnover and costs indicators are shown as lines with markers related to the right vertical axis. The detailed value indicators are presented in line with the value chain structure starting with the sales turnover index and continuing with cost indices in distribution, production and procurement.

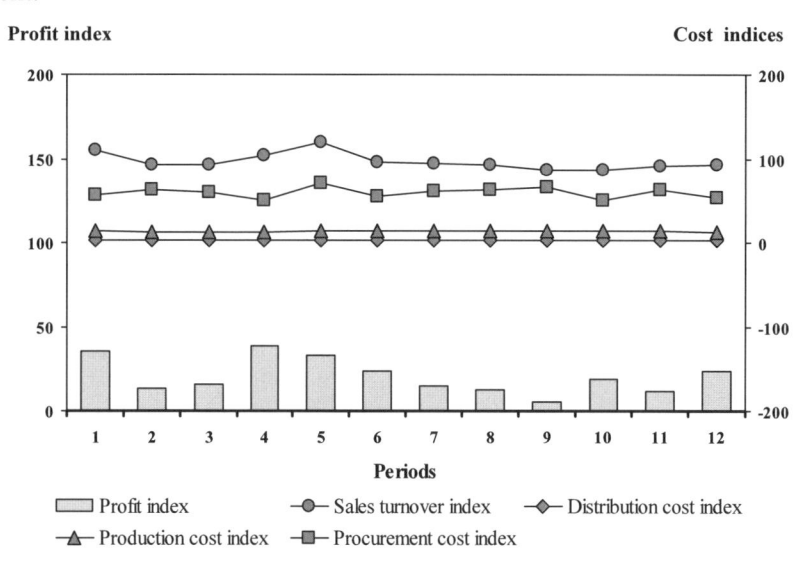

Fig. 76 Basis value plan

The initial view on total values reveals the characteristics of a commodity value chain introduced in the work's motivation (see fig. 1): profits are monthly volatile as it can be seen in fig. 76.

Secondly, the profit volatility is mainly driven by sales and procurement value volatility and the respective ratio of sales turnover to procurement costs. The higher the ratio of sales turnover to procurement costs, the better the respective profit index.

In consideration of total values across the entire value chain, the importance of the single value chain steps gets transparent. In proportion, management of sales and procurement values are much more important to the company's overall profitability than managing the distribution and production costs. In this case, production and distribution costs are relatively stable. Since related cost parameters are stable, consequently distribution and production volumes should remain on a relatively constant level.

The underlying volumes are analyzed in the following. Sales volumes – spot and contract – are near to demand. It is assumed that spot sales are lower or equal to the spot demand. Consequently, underlying sales prices are sufficiently high compared to supply costs, since all businesses are nearly fulfilled as it can be seen in fig. 77.

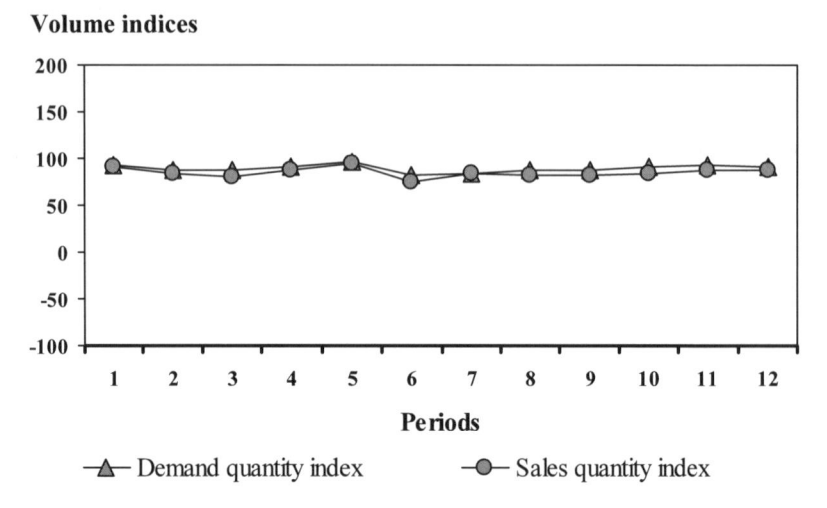

Volume indices

Fig. 77 Sales volume plan

Sales volumes by period follow the same pattern as sales turnover does with a peak in the middle periods. In conclusion, the overall demand volume and prices are sufficiently attractive to be served.

Distribution quantities cover transportation, transit and local inventories. Transportation quantities result from the overall material balances and indices follow a certain corridor as shown in fig. 78.

Volume indices

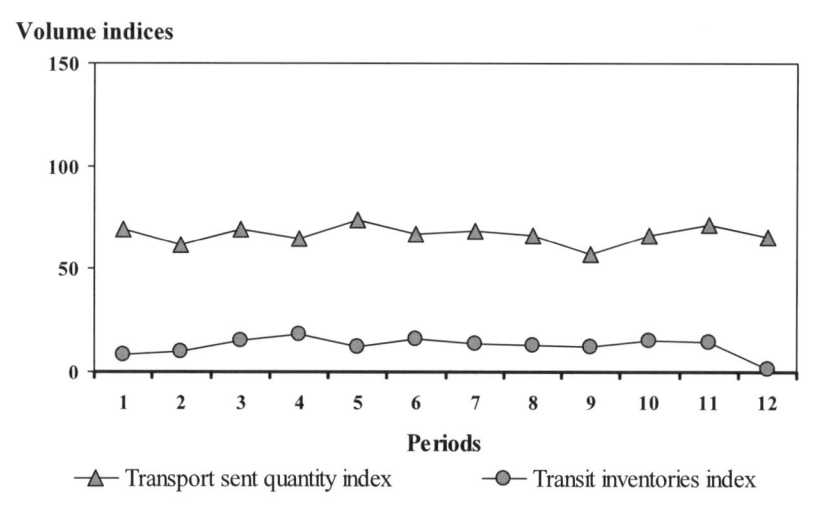

Fig. 78 Transportation and transit inventory volume plan

Transit inventories for transcontinental shipments increase during the first periods and drop at the end of the planning horizons. The increase at the beginning results from lower actual shipments in the starting periods and the time lag to build up the "pipeline flow" of transit inventories on the vessels. The transit inventory dropping at the end is caused by the plan cut with missing sales quantities after period 12. Since planning focus lies on the first six to nine months in practice, this inaccuracy at the end is acceptable from a value chain planning perspective.

Inventories in the first months are relatively high compared to the minimum inventory index due to higher actual inventories at the beginning of the planning horizon as shown in fig. 79.

210   6 Model Implementation and Case Study Evaluation

Volume indices

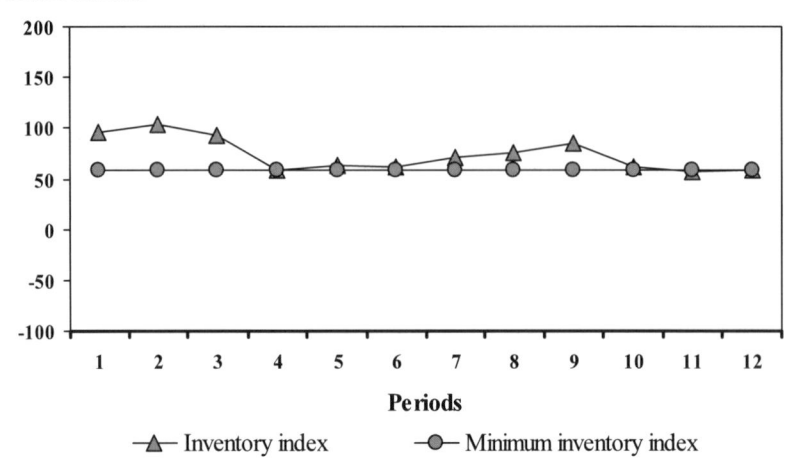

Fig. 79 Inventory volume plan

Subsequently, inventories are dropped down to minimum with a slight increase in the third quarter of the planning horizon. The inventory increase is mainly driven by raw material procurement decisions in combination with production quantities.

Production analysis considers total capacity volume and total production quantity indices across all considered production steps of the value chain. Production quantities are near to capacity. Therefore, sales decisions are sufficient to utilize production capacities as shown in fig. 80.

Volume indices

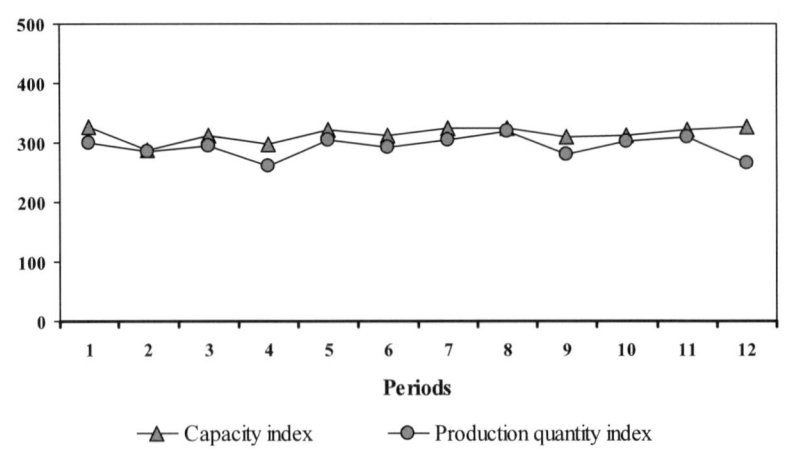

Fig. 80 Production volume plan

Spot and contract procurement quantity planning is shown in the next chart. The procurement value volatility is mainly driven by volume volatility as shown in fig. 81.

Volume index

[Chart: Procurement quantity index over periods 1-12, values approximately: 450, 500, 410, 180, 520, 370, 520, 460, 490, 270, 420, 400]

Periods

─▲─ Procurement quantity index

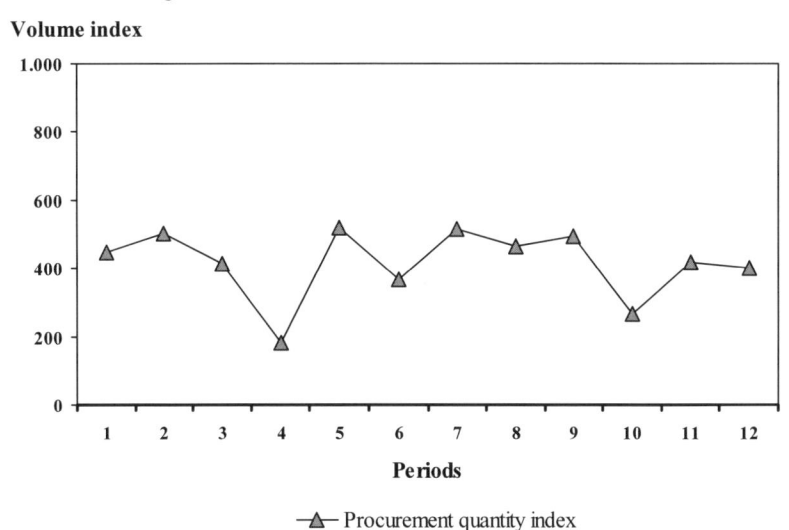

Fig. 81 Procurement volume plan

Volatile raw material prices lead to risk-hedging procurement decisions within the given procurement flexibility: more raw material is purchased within periods of low prices compared to periods of higher prices. This is the cause for increasing inventories within the ninth period: raw materials were procured during the previous periods due to better prices and put on stock. Capital costs for holding inventory are negligible compared to procurement cost savings. These results prove the importance of defining not only minimum and maximum inventories from a logistical perspective to ensure delivery capability or to consider physical warehousing boundaries. Maximum bandwidth inventories in addition needs to be defined considering the inventory function for risk-hedging of raw material costs.

Basis for calculating capital costs on transit and local inventories are the planned product values. The model supports future inventory value planning based on the raw material price offers. Fig. 82 shows results of the inventory value planning.

Product value index

[Chart: Future inventory value plan, showing product value index across 12 periods for Raw material, Product A, Product B, Product C, Product D, and Product E]

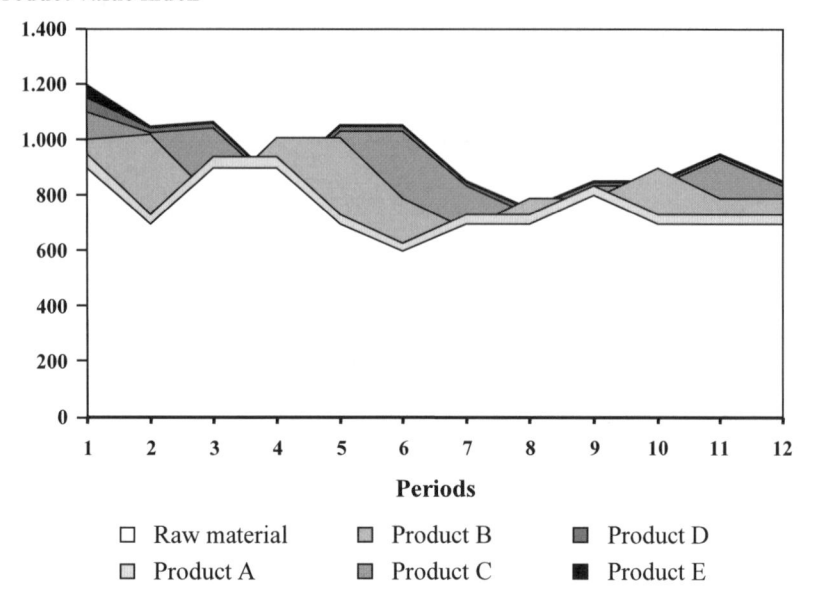

Fig. 82 Future inventory value plan

The raw material product value shown in the foreground of the chart is related to the procurement price offers. Subsequently, the following products are listed based on the raw material. The production step costs for each product are the values-added on the raw material value. In addition, an assumed timestamp is considered reflecting lead times of products through the value chain: therefore, price changes of the raw material would impact the value of e.g. product E with some periods of delay.

The spot demand elasticity analysis algorithm has also been analyzed and presented in the sales model (see table 24). Two products in two sales locations with a significant number of customers are analyzed with respect to spot sales elasticity: customer demands are ranked by price and the price-quantity function of cumulated spot sales quantities. The average price is determined over 12 periods. Fig. 83 shows the results of the elasticity analysis.

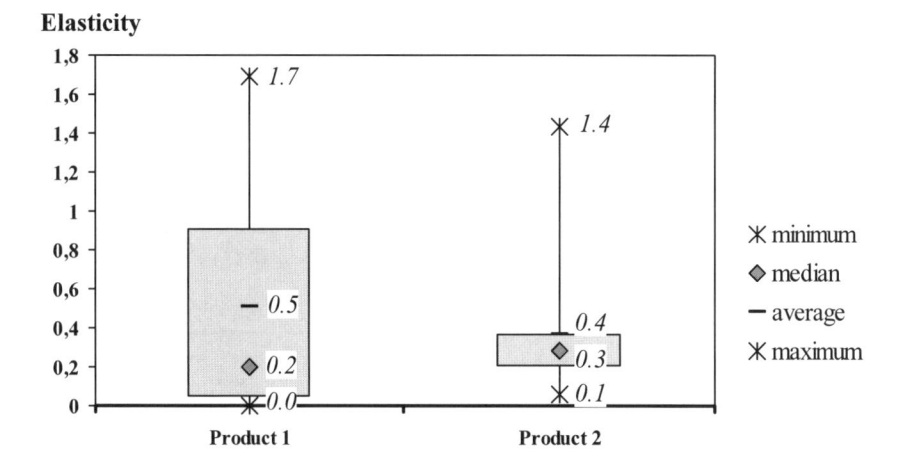

Fig. 83 Elasticity analysis example

The figure shows minimum, average, median and maximum elasticity for product 1 and product 2 respectively across 12 months. The average elasticity for product 1 across all 12 months is 0.5, for product 2 0.4 but are volatile analyzed for 12 months. The number of customers for one product and one location varied each month between 10 and 36. The R-squared value for the linear regression varied monthly between 0.4 and 0.99.

Without having conducted a full elasticity analysis across the entire portfolio, the analysis helps to prove market perceptions such as a higher elasticity exist in one market compared to another market or comparing elasticity between products being perceived to have a different elasticity. The statistical quality of the linear regression analysis in selected months is considered as good in terms of the number of customers involved and the R-squared value proving the applicability of the approach.

This simple analysis shows that there are price differences within regional price-quantity forecasts reflected by the elasticity greater than 0 leading to an average price increase, if sales quantities are lower than the total demand quantity. Secondly, elasticities are not stable but differ each period in analogy to demand quantity and prices.

The next analysis is related to campaign planning developed in the production model. Two multi-purpose resources with 3 and 5 process groups including a process group for change-overs are considered. The maximum campaign number per period and resource is set to 3, resulting in two finished product campaigns and one change-over campaign required for change. The campaign plan is shown in fig. 84.

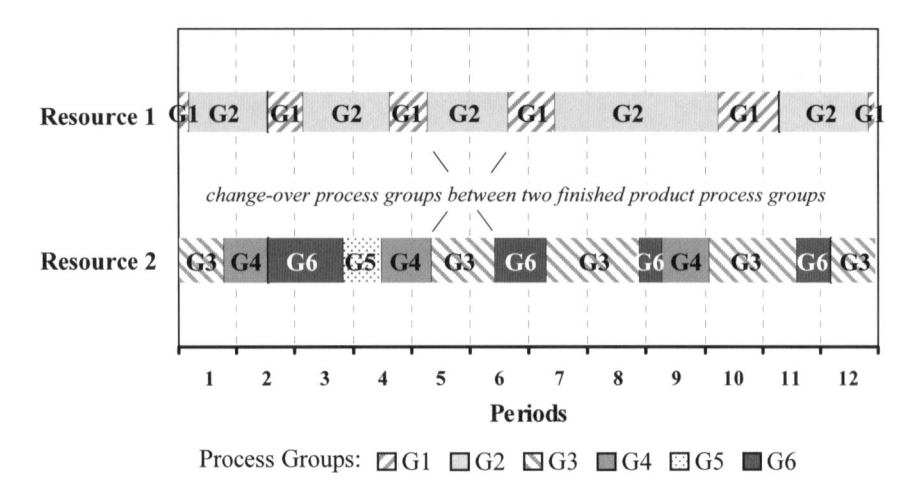

Fig. 84 Production campaign plan

Resource 1 begins with two campaigns and one change-over per period and dedicates the resources within period 8 and 9 to one process group. Resource 2 has more process groups and has to be changed every period. Consequently, inventory is required bridging periods with no campaign assuming constant demand, what should be investigated as one of the following scenario experiments.

6.2.3 Value Scenario Evaluation

Value scenarios relate to value parameters used across the value chain like currency exchange rates or interest rates. The impact of currency exchange rate scenarios on total volumes and values is investigated. The exchange rate from currency C1 to currency C2 across the 12 periods is applied. Then, the exchange rate of currency C1 is varied from a basis exchange rate assuming a depreciation or appreciation of the respective currency. Resulting, the volume indices for total sales, inventory, utilization and procurement as well as the value index of total profit on discounted earnings before tax level are compared. In addition, the ratio of total turnover to total procurement costs named VA index is evaluated. Fig. 85 illustrates experiment results.

Profit index   **All other indices**

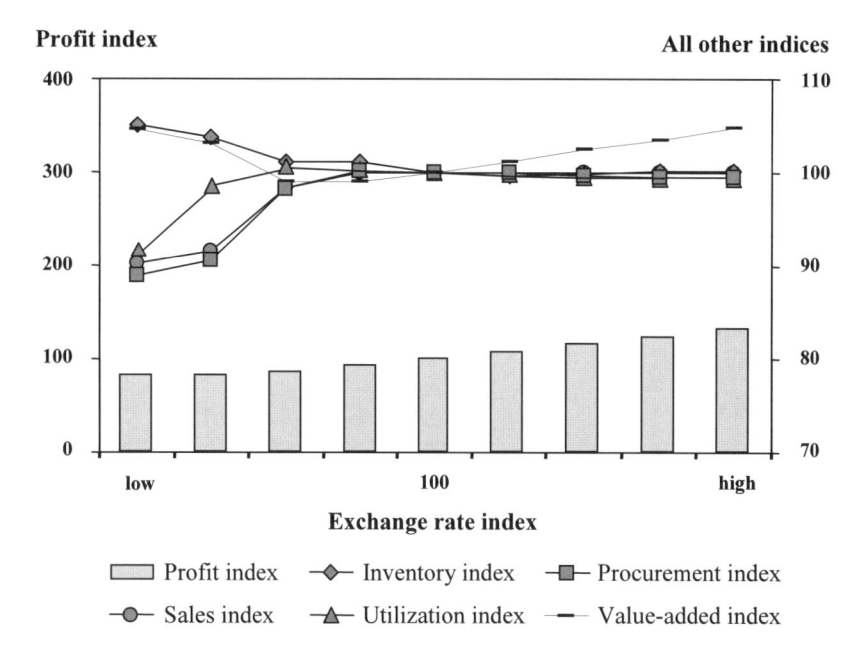

Fig. 85 Exchange rate scenario evaluation

Fig. 85 shows the different exchange rate index experiments on the horizontal axis with the basis experiment indexed with 100. The total profit index is represented by the column bar related to the left vertical axis. The volume indices for sales, inventory, production and procurement as well as the value-added index are represented by the lines with markers related to the right vertical axis. This figure structure and the sequence of indices oriented at the value chain structure will be used also in the following experiments.

An appreciation of currency C1 compared to currency C2 does lead to a profit increase but no volume increase starting from a situation of full utilization. In conclusion, the C1 appreciation has only a value, but no volume effects. The value-added index improves constantly for these scenarios due to the fact of more sales being conducted in the C1 regions while supply costs are on a C2 basis. Consequently, a strong C1 depreciation leads to a reduction of all volume indices including sales, production and procurement, since sales prices lose value due to the depreciated currency. The VA index drops to a minimum point. From this point, volumes are reduced in the optimization leading to better profits compared to a continuation of full-utilization policies. The VA-index improves again when volumes are reduced: sales turnover remains constant but procurement costs within the index can be reduced. The inventory index is higher in a situation of lower volumes since starting inventories at the beginning of the planning period are not reduced as fast as in the basis scenario and remain longer on stock.

6.2.4 Sales Scenario Evaluation

Sales scenario evaluation considers the impact of sales prices, sales flexibility and elasticity on volumes and values. Initially, sales prices are varied starting from a basis plan and consider the impact on volumes and values shown in fig. 86.

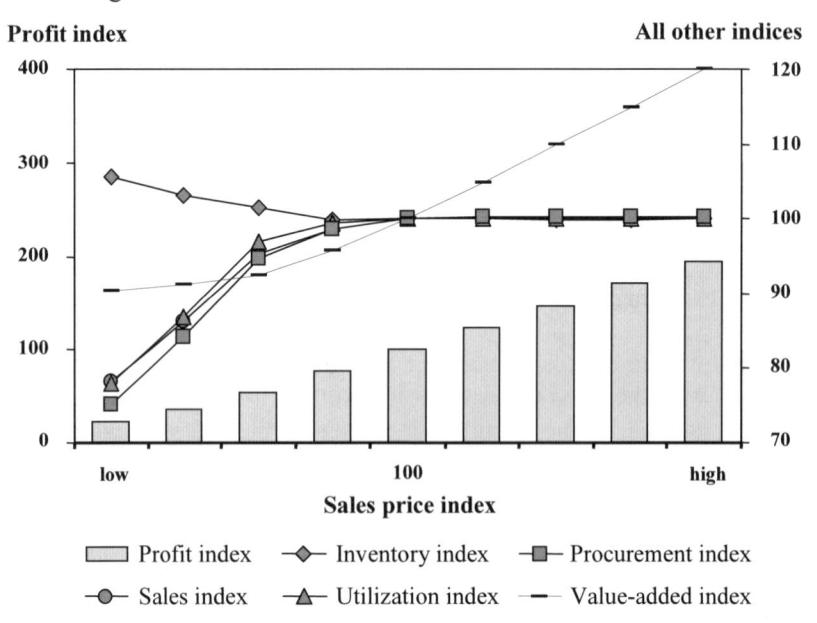

Fig. 86 Sales price scenario evaluation

Results are no surprise: increasing sales prices lead to larger profits but not to higher volumes, since the value chain is already utilized. Lower sales prices impose a reduction of volumes, since increasingly fewer sales opportunities and prices compensate for the supply costs. In addition, it is called into mind that linear recipe functions in production lead to lower volumes with lower raw material consumption rates and consequently lower supply costs.

Secondly, the impact of spots sales flexibility on volumes and values is considered. The minimum spot sales share boundary is increased from 0% – spot sales demand can be cut down to 0 – to higher shares shown in fig. 87.

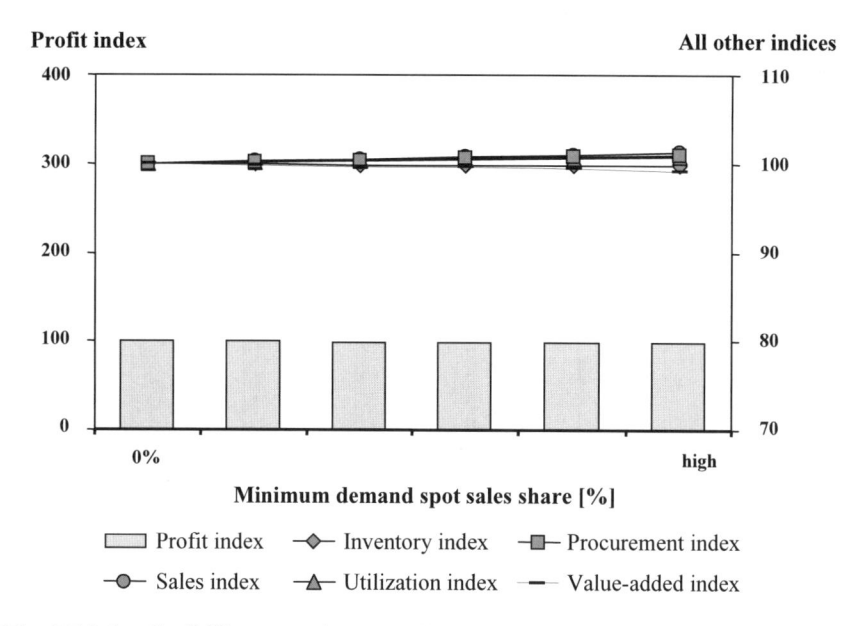

[Figure showing bar and line chart with Profit index (left axis, 0-400) and All other indices (right axis, 70-110) vs Minimum demand spot sales share [%] ranging from 0% to high. Legend: Profit index, Inventory index, Procurement index, Sales index, Utilization index, Value-added index.]

Fig. 87 Sales flexibility scenario evaluation

Limited optimization flexibility should lead to lower profits compared to full optimization flexibility, since spot sales boundaries have to be considered in the second case that would not be served in the optimum case. But in the specific case, limiting sales flexibility has only limited impact on volumes and values.

Elasticity in the third experiment is varied from 0 – no price effects in case of sales volume changes compared to demand quantity – to 1.0 for external spot sales. The higher the elasticity, the higher is the underlying price effect. Fig. 88 reveals that elasticity has direct influence on profits and volumes.

Profit index   **All other indices**

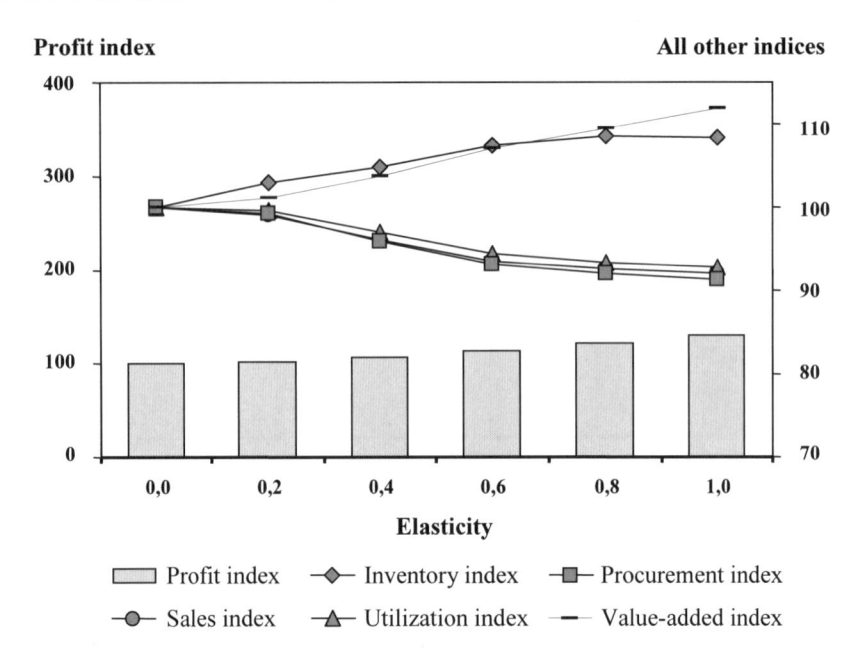

[Chart showing Elasticity (0.0 to 1.0) on x-axis, with bars for Profit index and lines for Inventory index, Procurement index, Sales index, Utilization index, and Value-added index]

Fig. 88 Elasticity scenario evaluation

Starting with elasticity 0 in the basis scenario, increasing elasticity leads to lower volumes in production, sales and procurement, since lower quantities lead to higher prices and higher profit can be realized with lower volumes. Consequently, the value-added index increases with increasing elasticity. The inventory index also grows due to the reduction of volumes and relatively high inventories at the beginning of the planning horizon requiring more time to be reduced.

Elasticity experiments rely on the developed turnover approximation method. The following model performance tests investigate the influence of partial quantity points on approximation accuracy and solution time. The more sections subdivide spot sales quantities into partial quantities, the better the approximation, but the more constraints and decision variables are required.

Table 32 shows the model performance: the total and the maximum relative turnover gap are analyzed to evaluate the accuracy of the turnover approximation depending on the number of partial quantity points; constraints, variables and solution time indicate the solution performance and model complexity.

Table 32 Turnover approximation performance test

Partial quantity points	4	14	24	44	64	84	104
Total relative turnover gap	1.45%	0.04%	0.02%	0.00%	0.00%	0.00%	0.00%
Max. relative turnover gap	10.94%	0.15%	0.04%	0.01%	0.01%	0.00%	0.00%
Constraints	12,745	16,585	20,425	28,105	35,785	43,465	51,145
Variables	14,799	18,639	22,479	30,159	37,839	45,519	53,199
Solution time in sec.	6.0	6.0	6.4	6.8	7.5	7.5	8.2

4 partial quantity points – the 0-point, minimum, demanded and maximum spot sales quantity – make the default case. A solution time of 6 seconds for nearly 15,000 variables is fast. However, the total approximated turnover is about 1.45% lower than the most accurate turnover in the case of 104 partial quantity points. In addition, extreme cases of product-location-period combinations exist with a 10.9% turnover gap. The approximation is improved by adding more partial quantity points. Although the number of constraints and variables increase significantly, solution times remain short, below 10 seconds. 44 partial quantity points already reached turnover gaps of less than 0.01%. In conclusion, 44 partial quantity points can be used as approximation basis as already used in the previous elasticity scenario experiment.

6.2.5 Distribution Scenario Evaluation

Distribution scenario evaluation considers inventory management and transportation time scenarios. Initially, the impact of maximum bandwidth inventory boundaries on profits and volumes is analyzed. Maximum bandwidth inventories are increased and decreased starting from a basis scenario as shown in fig. 89.

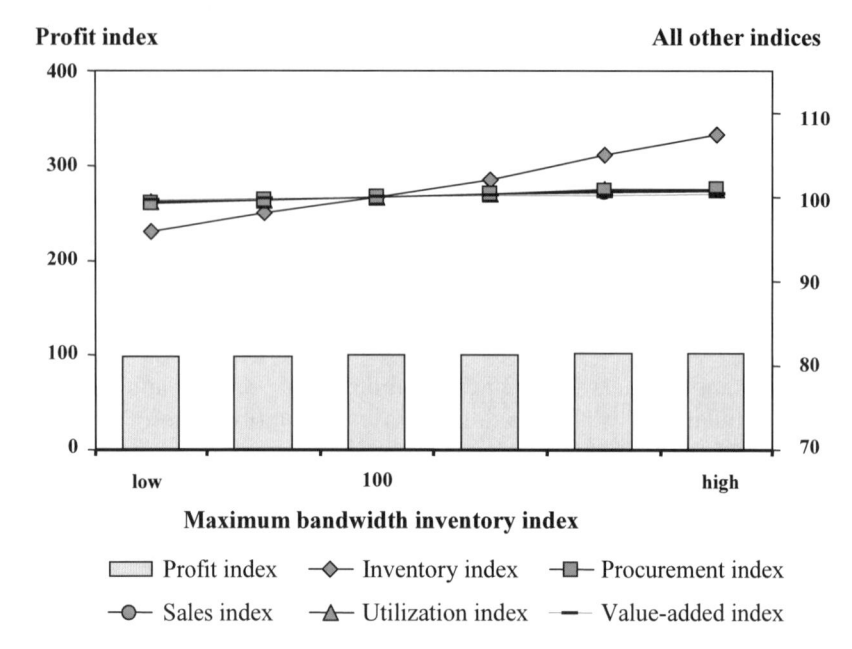

Fig. 89 Maximum bandwidth inventory scenario evaluation – continuous

One hypothesis is that an increasing maximum bandwidth inventory provides more optimization flexibility and hence better profits at the expense of higher inventories. In this case, inventories increase indeed with higher maximum bandwidth inventories, but inventory flexibility does not significantly compensate for higher capital costs and profit remains relatively stable. The opposite effect can be observed at maximum bandwidth inventories: inventories are reduced overall with no significant impact on profits in the specific case.

Repeating the experiment for campaign production may lead to a more differentiated picture, since inventory has the primary function to bridge campaigns and to ensure continuous delivery capability between campaigns. However, results do not show a clear tendency in fig. 90.

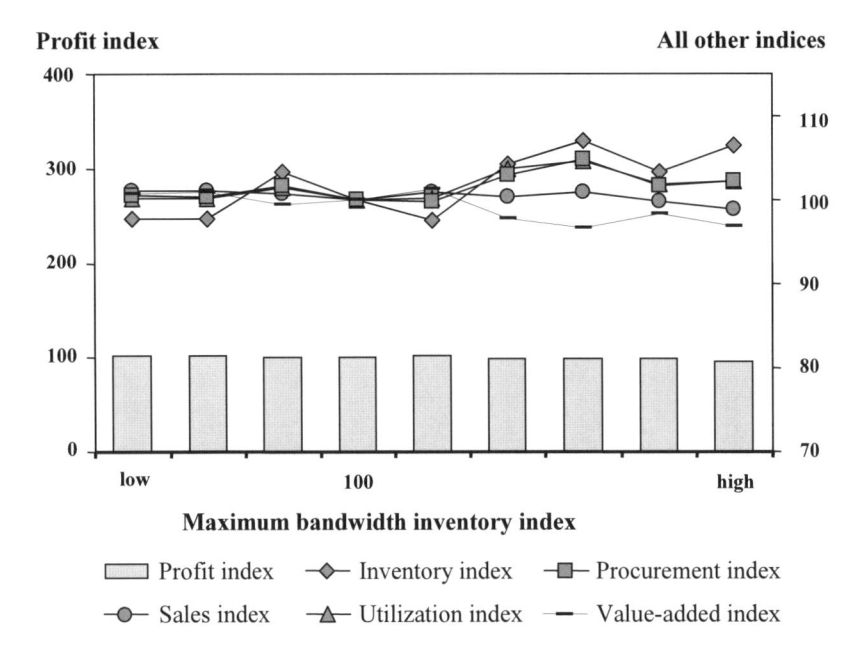

Fig. 90 Maximum bandwidth inventory scenario evaluation – campaign

Higher maximum bandwidth inventories lead to higher inventories, however, profits and other volume indices have no clear tendencies and profits even decrease slightly with higher inventory flexibility. These results can be explained by a relative MIP gap of 1% with lower profits being possible within this tolerance interval especially in campaign production, where many change-over decisions based on integer variables have to be compared.

Thirdly, different transportation times for transcontinental shipments are distinguished starting with basis transportation times measured in days an indexed with 100 as shown in fig. 91.

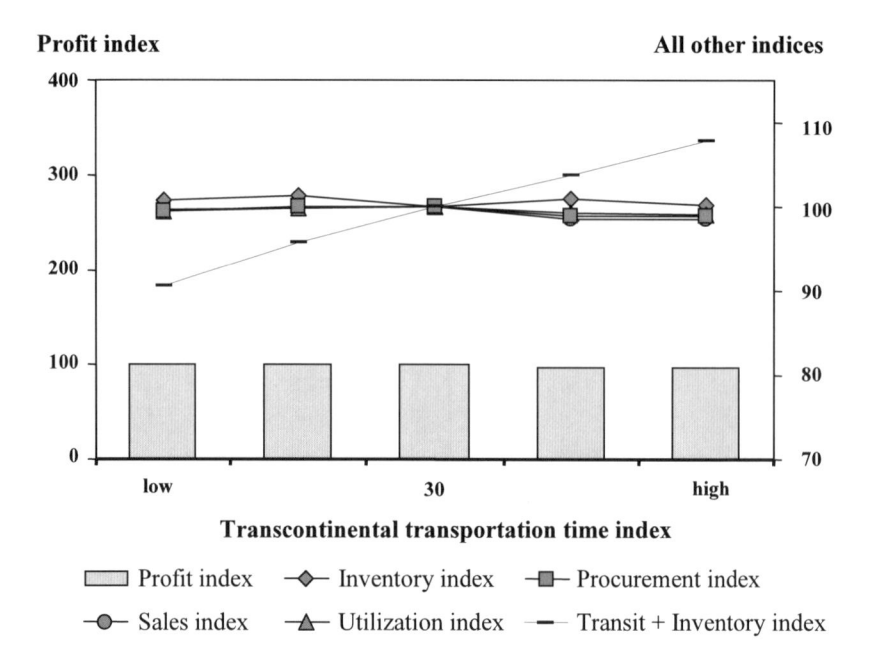

Fig. 91 Transportation time scenario evaluation

Experiment results prove that longer transportation times lead to higher transit inventories and lower profits due to higher capital costs for transit inventories.

6.2.6 Production Scenario Evaluation

Production scenario evaluation investigates the influences of production and campaign control parameters on volumes and values. All experiments share the hypothesis that restrictive production control leads to lower profits due to lower optimization flexibility.

Throughput smoothing is an important planning requirement. The impact of different production variance scenarios on profits and volumes is analyzed. A production variance of for example 20% means that the average resource throughput of the following periods can be only 20% higher or lower compared to the previous period. The production variance is varied from 100% - meaning no throughput smoothing restrictions - to more restrictive production variances as shown in fig. 92.

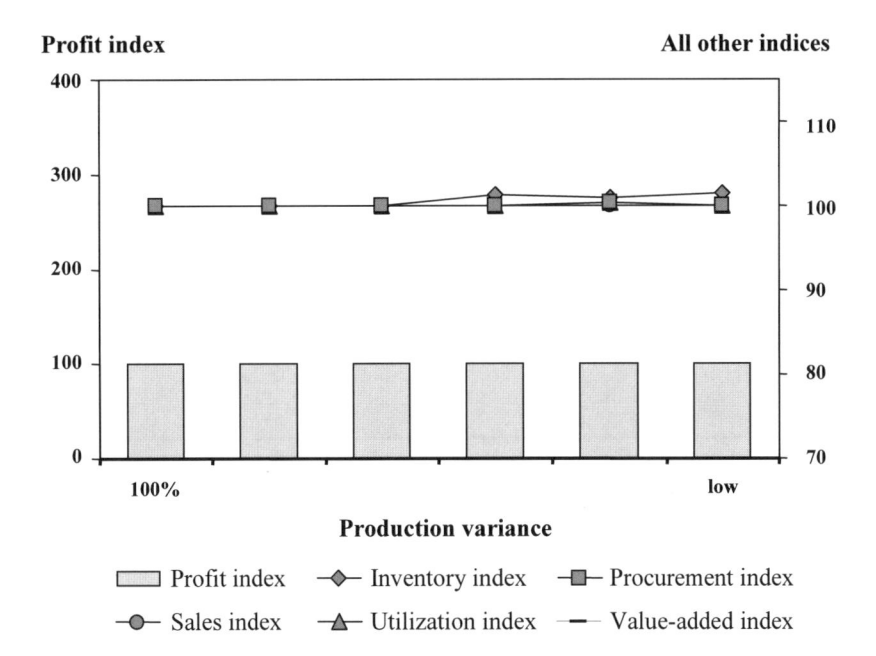

Fig. 92 Production variance scenario evaluation

Due to high production utilization and relatively constant throughput levels in the basis plan, throughput smoothing is not critical in this case situation. Therefore, a more restrictive smoothing has only limited influence on volumes and profits and leads to slightly increased inventories.

Secondly, we consider minimum utilization scenarios as control parameters. Minimum utilization has to be set if required by production processes e.g. in order to ensure process stability and product quality. But minimum utilizations defined higher than required may lead to lower profits due to less optimization flexibility as shown in fig. 93.

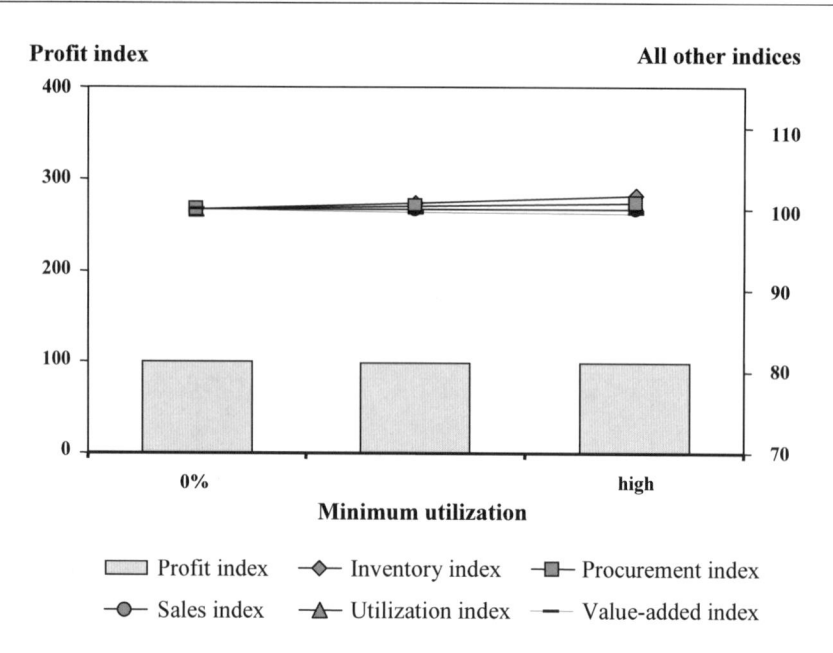

Fig. 93 Minimum utilization scenario evaluation

However, minimum utilization scenarios do not influence profits and volumes as assumed due to the same reason as in case of production variance: the basis plan already led to a situation of high utilization, minimum utilization limits are not a hard constraint in the specific case.

Thirdly, different recipe function gradients in production are considered. Starting with a basis recipe function, planning results for a higher or lower recipe function gradient are compared as it can be seen in fig. 94.

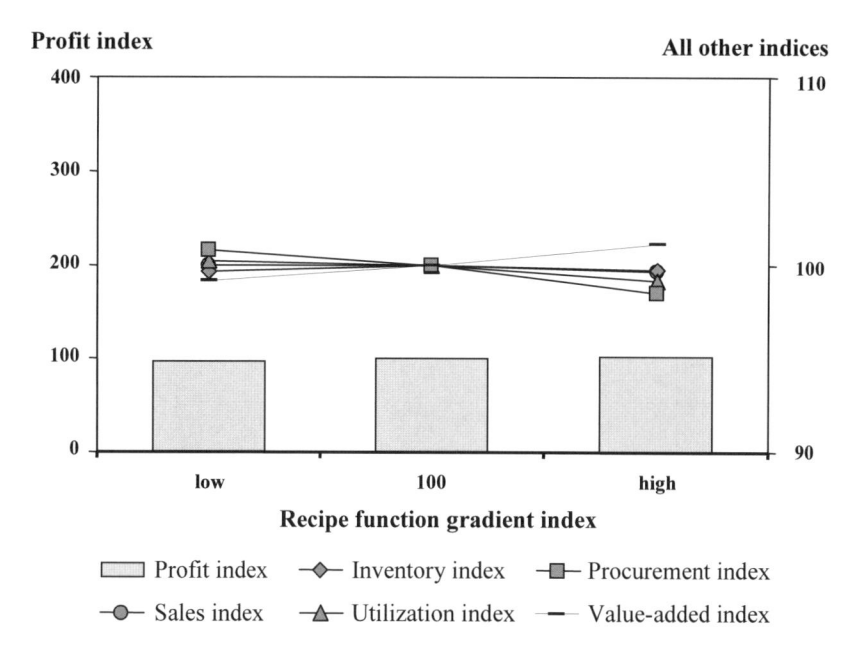

Fig. 94 Recipe function scenario evaluation

Higher recipe function gradients lead to slightly higher profits and lower volume indices. The reason is that higher gradients mean also a reduction of production quantities resulting into lower raw material consumption rates compared to the basis scenario. Lower recipe function gradients lead to lower profits and slightly higher volume indices, since the raw material consumption rates do not decrease as fast as within the basis or high gradient scenario.

While previous experiments focused on volume constraints, now campaign planning experiments are designed. First the minimum campaign time measured in hours is varied from no restrictions (1h) to long minimum campaign times reflecting the planner's experience in optimal lot sizes and campaign run times. As shown in fig. 95 profit decreases slightly, production volumes and hence utilization decreases and inventories increase, since higher minimum campaign run times limit change-over optimization decisions.

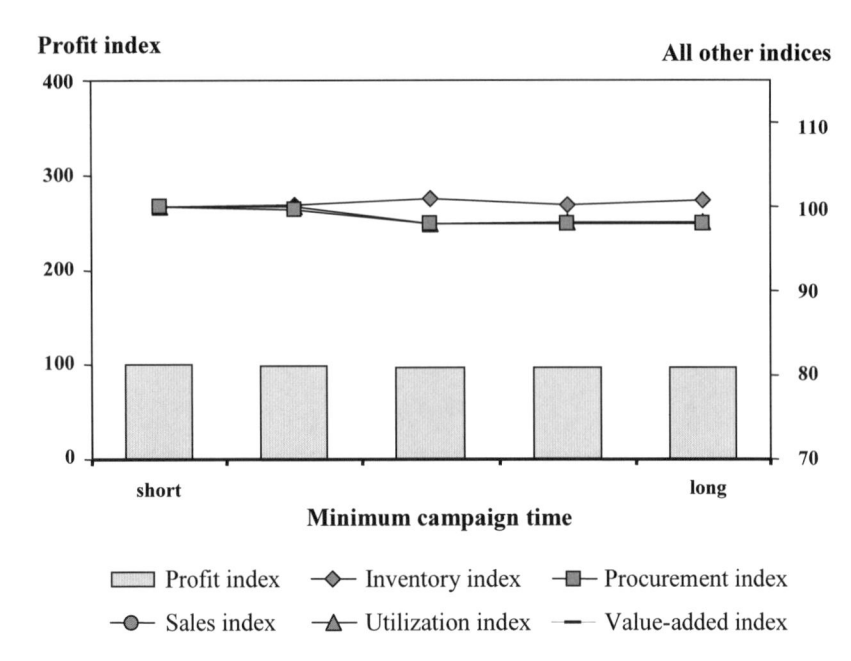

Fig. 95 Minimum campaign time scenario evaluation

In practice, this experience can lead to the situation that planner and production have to review applied campaign run times based on experience and to compare them with optimization results.

Finally, different maximum campaign scenarios are compared. As introduced, three campaigns per resource and period are set as a limit based on planner's experience.

The maximum campaign scenario with 5 and 7 maximum campaigns is compared in fig. 96.

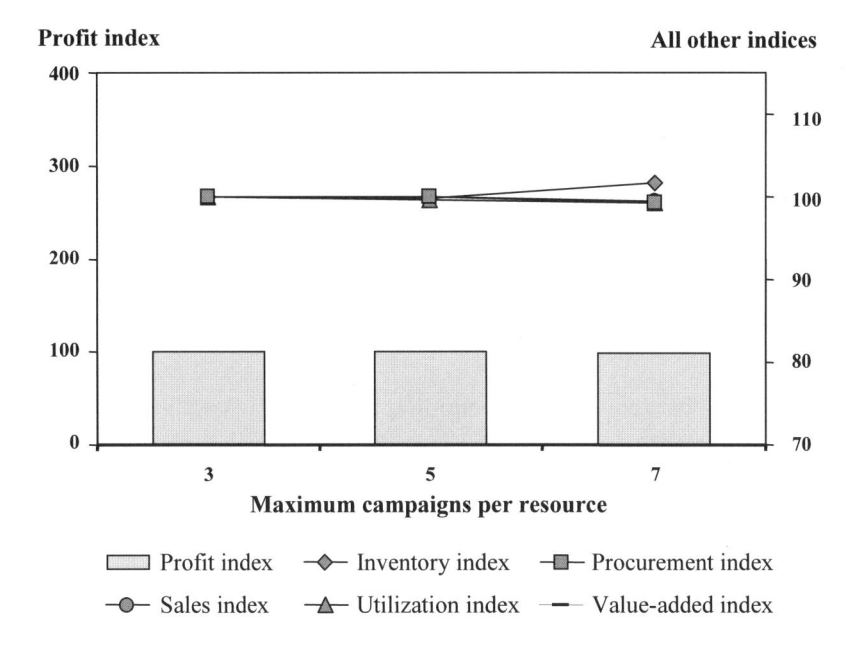

Fig. 96 Production campaign scenario evaluation

The experiment supports the planner's experience: allowing more degrees of freedom does not lead to higher profits and changes of volumes outside an MIP gap tolerance of 1%. The alternative plan uses also not more than 3 campaigns as maximum per period. Surprisingly more campaigns do not necessarily lead to lower inventory volumes as one might expect; reason is that the optimization model does not minimize costs by optimizing change-overs against inventory holding costs alone but maximizes overall profit across the value chain, which can lead also to solutions with higher inventories to support more valuable products or hedge risks of raw material prices.

The maximum number of campaigns is a critical parameter impacting model performance, since an increased number of campaigns results in more variables as well as longer run time as shown in table 33.

Table 33 Production campaign influence on model performance

Maximum campaigns	3	5	7
Constraints	14,785	17,161	19,537
Variables	15,723	17,883	20,043
Iterations	5,682	6,712	8,472
Run time	21.6 sec	28.7 sec	42.5 sec

Extending the number of maximum campaigns from 3 to 7 leads to a wider value range for the three campaign-indexed binary variables steering change-over decisions:

- The binary variable α_{rct}^{Pcamp} deciding if a campaign is active or not
- The campaign mode α_{rgct}^{Pmode} matching active process groups with active campaigns
- The change-over variable $\gamma_{rg_1g_2c_1c_2t}^{Pchange}$ deciding if a change-over between process groups and campaigns takes place or not

The branch and bound algorithm applied to solve the mixed integer linear program requires more iterations, since the respective decision tree has more nodes to be validated when extending the number of possible campaigns per month.

Thanks to block planning and grouping of single production processes into process groups as well as limiting campaign change-overs in the case of commodity production to three campaigns per months including one for change-over, the model is sufficiently capable to be used for a monthly planning purpose.

6.2.7 Procurement Scenario Evaluation

Finally, we compare procurement price scenarios for key raw materials from low to high raw material prices. The results shown in fig. 97 are the mirror of the sales price experiments conducted before.

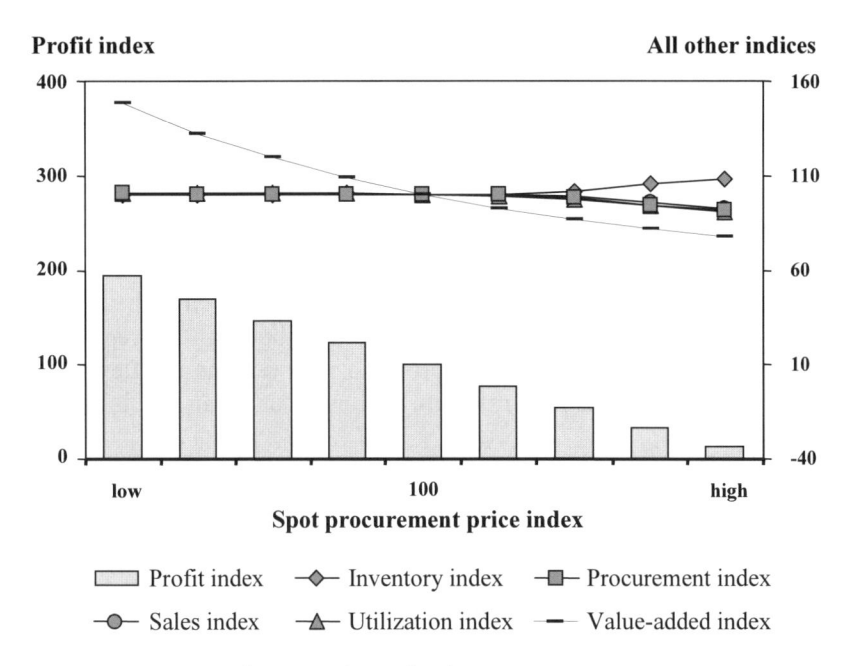

Fig. 97 Procurement price scenario evaluation

Low procurement prices lead to a very positive value-added index and hence to higher profits compared to a basis scenario. Low procurement prices have no volume effect, since production quantities cannot be increased in the situation of full utilization. High raw material prices result in a reduction of volume indices.

Comparing value scenarios like exchange rate, sales price, elasticity and procurement price experiments with the control scenarios, value scenario influence on profits and volumes is significantly higher than the influence of volume control scenario experiments in the specific case.

6.3 Opportunities for Model Extensions

The developed model serves as a basis for extension addressing additional planning requirements such as regional sales planning, robust planning with price uncertainties and price planning using simulation. Regional sales planning means the implementation of the global plan on regional level in the last phase of the planning process considering regional price and cost differences between customers and articles. Robust planning addresses the requirement to incorporate sales price uncertainties of commodities into the model. Price simulations support pricing decisions by identifying profit-optimal prices or price limits with respect to production utilization levels.

6.3.1 Regional Sales Planning

The global sales plan serves as a basis for regional sales planning as defined in the value chain planning process (see section 4.1.2). While contract sales is executed in the region as contractually agreed with single customers, the global spot sales plan has to be distributed in the regions on a detailed customer and article level providing the regions the flexibility to allocate the overall volume to different customers as illustrated in fig. 98.

Global level

Global sales location — Sales location 1, Product A

Global spot sales plan
Σ Sales quantity: 1.000 t
$\varnothing$ Sales price: 1.000 €/t
Σ Sales turnover: 1 mio. €

Regional level

Regional customer cluster: Customer A Article AI, Customer B Article AI, Customer C Article AII

Regional spot sales plan

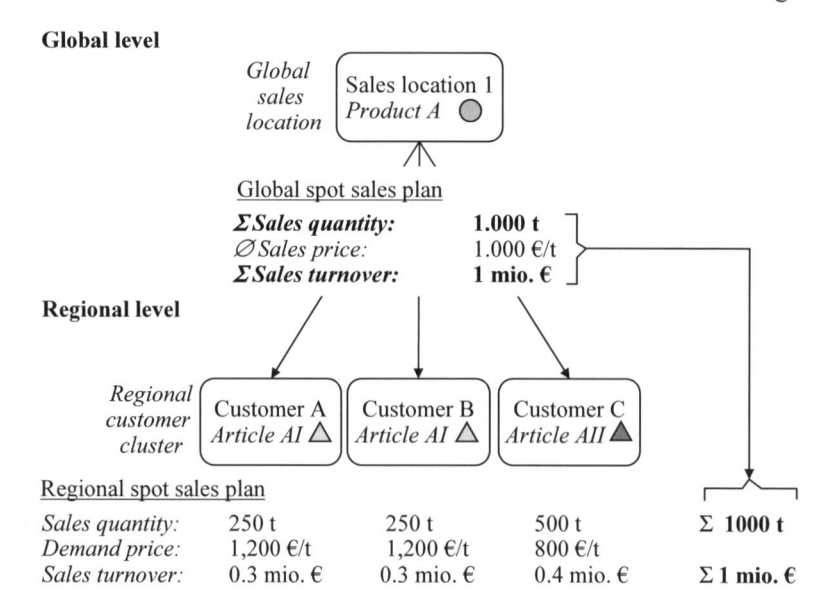

	Customer A	Customer B	Customer C	
Sales quantity:	250 t	250 t	500 t	Σ 1000 t
Demand price:	1,200 €/t	1,200 €/t	800 €/t	
Sales turnover:	0.3 mio. €	0.3 mio. €	0.4 mio. €	Σ 1 mio. €

Fig. 98 Regional spot sales planning

The regional spot sales planning considers price and cost differences between regional customers and individual articles constrained by having to meet the total sales volume *and* turnover targets on global level.

Regional Basis Indices and Sets

The regional sales planning level is oriented by the planning object hierarchies presented in the global planning framework in section 5.2.1. Planning objects on regional level are more detailed in comparison to the global level in order to further consider regional price and cost differences.

6.3 Opportunities for Model Extension

Since packaging costs are considered as optimization criterion on a regional level, regional sales planning is conducted on an article-level $a \in A$ differentiating packaging types such as bulk, bags, etc. with the respective packaging costs. Multiple articles are related to one product defined in the index set $\{a,p\} \in I^{S5}$, $\forall a \in A$, $p \in P$. Secondly, regional sales planning is conducted for individual customers or groups of customers defined as customer clusters $k \in K$. Considering individual customers, allows differentiating price differences between customers within the regional sales planning. Customer clusters are uniquely associated to one global sales location defined in the index set $\{k,l\} \in I^{S6}$, $\forall k \in K$, $l \in I^{Sl}$. Customer articles are defined by the tuple $\{a,k\} \in I^{S7}$, $\forall a \in A$, $k \in K$. All relations of regional customer clusters and articles to global locations and products are defined in the index set $\{a,p,k,l\} \in I^{S8}$, $\forall \{k,l\} \in I^{S3}$, $\{a,p\} \in I^{Sap}$, $\{a,k\} \in I^{S7}$. These sets serve as basis for regional planning linking the regional plan with the global plan.

Regional Sales Control, Demand Input Data and Decision Variables

Regional sales planning translates the global sales and turnover targets into the regional level considering regional demand plans. The global contract sales plan is equal to the global demand. As a consequence, the regional contract sales plan is equal to the regional demand plan, since no sales quantity flexibility exists and prices are fixed by contract for each customer cluster. Regional sales planning is focused on regional spot sales decisions with sales flexibility existing.

Regional sales flexibility is controlled using minimum and maximum spot sales flexibility: $R_{ak}^{SR\min s}$ and $R_{ak}^{SR\max s}$ are minimum and maximum spot sales quantity shares applied to the regional spot demand quantity by customer and article, $R_{ak}^{SR\min a}$ and $R_{acc}^{SR\max a}$ are minimum and maximum absolute regional spot sales quantities, all defined by $\forall \{a,k\} \in I^{S7}$. Here, it is assumed that the elasticity can be based on regional customer demand and that full sales quantity flexibility exists as assumed also in the elasticity analysis algorithm presented in table 24. In this case, regional spot sales boundaries are set to 0% as a minimum sales share and to 100% as a maximum sales share.

The regional demand input data consists of monthly spot demand quantity q_{akt}^{SRs} and spot demand price p_{akt}^{SRs} by article and customer cluster $\forall \{a,k\} \in I^{S7}$, $t \in T$. These regional businesses differ not only by price, but also by sales and distribution costs for the individual customer or article. Payment terms r_k^{SRpt}, $\forall k \in K$ measured in days reflect the specific number of days the company concedes the customer for order payment. Higher payment terms lead to increased working capital due to debts outstanding longer and consequently to higher capital costs.

Secondly, customer-specific variable selling cost shares r_k^{SRsc}, $\forall k \in K$ are applied as a percentage to net turnover and comprise customer-specific sales costs like insurances, bank charges or import tariff costs for the customer or the related country. Regional transportation costs c_{ak}^{RStc}, $\forall \{a,k\} \in I^{S7}$ reflect costs differences between articles and/or customers for transportation within the sales location. Finally, article-specific packaging costs c_{ak}^{RSpc}, $\forall \{a,k\} \in I^{S7}$ in the sales location currency on a currency per ton basis are considered.

Regional sales planning has to decide the regional spot sales quantity x_{akt}^{SRs} and the regional spot sales turnover y_{akt}^{SRs}, $\forall \{a,k\} \in I^{S7}$, $t \in T$.

Regional Spot Sales Planning Objective Function

Regional sales planning objective is to maximize discounted regional spot sales profit considering sales turnover and the described sales- and distribution-oriented costs:

$$\max z^R = \sum_{t \in T} \left\{ \left[\sum_{\{a,k\} \in I^{S7}} y_{akt}^{SRs} \right. \right. \quad \text{Net spot sales turnover} \tag{118}$$

$$- \sum_{\{a,k\} \in I^{S7}} \left(y_{akt}^{SRs} \cdot \frac{r_k^{SRpt} \cdot \varphi_t \cdot d_t}{365} \right) \quad \text{Spot sales payment terms}$$

$$- \sum_{\{a,k\} \in I^{S7}} \left(y_{akt}^{SRs} \cdot r_k^{SRsc} \right) \quad \text{Variable spot selling costs}$$

$$- \sum_{\{a,k\} \in I^{S7c}} \left(x_{akt}^{SRs} \cdot c_{ak}^{SRtc} \right) \quad \text{Regional transportation costs}$$

$$\left. - \sum_{\{a,k\} \in I^{S7}} \left(x_{akt}^{SRs} \cdot c_{ak}^{SRpc} \right) \right] \quad \text{Packaging costs}$$

$$\left. / \left[(1 + \frac{\varphi \cdot d_t}{365})^t \right] \right\} \quad \text{Net present value factor}$$

The regional optimization is focused on sales values and remaining regional sales decisions that have to be taken in the regions. The regional objective function does not intend to reflect the company's profit and loss situation as completely as possible being already done on global level. Therefore, contract sales are also excluded from the model, since they are already decided in the fixed contracts.

Regional Spot Sales Planning Constraints

Consequently, regional model constraints are focused on spot sales. The spot sales turnover is the sum of regional spot sales quantities and the spot sales demand price assuming to be the demand price to be not renegotiated.

$$y_{akt}^{SRs} = x_{akt}^{SRs} \cdot p_{akt}^{SRs} \qquad \forall \{a,k\} \in I^{S7}, \, t \in T \qquad (119)$$

The regional spot sales quantity has to remain within relative and absolute quantity boundaries.

$$R_{ak}^{SR\min s} \cdot q_{akt}^{RSs} \le x_{akt}^{SRs} \le q_{akt}^{RSs} \cdot R_{acc}^{SR\min s} \qquad \forall \{a,k\} \in I^{S7}, \, t \in T \qquad (120)$$

$$R_{ak}^{SR\min a} \le x_{akt}^{SRs} \le R_{ak}^{SR\max a} \qquad \forall \{a,k\} \in I^{S7}, \, t \in T \qquad (121)$$

The sum of regional spot sales quantities needs to be equal to the global spot sales quantity within the same sales location.

$$x_{plt}^{Ss} = \sum_{\{a,p,k,l\} \in I^{S8}} x_{akt}^{SRs} \qquad \forall \{p,l\} \in I^{S2}, \, t \in T \qquad (122)$$

Global spot sales turnover has to be equal to the regional spot sales turnover.

$$y_{plt}^{Ss} = \sum_{\{a,p,k,l\} \in I^{S8}} y_{akt}^{SRs} \qquad \forall \{p,l\} \in I^{S2}, \, t \in T \qquad (123)$$

The constraints ensure that global plans are executed on regional level and serve as a stable framework for the respective operations level. In addition, they provide flexibility and degrees of freedom for regional sales organizations in considering regional market and customer specifics within the framework of global volume and value objectives.

6.3.2 Robust Planning with Price Uncertainties

Up to this point, it is assumed that prices are deterministic, which is true for contract demand and procurement but is not necessarily true for spot demand and procurement prices. Therefore, an important value chain planning requirement is the consideration of uncertain prices and price scenarios. Now, uncertain spot demand prices are under consideration and it is illustrated how price uncertainty can be integrated into the model in order to reach *robust* planning solutions.

Robust planning is a specific research area within Operations Research (Scholl 2001). Generally, robustness can be defined as the *insensitivity of an object or system against (stochastic) external influences* (Schneeweiß 1992 reviewed by Scholl 2001, p. 93). A plan is robust, if the realization of the plan – also in a slightly modified form - leads to good and/or acceptable results with respect to the pursuit objectives for nearly all possible occurring scenarios (Scholl 2001, p. 93). Robustness is not only relevant in tactical planning or operative scheduling but also in other areas such as product design where design parameters needs to be determined in a way that with a set of possible scenarios determined by stochastic parameters a targeted probability to reach a feasible product design is reached (Olieman 2004a; Olieman 2004b). Theoretic papers related to robustness trying to approach industrial planning practice exists also for the chemical industry (Suh/Lee 2001).

In the considered value chain planning problem, the uncertainty of spot sales prices impacts the profitability of the overall value chain plan, since volume decisions can lead to profit-suboptimal plans, if the average sales price cannot be realized as planned. Therefore, price volatility is considered as an external (stochastic) influence in the considered value chain planning problem. The following model extensions account for this uncertainty and try to derive methods to achieve more robust plans with respect to profit results with contributions from Habla (2006). The objective of the proposed modeling approach is to maximize profit for the entire value chain network. It is assumed that the company behaves risk-averse in face of the price uncertainty.

Price uncertainty is reflected by alternative price scenarios $o \in O$. To model the volatility of market prices, a price factor δ_{plot}^{Ss} for spot demand prices e.g. 0.8, 1.0 and 1.2 and a corresponding subjective scenario probability ω_o^{Ss} valid for the entire planning horizon have to be defined by management. Typically, three scenarios *"worst"*, *"best"* and *"average"* are used in order to limit the complexity and keep scenario planning pragmatic. The price scenario philosophy of the company is to have only one single spot sales volume plan x_{plt}^{Ss} that is executed in the market at different price levels p_{plt}^{Ss}. In addition, we assume identical price-quantity functions i.e. identical spot demand elasticities, for all price scenarios.

Fig. 99 illustrates the concept of scenario-based price-quantity functions, which basically describe the dependency of sales price p on quantity x. With price-quantity function $p(x)$ the resulting turnover is given as $p(x) \cdot x$. In addition, to given input data, *sales control data* are defined by the planner executing sales and marketing business rules to set the boundaries for spot sales quantities. Control parameters $X_{plt}^{Ss\,min}$ and $X_{plt}^{Ss\,max}$ indicate the minimum and maximum spot demand that needs to be fulfilled.

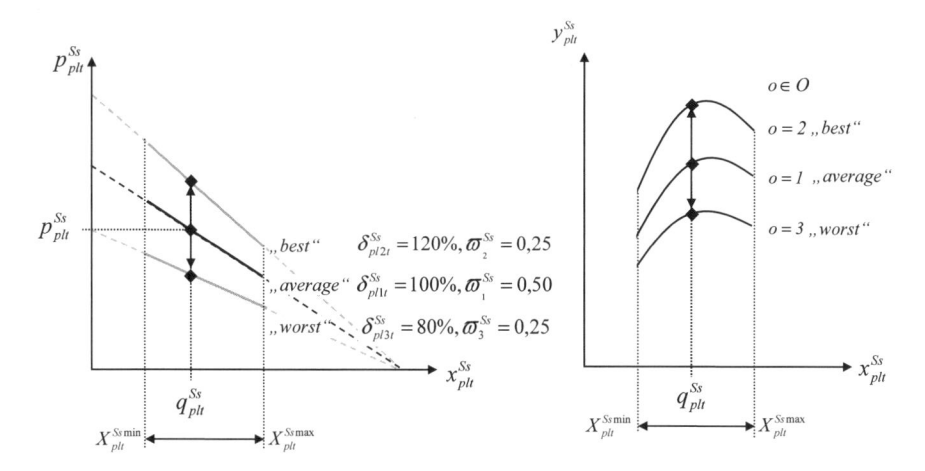

Fig. 99 Price-quantity function and turnover curve with price scenarios

The scenario-dependent price-quantity function can be determined as:

$$p_{plot}^{Ss}(x_{plt}^{Ss}) = \delta_{plot}^{Ss} \cdot \left[-\varepsilon_{plt}^{Ss} \cdot \frac{p_{plt}^{Ss}}{q_{plt}^{Ss}} \cdot x_{plt}^{Ss} + (1+\varepsilon_{plt}^{Ss}) \cdot p_{plt}^{Ss} \right] \quad (124)$$

$$\forall \{p,l\} \in I^{S2}, \ o \in O, \ t \in T$$

Secondly, the scenario-dependent turnover function can be determined as:

$$y_{plot}^{Ss}(x_{plt}^{Ss}) = \delta_{plot}^{Ss} \cdot p_{plot}^{Ss}(x_{plt}^{Ss}) \cdot x_{plt}^{Ss} \quad (125)$$

$$= -\varepsilon_{plt}^{Ss} \cdot \frac{p_{plt}^{Ss}}{q_{plt}^{Ss}} \cdot \delta_{plot}^{Ss} \cdot (x_{plt}^{Ss})^2 + (1+\varepsilon_{plt}^{Ss}) \cdot p_{plt}^{Ss} \cdot \delta_{plst}^{Ss} \cdot x_{plt}^{Ss}$$

$$\forall \{p,l\} \in I^{S2}, \ o \in O, \ t \in T$$

The concept of scenario-dependent turnover functions represent a significant advantage of demand price scenarios compared to demand quantity scenarios, since the scenario price factors can be directly applied to model turnover in the objective function of the optimization model without affecting quantity constraints of the model. This advantage might change the perspective on demand uncertainty from quantity scenarios towards price scenarios related to a defined sales quantity. This is even more practicable, since prices can be changed faster in practice compared to production volumes and material flows. In particular in the production of chemical commodities, considerable change-over times of the processing equipment have to be considered. Moreover, transportation lead times and limitations on transit stock often reduce the flexibility to adjust production quantities and redirect material flows on short notice.

Optimization Strategies

The objective of the proposed modeling approach is to maximize profit for the entire value chain network. Two optimization strategies can be applied incorporating spot sales price scenarios to reflect price uncertainty:

- *One-phase optimization:* Maximize expected profit across one or multiple price scenarios. This approach corresponds to the classical "expect value" maximization known from decision theory.
- *Two-phase optimization:* Maximize expected profit across multiple price scenarios subject to the constraint that a given minimum profit value is reached. From a practical point of view, this approach seems to be more appropriate in situations where a high variability of profit can be expected and the risk of low profit outcomes shall be minimized.

The one-phase optimization strategy considers one or multiple spot price scenarios. Each scenario is characterized by the spot price factor, which expresses possible spot price levels (e.g. 0.8, 1.0 and 1.2) for each relevant product-location combination pl, period t and scenario s. Each scenario has a subjective probability. While supply decisions remain unchanged, the various spot price scenarios lead to multiple turnover scenarios that are realized with the same spot sales quantity. Since price scenarios are represented by specific price factors, they can be directly applied to model spot turnover in the objective function.

The objective function for a single scenario is defined as follows:

$$z_o = \sum_{t \in T} \left[\sum_{\{p,l\} \in I^{S2}} y_{plt}^{Ss} \cdot \delta_{plot}^{Ss} + \sum_{\{p,l\} \in I^{S2}} p_{plt}^{Sc} \cdot q_{plt}^{Sc} - v_t^{Supply} \right] \quad (126)$$

In this simplified case, all distribution, production and procurement costs are summarized under period-specific supply costs v_t^{Supply}. The scenario profit z_o is calculated by the scenario spot sales turnover multiplied with the respective scenario factor δ_{plot}^{Ss} plus the contractually agreed turnover less the supply costs.

The expected profit determines the average profit across all price scenarios weighted with their scenario probability. The expected profit function can be defined as follows:

$$\max z^{exp} = \sum_{t \in T} \left[\sum_{\{p,l\} \in I^{S2}} \sum_{o \in O} y_{plt}^{Ss} \cdot \delta_{plot}^{Ss} \cdot \varpi_o^{Ss} + \sum_{\{p,l\} \in I^{S2}} p_{plt}^{Sc} \cdot q_{plt}^{Sc} - v_t^{Supply} \right] \quad (127)$$

The expected profit across multiple scenarios provides a more realistic picture of the future profit situation compared to one single scenario. However, scenarios are consolidated and averaged in one total number with their probability weights. The planner would have no information about potential worst case profits as a profit basis and might like to sacrifice expected profit opportunities for safety in exchange. This is addressed by the two-phase optimization approach.

Two-phase Profit Optimization

The two-phase optimization strategy (see fig. 100) first maximizes the minimum scenario profit, which is alwayss lower or equal to all single scenario profits z_o, where z_o is defined as shown in equation 126.

This first phase determines the best minimum profit z^{min} from all scenarios. z^{min} is then fixed as baseline profit z^{min*} for the second phase of the optimization, during which the expected profit z^{exp} is maximized across all scenarios given the constraint that each scenario profit z_o reaches the minimum scenario profit z^{min*}.

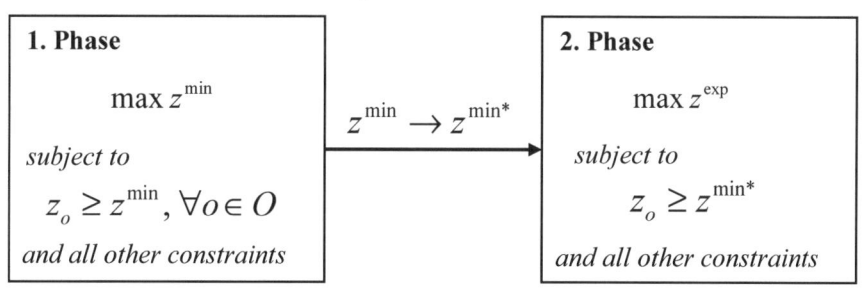

1. Phase	2. Phase
max z^{min}	max z^{exp}
subject to	subject to
$z_o \geq z^{min}, \forall o \in O$	$z_o \geq z^{min*}$
and all other constraints	and all other constraints

with transition $z^{min} \to z^{min*}$ between phases.

Fig. 100 Two-phase optimization approach

This approach is proposed by Chen/Lee (2004) to reach more robust solutions considering probabilistic for in this case demand quantity scenarios without considering price uncertainty.

Robust Planning Evaluation

This model extension is tested with *ILOG OPL Studio 3.71*® using *ILOG CPLEX 9.1*® and examined industry case test data on an *Intel Pentium 4 Processor*® with 1,598 Mhz and 256 MB RAM. The extension is tested for an excerpt of the value chain network including nine sales locations, one procurement location and one production and having one multi-purpose and one continuous production resource as shown in fig. 101.

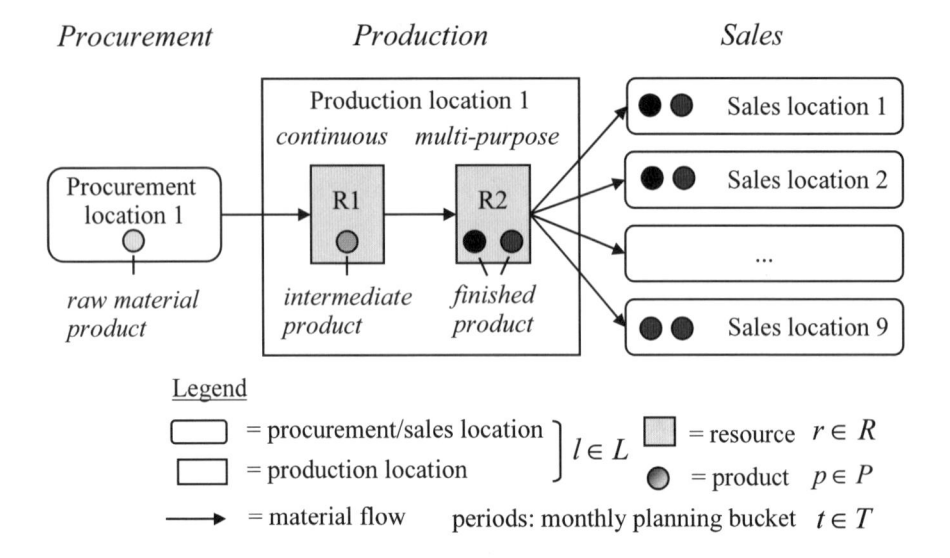

Fig. 101 Value chain network excerpt used for robust planning testing

The scale of this focused value chain network is shown in table 34.

Table 34 Case data scale for testing robust planning model

Basic elements	Scale
Products	50
- Finished	48
- Intermediate	1
- Raw material	1
Locations	11
- Sales	9
- Production	1
- Procurement	1
Resources	2
- Continuous	1
- Multi-purpose	1
Periods	6

In an experiment, we compare the optimization strategies introduced for different spot price scenarios. Two alternative demand spot price scenarios "best case" and "worst case" with equal probability of 0.25 are defined in addition to the standard scenario with probability 0.5. The best case assumes a continuous price increase while the worst case assumes a continuous price decrease. Consequently the expected profit is the average of the best and worst case scenario results and equal to the standard scenario.

Fig. 102 shows the numerical results. The results of the first period are indexed at 100 in order to compare the results of the subsequent periods compared the first period. Results of the one-phase optimization strategy are relatively constant sales quantities and expected profits slightly below the index level of 100. Executing this plan can lead to very positive best-case scenario profits but also to very negative profits, if the worst-case price scenario occurs.

Less extreme plans can be reached with the two-phase optimization strategy compared to the one-phase optimization approach: scenario profits are nearer by and the worst case scenario is comparably better than in the one-phase-optimization strategy. The overall plan in sales, production and procurement is more cautious with lower sales quantities and lower expected profits as the pay-off for better minimum profits.

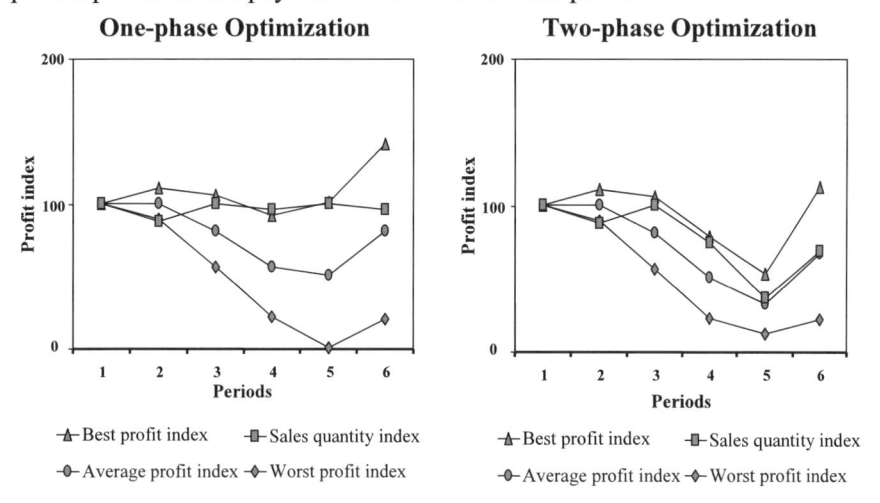

Fig. 102 Comparing 1-phase and 2-phase optimization strategy by periods

Fig. 103 shows all scenario profits in the one-phase and the two-phase optimization case as well as the sales quantity index: the two-phase optimization results do not disperse as strong as the one-phase-optimization. Besides, the worst case scenario is comparably better than the worst case scenario of the one-phase-optimization strategy. The plan is more cautious: supply quantities are reduced leading to lower expected profits but better minimum profits in the worst case scenario. Although robustness is not measured it get's visible in the numerical tests for the 2-phase optimization approach.

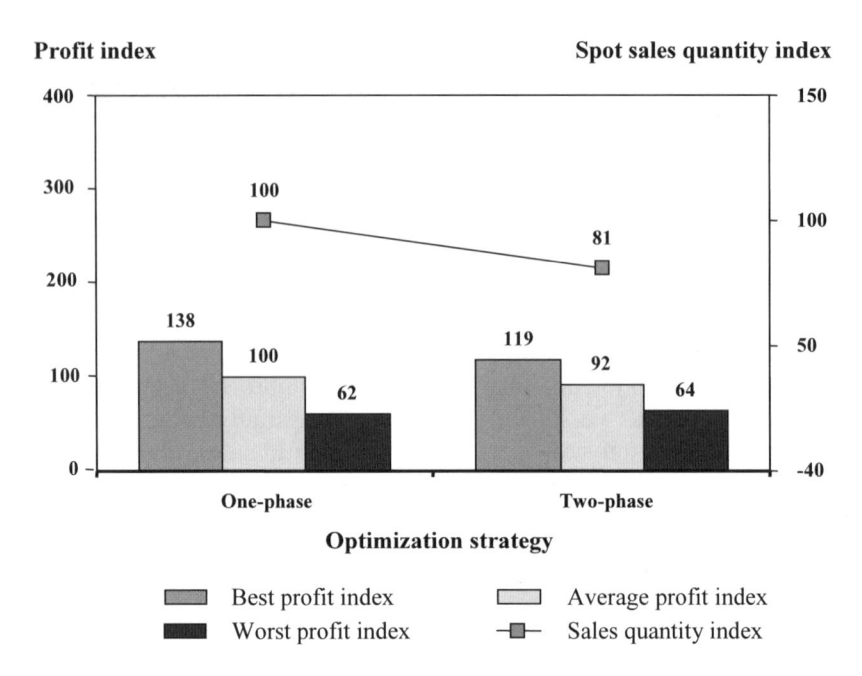

Fig. 103 Comparing 1-phase and 2-phase optimization strategy by profits

To conclude, the 2-phase optimization results in lower average profits. In the real application, planners might also vary the subjective weights for the different scenarios or set alternative minimum profit levels. This way additional information on the robustness of the obtained solution and a better understanding of the complex relationships between volumes and values in a price-volatile commodity business could be gained. This approach can be further extended e.g. by defining a robustness measure to be optimized explicitly (Olieman/Hendrix 2005).

6.3.3 Price Planning Using Simulation-based Optimization

The models presented so far, helped to determine profit-optimal plans by volumes and values. However, the optimization can result in under-utilization of capital-intensive production resource, which is not a desired state. In this situation two questions are raised mainly by sales and marketing:

- Which sales prices are profit-optimal fully utilizing a specific capacity?
- Which sales prices are price limits before reducing capacity utilization?

These questions get even more complex, if multiple products and businesses compete for production capacity – e.g. one product in two sales locations or two products against each other.

Utilization-optimal prices for these businesses can be systematically identified using simulation-based optimization of prices with contributions from Kurus (2006).

Core idea is to simulate various price scenarios for single or competing businesses and to conduct the optimization several times in order to identify price limits leading to full utilization of production.

In literature simulation and simulation-based optimization is focused on supply chain management areas such as production (Smith 2003; Wullink et al. 2004), inventory (Siprelle et al. 2003), transportation or integrated supply chain networks (Preusser et al. 2005).

The simulation-based optimization approach is illustrated in fig. 104 (see also Preusser et al. 2005, p. 98).

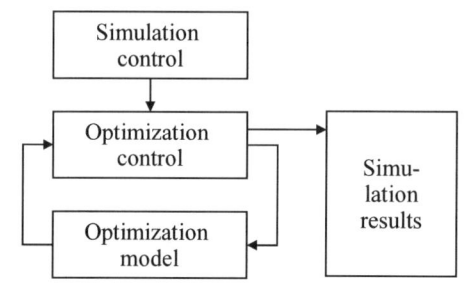

Fig. 104 Simulation-based optimization approach

The simulation control includes the methods of generating price simulation scenarios either manually, equally distributed or using stochastic distribution approaches such as normal distribution. In addition, the number of simulation scenarios e.g. 50 is defined. The optimization control covers preprocessing and postprocessing phases steering the optimization model. The optimization model is then iteratively solved for a simulated price scenario and optimization results including feasibility of the model are captured separately after iteration. Simulation results are then available for analysis.

Fig. 105 illustrates the case of equally distributed generation of price scenarios around the demand point of two competing products with the two prices $p1$ and $p2$. The planner simulates prices +/- 10% around the respective demand prices.

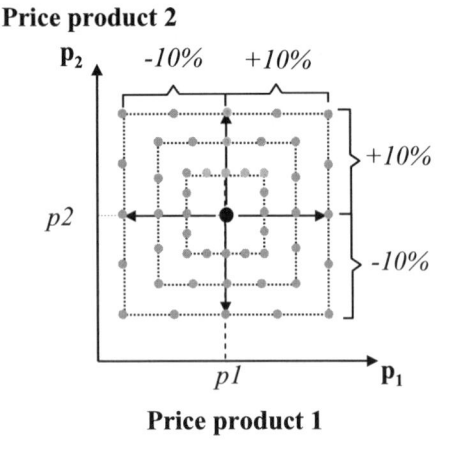

Fig. 105 Price scenarios

The evenly distributed price points ensure result analysis maps based on a standard grid. Core analysis of simulation results considers profit and utilization of the value chain as illustrated in fig. 106.

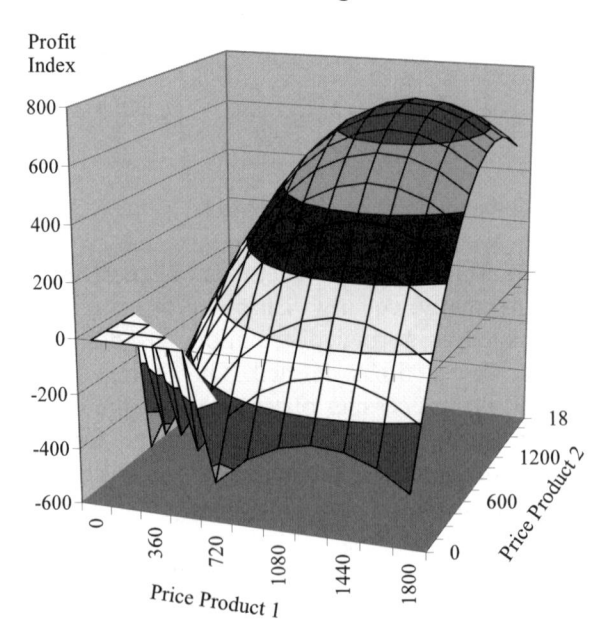

Fig. 106 Profit map example

In this simple example, two sales products compete for limited production capacity. Different sales prices for both products are simulated and the total profit dependent on price constellation is shown in a profit map. The profit in this simple example consists of sales turnover for the two products less production and raw material procurement costs. The map illustrates profit dynamics depending on sales prices: profit-optimal price constellations get transparent. However, profit-maximizing price constellations are often hard to realize in the market and hence are not of primary decision relevance.

Additionally, limit prices can be identified to show when production has to be decreased in order to ensure optimal profit. Limit prices support marketing decisions on minimum prices to be reached to ensure production utilization. In a simplified example with three resources – a continuous resource is a capacity bottleneck and two subsequent campaign resources produce the competing products 1 and 2 – the respective utilization maps show the utilization dynamics depending on sales prices illustrated in fig. 107.

Utilization of all resources is strongly increased with a sales price increase of product 1 and product 2. The continuous resource utilization is increased to 100% supplying the raw material for product 1 and product 2 on the respective campaign resources. Since the capacity of resource 3 is not sufficient to supply resource 1 and resource 2 at full utilization at the same time, the available capacity needs to be allocated either on resource 1 or resource 2. It gets transparent that resource 1 with product 1 are fully utilized up to 100%, while utilization of resource 2 with product 2 is reduced, since the product 2 businesses is less attractive compared to product 1 in this case.

The very simple 3-D-visualization of price simulation results for competing businesses can foster the understanding of value chain dynamics. Limit and target prices can be determined based on the simulation results.

These simple examples can only show the opportunity to further extend the value chain planning model usage for decision support integrated in simulation-based optimization architecture. There is an opportunity for further industry-oriented research to better understand production-price dynamics in different types of value chain networks.

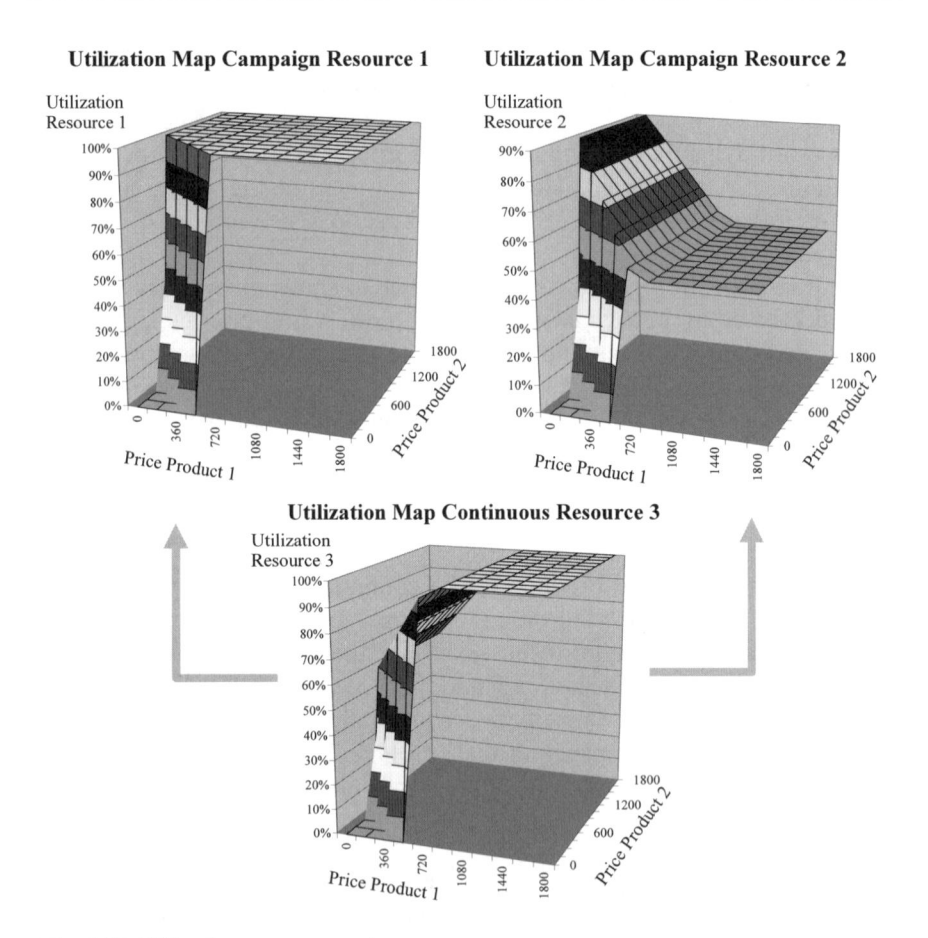

Fig. 107 Utilization map examples

6.4 Conclusions

The model evaluation by means of industry test data proved the importance of integrated volume and value decisions throughout the entire value chain. In particular, sales and procurement prices, exchange rates and demand elasticity have high influence on overall values and volume decisions. Model solution times below one minute on a desktop PC are acceptable for tactical value chain planning in the monthly planning process for the applied industry case data. Model extensions provide further decision support opportunities for regional sales planning, robust planning incorporating price uncertainties or support price decisions using simulation-based optimization.

The case study demonstrated how the company can use the developed model in decision support. Having implementing the global value chain planning process and model the company could significantly improve overall profitability of the business. Specifically, the spot price mechanism used to better coordinate sales and supply decisions showed a significant impact for the company.

7 Summary, Conclusions and Outlook

In this study, two research questions have been investigated: *1. How volumes and values within the value chain can be managed in an integrated way* and, especially, *2. How a global commodity value chain within the chemical industry can be planned by volumes and values.*

A value chain planning model has been developed to integrate volume and value decisions within the value chain. Value chain planning is part of value chain management to integrate strategy, planning and operational decisions across the value chain. This value chain management combines separate research areas focusing either on supply, demand or values. It is based on methods like reference models, simulation, optimization, analysis and visualization to support decisions.

Specifically, a global value chain planning model for a company-internal commodity value chain network has been developed within the process industry. Balancing sales turnover with raw material procurement costs both volatile in volumes and values is the primary task in commodity value chain planning. The global scope poses additional requirements on planning of handling exchange rates and multi-period transportation time and transit inventories between continents. The value chain planning requirements coverage by state of the art literature is analyzed for the specific problem. Literature focuses either on global models, chemical industry models in production and distribution or models handling demand uncertainty by quantity. An integrated volume and value planning approach specifically for chemical commodities is missing so far.

So, the global value chain planning model covers the formulated requirements as illustrated in fig. 108.

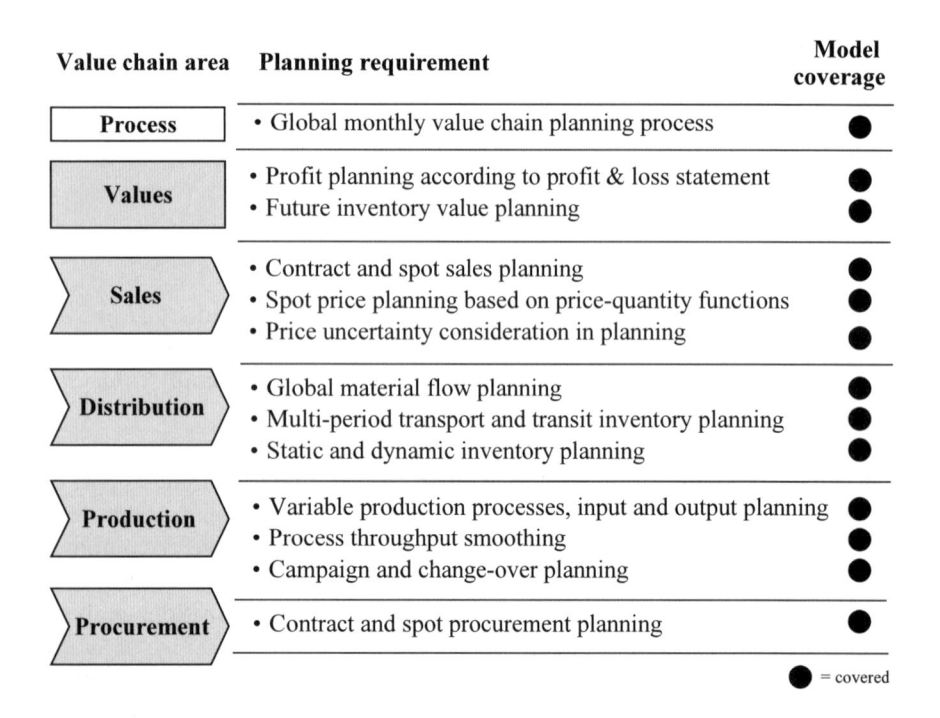

Value chain area	Planning requirement	Model coverage
Process	• Global monthly value chain planning process	●
Values	• Profit planning according to profit & loss statement • Future inventory value planning	● ●
Sales	• Contract and spot sales planning • Spot price planning based on price-quantity functions • Price uncertainty consideration in planning	● ● ●
Distribution	• Global material flow planning • Multi-period transport and transit inventory planning • Static and dynamic inventory planning	● ● ●
Production	• Variable production processes, input and output planning • Process throughput smoothing • Campaign and change-over planning	● ● ●
Procurement	• Contract and spot procurement planning	●

● = covered

Fig. 108 Value chain planning requirements coverage by the model

Several new approaches have been developed in the model:

- Global profit optimization consistent with profit and loss statements demonstrates how to integrate the value and volume views in controlling, sales & marketing, supply chain management, production and procurement.
- Future inventory planning approach to anticipate future inventory values in the value chain network based on future raw material price forecasts.
- Elasticity analysis algorithm as pragmatic approach to determine average price elasticity of aggregated demand forecasts that analyzes underlying customer price-quantity demand.
- A piecewise linear turnover approximation supports effective and accurate decision making on sales turnover based on price-quantity functions and elasticity as an alternative to exact quadratic optimization.
- Global transportation and transit inventory planning differentiates sent and received transportation quantity allocation cases and calculates transit inventories and capital costs on the transportation lane.

- Production process planning extended by throughput smoothing and planning of variable raw material consumption using linear recipe function.

The model has been evaluated by means of a global commodity industry case. The evaluation proved the importance of value chain planning to integrate volume and value decisions from sales to procurement: exchange rate, sales and raw material price and elasticity scenarios have key influences on total profit and volume planning decisions within the global value chain network.

Outlook and Areas for Further Research

The integrated concept of value chain management provides opportunities for further interdisciplinary research questions that integrate separated research areas in sales, marketing, controlling, operations research, supply chain management, logistics and procurement. The value chain planning approach can be validated or extended for specialty chemicals or for other process industries or in the discrete sector confronted with increasing raw material and sales price volatility having traditionally focused on volume planning alone. Examples are the high tech, automotive, manufacturing and consumer goods industries.

Additional research questions may exist related to other concept elements within the value chain management framework:

- Value chain strategy
  - How can sales and procurement strategy, network design and product strategy decisions be integrated?
  - How can product strategies in the market be integrated with complexity costs, product life cycle decisions and supply network design?
  - What is the right integrated spot/contract split in sales and procurement?
  - What is the appropriate inventory level within the entire value chain considering risk-hedging of raw material and sales prices?
- Value chain operations
  - How can order schedules be integrated throughout the value chain in sales, production, distribution and procurement considering profitability or order business rules?
- Negotiation and collaboration
  - How can spot/contract sales and procurement flexibility rules be integrated into negotiation and collaboration agreements?
  - How should collaborative planning and bidding processes be ideally designed within the rolling monthly planning?

- Which indicators, mutual service level and bonus-malus agreements have to be agreed and measured between companies?
- Support and service functions
  - Returning to Porter's original value chain, how can company services and support functions like IT, HR or Finance be integrated into strategy, planning and operations as an extended value chain management framework?
- Macro-perspective on value chains
  - Value chains are embedded and influenced by their macro-environment e.g. internationally, politically, technologically, socially, legally and/or environmentally: tax legislation, shortages of energy and natural resources, socio-demographic changes and/or specific legislations such as the EU chemicals legislation are some examples that have impact on value chain strategy, planning and operations. Hence, the influence and systematic consideration of these factors in value chain management on the strategic level is a further interesting research area looking beyond the focused business perspective onto companies and markets (see also van Beek 2005).

All research questions share the characteristic of investigating value chain processes and decisions holistically like in an integrated ecosystem. Operations Research methods and Information Technology provide the capabilities to be successful in this interdisciplinary research.

References

A.D. Little (2003) Supply Chain Management in der chemischen Industrie. URL: http://www.adlittle.de/downloads/artikel/scm_in_der_chemischen_industrie.pdf, Date: 19.03.2007

A.T. Kearney (2003) Kostensenkung hat oberste Priorität - Studie "Challenges 2003" offenbart neue Herausforderungen für die Industrie. URL: http://www.innovations-report.de/html/berichte/wirtschaft_finanzen/bericht-16356.html, Date: 19.03.2007

A.T. Kearney (2004), Creating Value through Strategic Supply Management. URL: http://www.atkearney.com/shared_res/pdf/AEP_2004_S.pdf, Date: 08.11.2005

Alicke K (2003) Planung and Betrieb von Logistiknetzwerken: unternehmensübergreifendes Supply Chain Management, 2nd edn. Springer, Berlin et al.

Al-Mudimigh S, Zairi M, Ahmed A (2004) Extending the concept of supply chain: the effective management of value chains. International Journal of Production Economics 87 (3): 309-320

Al-Sharrah GK, Alatiqi I, Elkamel A, Alper E (2001) Planning an Integrated Petrochemical Industry with an Environmental Objective. Industrial & Engineering Chemistry Research 40: 2103-2111

Al-Sharrah GK, Alatiqi I, Elkamel A (2003) Modeling and Identification of Economic Disturbances in the Planning of the Petrochemical Industry. Industrial & Engineering Chemistry Research 42: 4678-4688

Alvarado UY, Kotzab H (2001) Supply Chain Management: The Integration of Logistics in Marketing. Industrial Marketing Management 30 (2): 183-198

Angerhofer BJ, Angelides MC (2000) System Dynamics Modelling in Supply Chain Management: Research Review, In: Joines JA, Barton RR, Kang K, Fishwick PA (eds) Proceedings of the 2000 Winter Simulation Conference, pp 342-351

Anjos MF, Cheng RCH, Currie CSM (2005) Optimal pricing policies for perishable products. European Journal of Operational Research 166 (1): 246-254

Anthony R (1965) Planning and Control Systems: A Framework for Analysis. Harvard University, Harvard Graduate School of Business Administration, Cambridge, MA

Aprile D, Garavelli AC, Giannoccaro I (2005) Operations planning and flexibility in a supply chain. Production Planning & Control 16 (1): 21-31

Arnold D (1995) Materialflusslehre. Vieweg, Braunschweig,

Arntzen B, Brown G, Harrison T, Trafton L (1995) Global Supply Chain Management at Digital Equipment Corporation. Interfaces 25 (1): 69-93

Asche F, Gjölberg O, Völker T (2003) Price relationships in the petroleum market: an analysis of crude oil and refined product prices. Energy Economics 25 (3): 289-301

Asgekar V (2004) The Demand Driven Supply Network. Supply Chain Management Review April 2004: 15-16

Barker MJ (1992) Marketing - An Introductory Text. 5th edn. Macmillan, London

Bartodziej P, Derigs U, Zils M (2007) O&D revenue management in cargo airlines – a mathematical programming approach. OR Spectrum 29: 105-121

Bartsch H, Bickenbach P (2002) Supply Chain Management mit SAP APO – Supply-Chain-Modelle mit dem Advanced Planner & Optimizer 3.1, 2nd edn. Galileo Press, Bonn

Beamon BM (1998) Supply chain design and analysis: Models and methods. International Journal of Production Economics 5 (5): 291-294

Berning G, Brandenburg M, Gürsoy K, Kussi JS, Mehta V, Tölle F (2004) Integrating collaborative planning and supply chain optimization for the chemical pro-cess industry (I) — methodology. Computers & Chemical Engineering 28 (2004): 913-927

Berning G, Brandenburg M, Gürsoy K, Mehta V, Tölle F (2002) An integrated system solution for supply chain optimization in the chemical process industry. OR Spectrum 24: 371–401

Bestmann U (1996) Kompendium der Betriebswirtschaftslehre, 8th edn. Oldenbourg, München et al.

Betge D, Leisten R (2005) Koordinationsansatz für ausgewählte Module von Advanced Planning and Scheduling-Systemen, In: Günther H, Mattfeld DC,. Suhl L (eds), Supply Chain Management und Logistik: Optimierung, Simulation, Decision Support. Physica, Heidelberg, pp 41-68

Bitpipe (2007) Value Chain Management. URL: http://www.bitpipe.com/tlist/Value-Chain-Management.html, Date: 19.03.2007

Biller S, Chan LMA, Swann J (2005) Dynamic pricing and the direct-to-customer model in the automotive industry. Electronic Commerce Research 5: 309-334

Bixby R (2005) More than Moore: The Ever Shrinking Optimization Time Horizon. Presentation at the GOR SCM AG, Frankfurt

Blömer F (1999) Produktionsplanung and -steuerung in der chemischen Industrie. DUV Gabler, Wiesbaden

Boeken P, Kotlik L (2001) Optimierung der Supply Chain in der pharmazeutischen Industrie, A.D. Little (ed.) Einkauf - Produktion - Logistik, pp 67-74

Bogataj M, Bogataj L (2004) On the compact presentation of the lead times perturbations in distribution networks. International Journal of Production Economics 88: 145–155

Born K (1999) Rechnungslegung nach IAS, US-GAAP und HGB im Vergleich. Schaeffer-Poeschel, Stuttgart

Bourbeau B, Crainic TG, Gendreau M, Robert J (2005) Design for optimized multi-lateral multi-commodity markets. European Journal of Operational Research 163 (2): 503-529

Boyd EA, Bilegan IC (2003) Revenue Management and E-Commerce. Management Science 49 (10): 1363-1386

Brenner W, Keller G (1994) Business reengineering mit Standardsoftware. Campus, Frankfurt et al

Budde F, Hofmann K, Frankemölle H (2002) Die Chemie stimmt, der Preis nicht - Höhere Profitabilität durch Exzellenz in der Preisgestaltung. Handelsblatt, 05.06.2002

Carroll W, Grimes R (1995) Evolutionary Change in Product Management: Experiences in the Car Rental Industry. Interfaces 25 (5): 84-104

CEFIC (2005) Facts and figures - The European chemical industry in a worldwide perspective: July 2005, The European Chemical Industry Council, Brussels.

Chakravarty AK (2005) Global plant capacity and product allocation with pricing decisions. European Journal of Operational Research 165 (1): 157-181

Champion S, Fearne A (2001) Supply Chain Management: A 'First Principles' Consideration of its Application to Wool Marketing. Wool Technology and Sheep Breeding 49 (3): 222-236

Chan FTS (2003) Performance Measurement in a Supply Chain. International Journal of Advanced Manufacturing Technology 21: 534–548

Chan FTS, Chung SH (2004) Multi-criteria genetic optimization for distribution network problems. International Journal of Advanced Manufacturing Technology 2004: 517-532

Charnsirisakskul K, Griffin P, Keskinocak P (2006) Pricing and scheduling decisions with leadtime flexibility. European Journal of Operational Research 171 (1): 153-169

Chen C, Lee W (2004) Multi-objective optimization of multi-echelon supply chain networks with uncertain product demands and prices. Computers & Chemical Engineering 28 (6-7): 1131-1144

Chen C, Wang B, Lee W (2003) Multiobjective Optimization for a Multienterprise Supply Chain Network. Industrial & Engineering Chemistry Research 42: 1879-1889

Chen IJ, Paulraj A, Lado AA (2002) Strategic purchasing, supply management and firm performance. Journal of Operations Management 22 (5): 505-523

Cheng L, Duran M (2004) Logistics for world-wide crude oil transportation using discrete event simulation and optimal control. Computers & Chemical Engineering 28 (6-7): 897-911

Cheng L, Subrahmanian E, Westerberg AW (2003) Design and planning under uncertainty: issues on problem formulation and solution. Computers & Chemical Engineering 27 (6): 781-801

Cheng L, Subrahmanian E, Westerberg AW (2004) Multi-objective Decisions on Capacity Planning and Production-Inventory Control under Uncertainty. Industrial & Engineering Chemistry Research 43: 2192-2208

Childerhouse P, Aitken J, Towill DR (2002) Analysis and design of focused demand chains. Journal of Operations Management 20: 675-689

Chopra S, Meindl P (2004) Supply Chain Management: Strategy, Planning and Operation, 2nd edn. Pearson Prentice Hall, Upper Saddle River

Christopher M (1992) Logistics and Supply Chain Management: Strategies for Reducing Cost and Improving Service, Pitman Publishing, London

Christopher M (1998) Logistics and Supply Chain Management, Pearson Prentice Hall, London et al.

Christopher M, Gattorna J (2005) Supply chain cost management and value-based pricing. Industrial Marketing Management 34 (2): 115-121

Clark E, Lesourd J, Thiéblemont R (2001) International commodity trading: physical and derivative markets, John Wiley & Sons, Chichester

Commodity Research Bureau (2005) The CRB Commodity Yearbook 2005, John Wiley & Sons, Chichester

COMTRADE (2005) Commodity Trade Statistics Database. URL: http://unstats.un.org/unsd/comtrade/default.aspx, Date: 15.09.05

Considine TJ (2001) Markup pricing in petroleum refining: a multiproduct framework. International Journal of Industrial Organizations 19 (10): 1499-1526

Corsten D, Gabriel C (2004) Supp ly Chain Management erfolgreich umsetzen: Grundlagen, Realisierung and Fallstudien, 2nd edition, Springer, Berlin et al.

Corsten H, Gössinger R (2001) Einführung in das Supply Chain Management, Oldenbourg, München et al.

Cross RG (2001) Ressourcen erkennen – Umsätze steigern: mit Revenue-Management neue Einnahmequellen erschließen, Ueberreuter Wirtschaft, Wien et al.

Curran T, Keller G (1998) SAP R/3 Business Blueprint: understanding the business process reference model, Prentice Hall, Upper Saddle River

Datta S, Betts B, Dinning M, Erhun F, Gibbs T, Keskinocak P, Li H, Li M, Samuels M (2004) Adaptive Value Networks, In: Chang YS, Makatsoris H, Richards H (eds) Evolution of Supply Chain Management. Kluwer Academic Publishers, Norwell, MA, pp 3-68

Deans GK, Kröger F, Zeisel S (2002) Merger Endgames - Strategien für die Konsolidierungswelle, Gabler, Wiesbaden

Defregger F, Kuhn H (2007) Revenue management for a make-to-order company with limited inventory capacity. OR Spectrum 29: 137-156

Delfmann W, Albers S (2000) Supply Chain Management in the Global Context. University of Cologne, Department of General Management, Business Planning and Logistics, Cologne, 102

Dicken P (1998) Global Shift. Transforming the World Economy, 3rd edn. Paul Chapman, London

Dickersbach JT (2004) Supply Chain Management with APO: Structures, Modelling Approaches and Implementation Peculiarities, Springer, Berlin et al.

Dobler DW, Lee LJ, Burt DN (1977) Purchasing and Materials Management, 3rd edn. McGraw-Hill, Boston et al.

Dolan R (1995) How Do You Know When the Price Is Right? In: Harvard Business Review, September: 174-183

Domschke W, Drexl A (2004) Einführung in Operations Research, 6th edn. Springer, Berlin et al.

Dudek G (2004) Collaborative Planning in Supply Chains: A Negotiation-Based Approach, Springer, Berlin et al.

Dudek G, Stadtler H (2005) Negotiation-based collaborative planning between supply chains partners. European Journal of Operational Research 163: 668–687

Enns ST, Suwanruji P (2003) A simulation test bed for production and supply chain modeling, In: Sánchez S, Ferrin PJ, Morrice DJ (Ed.) Proceedings of the 2003 Winter Simulation Conference, pp 1174-1182

Eppen GD, Martin KA, Schrage L (1989) A Scenario Approach to Capacity Planning. OR Practice 37 (4): 517-527

Faber R, Jockenhövel T, Tsatsaronis G (2005) Dynamic optimization with simulated annealing. Computers & Chemical Engineering 29: 273–290

Ferdinand A, Haeger C (2001) Restrukturierung des europäischen Produktionsnetzwerkes am Beispiel der BASF-Gruppe. In: A.D. Little (eds) Einkauf - Produktion - Logistik, pp 21-30

Fisher ML (2004) The Lagrangian Relaxation Method for Solving Integer Programming Problems. Management Science 50 (12): 1861-1871

Fisher M, Ramdas K, Zheng Y (2001) Ending Inventory Valuation in Multiperiod Production Scheduling. Management Science 45: 679-692

Fleischmann B (2004) Distribution and Transportation Planning. In: Stadtler H, Kilger C (eds) Supply Chain Management and Advanced Planning, 3rd edn. Springer, Berlin et al., pp 229-244

Fleischmann B, Meyr H (1997) The general lot sizing and scheduling problem. OR Spectrum 19 (1): 11-21

Fleischmann B, Meyr H (2003) Planning Hierarchy, Modeling and Advanced Planning Systems. In: Graves SC, De Kok AG (eds) Supply Chain Management. North-Holland, Amsterdam, pp 1-56

Fleischmann B, Meyr H, Wagner M (2004) Advanced Planning. In: Stadtler H, Kilger C (eds) Supply Chain Management and Advanced Planning, 3rd edn. Springer, Berlin et al., pp 81-108

Fleischmann M, Hall JM, Pyke DF (2004) Smart Pricing. MIT Sloan Management Review 45 (2): 8-13

Flint D (2004) Strategic marketing in global supply chains: Four challenges. Industrial Marketing Management 33 (1): 45-50

Forman H, Hunt JM (2005) Managing the influence of internal and external determinants on international industrial pricing strategies. Industrial Marketing Management 34 (2): 133-146

Forrester JW (1961) Industrial Dynamics. MIT Press, Cambridge, MA

Franke S (2004) Einführung von SCM-Systemen bei der BASF AG Ludwigshafen – Erfahrungen der Geschäftseinheit Styrolpolymere mit SAP APO DP. In: Busch A, Dangelmaier W (eds) Integriertes Supply Chain Management. Gabler, Wiesbaden, pp 285-300

Franke S (2005) Simultanplanung der BASF Polystyrol-Produktion. Presentation at the GOR SCM AG, Frankfurt.

Friedrich M (2000) Konzeption eines Componentware-basierten Supply-Chain-Management-Systems für kleine and mittlere Unternehmen. University of Erlangen.

Frontline Solutions (2005) Supply Chain Spending Shifts to Demand Management. URL: http://www.innovateforum.com/innovate/article/ articleDetail.jsp?id=178130, Date: 19.03.2007

Fu MC (2002) Optimization for Simulation: Theory vs. Practice. INFORMS Journal on Computing 14: 192-215

Garcia-Flores R, Wang XZ (2002) A multi-agent system for chemical supply chain simulation and management support. OR Spectrum 24: 343–370

Geman H (2005) Commodities and commodity derivatives – Modeling and Pricing for Agriculturals, Metals and Energy, John Wiley & Sons, Chichester

Genin P, Lamouri S, Thomas A (2005) Sales and Operations Planning Optimisation. In: Dolgui A, Soldek J, Zaikin O (eds) Supply Chain Optimisation, pp 191-204

Gibson W (1998) Getting a grip on the supply chain. Chemical Engineering November: 35-39

Gjerdrum J, Shah N, Papageorgiou LG (2001) Transfer Prices for Multienterprise Supply Chain Optimization. Industrial & Engineering Chemistry Research 40: 1650-1660

Goetschalckx M (2004) Strategic Network Planning. In: Stadtler H, Kilger C (eds) Supply Chain Management and Advanced Planning, 3rd edition, Springer, Berlin et al., pp 117-138

Goetschalckx M, Vidal CJ, Dogan K (2002) Modeling and design of global logistics systems: A review of integrated strategic and tactical models and design algorithms. In: European Journal of Operational Research 143 (1): 1-18

Götze U (2004) Kostenrechnung und Kostenmanagement, 3rd edn. Springer, Berlin et al.

Götze U, Bloech J (2004) Investitionsrechnung, 3rd edn. Springer, Berlin et al.

Gosavi A, Ozkaya E, Kahraman AF (2007) Simulation optimization for revenue management of airlines with cancellation and overbooking. OR Spectrum 29: 21-38

Grunow M (2001) Management von Produktions- und Distributionsnetzwerken in der chemischen Industrie. In: Sebastian H, Grünert T (eds) Logistik management, supply chain management and electronic business. Teubner, Stuttgart et al., pp 323-335

Grunow M, Günther HO (2001) Logistiknetzwerke in der chemischen Industrie: Einsatzfelder von APS Systems. Presentation at the GOR SCM AG, St. Leon-Rot

Grunow M, Günther HO, Lehmann M (2003a) Campaign planning for multi-stage batch processes in the chemical industry. In: Günther HO, van Beek P (eds) Advanced Planning and Scheduling Solutions in Process Industry. Springer, Berlin et al., pp 73-106

Grunow M, Günther HO, Yang G (2003b) Plant co-ordination in pharmaceutics supply networks. In: Günther HO, van Beek P (eds) Advanced Planning and Scheduling Solutions in Process Industry. Springer, Berlin et al., pp 261-294

Grunow M, Günther HO, Lehmann M (2004) Dispatching multi-load AGVs in highly automated seaport container terminals. OR Spectrum 26: 211-235

Gunasekaran A, Ngai EWT (2004) Information systems in supply chain integration and management. European Journal of Operational Research 159: 269–295

Günther HO (2005) Supply Chain Management and Advanced Planning Systems - A Tutorial. In: Günther H, Mattfeld DC, Suhl L (eds), Supply Chain Management und Logistik: Optimierung, Simulation, Decision Support. Physica, Heidelberg, pp 3-40

Günther HO, Grunow M, Neuhaus U (2006) Realizing block planning concepts in make-and-pack production using MILP modeling and SAP APO$^©$. International Journal of Production Research 44 (18-19): 3711-3726

Günther HO, Tempelmeier H (2003) Produktion und Logistik, 5th edition, Springer, Berlin et al.

Günther HO, van Beek P (eds) (2003) Advanced Planning and Scheduling Solutions in Process Industry, Springer, Berlin et al.

Günther HO, van Beek P (2003) Advanced Planning and Scheduling in Process Industry. In: Günther HO, van Beek P (eds) Advanced Planning and Scheduling Solutions in Process Industry. Springer, Berlin et al., pp 1-9

Günther HO, van Beek P, Grunow M, Lütke Entrup M (2005) Coverage of shelf life in APS systems. In: Günther H, Mattfeld DC, Suhl L (eds) Supply Chain Management und Logistik: Optimierung, Simulation, Decision Support. Physica, Heidelberg, pp 135-156

Günther HO, van Beek P, Grunow M, Lütke Entrup M, Seiler T (2004) MILP approaches to shelf life integrated planning and scheduling in yogurt production. Technical University of Berlin, Department of Production Management, Berlin

Gupta A, Maranas CD (2003) Managing demand uncertainty in supply chain planning. Computers & Chemical Engineering 27 (8-9): 1219-1227

Gupta A, Maranas CD (2004) Real-Options-Based Planning Strategies under Uncertainty. Industrial & Engineering Chemistry Research 43: 3870-3878

Guvenen O (1998) International commodity market models and policy analysis. Kluwer, Dordrecht

Habla C (2006) Planning and optimization of global supply network in the process industry, Technical University of Berlin

Hallwood P (1979) Stabilization of international commodity markets. Jai Press, Greenwich

Ham H, Kim TJ, Boyce D (2005) Implementation and estimation of a combined model of interregional, multimodal commodity shipments and transportation network flows. Transportation Research Part B (39): 65–79

Hartmann E (2002) B-to-B Electronic Marketplaces. DUV Gabler, Wiesbaden

Harvard Business Review (2000) Managing the value chain. Harvard Business School Press, Boston

Hauth M (1998) Hierarchisch integrierte Planungsansätze in der Prozessindustrie. DUV Gabler, Wiesbaden

Heckmann P, Shorten D, Engel H (2003) Supply Chain Management at 21 - The Hard Road to Adulthood. Industry Study of Booz Allen Hamilton Inc.

Heikkilä J (2002) Form supply to demand chain management: efficiency and customer satisfaction. Journal of Operations Management 20: 747-767

Heisig G, Minner S (1999) ILOG OPL Studio - Version: 2.0. OR Spectrum 21: 419-427

Hieber R (2001) Supply Chain Management: A Collaborative Performance Measurement Approach. vdf Hochschulverlag, ETH Zürich

Hill JA, Berry WL, Leong GK, Schilling DA (2000) Master production scheduling in capacitated sequence-dependent process industries. International Journal of Production Research 38 (18): 4743-4762

Hofmann S (2004) Kunststoff-Verarbeiter in der Klemme - Rasanter Preisanstieg setzt Margen unter Druck - Engpässe bei Standard-Kunststoffen. Handelsblatt, 13.12.2004

Holmström J, Främling KTJ, Kärkkäinen M, Ala-Risk T (2002) Implementing collaboration process networks. The International Journal of Logistics Management 13 (2): 39-50

Homburg C, Beutin N, Jensen O (2005) Preismanagement für Industrieunternehmen. FAZ, 24.10.2005

Homburg C, Schneeweiss C (2000) Negotiations Within Supply Chains. Computional & Mathematical Organization Theory 6: 47-59

Hostettler S (2002) Economic Value Added (EVA), 5th edn. Paul Haupt, Bern

Huang H (2002) Pricing and logit-based mode choice models of a transit and highway system with elastic demand. European Journal of Operational Research 140: 562-570

Humphreys PK, Lo VHY, McIvor RT (2000) A decision support framework for strategic purchasing. Journal of Materials Processing Technology 107 (1-3): 353-362

Hwarng HB, Chong CSP, Xie N, Burgess TF (2005), Modelling a complex supply chain: understanding the effect of simplified assumptions. International Journal of Production Research 43 (13): 2829-2872

Inderscience (2007) International Journal of Value Chain Management (IJVCM). URL: http://www.inderscience.com/browse/index.php?journalID=63#objectives, Date: 19.03.2007, 20

Jackson JR, Grossmann IE (2003) Temporal Decomposition Scheme for Nonlinear Multisite Production Planning and Distribution Models. Industrial & Engineering Chemistry Research 42: 3045-3055

Jammernegg W, Paulitsch M (2004) Portfolio Procurement Strategies and Speculative Inventory for Risk-Hedging Supply Chains. Proceedings of the EurOMA Conference INSEAD Fontainebleau: 323-332.

Jang Y, Jang S, Chang B, Park J (2002) A combined model of network design and production/distribution planning for a supply network. Computers & Industrial Engineering 43 (1-2): 263-281

Jänicke W (2001) Regelkreise bei der Produktions- und Bedarfsplanung für Systeme chemischer Mehrzweckanlagen. Chemie Ingenieur Technik 73: 1192-1195

Jetlund AS, Karimi IA (2004) Improving the logistics of multi-compartment chemical tankers. Computers & Chemical Engineering 28 (8): 1267-1283

Jörns CT (2004) Zusammenarbeit in dynamischen Supply Chain-Netzwerken, In: Scheer AW (ed) Innovation durch Geschäftsprozessmanagement. Springer, Berlin et al., pp 35-56

Jung JY, Blau G, Pekny JF, Reklaitis GV, Eversdyk D (2004) A simulation based optimization approach to supply chain management under demand uncertainty. Computers & Chemical Engineering 28: 2087–2106

Kaeseler J (2004) Value Chain Management in der Gebrauchsgüterindustrie, In: Beckmann H (ed) Supply Chain Management: Strategien und Entwicklungstendenzen in Spitzenunternehmen. Springer, Berlin et al., pp 227-260

Kallrath J (2002a) Planning and scheduling in the process industry. OR Spectrum 24: 219-250

Kallrath J (2002b) Gemischt-ganzzahlige Optimierung: Modellierung in der Praxis. Vieweg, Braunschweig et al.

Kallrath J (2003) Combined strategic and operational planning - a MILP success story in chemical industry. In: Günther HO, van Beek P (eds) Advanced Planning and Scheduling Solutions in Process Industry. Springer, Berlin et al., pp 201-228

Kaplan R, Norton D (1997) Balanced Scorecard: Strategien erfolgreich umsetzen, Schäffer Poeschel, Stuttgart

Karmarkar U, Lele M (2005) The Marketing/Manufacturing Interface: Strategic Issues. In: Chakravarty A, Eliashberg J (eds) Managing Business Interfaces, pp 311-328

Kazaz B, Dada M, Moskowitz H (2005) Global Production Planning under Exchange-Rate Uncertainty. In: Management Science 51 (7): 1101-1119

Keller G, Teufel T (1997) R/3 prozessorientiert anwenden: iteratives Prozess-Prototyping zur Bildung von Wertschöpfungsketten. Addison-Wesley-Longmann, Bonn et al.

Kennedy Information (2005) Operations Management Consulting Growth Shifts From Supply Chain Management to Ends of Value Chain. URL: http://www.marketwire.com/mw/release_html_b1?release_id=95751, Date: 22.09.2005

Kilger C, Schneeweiss L (2004) Demand Fulfilment and ATP. In: Stadtler H, Kilger C (eds) Supply Chain Management and Advanced Planning. 3rd edn. Springer, Berlin et al., pp 179-196

Kleijnen, JPC (2005a) An overview of the design and analysis of simulation experiments for sensitivity analysis. European Journal of Operational Research, 164, pp 287–300

Kleijnen JPC (2005b) Supply chain simulation tools and techniques: a survey. International Journal of Simulation & Process Modelling 1 (1/2): 82-89

Kline C (1976) Maximizing Profits in Chemicals. Chemtech 6 (2): 110-117

Klose A, Lidke T (2005) Lagrange-Ansätze zur Lösung des Transportproblems mit Fixkosten, In: Günther HO, Mattfeld DC, Suhl L (eds), Supply Chain Management und Logistik: Optimierung, Simulation, Decision Support. Physica, Heidelberg,, pp 507-530

Knolmayer G, Mertens P, Zeier A (2000) Supply Chain Management auf Basis von SAP-Systemen: Perspektiven in der Auftragsabwicklung für Industriebetriebe. Springer, Berlin et al.

Knolmayer G, Mertens P, Zeier A (2002) Supply Chain Management Based on SAP systems: Order Management in Manufacturing Companies. Springer, Berlin et al.

Koçlar A, Süral H (2005) A note on "The general lot sizing and scheduling problem". OR Spectrum 27: 145-146

Kotler P, Keller K (2005) Marketing Management. 12th edn. Pearson Prentice Hall, Upper Saddle River

Kremin-Buch B (2001) Internationale Rechnungslegung, 2nd edn. Gabler, Wiesbaden

Krenek MR (1997) Improve global competitiveness with supply-chain management - Manufacturers must rethink how, when, where and why they produce goods. Hydrocarbon Processing 76 (5): 97-100

Krever M, Wunderink S, Dekker R, Schorr B (2005) Inventory control based on advanced probability theory, an application. European Journal of Operational Research 162 (2): 342-358

Kurus D (2006) Simulation-based optimization model for supply chain planning of commodities in the chemical industry Technical University of Berlin

Lababidi HMS, Ahmed MA, Alatiqi IM, Al-Enzi AF (2004) Optimizing the Supply Chain of a Petrochemical Company under Uncertain Operating and Economic Conditions. Industrial & Engineering Chemistry Research 43: 63-73

Labys WC (1973) Dynamic Commodity Models: Specification, Estimation and Simulation, Lexington Books, Lexington

Labys WC (1975) Quantitative Models of Commodity Markets, Ballinger, Cambridge, MA

Lakhal S, Martel A, Kettani O, Oral M (2001) On the optimizaton of supply chain networking decisions. European Journal of Operational Research 2: 259-270

Large R (2000) Strategisches Beschaffungsmanagement. Gabler, Wiesbaden

Laudicina PA (2004) World out of Balance. McGraw-Hill, Boston et al.

Lee JL, Billington C (1995) The Evolution of Supply-Chain-Management Models and Practice at Hewlett-Packard. Interfaces 25 (5): 42-63

Lee LH, Chew EP, Sim MS (2007) A heuristic to solve a sea cargo revenue management problem. OR Spectrum 29: 123-136

Lee YH (2001) Supply Chain Model for the Semiconductor Industry of Global Market. Journal of Systems Integration 10 (3): 189-206

Levis AA, Papageorgiou LG (2004) A hierarchical solution approach for multi-site capacity planning under uncertainty in the pharmaceutical industry. Computers & Chemical Engineering 28: 707–725

Loos P (1997) Produktionslogistik in der chemischen Industrie, betriebstypologische Merkmale und Strukturen. DUV Gabler, Wiesbaden

Lütke Entrup M (2005) Advanced Planning in Fresh Food Industries. Physica-Verlag, Heidelberg et al.

Mallik S, Harker PT (2004) Coordinating supply chains with competition: Capacity allocation in semiconductor manufacturing. European Journal of Operational Research 159 (2): 330-347

Maloni M, Benton WC (1999) Power influences in the supply chain. The Ohio State University, Fisher College of Business

Mandal P, Gunasekaran A (2002) Application of SAP R/3 in on-line inventory control. International Journal of Production Economics 75: 47-55

Marn MV, Rosiello RL (1992) Managing Price, Gaining Profit. Harvard Business Review 70 (5): 84-94

Marquez, AC, Blanchar C (2004) The procurement of strategic parts. Analysis of contracts with suppliers using a system dynamics simulation model. International Journal of Production Economics 88 (1): 29-49

Mason S (2002) Simulation software buyer´s guide. IIE Solutions May: 45-51

McAfee R, McMillan J (1987) Auctions and Bidding. Journal of Economic Literature 25: 699-738

McGill JI, van Ryzin GJ (1999) Revenue Management: Research Overview and Prospects. Transportation Science 33 (2): 233-256

McGuffog T, Wadsley N (1999) The general principles of value chain management. Supply Chain Management: An International Journal 4 (5): 218-225

McWilliams G (2001) Lean Machine: How Dell Fine-Tunes Its PC Pricing to Gain Edge in A Slow market. Wall Street Journal, 08.06.2001

Meadows DL (1970) Dynamics of Commodity Production Cycles. Wright-Allen, Cambridge, MA

Meffert H (1998) Marketing: Grundlagen marktorientierter Unternehmensführung: Konzepte – Instrumente – Praxisbeispiele, 8th edn. Gabler, Wiesbaden

Melzer-Ridinger R (2004) Materialwirtschaft und Einkauf, Band 1: Beschaffung und Supply Chain Management, 4th edn. Oldenbourg, München et al.

Mentzer JT, DeWitt W, Keebler JS, Soonhong M, Nix NW, Smith CD, Zacharia ZG (2001) Defining Supply Chain Management. Journal of Business Logistics 22 (2): 1-25

Merkuryeva G (2005) Response Surface-based Simulation Metamodelling Methods, Dolgui A, Soldek J, Zaikin O (eds) Supply Chain Optimization: Product/Process Design, Facility, Location and Flow Control. Springer, Berlin et al., pp 205-216

Meyr H (2004a) Supply chain planning in the German automotive industry. OR Spectrum 26: 447-470

Meyr H. (2004b) Forecast Methods. In: Stadtler H, Kilger C (eds) Supply Chain Management and Advanced Planning, 3rd edn. Springer, Berlin et al., pp 461-472

Meyr H, Stadtler H (2004) Types of Supply Chains. In: Stadtler H, Kilger C (eds) Supply Chain Management and Advanced Planning, 3rd edn. Springer, Berlin et al., pp 65-80

Meyr H, Wagner M, Rohde J (2004) Structure of Advanced Planning Systems, In: Stadtler H, Kilger C (eds) Supply Chain Management and Advanced Planning, 3rd edn. Springer, Berlin et al., pp 110-137

Milgrom P (1989) Auctions and Bidding: A Primer. Journal of Economic Perspective 3 (3): 3-22

Miller T (2002) Hierarchical Operations and Supply Chain Planning. Springer, London et al.

Minner S (2003) Multiple-supplier inventory models in supply chain management: A review. International Journal of Production Economics 81-82: 265-279

Monczka R, Trent R, Handfield R (2004) Purchasing and Supply Chain Management, 3rd edn. South Western College Publishing, Mason, OH

Moon MA, Mentzer JT, Thomas Jr. DE (2000) Customer Demand Planning at Lucent Technologies: A Case Study in Continuous Improvement through Sales Forecast Auditing. In: Industrial Marketing Management 29 (1): 19-26

Munson CL, Rosenblatt MJ (2001) Coordinating a three-level supply chain with quantity discounts. In: IIE Transactions 33: 371-384

N.N. (2005a) Silk road. Wikipedia, The Free Encyclopedia. URL: http://en.wikipedia.org/wiki/Silk_Road, Date: 14.10.2005

N.N. (2005b) Trade. Wikipedia, The Free Encyclopedia. URL: http://en.wikipedia.org/wiki/Trade, Date: 14.10.2005

N.N. (2005c) Silk road. Britannica Concise Encyclopedia. URL: http://www.britannica.com/ebc/article-9378681?query=Silk%20road&ct=, Date: 14.10.2005

N.N. (2005d) Blickpunkt Kapazitätsmanagement - Revenue Management gewinnt in der Prozessindustrie an Bedeutung. Frankfurter Allgemeine Zeitung, Frankfurt, 09.10.2005

N.N. (2006a) Income statement. Wikipedia, The Free Encyclopedia. URL: http://en.wikipedia.org/wiki/Profit_and_loss_statement, Date: 24.07.2006

N.N. (2006b) Economic Value Added. Wikipedia, The Free Encyclopedia. URL: http://de.wikipedia.org/wiki/Economic_Value_Added, Date: 27.07.2006

N.N. (2006c) Marksituation. Wikipedia, Die freie Enzyklopädie. URL: http://de.wikipedia.org/wiki/Marktsituation, Date: 27.07.2006

N.N. (2006d) Preis-Absatz-Funktion. Wikipedia, Die freie Enzyklopädie. URL: http://de.wikipedia.org/wiki/Preis-Absatz-Funktion, Date: 27.07.2006

N.N. (2006e) Preiselastizität. Wikipedia, Die freie Enzyklopädie. URL: http://de.wikipedia.org/wiki/Preiselastizit%C3%A4t, Date: 27.07.2006

N.N. (2006f) Logistics. Wikipedia, The Free Encyclopedia. URL: http://en.wikipedia.org/wiki/Logistics, Date: 24.07.2006

N.N. (2006g) Chronologie der chemischen Entdeckungen. In: Wikipedia, Die freie Enzyklopädie. URL: http://de.wikipedia.org/wiki/Chronologie_der_chemischen_Entdeckungen, Date: 10.07.2006, 2006

N.N. (2006h) Discoveries of the chemical elements. In: Wikipedia, The Free Encyclopedia. URL: http://en.wikipedia.org/wiki/Timeline_of_chemical_element_discovery, Date: 10.07.2006

N.N. (2006i) Geschichte der Chemie. Wikipedia, Die freie Enzyklopädie. URL: http://de.wikipedia.org/wiki/Geschichte_der_Chemie, Date: 24.10.2006

N.N. (2006j) Commodity. Wikipedia, The Free Encyclopedia. URL: http://en.wikipedia.org/wiki/Commodity, Date: 24.10.2006

N.N. (2006k) WACC-Ansatz. Wikipedia, Die freie Enzyklopädie. URL: http://de.wikipedia.org/wiki/WACC-Ansatz, Date: 02.05.2006

N.N. (2007) Timestamp. Wikipedia, The Free Encyclopedia. URL: http://en.wikipedia.org/wiki/Timestamp, Date: 27.05.2007

Nagurney A, Cruz J, Matsypura D (2003) Dynamics of global supply chain supernetworks. Mathematical and Computer Modelling 37 (9-10): 963-983

Neubert R, Görlitz O, Teich T (2004) Automated negotiations of supply contracts for flexible production networks. International Journal of Production Economics 89: 175-187

Neuhaus U, Günther HO (2006) Development of a reactive scheduling system for application in the process industry, In: Botta-Genoulaz V (ed) ILS2006, Proceedings of the First International Conference on Information Systems, Logistics and Supply Chain. Lyon

Neumann K, Schwindt C, Trautmann N (2000) Short-Term Planning of Batch Plants in Process Industries. In: Kischka P, Leopold-Wildburger U, Möhring RH, Radermacher FJ (eds) Models, Methods and Decision Support in Management Physica, Heidelberg, pp 211-226

Neumann K, Schwindt C, Trautmann N (2002) Advanced production scheduling for batch plants in process industries. OR Spectrum 24: 251-279

Nielsen MJ, Schwartz ES (2004) Theory of Storage and the Pricing of Commodity Claims. Review of Derivatives Research 7: 5–24

Nienhaus J (2005) Modeling, Analysis and Improvement of Supply Chains - a Structured Approach, ETH Zürich

Nienhaus J, Schnetzler M, Sennheiser A, Weidemann M, Glaubitt K, Pierpaoli F (2003) Trends in supply chain management - Results of a study among more than 200 companies. Swiss Federal Institute of Technology, BWI Center for Enterprise Sciences, Zurich

Nygreen B, Christiansen M, Haugen K (2000) Modeling Norwegian petroleum production and transportation. Annals of Operations Research 82: 251-268

Olieman N, Hendrix EMT (2005) Global Optimisation Challenges in Robustness Programming Bounding Methods. Proceedings of GO 2005: 1-6

Olieman N (2004a) Methods for optimal robust product design. Presentation at the Operations Research 2004 International Conference, Tilburg, The Netherlands

Olieman N (2004b) Optimal robust product design. Presentation at the 29th Conference on the Mathematics of Operations Research, Lunteren, The Netherlands

Oliver R, Webber M (1982) Supply Chain Management: Logistics catches up with strategy. In: Booz, Allen & Hamilton, Outlook and in: Christopher M (ed), Logistics - the strategic issue. Chapman & Hall, London, pp. 61-75

Persson JA, Göthe-Lundgren M (2005) Shipment planning at oil refineries using column generation and valid inequalities. European Journal of Operational Research 163: 631–652

Phillips RL (1999) Pricing and Revenue Management – Driving Profit Improvement from CRM. CRM Project 1:1-7

Pibernik R (2005) Advanced available-to-promise: Classification, selected methods and requirements for operations and inventory management. International Journal of Production Economics 93-94 (1): 239-252

Pibernik R, Sucky E (2005) Master Planning in Supply Chains. In: Günther HO, Mattfeld DC, Suhl L (eds) Supply Chain Management und Logistik: Optimierung, Simulation, Decision Support. Physica, Heidelberg, pp 69-94

Pistikopoulos EN, Vassiliadis CG, Arvela J, Papageorgiou LG (2001) Interactions of Maintenance and Production Planning for Multipurpose Process Plants - A System Effectiveness Approach. Industrial & Engineering Chemistry Research 40: 3195-3207

Poesche J (2001) Agile Produktion – Voraussetzungen für das Supply Chain Management in der chemischen Industrie, FB/IE 2: 65-70.

Pontrandolfo P, Gosavi A, Okogbaa OG, Das TK (2002) Global supply chain management: a reinforcement learning approach. International Journal of Production Research 40 (6): 1299-1317

Popper K (1959) The Logic of Scientific Discovery. Hutchinson & Co., London, UK

Porter M (1985) Competitive Advantage: Creating and Sustaining Superior Performance. Free Press, New York et al.

Preusser M, Almeder C, Hartl RF, Klug M (2005) LP Modeling and Simulation of Supply Chain Networks, In: Günther HO, Mattfeld DC, Suhl L (eds) Supply Chain Management und Logistik: Optimierung, Simulation, Decision Support. Physica, Heidelberg, pp 95-114

Pyke DF, Johnson ME (2005) Real-Time Profit Optimization: Coordinating Demand and Supply Chain. URL: http://www2.cio.com/higher/report3489.html, Date: 31.03.2005

Rabe M (1998) Einführung. In: Kuhn A, Rabe M (eds) Simulation in Produktion und Logistik: Fallbeispielsammlung. Springer, Berlin et al., pp 1-10

Rammer C, Heneric O, Legler H (2005) Innovationsmotor Chemie 2005 – Leistungen und Herausforderungen. Zentrum für Europäische Wirtschaftsforschung, Mannheim

Reiner G (2005) Customer-oriented improvement and evaluation of supply chain processes supported by simulation. International Journal of Production Economics 96 (3): 381-395

Reiner G, Jammernegg W (2005) Bewertung unterschiedlicher Beschaffungsstrategien für Risk-Hedging Supply Chains unter Berücksichtigung intermodaler Transportprozesse. In: Günther HO, Mattfeld DC, Suhl L (eds) Supply Chain Management und Logistik: Optimierung, Simulation, Decision Support. Physica, Heidelberg, pp 115-134

Reiner G, Natter M (2007) An encompassing view on markdown pricing strategies: an analysis of the Austrian mobile phone market. OR Spectrum 29: 173-192

Revsine L, Collins D, Johnson W (2004) Financial Reporting and Analysis. 3rd edn. Pearson Prentice Hall, Upper Saddle River

Roche J (1995) Forecasting Commodity Markets: Using Technical Fundamental and Econometric Analysis, Probus, London

Rohde J, Wagner M (2004) Master Planning. In: Stadtler H, Kilger C (eds) Supply Chain Management and Advanced Planning, 3rd edn. Springer, Berlin et al., pp 159-178

Rohde J, Meyr H, Wagner M (2000) The Supply Chain Planning Matrix. PPS-Management 5 (1): 10-15

Scharlacken JW, Harland D (1997) Global Supply Chain Planning: Synchronizing Operations and Logistics with the Pulse of the International Marketplace. 40th APICS International Conference Proceedings: 211-219

Schaub A, Zeier A (2003) Eignung von Supply-Chain-Management-Software für unterschiedliche Betriebstypen und Branchen untersucht am Beispiel des Produktionsprozessmodells zum System SAP APO. Universität Erlangen-Nürnberg, Bayrischer Forschungsverbund Wirtschaftsinformatik, FWN-2000-004

Schneeweiß C (1992) Planung 2: Konzepte der Prozess- und Modellgestaltung. Springer, Berlin et al.

Scholl A (2001) Robuste Planung und Optimierung. Physica, Heidelberg

Schönsleben P (2004) Integrales Logistikmanagement – Planung und Steuerung der umfassenden Supply Chain, 4th edn. Springer, Berlin et al.

Schuster EW, Allen SJ, D'Itri MP (2000) Capacitated materials requirements planning and its application in the process industries. Journal of Business Logistics 21 (1): 169-187

Secomandi N, Abbott K, Atan T, Boyd EA (2002) From Revenue Management Concepts to Software Systems. Interfaces 32 (2): 1-11

Seifert RW, Thonemann UW, Hausman WH (2004) Optimal procurement strategies for online spot markets. European Journal of Operational Research 152 (3): 781-799

Sen W, Pokharel S, YuLei W (2004) Supply chain positioning strategy integration, evaluation, simulation and optimization. Computers & Chemical Engineering 46 (4): 781-792

Sery S, Presti V, Shobrys DE (2001) Optimization Models for Restructuring BASF North America's Distribution System. Interfaces 31: 55-65

Shah N (2005) Process industry supply chains: Advances and challenges. Computers & Chemical Engineering 29 (6): 1225-1236

Shapiro JF (2001) Modeling the Supply Chain, Dubuxury, Pacific Grove

Shapiro JF (2004) Challenges of strategic supply chain planning and modeling. Computers & Chemical Engineering 28: 855–861

Shapiro JF, Sinhal V, Wagner S (1993) Optimizing the Value Chain. Interfaces 23 (2): 102-117

Shih L (1997) Planning of fuel coal imports using a mixed integer programming method 51: 243-249

Short P (2005) Global Top 50. Chemical & Engineering News 83 (29): 20-23

Silver EA, Pyke DF, Peterson R (1998) Inventory Management and Production Planning and Scheduling, 3rd edn. Wiley, New York

Siprelle AJ, Parsons DJ, Clark RJ (2003) Benefits of Using a Supply Chain Simulation Tool to Study Inventory Allocation. In: Chick S, Sánchez PJ, Ferrin D, Morrice DJ (eds) Proceedings of the 2003 Winter Simulation Conference, pp 238-245

Sittig M (1972) Polyamide Fiber Manufacture, Noyes Data Corporation, Park Ridge

Skiscim C (2001) OPL Studio 3.1. OR/MS Today April 2001: 70-73

Smith B, Leimkuhler J, Darrow R (1992) Yield Management at American Airlines. Interfaces 22 (1): 8-31

Smith, JS (2003) Survey on the use of simulation for manufacturing system design and operation. Journal of Manufacturing Systems 22 (2): 157-171

Specker A (2001) Modellierung von Informationssystemen: ein methodischer Leitfaden zur Projektabwicklung. vdf-Hochschulverlag, Zürich

Spengler T, Rehkopf S, Volling T (2007) Revenue management in make-to-order manufacturing – an application to the iron and steel industry. OR Spectrum 29: 157-171

Spitter JM, Hurkens CAJ, de Kok AG, Lenstra JK, Negenman EG (2005) Linear programming models with planned lead times for supply chain operations planning. European Journal of Operational Research 163: 706–720

Stadtler H (2004a) Supply Chain Management - An Overview. In: Stadtler H, Kilger C (eds) Supply Chain Management and Advanced Planning. 3rd edn. Springer, Berlin et al., pp 9-36

Stadtler H (2004b) Purchasing and Material Requirements Planning. In: Stadtler H, Kilger C (eds) Supply Chain Management and Advanced Planning. 3rd edn. Springer, Berlin et al., pp 215-228

Stadtler H, Kilger C (eds) (2005) Supply Chain Management and Advanced Planning. 3rd edn. Springer, Berlin et al.

Staudigl R (2004) Chemieindustrie: Herausforderungen und Antworten. Chemie Ingenieur Technik 76 (1-2): 21-29

Suh M, Lee T (2001) Robust Optimization Method for the Economic Term in Chemical Process Design and Planning. Industrial & Engineering Chemistry Research 40: 5950-5959

Supply Chain Council (2006) Supply-Chain Operations Reference-model - SCOR Version 7.0 Overview. Supply Chain Council, http://www.supply-chain.org

Sürie C (2005a) Campaign planning in time-indexed model formulations. International Journal of Production Research 43 (1): 49-66

Sürie C (2005b) Abbildungsfehler in zeitdiskreten Optimierungsmodellen – Auftreten und Maßnahmen zu ihrer Behebung. In: Günther HO, Mattfeld DC, Suhl L (eds) Supply Chain Management und Logistik: Optimierung, Simulation, Decision Support. Physica, Heidelberg, pp 205-222

Sürie C, Wagner M (2004) Supply Chain Analysis. In: Stadtler H, Kilger C (eds) Supply Chain Management and Advanced Planning. 3rd edn. Springer, Berlin et al., pp 37-64

Talluri S, Narasimhan R (2004) A methodology for strategic sourcing. International Journal of Operational Research 154 (1): 236-250

Tallury KT, Van Ryzin GJ (2005) The Theory and Practice of Revenue Management. Springer, New York

Tang O, Grubbström RW (2002) Planning and replanning the master production schedule under demand uncertainty. International Journal of Production Economics 78 (3): 323-334

Teich T (2002) Extended Value Chain Management - ein Konzept zur Koordination von Wertschöpfungsnetzen, Technische Universität Chemnitz, Fakultät für Wirtschaftswissenschaften

Tekin E, Sabuncuoglu I (2004) Simulation optimization: A comprehensive review on theory and applications. IIE Transactions 36: 1067-1081

Teufel T, Röhricht J, Willems P (2000) SAP-Prozesse: Finanzwesen und Controlling. Addison-Wesley Longman, Bonn et al.

Timpe CH, Kallrath J (2000) Optimal planning in large multi-site production networks. European Journal of Operational Research 126 (2): 422-435

Todd M (2004) Industry buyers lift ethylene. European Chemical News 80 (2087): 13

Trautmann N (2001) Anlagenbelegungsplanung in der Prozessindustrie. DUV Gabler, Wiesbaden

Trombly M (2000) Value-Chain management. URL: http://www.computerworld.com/printthis/2000/0,4814,45129,00.html., Date: 15.12.04

Tyworth JE, Zeng AZ (1998) Estimating the effects of carrier transit-time performance on logistics cost and service. Transportation Research Part A: Policy and Practice 32 (2): 89-97

Ulrich P, Hill W (1976) Wissenschaftstheoretische Grundlagen der Betriebswirtschaftslehre - Teil II. Wirtschaftswissenschaftliches Studium 5 (8): 345-350

Ünal A, Draman M, Altinel IK, Bajgoric N, Geriskovan AI (2002) Clone-based modelling for optimal production planning in process industries. International Journal of Production Research 40 (16): 4041-4059

van Beek P (2005) Quantitative Chain Modeling: The use of OR models for better understanding chain processes. Wageningen University

van der Vorst JG (2000) Effective Food Supply Chains: Generating, modeling and evaluating supply chain scenarios. Ponsen & Looijen, Wageningen

van Hentenryck P, Michel L (2002) The Modeling Language OPL - A Short Overview. In: Voß S, Woodruff D. (eds) Optimization Software Class Libaries, Kluwer Academic Publishers, Boston, Mass., pp. 263-294

van Landeghem H, Vanmaele H (2002) Robust planning: a new paradigm for demand chain planning. Journal of Operations Management 20: 769-783

van Weele AJ, Rozemeijer FA (1996) Revolution in purchasing: Building competitive power through proactive. European Journal of Purchasing & Supply Management 2 (4): 153-160

Varian H (1994) Mikroökonomie, 3rd edn. Oldenbourg, München et al.

Vicens E, Alemany ME, Andres C, Guarch JJ (2001) A design and application methodology for hierarchical production planning decision support systems in an enterprise integration context. International Journal of Production Economics 74: 5-20

Vidal CJ, Goetschalckx M (2001) A global supply chain model with transfer pricing and transportation cost allocation. European Journal of Operational Research 129 (1): 134-158

Wagner M (2004) Demand Planning. In: Stadtler H, Kilger C (eds) Supply Chain Management and Advanced Planning, 3rd edn. Springer, Berlin et al., pp 139-158

Wallace TF (ed) (1992) APICS Dictionary, 7th edn. American Production and Inventory Control Society, Falls Church VA

Wang R, Liang T (2004) Application of fuzzy multi-objective linear programming to aggregate production planning. Computers & Industrial Engineering 46: 17-41

Wasner M, Zäpfel G (2003) An integrated multi-depot hub-location vehicle routing model for network planning of parcel service. International Journal of Production Economics 90: 403-419

Willems I, Pirk K, Eulitz B (2002) How to boost your profits. Containerisation International May: 46-49

Williams T, Maull R, Ellis B (2002) Demand chain management theory: constraints and development from global aerospace supply webs. Journal of Operations Management 20 (6): 691-706

Winkelmann P (2005) Marketing und Vertrieb. 4th edn. Oldenbourg, München et al.

Wöhe G (2002) Einführung in die Allgemeine Betriebswirtschaftslehre. 21st edn. Vahlen, München

Wullink G, Gademann AJRM, Hans EW, van Harten A (2004) Scenario-based approach for flexible resource loading under uncertainty. International Journal of Production Research 42 (24): 5079-5098

Xia M, Stallaert J, Whinston AB (2005) Solving the combinatorial double auction problem. European Journal of Operational Research 164: 239–251

Yang G (2005) Produktionsplanung in komplexen Wertschöpfungsnetzwerken – Ein integrierter Ansatz in der chemischen Industrie. Technical University of Berlin, Department of Economics and Management

Yano C, Gilbert S (2005) Coordinated Pricing and Production/Procurement Decisions: A Review. In: Chakravarty A, Eliashberg J (eds) Managing Business Interfaces, Springer, Berlin et al., pp 65-104

Zeier A (2002) Identifikation und Analyse branchenspezifischer Faktoren für den Einsatz von Supply-Chain-Management-Software - Teil II: Betriebstypologische Brachensegmentierung. Universtität Erlangen-Nürnberg, Bayrischer Forschungsverbund Wirtschaftsinformatik, FWN-2002-002-005

Zeier A (2002) Identifikation und Analyse branchenspezifischer Faktoren für den Einsatz von Supply-Chain-Management-Software. Universtität Erlangen-Nürnberg, Bayrischer Forschungsverbund Wirtschaftsinformatik, FWN-2002-002

Zhang J (2005) Transshipment and its Impact on Supply Chain Members' Performance. Management Science 51 (10): 1534-1539

Zhou T, Cheng S, Hua B (2000) Supply Chain Optimization of Continuous Process Industries with Sustainability Considerations. Computers & Chemical Engineering 24: 1151-1158

Zimmer K (2001) Koordination im Supply Chain Management: ein hierarchischer Ansatz zur Steuerung der unternehmensübergreifenden Planung. DUV Gabler, Wiesbaden

Zimmermann K (2003) Supply Chain Balanced Scorecard: unternehmensübergreifendes Management von Wertschöpfungsketten. DUV Gabler, Wiesbaden